WITHDRAWN

Critical Essays on
SALMAN RUSHDIE

CRITICAL ESSAYS ON BRITISH LITERATURE

Zack Bowen, General Editor
University of Miami

Critical Essays on
SALMAN RUSHDIE

edited by
M. KEITH BOOKER

G. K. Hall & Co.
New York

Copyright © 1999 by G.K. Hall & Co.

All rights reserved. No part of this book may be reproduced or transmitted in any form or by any means, electronic or mechanical, including photocopying, recording, or by any information storage and retrieval system, without permission in writing from the Publisher.

G. K. Hall & Co.
1633 Broadway
New York, NY 10019

Library of Congress Cataloging-in-Publication Data

Critical essays on Salman Rushdie / edited by M. Keith Booker.
    p. cm. — (Critical essays on British literature)
    Includes bibliographical references and index.
    ISBN 0-7838-0429-6 (alk. paper)
    1. Rushdie, Salman—Criticism and interpretation. 2. Rushdie, Salman. Midnight's children. 3. Islam and literature. 4. India— In literature. I. Booker, M. Keith. II. Series
PR6068.U57Z598   1999
823'.914—dc21   99-20986
                                                              CIP

This paper meets the requirements of ANSI/NISO Z3948-1992 (Permanence of Paper).

10 9 8 7 6 5 4 3 2

Printed in the United States of America

For Epifanio San Juan Jr.,
In appreciation of all you have done over the years to make the study of literature and culture a tool of liberation rather than domination

Contents

♦

General Editor's Note	ix
Publisher's Note	xi
Introduction:	
Salman Rushdie: The Development of a Literary Reputation	1
M. Keith Booker	
"Marching In from the Peripheries":	
Rushdie's Feminized Artistry and Ambivalent Feminism	16
Ambreen Hai	
Reading the Rushdie Affair: "Islam," Cultural Politics, Form	51
Aamir R. Mufti	
Rushdies's *Dastan-e-Dilruba*:	
The Satanic Verses as Rushdie's Love Letter to Islam	78
Feroza Jussawalla	
The Cultural Politics of Rushdie Criticism: All or Nothing	107
Timothy Brennan	
An Invitation to Indian Postmodernity:	
Rushdie's English Vernacular as Situated Cultural Hybridity	129
Bishnupriya Ghosh	
The Moor's Last Sigh and India's National Bourgeoisie:	
Reading Rushdie through Frantz Fanon	154
Farhad B. Idris	
"The Mirror of Us All": *Midnight's Children* and	
the Twentieth-Century Bildungsroman	169
Dubravka Juraga	

"This Angrezi in which I am forced to write":
On the Language of *Midnight's Children* 188
    Michael Gorra

Allegorizing the Emergency: Rushdie's *Midnight's Children* and
Benjamin's Theory of Allegory 205
    Todd M. Kuchta

Rewriting History and Identity: The Reinvention of
Myth, Epic, and Allegory in Salman Rushdie's
Midnight's Children 225
    Michael Reder

Victim into Protagonist? *Midnight's Children* and
the Post-Rushdie National Narratives of the Eighties 250
    Josna E. Rege

Midnight's Children, History, and Complexity:
Reading Rushdie after the Cold War 283
    M. Keith Booker

Notes on Contributors 315
Index 317

General Editor's Note

♦

The Critical Essays on British Literature series provides a variety of approaches to both classical and contemporary writers of Britain and Ireland. The formats of the volumes in the series vary with the thematic designs of individual editors and with the amount and nature of existing reviews and criticism, augmented, where appropriate, by original essays by recognized authorities. It is hoped that each volume will be unique in developing a new overall perspective on its particular subject.

In his introduction, Keith Booker establishes the basis for Rushdie's reputation as one of the most important writers in Western literature in the last 25 years, and then goes on to describe the critical problems involved with an author writing simultaneously in two literary traditions, British and Indian, and composing the whole in English. Rushdie never shied away from controversial representations. After incurring Islam's censure, Rushdie continued to be the center of controversy. His last two books were banned in India. Booker traces the hybridity of his work, which some Indian critics have questioned as authentically Indian.

The more sensational debate over religio-political issues in *The Satanic Verses* led to a shift of critical emphasis from *Midnight's Children* to the later book, an emphasis that is currently reversing itself as *Midnight's Children* becomes more widely read and more fully appreciated by an increasingly attentive intellectual audience.

Half the selected essays in the volume deal with works other than *Midnight's Children,* and half deal with that major novel. Booker sought "to capture the freshest and most current trends in Rushdie scholarship in the West." In his doing so the readers of this groundbreaking volume are treated to eight new essays especially written for publication here. These essays, which are largely representative of current interest in postcolonial studies and their political ramifications, see Rushdie both as an advocate of global liberation and as cooperating with the hegemony. Booker's own concluding essay finds Rushdie's affinity with postmodernist writing even more pronounced than that with the issues of postcolonialism.

ZACK BOWEN
University of Miami

Publisher's Note

♦

Producing a volume that contains both newly commissioned and reprinted material presents the publisher with the challenge of balancing the desire to achieve stylistic consistency with the need to preserve the integrity of works first published elsewhere. In the Critical Essays series, essays commissioned especially for a particular volume are edited to be consistent with G. K. Hall's house style; reprinted essays appear in the style in which they were first published, with only typographical errors corrected. Consequently, shifts in style from one essay to another are the result of our efforts to be faithful to each text as it was originally published.

Introduction

◆

Salman Rushdie: The Development of a Literary Reputation

M. KEITH BOOKER

Salman Rushdie has undoubtedly been one of the most important writers in world literature in the past quarter of a century. For example, Rushdie's *Midnight's Children,* having won the prestigious Booker Prize in 1981 and then having subsequently been awarded the special 25th-anniversary "Booker of Bookers" in 1994, has some claim to being the most honored novel produced by a writer from the British commonwealth since World War II. Rushdie has, in fact, long been a favorite of the Booker committee, having also been shortlisted in 1983 for *Shame,* in 1988 for *The Satanic Verses,* and in 1995 for *The Moor's Last Sigh.* Moreover, Rushdie's importance goes beyond his own work as a novelist. For one thing, he has emerged as a major commentator on Indian and other postcolonial culture. For another, the critical and commercial success of *Midnight's Children* can be credited with playing a key role in the recent explosion of English-language novels coming out of India, with writers as varied as Vikram Seth, Rohinton Mistry, Nayantara Sahgal, Shashi Tharoor, Allan Sealy, Farrukh Dhondy, Amitav Ghosh, Bapsy Sidhwa, Shashi Deshpande, and Arundhati Roy (herself a Booker Prize winner) all being sometimes grouped under the rubric of "Rushdie's children" to indicate the pathbreaking importance of Rushdie's most important novel. Meanwhile, earlier writers such as G. V. Desani, M. Anantanarayanan, and even Raja Rao have gained retrospective prominence by being identified as Rushdie's forebears.

There is, of course, a danger that this "Rushdie's children" model of literary history will overestimate Rushdie's importance and obscure other important trends in Indian literature. Not only does it lump together too many very different writers in a single category but it leaves out important English-language writers (such as Mulk Raj Anand, Manohar Malgonkar, and even R. K. Narayan) who simply will not fit in. And this is not to mention the way such attention to the recent Indian novel in English places undue weight on works in that former colonial language as opposed to those written in India's various "vernacular" languages—a difficulty Rushdie has done little to correct with his own recent unapologetic proclamations of the central importance of English-language fiction in the cultural production of postcolonial India.[1] In the meantime, this emphasis on Rushdie's importance to contemporary Indian literature obscures the fact that Rushdie's own work is rooted in both the Indian and the Western (especially British) cultural traditions. And the situation is complicated still further because it is largely Rushdie's reception by Western critics (and groups such as the Booker Prize committee) that makes him seem such a prominent figure in Indian literature, even though his last two novels were banned in India.

There are many reasons for Rushdie's critical prominence in the West, not the least of which is that he is simply an extremely gifted author who produces very impressive works of fiction. That is, Rushdie's works match up extremely well to criteria of literary quality that have been widely accepted among Western critics during the two decades of Rushdie's career as a writer. Rushdie's works are extremely complex, reflect a number of different cultural positions and viewpoints, and employ a rich variety of literary techniques, conveyed through a lively literary language that many critics have seen as an effective representation of the heteroglossia of postcolonial Indian culture. Moreover, the particular techniques and strategies Rushdie employs in his fiction correspond to those that have been popular among critics in recent years. For example, his use of irony, parody, and exuberant carnivalesque imagery and language have for many critics made him a paragon of postmodernism. At the same time, his particular cultural roots and the particular subject matter of his fiction have led many critics to see him as an exemplary postcolonial writer.

Indeed, Rushdie's critical prominence in the West is related in a very direct way to the turn toward political engagement that has marked Western literary criticism in recent years. And Rushdie has gained particular prominence because the nature of the political issues addressed in his work corresponds well to the growing interest in multicultural, especially postcolonial, cultures that has comprised some of the most vital trends in Western literary scholarship in the past decade. For example, the ability of Rushdie's texts to draw on both Eastern and Western cultural traditions, along with Rushdie's own special cultural hybridity as a Muslim from India who has lived most of his life and done all of his writing in Great Britain, has been particularly attractive to postcolonial critics, such as Homi Bhabha and Sara Suleri, for whom cultural hybridity is a crucial critical category. On the other hand, the very hybridity of Rushdie's work has been controversial as well, and many Indian critics have rejected his work as representative of Indian literature because Rushdie's work (like Rushdie himself) is so extensively rooted in Western literary traditions.

Such controversies, of course, have not necessarily diminished the critical attention afforded Rushdie's work. Indeed, the development of Rushdie's literary reputation has been fueled by controversy in rather obvious ways. However, Rushdie's first novel, *Grimus*, generated no controversy and got essentially no critical attention when it was first published in 1975. A sort of science fiction fantasy that grows out of a complex (and perhaps somewhat pretentious) dialogue with both Sufi mysticism and the Western literary tradition, *Grimus* clearly anticipates many of the central characteristics that have come to be associated with Rushdie's work, though Rushdie himself has acknowledged that the book was an apprentice piece in which he had not yet gained control of his considerable talents. *Grimus*, in fact, would have been all but forgotten had not Rushdie's later achievements brought retroactive attention to it. Among other things, Rushdie's critical attention later grew to the point that book-length studies devoted to his work began to appear, and *Grimus* is generally discussed as a matter of course in those works. Even today (in March of 1998), a search of the on-line MLA Bibliography yields only four articles devoted specifically to *Grimus*, only one of which appeared before the *Satanic Verses* controversy thrust Rushdie into the limelight in a new and unprecedented way.

Obviously, then, it is with the publication of *Midnight's Children* in 1981 that the story of Rushdie's literary reputation really begins. Not only did the book receive numerous enthusiastic reviews (and the Booker Prize) but it also began to generate serious scholarly commentary. Indeed, *Midnight's Children* received considerably more attention even than most Booker Prize winners, and Rushdie was quickly established as a serious writer who dealt with important and substantive issues in works of genuine literary merit. Many of the parameters that still tend to dominate Rushdie criticism today were established in these early years. For example, many critics were impressed by the energetic and innovative language of Rushdie's text, and particularly by his ability to enrich the English language with Indian accents. Thus Maria Couto notes that in *Midnight's Children*,

> Rushdie uses phonemes and word patterns to suggest the vigour and liveliness of folk culture, the pace and variety of Indian life, the mythology of Bom-

bay films, the brash exuberance of affluence, the violence simmering and on the boil.... His prose, liberally sprinkled with Urdu, Hindi, and Sanskrit names, the deliberately uncontrolled flow of sentence with repetition and sonorous content, suggests the chant of Indian traditional texts.[2]

Rushdie himself contributed to this critical emphasis on his language (and also thereby helped to establish his own credentials as a commentator on postcolonial culture) with a now-famous article in the London *Times* in which he argued that he was trying in his work to "decolonize" the English language. Meanwhile, he cited numerous postcolonial writers as his predecessors in this effort, placing special emphasis on the Irish trinity of Joyce, Beckett, and Flann O'Brien.[3]

Critics also quickly concluded (for equally obvious reasons) that history was a major issue in *Midnight's Children,* and numerous essays began to appear that attempted to clarify the specific nature of Rushdie's engagement with Indian history. Uma Parameswaran's 1983 article, which discusses both *Grimus* and *Midnight's Children,* is typical of early critical commentaries on the treatment of history in Rushdie's work. Parameswaran indicates both Rushdie's productive use of specific historical information and his attempt to comment on the nature of history itself, particularly in ways that challenge or even "spoof" traditional historical accounts.[4] Such a dual focus has remained crucial to critical studies of *Midnight's Children* ever since.[5] Parameswaran also indicates the clear connections between Rushdie's technique in *Midnight's Children* and that of predecessors such as Günter Grass and Gabriel García Márquez. And given the obvious engagement of *Midnight's Children* with any number of other texts, it is not surprising that studies of Rushdie's dialogue with various predecessor texts became a popular genre of Rushdie criticism early on. Grass and García Márquez have generally remained the most prominent among these, contributing to a growing emphasis on the use of "magic realism" in Rushdie's work.[6]

Rushdie's next novel, *Shame,* has been considered by most critics to be a somewhat less important work than *Midnight's Children,* but its publication in 1983 certainly did nothing to diminish Rushdie's growing critical reputation. Indeed, *Shame* was well received by critics (for many of the same reasons that *Midnight's Children* had been) while at the same time drawing additional critical attention to issues such as gender. Further, the more blatantly metafictional nature of *Shame* helped to solidify Rushdie's reputation as a postmodernist writer. Still, *Shame* received relatively little serious critical attention on its publication; the most important criticism on the book was not published until several years later, especially after the *Satanic Verses* affair.[7]

Critical attention paid even to the already prominent *Midnight's Children* picked up considerably after that controversy, though the earlier trend toward critical celebration of Rushdie's novel, especially with regard to his treatment of history, began at this time to be supplemented by a certain amount of skepticism.[8] The fact is that Rushdie is best known in the West not because *Midnight's Children* has been judged by the Booker Prize committee to be the finest novel produced in the British commonwealth since 1969 but because the publication of *The Satanic Verses* in 1988 led Rushdie to be condemned by numerous Islamic groups as a blasphemer; Iran's Ayatollah Khomeini, on Valentine's Day of 1989, offered a considerable bounty to anyone responsible for putting Rushdie to death.

Of course, *The Satanic Verses* is, by conventional Western standards, an impressive literary achievement in its own right. It has thus generated a large amount of relatively conventional critical commentary, much of it following in paths already laid down by criticism of Rushdie's earlier work, especially *Midnight's Children*. There were, for example, attempts to relate *The Satanic Verses* to the Western literary tradition, such as my own reading of the book in conjunction with Joyce's *Finnegans Wake*.[9] There were also essays that surveyed the treatment of familiar themes such as history and gender in the book, and there were those that explored the book's dialogic language and use of various literary devices typical of postmodernism.[10] But most of these essays were haunted by the fatwa, while most commentary on Rushdie in the wake of this controversy dealt with the controversy itself, in the midst of which Rushdie moved from the pages of scholarly journals to a featured place in mainstream newspapers and television news broadcasts, calling attention to certain literary issues in unprecedented ways. The controversy generated an immediate outpouring of support for Rushdie in the West, much of which showed a disturbingly blatant tendency to employ Orientalist stereotypes in describing Rushdie's condemnation as evidence of the savagery and brutality of Khomeini in particular and Islam in general.[11] And this stereotyping occurred not just in editorials in the popular press but in scholarly essays and in book-length studies of the controversy.[12]

More thoughtful commentary, including much of a scholarly variety, followed, however, and the controversy has now generated a whole family of other critical essays dealing specifically with the relationship of Rushdie's book to Islam and Islamic cultural traditions.[13] The latter address extremely important and fundamental issues involving the nature of the relationship between art and reality, the complexity of intercultural encounters, and the like. Moreover, the controversy raised issues that went well beyond the literary and cultural, among other things drawing needed attention to the complex and difficult status of immigrant communities in postimperial Britain. At the same time, the inherently controversial nature of discussions involving *The Satanic Verses* has sometimes led to heated exchanges, even in scholarly journals, such as that between Timothy Brennan and Aamir Mufti in the pages of *Social Text*.[14]

Astonishingly, more than 60 books have now been published, in various languages, dealing either in whole or in a large measure with the *Satanic Verses* affair and the issues it raised. In comparison, approximately half a dozen book-length critical discussions of Rushdie's fiction have appeared worldwide, which gives some indication of the extent to which traditional literary scholarship on Rushdie's work has been dwarfed by the controversy surrounding *The Satanic Verses* and the Islamic reaction to it. In the meantime, Rushdie has been in hiding (though in a curiously visible, media-savvy way) throughout the controversy while continuing to write. In addition to his own extensive commentary on the *Satanic Verses* affair, he has produced three more books of fiction since *The Satanic Verses,* including *Haroun and the Seas of Stories* (1990), ostensibly a work intended for children), and *East, West* (1994), a collection of short stories dealing centrally with encounters between Eastern and Western cultures. Rushdie's latest novel, *The Moor's Last Sigh* (1995), was well reviewed and was also short-listed for the Booker Prize. It is still too early to determine the ultimate critical fate of the book, though initial responses have been largely positive.[15] It does, however, appear to be a major work and can be seen as something of a return to the vein of his earlier works, such as *Midnight's Children.*

During the past decade, as these new works have appeared, criticism of Rushdie's work has continued to be haunted by the controversy surrounding *The Satanic Verses,* though it is becoming increasingly clear that this controversy has provided a tremendous boost to Rushdie's prominence as a figure of Western critical attention. At this writing, a search of the on-line MLA database for "Salman Rushdie" yields 322 publications, which is an impressive number when one compares, for example, the results of a similar search for "Nadine Gordimer," which yields 248 entries for a postcolonial author who has also won a Booker Prize and who has been around far longer than Rushdie, published far more books, and even been awarded a Nobel Prize for Literature.[16] The contribution of the *Satanic Verses* affair to the critical attention given Rushdie's work can be seen from the fact that an amazing 267 of the articles on Rushdie's works were published from 1989 onward, and 219 were published in the period from 1989 to 1993, when the controversy was at its height. Further, 128 of the publications on Rushdie also list "Satanic Verses" in the Subject field, whereas only 93 list "Midnight's Children," even though the latter book is widely acknowledged as Rushdie's most important in a literary sense. Finally, it should be noted that 63 of the 93 items on *Midnight's Children* were published from 1989 onward, indicating a significant increase in critical attention to that novel after the controversy surrounding *The Satanic Verses.*

Perhaps even more indicative of Rushdie's canonical status are the book-length studies devoted to his work, of which there are now three published in the West, in addition to two collections of critical essays (of which the present volume is the second).[17] All of these volumes appeared after *The Satanic Verses* first appeared in 1988, though it should be pointed out that Timothy Brennan's *Salman Rushdie and the Third World* grew out of a dissertation completed in 1987. Indeed, Aijaz Ahmad, responding to Fredric Jameson's complaint that Third World literature is excluded from the Western canon, has adduced Brennan's dissertation as evidence that Rushdie is, in fact, canonical in the West.[18] And if Brennan's dissertation already conferred canonicity on Rushdie, consider the almost mind-boggling fact that as of this writing, there are now (according to the Dissertation Abstracts Online Database) more than 60 dissertations devoted at least in part to Rushdie. Most of these are comparative studies dealing with Rushdie and other writers, with readings of Rushdie in conjunction with James Joyce being especially popular. Meanwhile, of the 11 dissertations devoted exclusively to Rushdie, only Brennan's was completed before the publication of *The Satanic Verses,* and several of the other 10 are devoted specifically to the controversy over that book.

As this volume is being compiled, at the end of the 1990s, Rushdie's work remains a crucial concern of Western literary studies, especially those that can be grouped under the rubric of "postcolonial studies." Critical discussions of Rushdie's work in this context remain generally positive, with many critics seeing Rushdie's work as a whole as an extended plea for intercultural tolerance and understanding. Rushdie criticism continues, in general, to see Rushdie's fiction as inherently opposed to dogmatism, authoritarianism, and fanaticism, both in its content—a rich combination of materials derived from various cultural perspectives—and in its use of a complex, dialogic language and style.[19] The current volume, which consists primarily of essays that have not been previously published, supplemented by several recently published essays, is intended to provide a reasonably representative picture of the concerns and inclinations of Rushdie criticism at the end of the twentieth century.

Of the 12 essays included in the current volume, 3 are by young scholars who completed dissertations at American universities dealing centrally with Rushdie and other Indian writers in the last few years, while three others are by doctoral candidates currently doing work related to Rushdie. The volume thus seeks to capture the freshest and most current trends in Rushdie scholarship in the West. The remaining essays are by scholars who have been publishing on Rushdie and other postcolonial cultural issues for a number of years, but four of the six "veteran" essays are original to this volume, so that they also capture new and recent trends in Rushdie criticism. This volume necessarily includes a relatively small sampling of current scholarship, of course, but several trends discernible from it appear to be valid. Perhaps the most obvious of these is that a decade after the *Satanic Verses* controversy, the weight of critical attention to Rushdie's work seems to be shifting back to *Midnight's Children,* the Rushdie novel that receives the most attention in this volume and that is increasingly becoming once again the most important focus of Rushdie criticism as a whole. As a result, the essays in this volume have been separated into two groups, one dealing with *Midnight's Children* and one dealing with Rushdie's other novels. Together, these essays provide a good cross-section of critical opinion regarding Rushdie's work at the end of the twentieth century, ranging from celebration of his texts as antiauthoritarian weapons in the battle for global liberation to criticism of those texts as thoroughly complicitous with the official discourses of the power of Western capitalism.

The volume begins with Ambreen Hai's excellent discussion of many of the issues raised by the complex treatment of gender in Rushdie's work. Examining Rushdie's novels from *Midnight's Children* to *The Moor's Last Sigh*, Hai finds, as have numerous critics before her, that Rushdie's representation of the feminine is marked by a deep ambivalence. However, Hai argues that this ambivalence in Rushdie's work is interesting not for its measurability as a mark of success or failure but rather for its contradictory efforts to conjoin discourses of colonialism and gender. For one thing, she argues, Rushdie uses figures of female artistry in changing and contradictory ways to represent his own postcolonial artistic and political work, and borrows or competes with what he sees as strategies of feminist revision to enable or situate his own postcolonial narration. For another, in relation or addition to these representations, Rushdie attempts feminist work by questioning certain patriarchal norms and recasting or foregrounding cultural and social injustices toward women. Thus he also seeks to transform the categories of both the feminine and the (formerly) colonized.

Aamir Mufti's essay is partly a response to the *Satanic Verses* controversy, though it includes significant discussion of that text itself. In particular, Mufti focuses on the "Rushdie affair" as a complex cultural (and political) event situated within the special context of Muslim South Asia that brings together, highlights, and restructures some of the central elements of contemporary Muslim life. Mufti is particularly concerned with the implications of this event for secular left intellectuals within the Muslim world, arguing that among other things, the official Islamic condemnation of *The Satanic Verses* highlights the participation (or at least acquiescence) of sections of the local elites (and of metropolitan interests) in the production of "Islam" and the rise of fundamentalist groups and parties in South Asia and across the Muslim world. Mufti concludes that while clearly needing to rethink its relationship to popular religious practices and to engage in new ways with progressive Islamic groups, the secular left cannot and must not pretend to be anything but that—secular. For Mufti, then, the left must avoid the pitfall of rejecting the politics of Third World secularism outright, thus aligning themselves with fundamentalist religious elements in the Third World, simply because they are in the Third World and opposed to American imperialism. At the same time, Mufti also warns that the secular left should distance itself from Rushdie's "visibly growing comfort in the corridors of metropolitan power."

Feroza Jussawalla's essay also centrally addresses the controversy over *The Satanic Verses*. Exploring the relationship of that novel to Islamic literary tradition, Jussawalla concludes that *The Satanic Verses* is a deeply Islamic book that can be understood only within specifically Indian Islamic traditions and that attempts to read the book essentially within the tradition of the Western novel have led to serious misperceptions of Rushdie's project. Particularly rejecting attempts to read *The Satanic Verses* within the context of postmodernism, Jussawalla notes that Rushdie's ambivalent attitude toward Islam in the book itself participates in a long tradition of Islamic texts. In particular, she argues that *The Satanic Verses* is best understood as an example of an Islamic poetic genre known as the *dastan-e-dilruba,* or love story created for the beloved. In this case, the beloved is Islam itself, thus emphasizing Rushdie's rootedness within Islamic culture despite his criticisms of Islamic fundamentalism. Jussawalla thus calls needed attention to important aspects of the background of Rushdie's most controversial novel that Western scholars might tend to miss. Her argument in dismissing the rather obvious influence of Western culture on the book may go too far, however, while her suggestion that scholars such as Brennan have entirely ignored the importance of the book's Islamic heritage may not be entirely fair.

In an essay that is at least partly a response to Mufti and Jussawalla (or at least to some of the issues addressed in their work), Timothy Brennan discusses the cultural politics of the *Satanic Verses* affair, focusing in particular on how controversies over the treatment of Islam in the novel have obscured important aspects of the book itself—sometimes even with Rushdie's collaboration. As Brennan points out, the novel deals primarily with the experience of England's immigrant community, while its political satire is aimed far more at the uncritical chauvinism of Thatcherite Britain than at religious intolerance in Khomeini's Iran. Meanwhile, Brennan argues, the attempts of "postcolonial" scholars, who live and work in the West but claim special cultural knowledge because of their South Asian or other Third World roots, to conscript Rushdie for their own agendas have tended to set aside (or make it dangerous to mention) certain basic aspects of his writing, like the central influence on his whole career of the novels of the Latin American boom or the crucial importance of Western popular culture to his writing.

Bishnupriya Ghosh's essay focuses primarily on *The Moor's Last Sigh* and represents a major contribution to early criticism on that work. In particular, Ghosh focuses on Rushdie's last novel in an effort to locate him as an "Indian postmodern," whose culture-specific use of English transforms the official language of global capital into a vernacular Indian language, a nonstandard, localized Bombay English that cannot be properly appreciated apart from the postcolonial context of its enunciation. Ghosh argues that her characterization of Rushdie's language explodes the tendency of most critical discussions of the Indian novel in English to oppose such novels to those written in Indian vernacular languages. She concludes that Rushdie's practice of a cultural hybridity situated in the very specific context of postcolonial Bombay undermines Western appropriations of his work into the discourses of postmodernism. While agreeing that Rushdie's work is in some sense postmodern, she argues that Rushdie's postmodernism is of a specifically Indian, postcolonial type that can be understood and appreciated only within the context of discourses (historical, linguistic, popular cultural) that are rooted in the same postcolonial context as Rushdie's fiction.

Farhad Idris's essay also focuses on *The Moor's Last Sigh*. Idris notes that Abraham Zogoiby, patriarch of the Zogoiby family, prospers phenomenally as a financial mogul in postcolonial India and argues that Abraham's success indicates India's growing bourgeois capitalism. But as Idris also notes, Abraham loses all his fortune in a spate of violence that grips the nation in the wake of the Babri mosque demolition by fanatic Hindus. His prospects and mischances thus mirror India's contemporary socioeconomic scene, scarred by corruption, communal strife, and various forms of political violence. Idris employs the work of Frantz Fanon, especially *The Wretched of the Earth,* to illuminate the forces underlying the grim political and economic realities of decolonized India. Even though India's colonial and postcolonial conditions are different in many respects from the African nations Fanon directly discusses, Idris finds that India, as presented by Rushdie in *The Moor's Last Sigh,* still well illustrates the findings of Fanon's work.

The first essay in the collection devoted specifically to *Midnight's Children* is Dubravka Juraga's study of the novel within the context of the traditional Western genre of the bildungsroman but with a recognition that this genre has been widely employed by postcolonial writers in recent decades. Juraga finds that in comparison to the works of postcolonial writers such as Gordimer, Barbados's George Lamming, Kenya's Ngugi wa Thiong'o, and India's Mulk Raj Anand, Rushdie's book remains trapped within Western conceptions of subjectivity. Moreover, Juraga finds that despite the rather transparent connection between the story of Saleem Sinai's life and the history of postcolonial India, *Midnight's Children* lacks the focus, central to the works of these other writers, on the building of alternative postcolonial cultural identities that escape the domination of the Western cultural tradition. Juraga's final conclusion is that read as a bildungsroman, Rushdie's novel appears to be fundamentally informed by a postmodernist worldview (and thus by the ideology of late capitalism), regardless of its surface engagement with postcolonial subject matter. Juraga's discussion also usefully suggests the relevance to Rushdie's work of the works of Russian emigré writers such as Sasha Sokolov and Vassily Aksyonov, thus indicating a rich context within which Rushdie has seldom been read.

The next several essays on *Midnight's Children* are somewhat more conventional in their view of the potential power of the book. For example, Michael Gorra's essay, extracted from a book in which he explores the work of Rushdie, Paul Scott, and V. S. Naipaul within the context of literary representations of postcolonial India, begins with a focus on the way in which Saleem Sinai functions in Rushdie's novel as an allegory of Indian national identity. Gorra then focuses on Rushdie's use of language to argue the richly intertextual nature of *Midnight's Children,* which is thereby shown to be extensively connected to a number of different cultural traditions, from the British colonialist literature of writers such as Kipling to the popular culture of the modern Bombay film industry. Gorra argues that Rushdie's use of a heteroglossic and intentionally impure English makes the book subversive of any range of monological ideologies, including not only the legacy of British colonialism but also such contemporary "purist" notions as the Hindu nationalism of the Bharatiya Janata Party. *Midnight's Children* thus becomes not only a celebration of Indian diversity but an exploration of the complexities of the postcolonial and postmodern self. Gorra ends with a note of discomfort that Rushdie's highly literary and ironic style tends to distance readers from emotional involvement in the text, making it very difficult, among other things, to genuinely care about the fates of the individual characters. All in all, however, he finds *Midnight's Children* a rich contribution to the discourse of Indian postcolonial identity.

Todd Kuchta's essay also argues the political power of *Midnight's Children* as a postcolonial novel by attempting to revise allegorical readings of *Midnight's Children;* he applies Walter Benjamin's writings on allegory to Rushdie's representation of the historical events that overshadowed his composition—as well as Saleem Sinai's narration—of the novel. Rushdie demythologizes the official rhetoric of modernization and discipline that justified Indira Gandhi's two-year Emergency rule by using recurrent allegorical images, especially the finger and hand, to link Gandhi's regime to the oppression of British imperialism. Benjamin's concept of allegory thus brings to *Midnight's Children* a recognition that the novel's fragmentary structure is neither politically effete nor epistemologically inept but rather an intervention into the repressed memory of modern Indian history.

In the next article, Michael Reder argues that Saleem Sinai, in the process of narrating *Midnight's Children,* offers an alternative historiography for India, one that emphasizes the individual's self-narration by employing a radically individualist historical discourse that challenges traditional notions of national myth and epic. Reder also argues that Rushdie challenges not only the traditional use of allegory found in colonial fiction and Indian criticism but also the allegorical interpretation of postcolonial texts. Saleem's narrative is most productively read "anti-allegorically," that is, against the grain, in opposition to his story's blatant or implied allegorical connections and meanings. For Reder, Rushdie ultimately asserts the primacy of individual narration over both official history and the idea of the nation-state.

Josna Rege's article sees *Midnight's Children* as an important breakthrough in attempts to explore India's postcolonial national identity through fiction. She notes that the book's treatment of themes such as fragmentation corresponds to the centrality of similar themes in contemporary global debates about nationalism. However, she reads Rushdie's book primarily within a specifically Indian context rather than the larger context of postcolonial cosmopolitanism, arguing that the book, in its complex treatment of

Saleem Sinai as a figure of the Indian nation, "enacts a discursive reconfiguration of the relationship between Self and Nation" in ways that have been inspirational for subsequent Indian novelists. Rege then briefly discusses a number of Rushdie's successors, including Namita Gokhale, Amitav Ghosh, Upamanyu Chatterjee, I. Allan Sealy, Boman Desai, Shashi Tharoor, and Nina Sibal, noting that these authors also tend to explore narratives of Indian national identity and that they do so in ways clearly influenced by *Midnight's Children*. For Rege, this legacy of influence helps to keep Rushdie's book relevant nearly two decades after its original publication, when it "remains a celebration of India, a paean to both unity and multiplicity, and both inspiration and challenge to a new generation."

The volume ends with my own essay on *Midnight's Children,* an essay that grows out of concerns that gradually developed in my own mind in the course of compiling and editing this volume. It also grows out of a growing discomfort with the ideas expressed in my own early essays on Rushdie's work, now written approximately a decade ago. In my essay "Beauty and the Beast," for example, I praise Rushdie for his ability to embrace contradiction and to deconstruct polar oppositions. But as Brennan has persuasively argued in his recent work *At Home in the World,* such claims that polar oppositions are overly simplistic (and typical of totalitarian political thought) have become an increasingly problematic cliché of literary studies, and especially postcolonial studies, in recent years.[20] Most prominent in the latter context are Sara Suleri's rejection of "alteritist" distinctions between East and West and Homi Bhabha's insistence that a "Manichean" opposition between colonizing and colonized cultures fails to comprehend the complexities of the cultural hybridity that results from the colonial encounter.[21]

Such visions of hybridity have been extremely fashionable in postcolonial studies in recent years, though the obvious influence of both poststructuralist and postmodernist ideas on them is problematic, to say the least. Bhabha in particular has come in for considerable criticism, as in Abdul JanMohamed's charge that Bhabha's poststructuralist perspective effaces the political realities of domination in the colonial situation or in E. San Juan's recent argument that Bhabha's "subordination of everything to the language metaphor and its exorbitant implications compels him to distort and render inutile the praxis-oriented" work of earlier Third World intellectuals such as Fanon.[22] Both JanMohamed and San Juan are writing from points of view strongly influenced by Marxist theory, and in my own view the fascination with complexity and concomitant horror of dual oppositions that has dominated much recent postcolonial theory can be attributed at least in part to a lingering anti-Marxism that shows the clear influence of Cold War stereotypes about the simplistic nature of the class-based oppositions so central to Marxism.

In the final essay, I explore this notion within the context of criticism of Rushdie's work. In particular, I read *Midnight's Children* as a historical novel and find that when compared with other examples of the same genre,

Rushdie's novel has far more in common with postmodernist works than with postcolonial ones. Moreover, I find that the challenges to the official historiography of the Enlightenment West that so many critics have found to be central to *Midnight's Children* lack force, partly because of their failure to explore the possibility of Marxist historiography as a viable alternative. Pursuing this notion, I find that a great deal of Rushdie's novel, especially its severe treatment of Indira Gandhi, seems based on an unstated anticommunist subtext and can be read as a continuation of the anticommunist discourse of the Cold War West. I then conclude that critics need to be wary of such possibilities before automatically endorsing Rushdie's work as subversive of the neocolonial hegemony of global capitalism simply because it explores narrative forms that violate the conventions of Western scientific historiography. Moreover, I argue that the odd dual tendency toward glorification of complexity and demonization of modernity that has been typical of postcolonial scholarship may itself be a continuation of Cold War stereotypes and thus should be treated with considerable skepticism.

Notes

1. See, for example, Salman Rushdie, "Damme, This Is the Oriental Scene for You!" *New Yorker* (23 and 30 June 1997): 50–61.
2. Maria Couto, "Midnight's Children and Parents," *Encounter* 58 (1982): 61–66, 63.
3. Salman Rushdie, "The Empire Writes Back with a Vengeance," *Times* (London) (3 July 1982): 8.
4. Uma Parameswaran, "Handcuffed to History: Salman Rushdie's Art," *Ariel* 14 (1983): 34–45.
5. See, for example, Rustom Bharucha, "Rushdie's Whale," *Massachusetts Review* 27 (1986): 221–37; David Lipscomb, "Caught in a Strange Middle Ground: Contesting History in Salman Rushdie's *Midnight's Children*," *Diaspora* 1, no. 2 (1991): 163–88; Neil ten Kortenaar, "*Midnight's Children* and the Allegory of History," *Ariel* 26, no. 2 (1995): 41–62.
6. On Rushdie and Grass, see Rudolph Bader, "Indian *Tin Drum*," *International Fiction Review* 11 (1984): 75–83; Patricia Merivale, "Saleem Fathered by Oskar: Intertextual Strategies in *Midnight's Children* and *The Tin Drum*, *Ariel* 21, no. 3 (1990): 5–21. On Rushdie and García Márquez, see Kumkum Sangari, "The Politics of the Possible," *Cultural Critique* 7 (Fall 1987): 157–86; Timothy Brennan, "Fantasy, Individuality, and the Politics of Liberation," *Polygraph* 1, no. 1 (1987): 89–99. See also Jean-Pierre Durix, "Magic Realism in *Midnight's Children*," *Commonwealth Essays and Studies* 8, no. 1 (1985): 57–63.
7. Some of the most important essays that deal centrally with *Shame* include M. D. Fletcher, "Rushdie's *Shame* as Apologue," *Journal of Commonwealth Literature* 21, no. 1 (1986): 120–32; Inderpal Grewal, "Salman Rushdie: Marginality, Women, and *Shame*," *Genders* 3 (November 1988): 24–42, Aruna Srivastava, " 'The Empire Writes Back': Language and History in *Shame* and *Midnight's Children*," *Ariel* 20, no. 4 (1989): 62–78; and Andrew Enda Duffy, "Engendering Monsters," *South Asian Review* 16, no. 13 (January 1992): 98–109. Books on broader subjects that feature chapters focusing on *Shame* include Sara Suleri, *The Rhetoric of English India* (Chicago: University of Chicago Press, 1992), and Aijaz Ahmad, *In Theory: Classes, Nations, Literatures* (London: Verso, 1992).

8. New essays that are at least in part critical of Rushdie's engagement with Indian history in *Midnight's Children* include David W. Price, "Salman Rushdie's 'Use and Abuse of History' in *Midnight's Children,*" *Ariel* 25, no. 2 (1994): 91–107, and Ronny Noor, "Misrepresentation of History in Salman Rushdie's *Midnight's Children,*" *Notes on Contemporary Literature* 26, no. 2 (1996): 7–8.

9. M. Keith Booker, "*Finnegans Wake* and *The Satanic Verses:* Two Modern Myths of the Fall," *Critique* 32, no. 3 (1991): 190–207. On *The Satanic Verses* and Joyce, see also Feroza Jussawalla, "Post-Joycean Sub-Joycean: The Reverses of Mr. Rushdie's Tricks in *The Satanic Verses,*" in *The New Indian Novel in English: A Study of the 1980s,* ed. Viney Kirpal (New Delhi: Allied Publishers, 1990), 227–38.

10. On *The Satanic Verses* and history, see Amin Malak, "Reading the Crisis: The Polemics of Salman Rushdie's *The Satanic Verses,*" *Ariel* 20, no. 4 (1989): 176–86 and Sourayan Mookerjea, "Irradiations of History: The Author, Cosmopolitanism, and *The Satanic Verses,*" *World Literature Written in English* 32, no. 2–33, no. 1 (1992–1993): 107–21. On gender in *The Satanic Verses,* see Gayatri Chakravorty Spivak, "Reading *The Satanic Verses,*" *Public Culture* 2, no. 1 (1989): 79–99 and Janet Mason Ellerby, "Narrative Imperialism in *The Satanic Verses,*" in *Multicultural Literatures through Feminist/Poststructuralist Lenses,* ed. Barbara Frey Waxman (Knoxville: University of Tennessee Press, 1993), 173–89. On dialogism and postmodernism in *The Satanic Verses,* see Gerald Marzorati, "Fiction's Embattled Infidel," *New York Times Magazine* (29 January 1989): 25 ff.; Mark Edmundsen, "Prophet of a New Postmodernism," *Harper's Magazine* 279 (December 1989): 62–71; M. Keith Booker, "Beauty and the Beast: Dualism as Despotism in the Fiction of Salman Rushdie," *ELH* 57 (1990): 977–97.

11. For a good discussion of the Orientalism of much of the discourse surrounding the *Satanic Verses* affair, see Anouar Majid, "Can the Postcolonial Critic Speak?: Orientalism and the Rushdie Affair," *Cultural Critique* 32 (Winter 1995–1996): 5–42.

12. For a good account of some of the early book-length reactions to the controversy, see Sara Suleri, "Whither Rushdie?," *Transition* 51 (1991): 198–212. Suleri notes, for example, the consistent appeal to Manichean oppositions that inform works such as Malise Ruthven, *A Satanic Affair: Salman Rushdie and the Rage of Islam* (London: Chatto and Windus, 1990). And she pulls no punches in her assessment of the Orientalist outrages of a work such as Daniel Pipes, *The Rushdie Affair: The Novel, the Ayatollah, and the West* (New York: Birch Lane Press, 1990). She notes, for example, that "if it were permissible to burn books," then Pipes's would surely be a good candidate (205).

13. See, for example, Sara Suleri, "Contraband Histories: Salman Rushdie and the Embodiment of Blasphemy," *Yale Review* 78, no. 4 (1989): 604–24, and Feroza Jussawalla, "Resurrecting the Prophet: The Case of Salman, the Otherwise," *Public Culture* 2, no. 1 (1989): 106–17. See also Jussawalla's "Rushdie's *Dastan-e-Dilruba*" and Aamir Mufti's "Reading the Rushdie Affair," reprinted in this volume.

14. See Brennan's response to complaints by scholars such as Mufti, Suleri, and Jussawalla that he has failed to appreciate the Islamic context of *The Satanic Verses* in "Rushdie, Islam, and Postcolonial Criticism," *Social Text* 31/32 (1992): 271–76. And see Mufti's counter-response to Brennan in "*The Satanic Verses* and the Cultural Politics of 'Islam': A Response to Brennan," *Social Text* 31/32 (1992): 277–82.

15. Paul Cantor, in one of the first formal critical pieces on *The Moor's Last Sigh,* praises the book for creating "a fictional world that mirrors the problematics of postcoloniality," thus describing the book in terms reminiscent of those typically used to describe *Midnight's Children* and *The Satanic Verses.* See Paul Cantor, "Tales of the Alhambra: Rushdie's Use of Spanish History in *The Moor's Last Sigh,*" *Studies in the Novel* 29, no. 3 (1997): 323–41, 336.

16. On the other hand, lest we get carried away, it should be pointed out that a search for "James Joyce" yields over 5,800 entries, and one for "William Shakespeare" yields a whopping total of more than 20,000! Reports from the right that "multiculturalism" has now com-

pletely supplanted the conventional canon in literary studies would seem from this statistic to be greatly exaggerated.

17. The book-length studies are Timothy Brennan, *Salman Rushdie and the Third World: Myths of the Nation* (London: Macmillan, 1989); J. Harrison, *Salman Rushdie* (New York: Twayne, 1992); Catherine Cundy, *Salman Rushdie* (Manchester, England: Manchester University Press, 1996). The other collection of essays is M. D. Fletcher, ed., *Reading Rushdie: Perspectives on the Fiction of Salman Rushdie* (Amsterdam: Rodopi, 1994).

18. Aijaz Ahmad, *In Theory: Classes, Nations, Literatures* (London: Verso, 1992), 111.

19. Typical of recent positive readings of the subversive nature of Rushdie's fiction are Kathryn Hume, "Taking a Stand while Lacking a Center: Rushdie's Postmodern Politics," *Philological Quarterly* 74, no. 2 (1995): 209–30; Jean M. Kane, "The Migrant Intellectual and the Body of History: Salman Rushdie's *Midnight's Children*," *Contemporary Literature* 37, no. 1 (1996): 94–118; and Neil ten Kortenaar, "Postcolonial Ekphrasis: Salman Rushdie Gives the Finger Back to the Empire," *Contemporary Literature* 38, no. 2 (1997): 232–59.

20. Timothy Brennan, *At Home in the World: Cosmopolitanism Now* (Cambridge, Mass.: Harvard University Press, 1997).

21. See Suleri, *The Rhetoric of English India;* Homi K. Bhabha, *The Location of Culture* (London: Routledge, 1994).

22. Abdul R. JanMohamed, "The Economy of Manichean Allegory: The Function of Racial Difference in Colonialist Literature," in *"Race," Writing, and Difference,* ed. Henry Louis Gates Jr. (Chicago: University of Chicago Press, 1986), 78–106, 78–79; Epifanio San Juan, *Beyond Postcolonial Theory* (New York: St. Martin's, 1998), 27.

"Marching In from the Peripheries": Rushdie's Feminized Artistry and Ambivalent Feminism

AMBREEN HAI

"The women are now moving to the center of my little stage....
{T}hey, not the men, were the true protagonists in the struggle."
—Rushdie, *The Moor's Last Sigh* (33)

I

In one of his striking asides in the unfolding narration of *Shame*, Rushdie-as-narrator pauses to remark:

> I had thought, before I began, that what I had on my hands was an almost excessively masculine tale, a saga of sexual rivalry, ambition, power, patronage, betrayal, death, revenge. But the women seem to have taken over; *they marched in from the peripheries of the story* to demand the inclusion of their own tragedies, histories, comedies, obliging me to couch my narrative in all manner of sinuous complexities, to see my "male" plot refracted, so to speak, through the prisms of its reverse and female side. It occurs to me that the women knew precisely what they were up to—that their stories explain, and even subsume, the men's.... So it turns out that my "male" and "female" plots are the same story, after all.[1] (emphasis added)

Rushdie begins by invoking the only-too-familiar binarisms "masculine/feminine," "center/periphery," and by ellipsis, "metropolis/colony," "colonizer/colonized." By deploying the militarist metaphor "marching in from the peripheries," he suggests that women and their stories can enact a reversal of power inequities and aggressively invade male "centrality" to "demand inclusion"—just as, by implication, postcolonial narratives like his own can "write

---

This essay was written specifically for this volume and is published for the first time by permission of the author.

back" to the so-called imperial "center" and "decolonize Britain."[2] But then he collapses the binarisms: the women's stories not only interrupt and "subsume" the "men's" but turn out to be "the same after all." By "refracting" the male stories in an "other" light, the "women"—both as subjects of the stories *and* as artists and mobile agents of change—transform the stories in content and in form and productively disorder the very categories of exclusion or definition.

This passage has often been quoted to adduce Rushdie's attempt (and unfortunate failure) at a purported feminism.[3] However, I find it exemplary because it also suggests that perhaps women's art—within Rushdie's art— can be revolutionary. First in *Shame,* and then recurrently throughout his subsequent work, from Bilquis and Rani Harappa, Zeeny Vakil and Ayesha, to Aurora, Uma, and Aei-ou in *The Moor's Last Sigh,* Rushdie will suggest increasingly both that women have a distinctive oppositional creativity, often because of their marginality, and that this power can be a trope that he can appropriate for, or that can be comparable to, his own construction of postcolonial artistic identity. This "feminized artistry" of the women he describes can then also become his own, a blueprint for his own postcolonial storytelling and politics. In this telling passage, by implicit self-analogy with what he chooses to represent as a "female" strategy, Rushdie suggests that his stories, too, can enact such a transformation on colonial or metropolitan ones, transforming not only what is defined as self/other, native/alien, but also dismantling the very grounds of such a binarism by being transformed themselves. Thus in an emblematic metanarratival self-reflexive moment in *The Satanic Verses,* whereas Gibreel Farishta attempts to "tropicalize London" in a powerful imagining of countercolonization (354), it is the *mother* of a dead resistance fighter who finally survives and succeeds in such a project, declaring to an assembly of immigrants in London: "Make no mistake. We are here to change things. I concede at once that we shall ourselves be changed.... We have been made again: but I say that we shall also be the ones to remake this society" (414).

Rushdie thus constructs a dual comparison—and perhaps competition—between two registers of alterity: feminist revision and postcolonial resistance. Like the women's stories, Rushdie's story interrupts itself—as a "feminine" move of interruption of its own "masculine" tale—to suggest Rushdie's own attempt at crossing boundaries of gender, at metamorphosing from male plot into female forms of "sinuous complexities." At the same time he also suggests that what is considered "feminine" might itself be changed by the oppositional force of his writing, that he too can be *feminist* in contesting culturally ascribed, constraining gender norms. (In this essay, I use the terms *female, feminine,* and *feminist* as, respectively, pertaining to women, sometimes for supposedly innate biological reasons; culturally, socially, or historically constructed and assigned traits; and a politically chosen position against patriarchy and sexism regardless of assignations of gender or sexuality.[4])

Yet such a metanarratival passage—and trend—nevertheless poses a number of problematic questions. How, for instance, might it serve Rushdie to cast postcolonial insurgency (narratival, national, artistic, or political) as "feminine"? How and why does he gender his storytelling—in what ways indeed does (or must) his story cross-dress to serve its own ends? How does Rushdie (re)envisage, reconstruct, or perhaps reify gender in order to orchestrate an idiom for postcolonial fictive or historiographic narration? What ideologies of gender—essentialist (based on the body or sexuality) or constructivist (assuming that gender is socially and discursively constructed) or heteronormative (built on the exclusive bipolarity of heterosexuality)—impel such translations?[5] What are the implications of mapping one form of disenfranchisement and self-enablement on another? At one point, Rushdie reflects soberly, and rightly (via Saladin Chamcha), on the dangers of conflating the different histories of slavery and of colonization, cautioning that neither should be collapsed into the other (*SV*, 415). But then does he proceed to enact the same kind of conflation in another register, mapping the histories of patriarchal and colonial subjugation on each other? In what ways is it possible to be critical and/or celebratory of such moves on his part?

In this essay I will make two interwoven arguments as I trace a dual impulse in Rushdie's writing, ranging from *Midnight's Children* to *The Moor's Last Sigh*. On the one hand, I will explore the ambiguous figure of the female migrant as artist and creator in these narratives. I will argue that: (1) Rushdie uses figures of female artistry in changing and contradictory ways to represent his own postcolonial artistic and political work, and borrows or competes with what he sees as strategies of feminist revision to enable or situate his own postcolonial narration; (2) in relation or in addition to these representations he attempts feminist work by questioning certain patriarchal norms and recasting or foregrounding cultural and social injustices toward women. Thus he also seeks to transform the categories of both the feminine and the (formerly) colonized.

On the other hand, as we will see, the shifting grounds of his self-asserted feminism become more complicated and ambivalent in different ways with each text. Thus I will also show that the feminist/revisionist impulse in Rushdie is countered by another quite contradictory though changing one. His narratives undermine their own (proto)feminist strains by regressing (perhaps because of a concurrent anxiety about effeminization/emasculation) into reifications of stereotypes of gender and sexuality, or odd ways of asserting a beleaguered masculinity, and into replaying surprisingly parochial and patriarchal discourses of gender and sexuality. This is manifested in a variety of ways, including plot or narrational structure, tone, representations of women, rhetorical tropes, and overarching symbolic structures that form a network, a set of resonances that collectively adumbrate not an isolated phenomenon but an entire way of seeing, a larger tendency and (in)coherent, if unconscious, ideology.

Even in the passage with which I began, what is particularly curious is the way in which, despite his good intentions, Rushdie genders both stories and the act of storytelling. At first it seems as if "male plots" are masculine by virtue of their themes, content, and subjects (they are about men and male things, sexual rivalry, power, patronage, etc.), while "femaleness" is conveyed primarily by absence of form (through "sinuous complexity" or the instrumentality of the proverbial vessel—a "prism" that can enable another way of seeing the same story). Rushdie's self-posturing as narrator, moreover, suggests an oddly unsteady position: it shifts from being first neutral (as if he were an umpire between the men and women), then male (by implication and possession—"my male plot"), and finally female (*his* narrative, too, has to be "couched" in womanly forms). Rushdie presents the richness of a double vision for his readers—he can see and see again, via both male and female plots. But an alternative reading of the "refraction" by women's stories of men's stories suggests instead that those women's stories are not to be seen in or for themselves but rather as alternative ways of reflecting on *men's* stories, so that the female plots at best can be appendages, supplemental but not integral in themselves.

The passage concludes with a proclamation of the narrator's feminist qualifications and a minatory prefiguring of the plot of *Shame*:

> It is commonly and I believe accurately said of Pakistan that her women are much more impressive than her men. . . . [T]heir chains, nevertheless, are no fictions. They exist. And they are getting heavier.
> *If you hold down one thing you hold down the adjoining.*
> In the end, though, it all blows up in your face. (*Shame*, 189; Rushdie's emphasis)

Combined with the self-conscious recognition of the problems of the women of Pakistan again are unselfconscious (and unfounded) assumptions of neutral objectivity. We may well wonder: to whom and on what grounds are the women "more impressive"—to themselves, or to a Westernized/masculine eye like Rushdie's own? And why, after all, is Pakistan a "she"—is it a counterpart to "Mother India?" Surely such gendering precisely returns to the familiar tropologies of nationhood that we have learned to recognize as problematic and that are amply echoed in this text in the ominously oppressive figures of destructive matriarchs, who include Bariamma (of whom I will say more later), head of the national family.[6]

Most critics who have addressed Rushdie's attempts at feminism have concentrated on either the problems or the achievements but not on how they work together or change, nor on the growing importance of tropes of women's art in his work. Moreover, the texts on which they focus remain

Shame and *The Satanic Verses*. I propose to trace, through the trajectory of Rushdie's work, the *shifting* contours and specific problems of each novel, to see how in each text the balance works a little differently, and to show how, across Rushdie's development in time, certain changes occur both in his feminized artistry and in his ambivalent feminism. In his early narratives, the female migrant, often endowed with magical powers of storytelling, song, or prophecy (Amina Sinai and Jamila Singer in *Midnight's Children,* Bilquis and Rani in *Shame*), is either a model or a competitor for the Rushdie narrator but is often ineffectual or remains marginal. By *The Satanic Verses,* Ayesha and Zeeny Vakil are central emblems of Rushdie's own narrative project: Ayesha embodies the force of a feminized revision and salvation of Islam, and Zeeny's philosophy alone articulates Rushdie's urgent understanding of cultural hybridity and migrancy. In *The Moor's Last Sigh,* Aurora and Uma have displaced male figures to become the central dualistic oppositional poles for reflexively emblematizing Rushdie's thorny concerns with postcolonial art, secularism versus communalism, and individual identity. However, as we will see, Rushdie's sexual stereotypes and misogynistic idiom are the bleakest in *Shame,* adjusted in *The Satanic Verses,* and definitely qualified by *The Moor's Last Sigh*. Some of these changes may in fact be a response to notable critiques by such critics as Aijajz Ahmad and Inderpal Grewal, but still other residues remain, or resurgences operate in new ways. I will begin with *Shame,* locating it at the center of both these trajectories, trace them back to *Midnight's Children* and *Grimus,* and then forward to Rushdie's more recent writing.

After the seminal work of Fanon or Said, which nevertheless retained the binarisms of colonial discourse, a second wave of postcolonial critics including Sara Suleri, Homi Bhabha, and Ann McClintock has taught us to read ambivalence in colonial discourse.[7] But it is still not a widespread practice to read postcolonial discourse as also equally ambivalent, as equally a palimpsest of conflicting ideologies. Rarely do critics of "Third World Literature," as Ahmad cautions us, read it against its grain or avoid the "complicity of a shared starting point" (Ahmad, 142). In the spirit of such an enterprise, I would like to explore the changing register of Rushdie's ambivalent feminism. If Rushdie's feminism is indeed an "honorable failure," as Gayatri Spivak generously terms that project in *The Satanic Verses,*[8] then I would also like to suggest that it is precisely the nodes of contradiction that are most interesting, and indeed inseparable. Postcolonial criticism as it is currently practiced sometimes tends to subsume texts to an overarching agenda or theoretical framework, which, though illuminating, can also overlook their subtlety and irreconcilable tensions. However, a more probing or nuanced, though theoretically informed, *reading* of the text may reveal a more self-knowing and complicated position, accounting for its more intractable twists and turns.

II

The feminism of *Shame,* which was inspired, as Rushdie himself describes, by the murder of a "dishonored" Pakistani girl in England by her own father (*Shame,* 123–26), has led critics such as Grewal and Ahmad rightly to question Rushdie's representations of female rage that only reinscribe male fear of female power as bestiality. In his expert analysis of the novel, Ahmad concludes:

> Rushdie is not, in the way Orwell always was, a misogynist plain and simple. Living in the contemporary milieu of the British Left, he has not remained untouched by certain kinds of feminism. . . . The complication is of a different order, and politically far more devastating than a mere lack of sympathy. It is only after taking into account that structure of sympathy and the kind of politics in which it is embedded that one can proceed to examine the more central issues in his representation of women. (Ahmad, 143)

Thus while acknowledging the "powerful images" of women and Rushdie's "vivid sympathies," Ahmad analyzes the text's crucial "disjuncture between particular episodes . . . (and) a generalized structure of representation" where "every woman, without exception, is sexually overdetermined; the frustration of erotic need . . . appears in every case to be the central fact of a woman's existence," and more particularly, where the central figure of female rage, embodied in the "Beast of Shame," replicates misogynistic stereotypes of "physiological insufficiency" and violently destructive seductiveness (Ahmad, 144–52). With his cogent readings I largely agree, though I would add that "powerful images" of women are surely not a sufficient condition for feminism (as Spivak has said of *The Satanic Verses* [Spivak, n. 15, 317]) and that the problem is not merely a subjective one of Rushdie's women characters being "dislikable and frequently repugnant" to us (Ahmad, 144). The challenge is not to make them more *attractive* (how would this gender and situate us as readers?) but rather to change such grounds of assessment to less compromised modes of representation.

Grewal also notes "a disjunction between the mode of inclusion in which the narrative [of *Shame*] is written, and the authoritative stance of the writer[,] . . . [which] breaks down a coalition between the writer and women" (Grewal, 25). Her main criticism is that Rushdie reinscribes Pakistani women's roles as passive and ineffective and fails to draw on an existing "history of struggle, instead . . . of subjection"—he suggests the need for "coalition" but neither depicts one as it is in fact taking place in Pakistan in the brutal context of General Zia's imposition of "Islamic Laws" or in Britain under a racist regime, nor creates one himself within the text (Grewal, 30, 41, 36–40). However, Grewal's readings make at least two presuppositions with which I take issue: one, that the locus of Rushdie's failure is his inability to offer an accurate representation of the real opposition offered by Pakistani women; two, that Rushdie's authoritative voice disallows the possibility of women's voices or agency and in fact breaks the analogy between marginalized writer and women by appropriating powers of narration that he denies to women (Grewal, 27, 29). While the first is a valid criticism especially in locating feminist struggles within the context of recent legalized discrimination in Pakistan, it risks suggesting that mimetic verisimilitude is a sufficient goal instead of changes in the structure of representation itself. More important, the second, by concentrating exclusively on the logic of exclusion/inclusion, overlooks the ways in which Rushdie both validates what he depicts as women's unusual powers of art and creative opposition and suggests that even if they may be ineffective or vulnerable precisely because of the powers of censorship and totalitarianism, *so may his own*. Thus neither Ahmad nor Grewal considers how Rushdie figures the possibilities of women's art—as his own.

I will begin with the foundational narrative of Bilquis, the mother and primal source of Shame, and by implication, perhaps, another origin for the novel. The archetypal migrant to the new postcolonial nation Pakistan, Bilquis is the girl whose past in India literally disappears in flames and whose beautiful naked body is rescued and reclothed by her future husband, the future president of Pakistan (as if the two were coterminous), just as her story is retold by her new family, re-covering her, in every sense, from the nakedness of her past. That this is a literal/metaphorical paradigm of the migrant and postcolonial nation as female is emphasized by Rushdie's comment "All migrants leave their past behind, although some try to pack it in to bundles and boxes. . . . [I]t is the fate of migrants to be stripped of history, to stand naked amid the scorn of strangers upon whom they see the rich clothing, the brocades of continuity and the eyebrows of belonging" (*Shame*, 64).

If migrancy must be understood in terms of the vulnerability of a singed, naked, nubile female body, or perhaps as emblematic of those who are forced to change homes and names, then Rushdie's deployment of such notions of femaleness seeks to cast a gendered disempowered condition as a generic one. As middle-class Pakistani women are routinely married by familial arrangement into new homes after dehumanizing processes of inspection and commodification, and forced to prove themselves again as members of a new family, so, he suggests, emigrants are the weaker partners who have to leave their pasts behind and seek refuge in a national marriage for which they must always remain grateful.

However, Rushdie also suggests that there is something uniquely female/marginal in the act of storytelling and that that migrancy-as-femaleness is ultimately a creative if transformative force.[9] As a condition of acceptance into the family, Bilquis has to tell her story, which then becomes part of the "family catalogue" of oft-retold tales of self-fashioning (*Shame*, 78). But if, in a parable of national self-invention as an imagined community, these tales in the retelling necessarily (re)define the family *to* the family, her migrant tale then also *changes* that sense of collective identity, as it blends into and transforms a sense of who and what that collective is.[10] It thus becomes the model for Rushdie's own migrant storytelling—as literal migrant from India to Pakistan, and to Britain, and as figurative migrant everywhere, a Westernized returnee to a culture suspicious of his "forked tongue," his claims to authority (*Shame,* 28). Moreover, it is precisely such migrants, he suggests, in *Shame* and in *The Satanic Verses,* who need to construct new stories and thus new nations and identities and who are indeed responsible for changing the world into which they march: "It is well known that the term "Pakistan" . . . was originally thought up in England by a group of Muslim intellectuals. . . . So it was a word born in exile which then went East, was borne-across or trans-lated, settling down on partitioned land. . . . Who commandeered the job of rewriting history? The immigrants, the *mohajirs* (*Shame,* 91; Rushdie's emphasis).

In the context of the violent sectarianism in Pakistan, where, despite being Muslim, the "mohajirs" who immigrated from India now face severe discrimination, Rushdie suggests that it is the mohajirs, the dispossessed, like the female arrivant, who in fact are responsible for the invention and construction of nationhood and identity, through the imagining and (self-) enabling of national narratives. (It is also historically true that the nationalist leaders who imagined and demanded the separation of Pakistan from British India were in fact such migrants.)

Of course, in telling her story the female migrant is also *dis*possessed of it. Bilquis's story is wrested from her and turned into the "mummifying" safety of familial and national matriarchal retelling, and Bilquis's urgent need for safety and home allows for her hasty co-optation into a patriarchal and national system (*Shame,* 74–80). Bilquis remains, however, even at the end, a figure whose femaleness suggests the potential for a powerful mobility that is linked with her prescience as a reader and artist. Although it is her daughter, the preternaturally mobile beast of Shame, who embodies the text's focal explosively cataclysmic rage of suppressed femininity, Bilquis's retreat into a "veil of solipsism" (229) enables her alone to predict and prepare for her presidential husband's downfall: like a silent Fury, she sews black shrouds, literally shaping the form that his death will take (275), and then cross-dresses him in women's clothes to deliver him into the hands of the three mothers (Fates) who engineer his death (290). Thus not only does she have the power to reverse agency and gender roles (now *she* clothes *him* and transforms his identity) but also to salvage and reshape the end of his story.

If Bilquis embodies the crucial and complex figure of the artist as both disabled and vengeful, Rushdie attempts, even in *Shame,* to identify yet another kind of female artistic creativity as another model for his own. It is Rani Harappa, whose exquisitely embroidered shawls become a daring exemplum of an alternate historiography that is attributed a centrality and unsurpassed tonal dignity at the core of *Shame.* In perhaps the most exquisite section of the entire novel, itself meticulously crafted with accumulating detail upon detail in a sentence that builds for six pages, Rushdie elaborately and ekphrastically describes Rani's art, figuring her husband's interminable reign of terror, and prefiguring the art of Aurora in *The Moor* (210–14).

Although both Grewal and Ahmad briefly note this episode, they dismiss it as either a "dignity of resignation" or an exemplum of ineffectuality, since as Grewal points out, Rani's work (which is actually directed at the reeducation of her daughter, successor to Iskander) in fact is suppressed and silenced by that daughter, who only "participates in the very regimes of oppression that ensure the suppression of women" (Ahmad, 144; Grewal, 30). However, first, if Rani's work is educational, transformative, and thus threatening enough to be censored, it must surely be politically potent (just as later, to make an obvious point, it would not help Rushdie to claim that *The Satanic Verses* was "only" a novel); second, it can hardly be to Rushdie's discredit to recognize that feminism is not a unifying banner for all women, that women leaders of postcolonial nations have a disgraceful record with regard to women's rights.[11] Rani's art remains a self-reflexive mirror of Rushdie's simultaneous self-glorification and vaunted but real anxiety about censorship, repeated only too often in the text itself—he too can both be silenced *and* speak subversively in another medium.[12]

At the same time, of course, it is well to remember that ekphrasis is a rivalrous art, that the very act of calling on the verbal to render the visual implicitly sets up a competition in which language seeks to assert its dominance over that other medium.[13] Thus Rushdie's narrative necessarily incorporates Rani's embroidery into itself, implicitly asserting its own superior ability to imagine and describe; but the flip side of that tension remains the uneasy sense that such otherness—of gender or medium—cannot ultimately be subsumed, that it will always remain outside, in excess of, the framing control of language. In discussing Achilles's shield, W. J. T. Mitchell writes: "The relation of epic to ekphrasis is . . . turned inside out: the entire action of the *Iliad* becomes a fragment in the totalizing vision provided by Achilles' shield." If, as he suggests, it is a characteristic of ekphrasis not merely to be framed *by* the text but to frame *it* instead, to have "imperial ambitions to take 'dominion everywhere,' " to be "all of literature in miniature," then it is Rani's shawls that have the "totalizing vision" that turns Rushdie's narrative into a fragment of itself, saying in miniature all that that text's garrulity cannot say.[14]

But while Rushdie casts his own—and by extension all—postcolonial art in the idiom of a feminized because marginalized yet potentially transformative craft like Rani's or Bilquis's, suggesting both its power and vulnerability, he also seeks to differentiate it from, and compete with, another kind of "female"-as-national storytelling, that of the archstoryteller, the grand matriarch, Bariamma (literally "Big Mother") herself. It is she who appropriates Bilquis's story: "Bariamma's mildly droning recital of the catalogue of family horrors had the effect of somehow defusing them, making them safe, embalming them in the mummifying fluid of her own incontrovertible respectability" (*Shame,* 79).

By retelling Bilquis's or the migrant's story as only *one* of many in a family's collective repertoire, Bariamma resituates and transforms that story. She changes it both externally by shifting its context (as a story defined by a happy teleology of safe conclusion and inclusion in a larger body) and internally by smoothing over its sharper, more "shameful" but subversive edges (i.e., by strategic omission of that which cannot belong in a triumphalist or self-enabling self-narration). This "mummification" (with a pun on deadly maternity), then, both deadens and preserves by clinical selection, creating a collectivity or "family" based on both remembering and forgetting. If this is Rushdie's misogynistically tinged national allegory of *Pakistani* self-censoring narration (i.e., Pakistan as female body thus preserves itself through such techniques of storytelling as history making and proganda), then by contrast, he suggests, his own narration is anything but "safe" or "mummified"—instead of draining the blood of his stories, depleting them of their (life) force, he insists on telling them whole, the "haram" with the "halal," the legitimate with the "unspeakable," the disallowed (*MC,* 64).[15] Unlike the safe, self-preserving domestication and chosen amnesias of national narrations, which he genders as matriarchal, he claims to take the risks of a storytelling that refuses, at least consciously, to succumb to self-censorship. Thus Rushdie insists on representing such limited national storytelling as the province of a grotesque matriarch, herself an allegory for a nation that could never be his home.[16]

Figures of artists and storytellers in Rushdie's narratives are by no means always women. Indeed, in an odd reversion to gender anxiety, Rushdie's male narrators are frequently emasculated beings, from Omar Khayyam in *Shame,* the "peripheral hero" (mis)named after a famous poet, a sorry successor who cannot write a word, to figures of impotence and putatively female corpulence like the effeminate and literally impotent Nadir Shah and Saleem Sinai in *Midnight's Children.* It is almost as if the anxiety of appropriating the forms of (re)production usually ascribed to women induces in Rushdie a need to subvert their powers, to return to stigmatizations of femaleness as a putative undermining of malehood. Nevertheless, women, linked with a certain essentialism by Rushdie to primal and bodily forces of reproduction, are associated with a potency of reproduction and cataclysmic transformation (ranging in *Midnight's Children* from Durga's endless supply of stories and Padma's procreative listening to Tavleen, the dynamite-breasted female bomber in *Satanic Verses,* the dangerous figure who enables the "re-birth" of the two central characters) to which Rushdie attributes a force of powerful insight, renewal, and regeneration that he suggests—even as he fears and undermines it—might be an apposite resource and model for postcolonial revisionary narration.

III

In this reconstitution of female art, *Shame* suggests something of an advance from *Midnight's Children*. Most critics who have considered the question of gender in the latter have attended to Padma, the unsatisfied desiring mistress and illiterate sounding board who waits on Saleem as he writes his gargantuan tale. While some critics range from celebrating her earthy link with "the common people" to wholesale denunciation of her exploited and subservient status both as character and figure, most agree that she "exists primarily to support Saleem in his quest for narrative order."[17] I would add that Padma—repeatedly presented as crucially enabling for Saleem's narration, often through figures such as the isosceles triangle, the base that enables his "apex" (*Shame*, 177)—also functions, to use Gerald Prince's terms, as the *narratee*, the figure *within* the text who serves to educate imagined real readers.[18] She is the butt of Saleem's narratorial supercilious explanations, which thus direct readers to accept the vagaries of his methodologies, to be more sophisticated than her desire for plot, closure, and linearity. But she also functions as a co-producer of his narrative, the aggressive partner to whom he has *already* told his story before he retells it—with her subsequent revisions—to us. She is an artist, but only in the sense that she is combined into a dualistic amalgam with Saleem (rather like the composite "I-Grimus"), and together they tell Rushdie's tale. They become an elaborate mechanism for internal commentary, self-interruption, and critique, for neither she nor Saleem can accomplish the exhausting task of storytelling without the other. And then there is Durga, the grotesquely productive washerwoman, whose inexhaustible supply of stories and milk outdoes Saleem's by the end. Or Parvati the witch, the third most important midnight's child, another member of the underclass whose magical powers of sorcery nevertheless cannot be allowed to compare with Saleem's procreative storytelling: her woman's body is at best able (predictably) only to co-produce Aadam, the joint child of the rivalrous pair, Saleem and Shiva; Parvati's body is finally shared and destroyed between them.

However, it is actually Jamila Singer, or the erstwhile "Brass Monkey," Saleem's sister, whose art suggests rivalrous potential for Rushdie's narrator. If Rushdie repeatedly sets Saleem up to be the microcosmic double of modern India, then Jamila is the fiery younger sister who comes to embody Pakistan; if Saleem's life work and identity is constituted by his historiographic reconstruction and narration of his life (which *is* a narration of his nation), then Jamila's transformed identity is to be both the "daughter" and "The Voice of (*her*) Nation," instructed by presidential fiat to make her voice "a sword for purity . . . a weapon with which we shall cleanse men's souls" (*Shame*, 375, 376). Saleem sets her up as a darkly antithetical parallel to himself, using her as a cautionary countermodel of the tragically co-opted artist, doomed to sing "troops to their deaths" (405) (thus collapsing two female stereotypes into one—compliance and Sirenhood), a blinded patriotic zealot against whom he can proudly define his own resistant art of "impurity," his secular Indian refusal to bow to the totalitarianism and self-righteous "cleansing" separatism of a Pakistan that founded itself on "purity."

Yet Rushdie's ambivalence here has several registers. Unlike the altogether self-distancing comparison he sets up with Bariamma's national storytelling, in *Midnight's Children* that rivalry with Jamila is as yet more complex and multidimensional. Although on the one hand Jamila embodies the negative horrors of acquiescence, gendered again as feminine submission to patriarchal and parochial national demands, on the other hand she also represents a concomitant desirability and an irrepressible quality of resistance, this time to the demands of Saleem's overpowering urge for possession and control, indeed a *Pakistani* resistance to India's desire for that sisterly land-as-body. It is worth recalling that Jamila's transformation from the fiercely independent, incendiary Brass Monkey to her new Pakistani self is not as disjunctive as it may at first seem. As Saleem's young sister and second-class citizen in a bourgeois family that privileged sons over daughters (an injustice of which Saleem—and Rushdie—are deeply self-aware as beneficiaries), she is also a figure for the underprivileged members of a newly decolonized national family, a minority that has to learn to hold her own.

She is born as a consequence of what her father takes to be a Hindu majority's discriminatory harassment of minorities—"freezing a Muslim's assets" (*Shame,* 157)—via this sexual pun Amina Sinai's wifely response leads to their conception of Jamila (158); early in life, she has to learn that "if she was going to get any attention in life, she would have to make plenty of noise" (175); as she grows she parallels violent colonial revolt against greater powers (like Nasser sinking ships in the Suez, she burns the family's shoes, impeding their "progress" [177]); as an adolescent, while regionalism breaks out all over India and each group demands its own rights, she single-handedly vanquishes the neoimperialist threat of American power embodied by Evie Burns and kicks her out (269–70). As Saleem remarks ruefully, "[T]here was a fierceness in her which none of the rest of us ever possessed" (269). Saleem's incestuous desire for her (which like all male sexual overtures in the text she fiercely and successfully repulses) can then be read as a figure for India's desire to incorporate Pakistan into itself, but it is also a figure for Rushdie's fascination and ultimately grudging respect for that intractable oppositionality, even when turned on himself. (This is not to suggest a consistent equivalence between Rushdie and his "unreliable narrator," from whom the author has taken care to distance himself.[19] But we can identify occasions of narratorial and authorial coincidence, especially in structures of desire and belief. Saleem's fallibility is restricted to his historical memory—and even that is linked with Rushdie's own.) That oppositionality becomes a figure for that gendered otherness—seen as a quality of female repudiation of male desire—that will not be subsumed even by the powers of his totalizing narrative. It is such "feminized artistry" as a politics of resistance that remains finally beyond the grasping limits of what Rushdie represents self-knowingly as his own overwhelming desire to possess—and to appropriate. Herein lies a peculiar quality of Rushdie's ambivalence: even as he renders as stereotypically female a beloved "other" art that he seeks to make his own, he at once also renders it as a ghostly outline of what he desires *and* desires his art to be. It is only later in *Shame* that he will split this duality into the polarized artists Rani and Bariamma.

IV

In both *Midnight's Children* and *Shame*, then, Rushdie makes certain crucial gestures toward constructing what he regards as female forms of creativity and politics that remain muted but that increasingly enable him to reflect in different ways within these texts on the politics and forms of his own work, that provide internal mirrors for aspects of his own art. The ambivalences of his feminism in both texts, however, are more disparate.

The feminism, if one can call it that, in *Midnight's Children* is limited to a tacit outrage at modes of gendering and cultural abuse, indirectly satirized in episodes such as the "hole in the sheet," which marvelously questions the self-contradiction of social practices that shroud women in inculcations of modesty and shame but then also instruct them to display their bodies flagrantly in premarital negotiations. Thus Naseem Ghani has no agency either in being positioned behind the perforated sheet or in having to display through that overdetermined "hole" sexual parts that include naked buttocks and breasts before her potential husband. Or, Saleem acknowledges guilt at his own privilege as firstborn son over his secondary sister Jamila, or indignation at the necklace of shoes cast on unmarried Parvati when her community discovers her pregnancy. Alternative or feminist modes of retaliation to such pressures or self-enablement that he can envisage in that text, however, are limited to Jamila's childish violence or to Padma's initiatory sexual overtures.

At the same time, such empathy remains restricted only to certain *kinds* of female troubles: the text also teems with misogynist stereotypes of malignant women, not only of the ubiquitous all-powerful "Widow" Indira Gandhi but also of the ominous matriarch, "Reverend Mother," whose angry, punishing silence smells like "a rotting goose-egg" (*MC,* 58), whose controlling dogmatic religiosity oppresses her husband into disappearance because she is a "succubus" who "swallows his soul" (329), and who can only be rendered grotesquely as a "prematurely old, wide woman, with two enormous moles like witch's nipples on her face" (41).[20] Or, Saleem's unmarried aunt Alia's vengefulness and envy of her twice-married sister "leaking out of her glands" infects the food she cooks and the baby clothes she sews (367), so that paradoxically her physical "aridity" produces "a tribe of [school] children and young adults . . . possessed by an ancient vengefulness." As Rushdie's discourse becomes more powerfully intense, dazzlingly innovative, and powerfully synesthetic, it also calls upon fairy-tale misogyny that relies on the physically grotesque and archaic cultural anxieties and fears to articulate itself. Unlike Arundhati Roy, who crucially and subtly contextualizes the malevolent but complex spinster aunt Baby Kochama in *The God of Small Things* with the sense of failure and obloquy heaped upon unmarried Indian women for being social and familial burdens, Rushdie remains oblivious to the structural and systemic cultural pressures that bear on such women and instead sees them in isolation as merely individualized instances of a generic female type.[21] It makes sense, then, that even Rushdie's celebration of women in this text is the function of a distanced and idealizing vision, which then also extends to his subsequent texts.

Almost as if it were an act of reparation, *Shame* is more overt in its foregrounding of its own feminist consciousness, as discussed previously, yet conversely it is also guilty of the most flagrant slippages. In addition to the inconsistencies between narratorial self-positioning and plot structure and modes of representation outlined by Ahmad, I want to focus on a particular quality of Rushdie's rhetoric, a tonality that suggests rather odd complications. Unlike *Midnight's Children*, *Shame* is extraordinary for the density of its language of sexuality that insistently, obsessively seems capable of imagining sexuality and politics only as coterminous, as obscenity, violence, and exploitation, with masculinity as that which insistently represents abusive power. The discourse of *Shame* itself regresses into an ethos in which even an abstraction such as "History" is a "mistress" for whom the ambitious Iskandar forsakes the beautiful Pinky Aurangzeb (his literal mistress), so that History becomes a female figure who "had been waiting for (him) to notice Her, . . . and from whom he will never escape" (*Shame,* 133) . The law (as opposed to male tribal revenge ethics) is "womanly" and to be disdained for its "minimum force" (108); Isky claims to build the country (Pakistan) like a "marriage" (200); and girls become "grown women" after their first sexual encounter (83, 114).

In the culminating moment of the text's buildup of the figure of Sufiya Zinobia, the retarded, monstrous, increasingly degenerate allegory of female rage, the repository of a culture's incapacity to feel shame, "shame's avatar" turns into a murderous beast: "Shame walks the streets of night. In the slums four youths are transfixed by those appalling eyes. . . . They follow her to the rubbish-dump of doom, rats to her piper. . . . *Down she lies; and what Shahbanou took upon herself is finally done to Sufiya.* Four husbands come and go . . . and then her hands reach for the first boy's neck. The others stand still and wait their turn" (*Shame,* 242; emphasis added).

In reversing the metaphor, by turning her into the "rapist," a female Ripper, Rushdie reifies, as Ahmad points out, "the oldest of the misogynist myths: the virgin who is really a vampire" (*Shame*, 148). But what is more interesting is that even in this moment of facile reversals (in which Islamic polygamy, permitting men to have four wives, is converted into a blasphemous polyandry), Rushdie's syntax slips back into the passive, as if his language cannot allow anything so unimaginable as a woman's body *not* prone and rapable. We may well ask of this narration, does Sufiya/Shame allow herself to be raped, and is she therefore stereotypically guilty of enticement and entrapment, or is she even as a "rapist" not describable in the active voice? At the crucial moment, this agent loses agency to "what is done *to* [her]," as if sexual violence ultimately can be rendered only in the archaisms of *her* shame and subjection, framed at best by her complicitous invitation and violent reprisal.

In another telling example, the fateful "duel" between Isky and Raza, transparent figures for Pakistan's two most power-hungry rulers, Zulfikar Ali Bhutto and Mohammed Zia-ul-Haq, begins emblematically with their instantaneous sexual and rivalrous desire for Pinkie (read Pakistan with a green-and-white flag), the Commander-in-Chief's wife: their "initial prize was the body of the Marshall's wife . . . excitingly on display, in a green sari worn dangerously low. . . . [T]his body is worth lingering over" (*Shame*, 112). And indeed, with insouciantly self-confessional prurience, the narrator does linger over this and many such bodies, as he invites his fellow readers to do.

What is striking about these accumulating examples is that they carry a rhetorical tenor that is altogether absent in *Midnight's Children*. Yes, Padma has "hairy forearms," and Amina Sinai's "rounded black buttocks" are slowly revealed to her hidden son's (and reader's) horrified but fascinated voyeurism, but that text delights at most in its own daring and bourgeois iconoclasm in imagining such things as a maternal sexuality usually shrouded in respect. And yes, structurally there too the women always take second place, always peripheral to Saleem's fascistic centrality. But the discourse of *Shame* reveals a difference because it takes on the tenor of what it seeks to write about, as if, caught in the claustrophobia of Pakistan's feudal stranglehold (quite the opposite of what Rushdie sees as India's generous openness), his language cannot separate itself from what it writes about.

In pithy but comically horrifying scenes, Rushdie seeks to depict the violent ethos of sexual, hierarchical, and inherited powers that prevail in the bleak landscapes—literal and psychic—of tribal and feudal anarchy. When, for instance, Isky steals feudal landlord Mir's "whore," his angry cousin retaliates by systematically looting and destroying Isky's domains and shouting at the absent Isky's helpless wife, Rani:

> "What do you know about the bullock's arsehole, madam? . . . That pizzle of a homosexual pig. . . . Sister fucking bastard. . . . A man's honour is in his women. . . . So when he took that whore from me he took my honour, tell him that. . . . I could have regained my honour by depriving him of his. Lady, I

could do to you anything, anything, and who would dare to say no? Here it is my law, Mir's law, that runs." (*Shame*, 102–3)

If forms of insults—actual and imagined—reveal a culture's deepest fears and poetic capacities, then, Rushdie suggests, surely these are quite telling. In such a heteronormative system, where the logic of rape for a rape prevails, where men's revenge is enacted upon "their" women's bodies, Mir's linguistic violence turns his rival's wife (like his house) into the medium through which he delivers his message. But when Rushdie himself describes the newly deflowered bride Rani Harappa as "oiled and naked on a bed before . . . a man who had just turned her into a grown woman" (*Shame*, 83), his own language and ideology become indistinguishable from that which they seek to castigate, furtively relishing and replicating—instead of distancing from—the imaginary that sees women as sexualized possessions, as having identity only by virtue of their sexual relation to male power, as reaching such "womanhood" only when acted upon or literally penetrated.

It could be argued that Rushdie's language in *Shame* is different because it is an example of postmodern parody, as Linda Hutcheon has defined it. If postmodern irony and satire operate by the parodic techniques of mimicry, by evoking the deleterious feudal modes of thinking that he deplores, Rushdie's language destabilizes by making visible by excess the sheer power of that feudalism.[22] This may be the case in part, but such a defense seems to me ultimately inadequate, for there is no technical feature here signaling distance or excess. Indeed, as theorists such as Paul de Man and J. Hillis Miller have pointed out, ironic subversion always runs the risk of reinforcing precisely what it seeks to subvert, since "the man who attempts to say one thing while clearly meaning another ends up by saying the first thing too, in spite of himself."[23] Rushdie's mimicry here is itself too unsteady, its slippages into feudal discourse too unselfconscious, its inhabitation of that ethos too easy. It fails when Rushdie allows the very discourse that he seeks to pillory to bleed into his own, in a return precisely of the repressed.

V

It is worth returning momentarily to *Grimus* to locate earlier stages, or points of beginning, to use Said's term, in both the trajectories of feminized artistry and dubious feminism in Rushdie's work.[24] In *Grimus,* there are no female artists at all. The grand overarching figure of the artist-as-magician, who enables thinking-into-being, is Grimus, an early but canny embodiment of the dangers of totalitarianism and the powers of art. Nevertheless, like Saleem with Padma, he still needs a female but servile accompanist in his magical mansion: first Bird-Dog, and then (when Grimus is replaced by his amalgamation with Flapping Eagle, "I-Grimus") the aptly named Media.

There is a certain incipient protofeminism in Flapping Eagle's indignation at Grimus's hypnosis and maltreatment of his sister, Bird-Dog, but it remains buried and isolated. Or, it may seem that Rushdie plays with the oppositional potential of gender blurring and the crossing of gender roles: the central protagonist, Flapping Eagle, begins as a hermaphrodite named Joe-Sue, at once both male and female. However, this remains an initial phase of indeterminacy and limbo, from which he graduates to the certainty of a more grounded identity, granted by the name of an eagle.[25] Thus even cross-dressing in all of Rushdie's narratives is not liberating, nor does it enable a transgressive disturbance or blurring of rigid boundaries or the status quo, as theorists such as Marjorie Garber have suggested for other contexts.[26] In every occurrence, a male figure cross-dresses on occasions that signify humiliation, defeat, or imminent death: Flapping Eagle is briefly dressed in Dolores's clothes as he passes out of a life of limbo to the mountain of his quest; Raza Hyder dons his wife's veil to escape shame, only to arrive at death; and the Moor enters the forbidden bastions of Vasco Miranda's folly, unknowingly en route to his final doom.

Meanwhile representations of women in *Grimus* range from cliché to cliché. "Strong" women are hideous (to a male sexualizing vision) and also aggressively inviting or vengeful. Dolores O'Toole, the pathetic "ugliest woman" ever seen, is a "hunch-backed crone," strong and "manly" (*Grimus*, 44, 46), whose grotesque sexual acts, inability to face the reality of a lover's desertion, and final suicide remain the peculiar butt of a ribald comic vision too pleased with its own daring. The early Bird-Dog, a "wild female animal" (15) and the "manly sister" of Flapping Eagle the hero (17), presents her brother on his 21st birthday with her lifted skirts in exchange for "*his* virginity" (23), while the aptly named Mrs. Livia Cram is a "human predator" (26), the "Old Woman of the Sea" (32) who devours men and whose "personal gigolo" Flapping Eagle becomes (30). Alternatively, there are the beautiful women: Irina and Elfrida, polarized as the desired and the desiring but both also repeatedly seen as "white witches, weaving their spell" (183, 205, 208); or the fantastical but vengeful Liv, La Belle Dame par excellence, whose final coup is to "destroy his masculinity" by arousal, rejection, and humiliation and thus prepare Flapping Eagle to meet and submit to Grimus (279); and of course the "sanctuary" whorehouse of Jocasta (an early study for the house of prostitutes in *The Satanic Verses*), whose inmates specialize in specific sexual arts.

But most telling is the key account of the goddess Axona, an obstacle of the "Inner Dimension" that Flapping Eagle has to overcome before he can ascend the Calf Mountain with Virgil Jones. Given the parallels to Dante, this encounter suggests also that this is a rite of passage for the poet, whose proof of condign merit is established thus:

Axona was on her feet, eyes blazing with wrath, but Flapping Eagle knew that behind that anger she was afraid. The Bone ... had foiled her perfect plan; and now she was at his mercy. He advanced upon her with slow deliberation.

Stay where you are, Unclean, she said, but her voice betrayed her.

I don't know what you are, said Flapping Eagle as he walked forward, but when I defile you, I am cleansed of my past. Cleansed of the guilt and shame.... To free myself, I must render Axona unclean. Do you understand?

He spoke the words with a gentle astonishment, like truths he had just understood.

Then he raped her. (*Grimus,* 109)

Flapping Eagle (then named Joe-Sue) was banished from his dark-skinned American Indian tribe because he was anomalous, a light-skinned "monster" who also confused gender boundaries as a hermaphrodite and thus brought "death" to the tribe (*Grimus,* 17–18). To his surprise here he discovers that the oppressively *fearsome* tribal deity responsible for that exile has turned out to be not male but "an old, dark, hawknosed, feathered woman." Axona thus embodies the most pernicious aspects of the exclusivist and violent urge for cultural authenticity: she keeps the tribe "pure" and enacts a traditional role of women—like Reverend Mother later—of cultural conservatism. (Perhaps belatedly his predicament is comparable to Rushdie's; Rushdie was also exiled quite dramatically by his community's unbending urge for purity. In some sense, *Grimus* could be read as an oblique account of Rushdie's own move from South Asia to Britain and of his assimilation into the desired colonial metropolis.)

Yet the crucial logic of this passage is that to assert and prove his supremacy, Flapping Eagle has to vanquish not the extraterrestrial Gorf (the colonizing figure who has actually masterminded his current dilemma) but his *past,* gendered as female, his own self-imprisoning "inner Dimensions," by making *her* impure. "To free myself, I must render Axona unclean"—what a dreadful announcement, on Rushdie's own part, if we were to see this as a program for *The Satanic Verse*s. (It is also a cruder version of Saleem's incestuous desire for Jamila.) Of course in Rushdie impurity is always valorized as positive, emblematic of cultural hybridity, mixing, and inclusiveness, whereas the desire for purity is always fraught, leading to bloodshed, separation, danger, totalitarianism. But here that battle between purity and impurity is cast in terms of gender—as the definitive test for the writer/poet led up the mountain by Virgil. Culture, the past, obstacles to poetic independence, are all seen as a threatening old woman, who can be made "impure" only in the clichéd form of sexual defilement. The writer, rebellious, desiring autonomy, now no longer Joe-Sue but fully gendered as male, must acquire his independence via the trope of sexual violation. Hence what is problematic is not only

Rushdie's representation of women but also a larger symbolic structure of allegory for imagining cultural entities as female, and (postcolonial) independence as an archaic form of female humiliation, an imaginary not too far from the feudalistic idiom of *Shame*.

Certainly it should be said that this is Rushdie's adolescent writing, extracted from a text that he has since repudiated (Hamilton, 101). But as we have seen, its problems persist—in different forms. At the same time it is important to note that this passage also includes a self-consciousness, a voicing of a writerly embarrassment and half-apology. When Flapping Eagle subsequently recounts this "encounter," Virgil bathetically remarks, "You really have to do something about your imagination. . . . It's so awfully lurid" (*Grimus*, 109). There is a self-knowing quality about Rushdie's worst excesses that is often overlooked by critics, a posture of looking at oneself askance in a double vision that is at once horrified at what he is doing even as he cannot stop himself from doing it—because it brings a secret enjoyment. Remnants of this double vision persist unflaggingly, reemerging in later texts, with a minimum of self-consciousness in *Shame*.

In a different version and valorization, *Midnight's Children* replays this national allegorization of woman in its famous opening episode of Naseem and the perforated sheet. Usually read either as an allegory of gender relations or of writer-reader relations, the episode suggests also the relation between makers of nationhood and of the imagined nation as desirable female body. For Aadam Aziz, dreaming of postcolonial independence and a secular nationalism, the body of his future wife also prefigures the Muslim dream of a partitioned India: "[T]he phantasm of a partitioned woman began to haunt him" (*MC*, 23). Here Rushdie exposes both postcolonial nationalism as a masculinist and exclusivist enterprise and its consequent prurience, its desire for independence, as a desire for an imagined female body, to be acquired in parts. Like the Axona episode, the axis of national allegory making is sexually charged and one-directional. At the same time, in his detailed and joyful writerly relish in partaking of Naseem's/India's body, Rushdie also partakes of that prurience, at once self-critical and participant.

The permutations of Rushdie's feminized artistry and ambivalent feminism remain always complex and mobile, not easily identifiable as a static dualism. His representations of feminine as postcolonial art begin properly with *Midnight's Children* and become stronger in *Shame,* though bifurcating what I think was a more promising figure of Jamila's song into the polarities of Rani and Bariamma, as silenced artist versus national self-censored invention. His feminism meanwhile grows more self-conscious with each text but also becomes more severely troubled by the increasingly problematic idiom, rhetoric, and allegory to which, with a peculiar self-knowingness, it resorts. In *The Satanic Verses* and *The Moor,* that feminist urge is stronger but is then undermined, though to a lesser degree, by new problems. In the former, for instance, earlier representations of female sexual frustration and repression are replaced by the opposite extreme of a voracious female sexual aggression; in the latter, women's ineffectuality is replaced by a feminism that is then dismissed derisively as lesbianism.

VI

Though there is as yet no full-length study of the problems of gender and sexuality in *The Satanic Verses,* many critics have commented briefly on either its recuperative or failed feminism. Yet what is striking is the disjunction in critical responses that focus on either one or the other. Most famously, Gayatri Spivak writes:

> One of the most interesting features about much of Rushdie's work is his anxiety to write woman into the narrative of history. Here again we have to record an honorable failure. . . . *The Satanic Verses* must end with Salahuddin Chamchawalla's reconciliation with *father* and nationality. . . . [T]he text is written on the register of male bonding and unbonding. . . . The two [male protagonists] are tortured by obsession with women, go through them, even destroy them, within a gender code that is never opened up, never questioned, in this book where much is called into question, so much is reinscribed. (Spivak, 223)

Harveen Mann sees Rushdie's efforts at feminism as a challenge to Islamic misogyny, but she also concludes that he only reinscribes those gender codes:

> In writing against the orthodox Islamic concern with female chastity, Rushdie goes too far in the opposite direction, casting his female characters as eroticized bodies. . . . [H]e has come uncomfortably close to replicating the Orientalist stereotypes of Eastern women as erotic, tempting appendages to male existence, and perhaps even more regrettably, to reinforcing Western notions of gender inequality as a mark of Islamic cultural inferiority. (Mann, 296, 297)

However, as if in opposition to both of these readings, Sara Suleri argues that Rushdie's project is a radical *feminization* (not effeminization) of Islam: "[Spivak's] reading does not pay sufficient attention to the crucial Ayesha episode, where the prophet is reembodied as a woman in contemporary Muslim India. . . . [T]he Ayesha sections do indeed attempt at opening the gender code."[27]

Yet none of the three accounts for the opposite argument to the one Spivak makes; if a disjunction is noted, one pole, it is suggested, overcomes the other. I would suggest that first, it is perhaps precisely the uniquely idiosyncratic (and critically frustrating) characteristic of Rushdie's work that such oppositions are held in balance in a tension that remains unresolvable, so that neither one quite overwhelms the other. This balance between feminism and a resurgent misogyny is by no means one that I would care to validate, but it does need to be recognized as such and not as one tendency overtaking the other. Second, Rushdie's modes of exercising feminism or misogyny are by no means constant; they change from text to text, so that the disjunctions in *The Satanic Verses* are of a different order from those in *Shame*.

To begin with, in *The Satanic Verses* the figures who represent a postcolonial artistic sensibility that is to be aspired to are women whose attributes are admirable not because they are held to be somehow essentially female but because their powers of understanding or will are precisely constructed and revisionary. Zeeny Vakil, dismissed by Mann as merely Chamcha's "female instructor" (*SV,* 296), is significantly both a doctor and an art critic who has a

> book on the confining myth of authenticity, that folklorist straitjacket which she sought to replace by an ethic of historically validated eclecticism, for was not the entire national culture based on the principle of borrowing whatever clothes seemed to fit, Aryan, Mughal, British, take-the-best-and-leave-the-rest? (*SV,* 52)

As the central embodiment of Rushdie's insistently radical philosophy of hybridity, Zeeny refutes the nationalist fundamentalisms that posit pure origins and identities and that occlude the historical mixing that is crucially formative of all cultures. Unlike the dangerously opportunistic chimerical self-construction of Uma in *The Moor's Last Sigh,* Zeeny upholds Aurora's defiant guiding principle: the "historically validated eclecticism" that insists on remembering instead of obliterating the diverse though conflicting historical traditions that create national cultures and that are key both to India's secular foundations and to Rushdie's increasingly urgent project in his last two novels. Indeed, he suggests, this art critic's twin *medical* abilities are necessarily coterminous with her *political* ones, for she represents the curative principle crucial for national and cultural health.

Zeeny's sexual relationship with Chamcha, though problematic, as I discuss later, should then be seen not merely as a literal one, for in this text heavily allusive of Blake's *Songs* and *The Marriage of Heaven and Hell,* sexuality becomes a powerful trope for the concretization of aspiration and desire, for the incarnation of the divine.[28] Zeeny represents the standard by which Chamcha continually fails and the understanding at which he finally arrives. At the very end, Chamcha may *reconcile* with father and nationality, as Spivak suggests, but only to be present at their *death,* only to bid that past farewell. The future lies not in that father's house but in Zeeny's "place," to which he turns, leaving behind the vistas of childhood, about to be bulldozed by the necessities of adulthood. "If the old refused to die, the new could not be born" (*SV,* 547). Spivak's assessment that "the last sentence [of the novel] records sexual difference in the idiom of casual urban fucking" (Spivak, 223) does not account for the somber tonality of mature realization and gratitude for the postapocalyptic possibility of regeneration. Reminiscent of Shakespeare's late romances, the ending of *The Satanic Verses* suggests that it is Zeeny's promised acceptance of history, impurity, and hybridity that might offer a solution—not a resting place but an avenue of hope for the ravages wrought by postcolonial communalism and fundamentalism. Only with the aftermath of both the "Rushdie affair" and India's grim decline in political affairs, in the bleak vision of *The Moor's Last Sigh*—where Zeeny reappears as the curator of Aurora's hybrid art and caretaker of that secular creativity and self-construction—will that hope be lost.

If, from *Shame* to *The Satanic Verses,* Rani has grown into Zeeny, then Bilquis has transmogrified into the much more prominent figure of Ayesha, living on and clothed in butterflies; in the two sections that mirror and transform the Mahound sections, she becomes the female migrant leader of archetypal postcolonial migrants and of believers in a promised future. Indeed, as Suleri suggests, Rushdie feminizes and rewrites the history of Islam (which dates its calendrical time from the moment of the Prophet's migration from Mecca to Medina) in terms of a contemporary female prophet who leads another group of faithful migrants to a more ambiguous end. But in the impossible ending of this extraordinary sequence, Rushdie suggests the feminization and opening not only of Islam but also of postcolonial narration, of Rushdie's own (re)constructive and imaginative project. Instead of closure, Ayesha insists on opening.

When Mirza Saeed, the last skeptic, a Westernized double of Chamcha, faces death, alone bereft of the miraculous sight of the parting Arabian Sea, he dreams of Ayesha, both of them drowning in a sea that seems both within and without him, and where he hears her shouting at him desperately to open:

> "Open," she was crying. "Open wide!" Tentacles of light were flowing from her navel and he chopped at them, chopped, using the side of his hand. "Open," she screamed. "You've come this far, now do the rest."—How could he hear her voice?—They were under water, lost in the roaring of the sea. . . . "Open," she said. He closed.
>
> He was a fortress with clanging gates.—He was drowning.—She was drowning too. . . . Then something within him refused that, made a different choice, and at the instant that his heart broke, he opened.
>
> His body split apart from his adam's apple to his groin, so that she could reach deep within him, and now she was all open, they all were, at the moment of their opening the waters parted, and they all walked to Mecca across the bed of the Arabian Sea. (*SV,* 507)

The "tentacles of light" binding the two, crying prophet and unbeliever refusing salvation, refer back intratextually to the crucial earlier moment between Mahound and Gibreel, also bound "navel to navel, by a shining cord of light, not possible to say which is dreaming the other. We flow in both directions along the umbilical cord" (*SV,* 110). If the umbilical cord represents both maternal source of nurture and of creation, here the cord is a bidirectional one of mutual dependence: neither one is child or mother, but *both* dream or imagine the other into being, *both* create and save each other, much as, in the emblematic opening of this text, the dual oppositions Gibreel and Saladin conjoined and miraculously survived (4–5).

Here, at the end of the Ayesha section, Mirza Saeed faces his opposition, the embodiment of his dreams—Ayesha, emblematic of a postcolonial piper, leading her followers to a vision that is real if they will believe it, incarnating both a Jamesian will-to-believe and Rushdie's central tenet that belief or the imagination constructs the reality we live (as it can construct our futures), a Blakean poet-turned-prophet. But interestingly, as with the Prophet Mahound and Gibreel, these two are also conjoined, the survival of each contingent on the other. In closing, Mirza drowns not only himself but her as well. It is in *opening,* in the same image of "unbuttoning ... from your adam's apple to your crotch," earlier applied to Gibreel and Alleluia's sexual spirituality, in the physical "blurring of the boundaries of the self" (*SV,* 314), that salvation lies. The savior here, then, is *neither* pole of an opposition, neither man nor woman, believer nor skeptic, but the mutuality of opening of a masculine body that must surrender its rigidly refusing maleness into femaleness, transforming both. Only then can death—of all kinds—be resisted.

Ayesha's injunction to open, then, is addressed not only to Mirza Saeed, to what is gendered as masculine exclusion and refusal, but also to the rigidities of Rushdie's multiple readers in the East *and* West, seeking alternatives to the death of imagination and possibility, to the stranglehold of binary oppositions. The Ayesha and Mirza duo becomes a metanarratival emblem of the relation between writer and audience, a paradigm beseeching Rushdie's readers to open, to blur boundaries of self and other, for only in that lies the possibility of postcolonial re-vision, reconstruction, salvation. If the racism of postcolonial Britain can turn immigrants into manticores, snakes, and other beasts because "they have the power of description, and we succumb to the pictures they construct" (*SV,* 168), then, Rushdie suggests, "we" have to reappropriate those images and recast them through the crucial and self-empowering act of the imagination—as indeed *The Satanic Verses* seeks to do—changing both the describers and the described. Thus Rushdie's postcolonial project recasts resistance as a feminist move, as that which moves across boundaries not just to exchange or invert opposition but to collapse it and to recast femaleness as that which aggressively enables opening, as cultural novelty and survival.

Rushdie's own avowed feminism in *The Satanic Verses* is evinced in his continual attempt to protest and revise the misogynistic construction of women not only in Islam (as Mann suggests) but also in the Judeo-Christian tradition of which it is a part, and to transform female representation by offering alternative possibilities. Thus early in the first Mahound section,

Gibreel blasphemously critiques not Mahound but the abandonment of Hagar by Ibrahim (Abraham) "the bastard," and the Muslim pilgrims' commemoration not of her survival in the desert but of his desertion (*SV,* 95). Or, Rushdie suggests, grotesquely ominous female figures such as Hind, Allat, and the Empress Ayesha are precisely misogynistically demonized oppositions constructed by the totalizing zeal of Mahound, Allah, and the Imam respectively, to which binarisms his paradigm of the prophet Ayesha provides the disturbing alternative, the third term inducing crisis. If Mahound's youngest wife, Ayesha, as protofeminist questions Mahound's polygamy, Salman the scribe suggests subversively that she is engineered into a compromised silence by the strategic arrival of Quranic Verses (386–87);[29] if sexually oppressed womanhood in *Shame* can only end in self-destructive apocalypse, in *The Satanic Verses* Mishal Sufiyan has learned to fight and survive; and if in *Shame* Rani's daughter suppresses and denies her own sexuality while Bilquis's daughter can control the proliferating excess of her body only by killing it, the daughters of a new generation in *The Satanic Verses* are sexually triumphantly independent. Indeed, in the aftermath of the so-called Rushdie affair, many Muslim women, including the Southall Black Sisters, upheld Rushdie for opening a space for dissent between the disabling binarisms of fundamentalism and ethical relativism.[30]

At the same time, though, even in the attempt to suggest the feminist potential of postcoloniality, *The Satanic Verses* certainly undermines its own revisionary status, reifying instead of reconstituting certain gender codes. As Spivak and Mann point out, Rushdie's narrative remains troubled by its overreliance not only on a register of "male bonding and unbonding" but also on unrevised stereotypes of gender and female sexuality. Alleluia Cone, Pamela Chamcha, Zeeny Vakil, and Rekha Merchant form an indefatigable desiring quartet for the sexual misdemeanors of the two male protagonists, replaying the tired roles of faithful lover or partner in sexual marathons, defined only in terms of their sexual relations with masculine heroes, their lives and experiences rendered in facile, sketchy clichés. Female power, anguish, joy, and meaning is rewritten solely in terms of a (hetero)sexuality that not only occludes other relations between women or men, or other material conditions, but also becomes an exclusively bodily trope for femaleness in general.

Yet there is a shift in the modes of Rushdie's patriarchal imagination, often as a response to earlier critics. Instead of the (relatively) ineffectual, sexually frustrated women that Ahmad and Grewal note in *Shame*, in *The Satanic Verses* and *The Moor's Last Sigh* women have become aggressively sexually independent, described in terms of a voracious hunger. Zeeny Vakil's project to "reclaim" Saladin casts her as sexually overwhelming and sacrilegious: she is "eating him alive" or "lunching on his naked thigh"; "She made love like a cannibal and he was her long pork" (*SV,* 52). Or, in a reversal of gender roles, Belle de Souza's "voluptuary hunger" complements her husband's "shy gentleness," which turns her into a Diana figure whose sexual hunger leads her to "hunt" other "lions and tigers" in his absence (*MLS*, 46, 44), while her daughter Aurora draws her future husband "to his doom" in a sex scene perfumed by spices, in which they "passionately . . . fed upon one another" (*MLS*, 89, 90).[31] But of course the mere reversal of binarisms is no solution, since women remain defined primarily, indeed exclusively, in terms of an obsessively projected, overblown hypersexuality. While clearly supposed to be an advance because it posits paradigms of action instead of *re*action, activity instead of passivity, Rushdie's discourse still bespeaks a projection of an alternate fantasy and indeed a certain fear of engulfment—both literal and metaphorical—by what is seen as a female power/sexuality threatening to malehood.

This rendering of even positively valorized women in terms of eating or hungering (transposing upper and lower orifices) echoes the overtly negative descriptions of grasping Livia Cramm or Flapping Eagle's entry into the cavernous regions of Bird-Dog's vagina in *Grimus* (86–88), or Rosa Diamond's demands on Gibreel, which set his "navel . . . on fire" (*SV*, 150). It extends into Rushdie's continued horror of grandmothers or matriarchs, always rendered as monstrous or sickening forces of consumption, a threat to masculinity, extending from the register of the sexual into the narratival and political. Reverend Mother, who seems to batten on her diminishing husband, is a succubus who lures men into "the matrimonial bed . . . and begins to swallow their souls" (*MC*, 329), just as Bariamma consumes everyone else's stories into her national master narrative (*Shame*, 79). In an analogous image that conflates female sexuality and destructive conjugality, Epifania de Gama "ate [her husband's] death as she had eaten his life; and grew" (*MLS*, 24), while her double (the Moor's other grandmother), "Roary Flory," drives her husband to abscond (*MLS*, 73–75). That this fear of sexuality is conjoined to a fear of political power becomes apparent when the same image reappears as the evil Empress Ayesha imagined by the exiled Imam as "his enemy, his other" (*SV*, 206), who swallows not just butterflies but the people of "Desh," his homeland—she is the mirror opposition whom he will vanquish, but then exactly replicate, "his mouth yawning open. . . . [A]s the people march through the gates he swallows them whole" (*SV*, 215). Yet while Rushdie presents this as the Imam's fear, his own discourse mirrors the same psychic structure in his representation of Pamela, Alleluia, and Zeeny.

In this questionable cultural imaginary, even Rosa Diamond's land as female body functions as the unrevised colonial trope on which the postcolonial immigrants Gibreel and Saladin land, echoing Saladin's desire to make love to the British queen as a masculine countercolonizing celebration of arrival in the desired metropolis (*SV*, 169). Yet it is worth noting that by now Rushdie's writing has developed a greater self-consciousness, so that even when it deploys the allegorical structure of female-as-national-body, seen earlier as Axona and Naseem, it figures his protagonist's male desire and fear as complicit in that construction.

In a dream, Saladin Chamcha recalls his phantasmagorical escape from the police hospital with the help of Hyacinth Phillips, his black physiotherapist, and her terrifying metamorphosis into the city of London, once loved and desired, now frighteningly unknown, a heart of darkness for this deracinated arrivant (*SV,* 254–55). Then, as she pulls him toward her in a dreaded sexual embrace, he flees, shouting: "Hubshees . . . savages. . . . Every morning you have to look at yourself in the mirror and see, staring back, the darkness: the stain, the proof" (255). This dense passage figures Chamcha's dread of his own blackness, his confrontation with self as other—and other as self, his colonized horror of a racialized and sexualized otherness, ironically inverted and superimposed on the colonial metropolis. Of course she rejects him as he rejects her. Thus Rushdie suggests, as does Blake in "London," that both kinds of immigrants have lost themselves in this doubly darkening city, both have come to see the other in the terms prescribed by a dominant racist system. Like the Inner Dimensions that Grimus fights, this phantasmagoric city as dark female body is as much an internal as an external landscape for Chamcha, trapping him in his own psychic horrors.

Yet we may question why, if darkness is the condition of this urban scape, it must be mapped on a racially demarcated female body. What inflections of gender, race, and sexuality does this overdetermined allegory carry? Horror is evoked here through recognizable tropes—Medusa hair, stereotypes of African features of body and land, sexuality as death (she is trying to drag him into a "grave")—that hark back to certain cultural fears and that are now transposed on or made a figure for the contortions of Chamcha's colonized imagination. While it remains impossible to distinguish the degree of separation between Chamcha's and Rushdie's modes of imagining, what I think is new in Rushdie's writing here is that his text nevertheless suggests a self-consciousness lacking in *Shame,* a complicating knowledge of the complicity of the male fear that projects its own horror in such terms.

VII

Early on in the narrative of *The Moor's Last Sigh,* the narrator remarks: "The women are now moving to the center of my little stage. . . . [T]hey, not the men, were the true protagonists in the struggle" (*MLS,* 33). Such a remark seems applicable not only to the trajectory of the narrative of that particular text but also perhaps to that of Rushdie's oeuvre. Instead of the dual protagonists who take center stage in the earlier narratives, pitting the narrator against his antithesis, each seemingly a polar opposite of the other who yet dissolves *into* the other (literally with Grimus–Flapping Eagle, eventually with Shiva-Saleem, Iskandar Harappa–Raza Hyder, Saladin Chamcha–Gibreel Farishta, Khattam Shud–the Shah of Blah), here we have the rivalrous duo

Aurora-Una, now battling over the ownership of the disabled narrator, Moraes Zogoiby, or the Moor—Othello turned object of desire. Certainly there are other men who dominate—Abraham, Mainduck, and of course Vasco Miranda—but the narratival structure here seems to have become a photographic negative of the earlier writings, in that the central gravitational pull comes from the twin stars Aurora-Una, around whom a plethora of male lovers-as-satellites orbit and who in turn are reflected and refracted through several more female figures, such as Zeeny Vakil and Aei-ou.[32] Aurora is the harbinger of a new dawn in art, a pure promise, while Una, seemingly her double, is also her antithesis, ungrounded in ethicality or belief, unmooring hybridity from desirability, embodying a chimerical and wanton opportunism, a perversion of Spenser's Una or oneness.

Both Aurora and Moraes (the Moor) represent aspects of Rushdie's writing self, now tragically split, in a dual self-portrait of the artist after the "Rushdie affair." Aurora is the culmination of Rushdie's female artists with revolutionary potential, now for the first time taking center stage. In a metanarrativalism that is unlike any earlier one, where the central writer-dreamer-narrator was always male, here Aurora is the embodiment and imagined fulfillment of Rushdie's own artistic aspirations: upholding the values of secularism and hybridity crucially constructed by the migrant, visionary writer, the teller of truths, defiant of censorship, creative of cultural survival and futurity, a "mother," as she is called, "of us all" (*MLS*, 160).[33] Yet here too Rushdie does not attempt a female narrator, *and* the narrator, Aurora's son, the Moor, is a self-representation of another dimension of Rushdie, the tired storyteller, awaiting death, a "Scheherazade" slouching toward his end. Ironically, her defiant art leads finally to her death, while his survival is predicated on the sly continuation of his storytelling. Since a fuller discussion of the questions of art, ekphrasis, and self-representation in this novel is deserving of another essay, I will limit myself here to sketching how Aurora constitutes the culmination of Rushdie's trajectory of feminized artistry, and how his resurgent patriarchal discourse returns to haunt the more muted feminism of this text.

The crucial turns in Aurora's fictive career echo with surprising biographical accuracy the turns and phases of Rushdie's career to date. Her work begins, as did his, in exile, in a state of banishment (though his was self-imposed—he left Pakistan in protest against its censoring restrictions to begin work in Britain): she is punished for her iconoclasm, for destroying her family's deities, but this precisely is the moment of birth for the artist defiant of restriction. Locked in her room, she covers the walls with an encyclopedic, panoramic vision of (world) history, which "pullulated with figures, human and animal, real and imaginary." As may have been said of *Midnight's Children*, her father proudly proclaims: " 'But it is the great swarm of being itself' " (*MC*, 59). Yet her painting embodies not just her own visions but also her "inner self" on display, also a self-portrait of creation (58). "Only God was absent," to be replaced by the artist. As Saleem is a microcosm and storyteller of the nation, so Aurora becomes Mother India, the central creative but human force throughout this text, who ironically begins to create by mourning the absence of her own mother (58–60). Thus from this inceptory moment, Rushdie both suggests the parallels between her art and his and links this paradigm of feminized artistry to a motherhood that is at once productive and destructive of his own work, ironizing the central trope of "Mother India who loved and betrayed and ate and destroyed and again loved her children" (60–61).

Thus the first phase of Aurora's art, her rise to fame in Bombay, parallels Rushdie's project in *Midnight's Children,* encompassing the range of the nation's subjects, "capturing history on charcoal" (*MLS,* 129–30), combining both microcosm and macrocosm and both politics and art at the heart of a secular nationalism directed against the forces of imperialism: "Aurora Zogoiby grew into the giant public figure we all know, that great beauty at the heart of the nationalist movement. . . . [H]er arrest after the Quit India Resolution of 1942 made her a national heroine . . . the new Chand Bibi, standing up against a different and even more powerful Empire" (116).

At the same time of course, like Rushdie, even at the height of fame, her subversiveness makes her suspect on all sides: "The sheer strangeness of the activity of art made her a questionable figure" (*MLS,* 130), a reaction that would culminate in disaster. Her next phase, one that we could compare to Rushdie's writing of *Shame,* is one torn between the alternate poles of realism and idealism, verisimilitude and fantasy, between "Abraham's dogmatic insistence on . . . a clear sighted naturalism that would help India describe herself to herself" and Vasco Miranda's "playful influence" urging her toward the "fantastic," the "epic fabulist," coupled with her own "instinctive dislike of the purely mimetic" (173–74).

But the crux of Aurora's career is her recognition of the vitality of hybridity, where, in her "famous" first set of "Moor" paintings, she uses "Arab Spain to re-imagine India" (*MLS,* 227), just as Rushdie, in *The Satanic Verses,* collapses binarisms, using Arab Islam to reimagine contemporary postcolonial migrations and forms of belief. Here, then, is the culmination of her art:

> The water's edge, the dividing line between two worlds, became in many of these pictures the main focus of her concern. She filled the sea with fish, drowned ships, mermaids, treasures . . . and on the land, a cavalcade of local riff-raff— . . . and other figures from history or fantasy or current affairs or nowhere. . . . At the water's edge strange composite figures slithered to and fro across the frontier of the elements. Often she painted the water-line in such a way as to suggest that you were looking at an unfinished painting which had been abandoned, half-covering another. But was it a waterworld being painted over the world of air, or vice versa? Impossible to be sure.
>
> "Call it Mooristan," Aurora told me. . . . "Place where worlds collide, flow in and out of one another, and washofy away." (226)

And Rushdie, via the Moor, himself hastens to explain this important metanarratival point: "In a way these were polemical pictures, in a way they were an attempt to create a romantic myth of the plural, hybrid nation. . . . Yes, there was a didacticism here, . . . but it was easy not to feel preached at, to revel in the carnival" (227).

"Mooristan," literally "the place of the Moor," evokes Othello's tragically hopeful interracial marriage and Moorish Spain's ethnic and religious diversity before its destruction by the monovision of Catholic Spain. But it is also the place of "more," and in Urdu, of the "moor" or peacock, of resplendence. This is the space of possibility, the promised land of "Palimpstine," where hybrid overlay is precisely the space of richness, possibility, the combination of the real and the ideal, the artist's blueprint for a postcolonial future. It is also thus an ironic "moor-ing" of identity on the balance of dualities, impurities, uncertainties, ambiguities, instead of on a hypothetical purity of origin. She is then truly Mother India, the promise of a new creation, but her visions in the end will not be allowed to prevail.

As with Rushdie' own fall, this star becomes victim to the forces of sectarianism and fundamentalism. Aurora goes into decline and retreats into an increasingly private world in her art, into a stage of black and white failing struggle with her opposition, Uma (*MLS*, 261). Her final "Moor" paintings, with the Moor as "narrator/narrated" (301), become, then, Rushdie's asymptotic representation of his own narrative within this narrative, his account of an artist's final work continuing in a death struggle with the forces against her.

Yet despite the seeming centrality of this female artist figure, the ambivalent puppeteer who pulls the strings is not Aurora but the Moor, a Rushdiean narrator who will outlast Aurora and whose story this finally becomes. Even though *women* may take center stage more often, Rushdie's *feminism* in this text, I would argue, is diminished from his project in *The Satanic Verses* and even in *Shame*. Perhaps this is because there seems to remain no grand system—such as the structure of Islamic belief or postcolonial nationalism—to be both loved and critiqued, to be entered imaginatively via a position of marginality, to be explored for its dualisms. Aurora represents the central figure of the artist not because she occupies a strategically oppositional position by virtue of a historically or culturally constructed gendering but rather because of an imputed biological essentialism, a troping of her reproductive as maternal/creative powers. Furthermore, with characteristic ambivalence, Rushdie's discourse presents her continually, as we have already seen, as a heavily and exclusively sexualized figure, both desiring and desired, in terms of a male heterosexual vision. Indeed, she can be valorized only in such terms—thus all the men around her either have sexual relations with her or turn evil (like Vasco Miranda or Mainduck) because of frustrated desire. In a new binarism of idealized versus whorish hybridity, her femaleness is then polarized against Uma's, whose artistic fulfillment of desire is cast as deeply pernicious.

In addition, earlier problems in Rushdie's discourse and narrative construction resurface, not only, as we have seen, in the representation of matriarchs and sexuality but also in newer ways. Feminism now is cast as a lesbianism in which the latter is presented as a term of opprobrium and discredit and not as a radical alternative. The Moor's third sister, Mynah, is a feminist lawyer whose activism leads her to militant or recuperative efforts against social ills such as bride burning, rape, and chemical abuse and who is killed by her own father's underground mafia. But there is a blurred line between *what* Rushdie represents as sexist and *how* he represents it as sexist. It is *his* joke that Mynah's feminist group WWSTP (for "We Will Smash This Prison"—so that feminism is exclusively understood as destructive militancy) is renamed by its detractors "Women Who Sleep Together Probably" (*MLS,* 243). That lesbianism is presented as a form of discreditation is illustrated by Moraes's dismissal of Mynah's suspicions of Uma upon Uma's allegation of Mynah's sexual advances toward her (250, 268–69). But Rushdie's own structure of allegory becomes collusive: the bird "mynah," after which Mynah is named (and that, unlike the nightingale, creates her own song), connotes in Urdu and Hindi a vacuous mimic who parrots without originality or purpose, suggesting that Mynah's feminism is indeed such an unthinking jingoism. Throughout the narrative, the three sisters are clearly appendages, all dying sudden and horrible deaths, while the Moor as narrator (and only son) retains his centrality to the end. It could be said that in the bleak ending of *The Moor's Last Sigh,* an indictment of contemporary India's decline into violence, corruption, and sectarianism, there are no promising survivors, except, however, for Nadia Wadia, whose disfigured face nevertheless holds out hope: "The city will survive. New towers will rise. Better days will come," she pronounces (377). But this is not a promise achieved in this text, either for India or for Rushdie's feminism.

VIII

Rushdie's unmistakable relish in and replay of very recognizably deleterious stereotypes, his returns to a discourse of ribaldry and gendered sexual rhetoric, his suspicion of feminism and matriarchy even as he seeks to promote them, suggest perhaps another form of belonging—this time not to the feminism and revisionary postcolonial artistry that pulls him one way but instead to another patriarchal code to which he cannot bid farewell. Where his chosen unbelonging between continents, cultures, and value systems might be a strategic one, his unbelonging between a purported feminism, a desire to recraft postcoloniality in terms of feminine revision, and a more dubious codification of sexual stereotypes is not altogether chosen.

Rushdie's last and autobiographical story in *East, West,* entitled "The Courtier," recounts vicariously the intercultural romance of his aging ayah (nanny) with the courtly doorman of his apartment building in London. In an inversion of the passage with which I began, where the "male" plot turns out also to be a "female" one, here Rushdie remarks that *his* story is the same as that of his domestic female servant, and so he turns *her* story into his: "I see now that it is not just their story, but ours, mine, as well" (*EW,* 178). The disingenuity of conflating such stark differences of class and gender notwithstanding, Rushdie suggests that when first his ayah, and then his family, painfully chose East over West, sacrificing romance to safety, returning to India because of the violence and racism of Britain, his own more courageous revision and appropriation of his ayah's story is to choose *not* to choose. In his famous final words, he declares with quite deliberate bravado:

> But I too have ropes around my neck, . . . pulling me this way and that, East and West, the nooses tightening, commanding, *choose, choose.*
> I buck, I snort, I whinny, I rear, I kick. Ropes, I do not choose between you. Lassoes, lariats, I choose neither of you, and both. Do you hear? I refuse to choose. (*EW,* 211)

This is certainly a fitting Rushdiean postscript to the Satanic affair—to refuse to be controlled by binarisms, to insist on the alogic of neither and both, to choose a "double unbelonging." However, as we read this paradigm in terms of the poles of feminism and patriarchal reification between which Rushdie alternates, here, I suggest, he does *not* make a choice not to choose—instead of agency, in this lies precisely an unchosen unbelonging. Yet as this essay attempts to show, even this betwixt and betweenness is not static—it slips, even within the same text, from the regrettably unselfconscious into the highly self-knowing, from misogyny to idealism, and shifts, across the trajectory of his writing, in the continually reconfigured relation between a resurgent obtuseness to questions of gender and an emphasis on feminism as an enabling force for postcolonial art.

What, then, are the implications of such ambivalence and alternation both for Rushdie's postcolonial revisionism and for us as readers? How does this undermine or compromise his project? Does Rushdie's writing end up becoming implicated in and sustaining of precisely the very ideologies it seeks to displace? Writing of a paradigmatic colonial text like *Heart of Darkness,* Bette London has argued that "race and gender [are] interlocking systems whose mutually authorizing relationships support the dominant cultural perspective" and that critical attempts to see these forces as independent of each other fail to address that mutually supporting inextricability.[34] How then are we to read the self-positioning of *post*colonial texts that also fall short of addressing such "interlocking" systems of power? Does Rushdie's failure to dismantle discourses of gender under a system of patriarchy (however culturally constructed) also reflect a failure to dismantle and revise adequately the very discourses of colonialism and history that his fictions seek to explore and critique?

While I would submit that yes, certainly, Rushdie's lapses into patriarchal discourse undermine significantly the scope and integrity of his efforts, there remain some additional complicating factors. What is interesting about this ambivalence in Rushdie's work is not its measurability as a mark of success or failure but rather its contradictory efforts to conjoin discourses of colonialism and gender, indeed, its self-critical growing recognition that the very definition of postcolonialism would be incomplete if it were not already posited on a critique of other discourses of power across intersecting axes of gender or class. As we have seen, increasingly until *The Moor's Last Sigh,* Rushdie actively seeks to cast postcolonial practice and cultural (re)construction as precisely analogous to and dependent on feminist work, and by implication attempts to redefine the categories of the feminine and the postcolonial. Even if he does not arrive at a point where the two may become unimaginable as independent, he does provide signposts to such a turn. Finally, our efforts as critics are surely geared not only to identify ideological blind spots, to know and "show the text as it cannot know itself"[35] (we are hardly exempt from being embedded in a conflux of ideologies ourselves), but also to recognize the unusual degree of agency and self-consciousness with which writings such as Rushdie's do seek, however imperfectly, to redress such ambivalence.

Notes

1. Salman Rushdie, *Shame* (New York: Aventura, 1983), 189; hereafter cited in the text. Sources for other works by Rushdie cited in this article are as follows: *Grimus* (1975, New York: Penguin, 1991); *Midnight's Children* (New York: Penguin, 1980), hereafter cited in the text as *MC; The Satanic Verses* (1988, New York: Penguin 1989), hereafter cited in the text as *SV; Imaginary Homelands* (New York: Penguin, 1991), hereafter cited in the text as *IH; East, West* (New York: Pantheon, 1994), hereafter cited in the text as *EW;* and *The Moor's Last Sigh* (New York: Pantheon, 1995), hereafter cited in the text as *MLS.*

2. Rushdie himself may be credited with the invention of the phrase "the empire writes back" in his famous piece "The Empire Writes Back with a Vengeance," *Times* (London), 3 July 1982, 8.

3. See in particular Aijaz Ahmad, "Salman Rushdie's *Shame:* Postmodern Migrancy and the Representation of Women," in *In Theory: Classes, Nations, Literatures* (New York: Verso, 1992), 123–58, n. 9; Inderpal Grewal, "Salman Rushdie: Marginality, Women, and Shame," *Genders* 3 (Fall 1988): 24–42, 25; Harveen Sachdeva Mann, " 'Being Borne Across': Translation and Salman Rushdie's *The Satanic Verses,*" *Criticism* 37, no. 2 (Spring 1995): 281–308, n. 35.

4. See Toril Moi, "Feminist, Female, Feminine," in *The Feminist Reader*, ed. Catherine Belsey and Jane Moore (Cambridge, England: Blackwell, 1989), 117–32. Throughout this text when I refer to women's art in Rushdie's writing, I do not mean to suggest that I subscribe to the notion that there is some inherently different essentialized art unique to all women. Rather, this is a shorthand for Rushdie's representations—either specific women have a unique kind of artistic power linked with their femaleness, or Rushdie makes a more generalized extension of this to women's art.

5. For an excellent, succinct exposition of the stakes in feminist analyses of gender between biologism and constructivism, see Linda Alcoff, "Cultural Feminism versus Post-Structuralism: The Identity Crisis in Feminist Theory," *Signs: Journal of Women in Culture and Society* 13, no. 3 (1988): 405–36. Since this is a wide and fast-growing field, I will restrict myself to the texts that I have found most useful: Diana Fuss, *Essentially Speaking: Feminism, Nature, and Difference* (New York: Routledge, 1990); Judith Butler, *Gender Trouble: Feminism and the Subversion of Identity* (New York: Routledge, 1995); Eve Sedgwick, "Gender Criticism," in *Redrawing the Boundaries*, ed. Stephen Greenblatt and Giles Gunn (New York: MLA, 1992): 271–302; and the recent anthology *Feminism and Sexuality: A Reader*, ed. Stevi Jackson and Sue Scott (New York: Columbia University Press, 1996).

6. On questions of the reinscription of gender in (post)colonial nationalist discourse, see Ann McClintock, "Family Feuds: Nationalism, Gender, and the Family," *Feminist Review* 44 (Summer 1993): 61–80.

7. Sara Suleri, *The Rhetoric of English India* (Chicago: Chicago University Press, 1992); Homi Bhabha, *The Location of Culture* (New York: Routledge, 1994); Ann McClintock, *Imperial Leather: Race, Gender, and Sexuality in the Colonial Conquest* (New York: Routledge, 1995).

8. Gayatri Chakravorty Spivak, "Reading *The Satanic Verses*," in *Outside in the Teaching Machine* (New York: Routledge, 1993), 223, 217–42.

9. This is not unlike Kipling's frequent assertions that writing is of a second order from doing, that storytellers are secondary to the agents who act the stories that writers subsequently narrate.

10. I refer here of course to Benedict Anderson's foundational argument on nations as "imagined communities" in Anderson, *Imagined Communities: Reflections on the Origins and Spread of Nationalism* (New York: Verso, 1991). See also Homi Bhabha, ed., *Nation and Narration* (New York: Routledge, 1990).

11. See, for example, Rajeswari Sunder Rajan, "Gender, Leadership, and Representation: The 'Case' of Indira Gandhi," in Rajan, *Real and Imagined Women: Gender, Culture, and Postcolonialism* (New York: Routledge, 1993), 103–28, for her discussion of South Asian and East Asian women leaders.

12. See, for example, *Shame*, 71–73. Indeed, *Shame* was banned in Pakistan soon after its publication.

13. See James A. Heffernan, *Museum of Words: The Poetics of Ekphrasis from Homer to Ashbery* (Chicago: Chicago University Press, 1993); John Hollander, *The Gazer's Spirit: Poems Speaking to Silent Works of Art* (Chicago: University of Chicago Press, 1995); W. J. T. Mitchell, "Ekphrasis and the Other," *South Atlantic Quarterly* 91 (1992): 695–719.

14. Mitchell, "Ekphrasis," 716.

15. I discuss this at more length in my "Fathered by History: Figurations of Family and the Writing of Empire" (Ph.D. diss., Yale University, 1994), 277–89.

16. Rushdie's antipathy to Pakistan—in contrast to India—is well known, as evidenced by the Pakistan sections of *Midnight's Children* and by the macabre tonality of *Shame* in comparison with the former. See also Ian Hamilton's recent biographical account, "The First Life of Salman Rushdie," *New Yorker* (25 December 1995 and 1 January 1996): 91–113.

17. Uma Parameswaran, "Handcuffed to History: Salman Rushdie's Art," *Ariel* 14, no. 4 (October 1983): 34–45, 44; Charu Verma, "Padma's Tragedy: A Feminist Deconstruction of

Midnight's Children," *Panjab University Research Bulletin* 20, no. 2 (October 1989): 59–65; Mann, 295.

18. The most important function of the narratee in the text, then, is to be the "relay between the narrator and the reader(s), or rather between the author and the reader(s)," to mediate between readers' expectations and writer's goals. Gerald Prince, "Introduction to the Study of the Narratee," in *Reader-Response Criticism: From Formalism to Post-Structuralism*, ed. Jane P. Tompkins (Baltimore, Md.: Johns Hopkins University Press, 1980), 21, 7–25.

19. See Rushdie's remarks in " 'Errata': Or, Unreliable Narration in *Midnight's Children*," in *Imaginary Homelands*, 22–25.

20. Rushdie's gender politics in his vitriolic depictions of Indira Gandhi are certainly questionable, especially when located within this larger structure of representation. For Saleem's/Rushdie's rivalrous relation with Indira Gandhi as controller of the nation, see Rajan, 111–13.

21. Arundhati Roy, *The God of Small Things* (New York: Random House, 1997).

22. Linda Hutcheon, *The Poetics of Postmodernism* (New York: Routledge, 1988); Hutcheon, *The Politics of Postmodernism* (New York: Routledge, 1989). More recently Hutcheon has argued, in *Irony's Edge: The Theory and Politics of Irony* (New York: Routledge, 1994), that the ironic stance makes itself impossible to locate definitively, even as subversive of dominant modes.

23. J. Hillis Miller, "*Heart of Darkness* Revisited," in *Heart of Darkness*, ed. Ross Murfin (New York: St. Martin's, 1996), 219.

24. Edward Said, *Beginnings: Intention and Method* (New York: Columbia University Press, 1985).

25. Certainly by the end that identity has transmuted again into the composite of Grimus and himself, "I-Grimus," but it remains emphatically and stereotypically masculine.

26. Marjorie Garber, *Vested Interests: Cross-Dressing and Cultural Anxiety* (New York: HarperCollins, 1993). For example, she writes: "The 'third' is that which questions binary thinking and introduces crisis—a crisis which is symptomatized by *both* the overestimation *and* the underestimation of cross-dressing. . . . [T]he interruption . . . reconfigures the relationship between the original pair, and puts into question identities previously conceived as stable, unchallengeable, grounded, and 'known' " (11, 13).

27. Sara Suleri, "Whither Rushdie?" *Transition* 51 (1991): 198–212, 209.

28. For instance, Alleluia reads *The Marriage of Heaven and Hell* (304), while Gibreel's vision are compared to Blake's (318). If "Without Contraries is no Progression," then the novel is predicated on the dualism of Gibreel and Chamcha, angel and devil, valorized by inversion, but then also, upon their necessary intertwining, their mutual need, for "[o]pposition is true friendship." Blake's "London" is repeatedly evoked, with Gibreel wandering through "chartered streets," bound precisely by "mind-forged manacles," encountering, for instance, the "lost soul" (322) or the "harlot's cry" in child-prostitutes on the streets (460). The conjoined polarities of innocence and experience intermesh, though the novel ends on a kind of innocence. The "Satanic Verses" are indeed Proverbs of Hell, validated in a Blakean vision that insists—as with the infamous episode of the whores that incarnates the desire of the devout—on the carnal as divine.

29. Rushdie recounts the apocryphal story of how Ayesha, the Prophet's favorite and youngest wife, is left behind inadvertently, is rescued by a young man, becomes subject to slanderous suspicion, and is exonerated by a supposed angelic Revelation, which, he adds, effectively silences her earlier questioning of the convenient timings of the verses.

30. Lisa Appignanesi and Sara Maitland, eds., *The Rushdie File* (Syracuse, N.Y.: Syracuse University Press, 1990), 238.

31. It is amusingly inappropriate, surely, for Rushdie to claim, as he does in his interview with *Playboy*, that this is his first sex scene. See *Playboy* 43, no. 4 (April 1996): 59; 49–62, 165.

32. Even the earliest reviewers of the novel recognized this shift. Thus Orhan Pamuk writes in the *Times Literary Supplement:* "The narrator of this richly textured, densely allusive tale is Moraes Zogoiby, but the true protagonist is his mother, Aurora da Gama, . . . the great creative mother figure of this novel" (8 September 1995): 3–4.

33. As Rushdie has said in the *Playboy* interview, "In [Aurora and her cohort of contemporary artists] I found affinities to my own ideas and work. It became easy for me to imagine myself in the skin of such a painter" (59). Later, he adds: "I also hope she's more than just a writer in disguise, . . . a painted word. . . . By the time I came to write the book, I actually knew her pictures very well—I had a clear sense of what they looked like. I just can't paint them" (60).

34. Bette London, "Reading Race and Gender in Conrad's Dark Continent," *Criticism* 31, no.3 (Summer 1989): 235–52.

35. Terry Eagleton, *Criticism and Ideology: A Study in Marxist Literary Theory* (London: Verso, 1978), 43.

Reading the Rushdie Affair: "Islam," Cultural Politics, Form

AAMIR R. MUFTI

Gayatri Spivak has argued that, in the case of *The Satanic Verses,* "the praxis and politics of life" intercept the aesthetic object to such a degree that a "mere reading" of the novel has become impossible.[1] In this essay, I shall examine the novel's "interception by" (and its intervention in) certain political contexts within the post-1979 Islamic world. The essay is not meant to provide an even partial reading of the text in traditional critical terms. Instead, it will focus on the "Rushdie affair" as a complex cultural (and political) *event* within the Islamic world, treating it as a constellation that brings together, highlights, and restructures some of the central elements of contemporary Muslim life. It is well known that Muslim South Asia, both "at home" and in diaspora, figured prominently in the crisis from the very beginning. Accordingly, it is the Indian context that provides the nucleus around which my argument will be built.

As has now become generally evident, the novel presents what is arguably the most serious literary challenge in recent years to the legitimacy of certain brands of contemporary "Islamic" politics. Some of the questions it confronts have been almost constantly present in the political discourse of much of the Islamic world for over a century, but have acquired their present form, as well as their current urgency, in the years since the Iranian Revolution of 1979: What kind of accommodation can Islam reach with "modernity" once "traditional" social structures have collapsed under the pressures of global capitalism? What is the place of women in a modern Islamic community? How is contemporary politics to be organized in accordance with Islamic tradition—and how is tradition to be interpreted? What place is there within Islam for claims—nationhood, citizenship, democracy, social and economic justice—that are identified with secularism and have their roots in the European Enlightenment? What is the role of Islam in the contemporary struggle against the economic, political and cultural imperialism of the West? What precisely, in this age of the globalization of economic, political and cultural forms, does it mean to be a Muslim?

Reprinted from *Social Text* 29, no. 4 (1992), with revisions supplied by the author.

What has given the novel its transgressive force is that instead of merely thematizing these familiar issues, it also forces a changing of the terms of the discussion itself. Its multi-layered engagement with the origin myth of Islamic orthodoxy, its "politics of offense" with respect to Islam,[2] have rightly been read as a forceful refusal to accept the cultural authority of the authoritarian political constellations and discourses, usually grouped under the label of fundamentalism, that have emerged across the Muslim world in the last decade and a half.[3] The term *fundamentalism* is notoriously slippery. The history of its abuse in the Reagan-Bush era, for instance, by the media and area studies establishment alike, is well known. Furthermore, as Ervand Abrahamian has shown, the term has little utility as a description of the doctrinal content of even such a paradigmatic movement of "Islamic militancy" as Khomeinism.[4] I therefore use the term, as will shortly become clear, in a very specific sense: as shorthand for the *public* and popular discourses of domestic and international militancy under the sign of "Islam" that have come to take remarkably similar shape across the Islamic world in recent years. The violence of the novel's reception in South Asia—and within the South Asian Muslim diaspora in Britain—is an accurate indicator of the anger generated by its insistence on a sweeping rearrangement and rethinking of the terms of Muslim public culture. It is the audacity of this insistence, enacted by an insider, and, as it were, in full view of the West, whose hostility to the world of Islam is both continuing and well known, that has been consistently glossed by the novel's Muslim detractors as "irreverence," "apostasy," and blasphemy.

It is my contention here that the affair surrounding *The Satanic Verses* forces us to reexamine notions of literary reception current in critical theory today. Conceptions of reception based on an almost Victorian image of the solitary bourgeois reader have allowed progressive commentators to more or less dismiss the novel as produced for (and consumed by) Western audiences alone.[5] Working under similar assumptions, Western accounts of the worldwide demonstrations against the book's publication have often expressed amazement at the passion of crowds that have obviously not read the book.[6] A reconceptualization of reception appropriate to the cultural realities of the present global conjuncture, I will argue, must account for forms of mass consumption other than reading in the narrower sense of that word. Extracts published in the print media, in English and in translation; commentary in print, on the airwaves, and from the pulpit; fantasticated representation in the popular cinema; rumors and hearsay—such are the means by which the novel has achieved circulation in the Islamic world.

I am arguing that this piecemeal and fitful reception at the popular level is not simply accidental, and that in a sense the novel even *requires* it. First of all, the novel's political project vis-à-vis contemporary "Islam"—to intervene in the public political conversation within the Muslim world—required breaking out of the minuscule anglophone audience to which the English-language writer in South Asia is traditionally confined. And secondly, the almost obsessive attention given in Rushdie's novels to the dynamics of mass communication—the fantasy-like distortions and fragmentation that events and objects go through in the process of entering the public sphere—the insistence in this novel on the "impurity" of any situation in the contemporary world, and the novel's self-conscious use of pastiche and nonlinear narrative, themselves point towards the filtered reception the novel has received. So the familiar and sinister-sounding charge, leveled by the likes of Roald Dahl and John Le Carré that Rushdie "knew what he was doing," must be stood on its head: by inserting itself in bits and pieces within the cultural politics of contemporary "Islam," the novel has indeed achieved—if one may speak of textual, rather than authorial, intention—what was already inscribed in and suggested by its very form.[7]

Furthermore, this "reception by pastiche" forces us to think again about the meaning and function of pastiche within the text itself. Entirely assimilable neither to the national-allegorical function attributed by Jameson to "Third-World literature," nor to the purely stylistic connotations of "the postmodern" as it has been conceptualized in recent critical theory, pastiche—that is, hybridity of form, in this case the juxtaposition and overlapping of realist, magical realist and modernist modes, the parodic rewriting of historical and religious narratives and of metropolitan texts, genres, and motifs, the use of the resources of literary as well as popular culture—takes on in Rushdie's text a deeply political and critical turn.[8] It is precisely this *ambivalence* of form—is the book about "real" events in Islamic history or is it pure fiction and fantasy?—that constitutes the space within which the novel is able to function as critique. Pastiche, in this context, is neither a purely formal question, nor merely the textual correlate of a hybrid "external reality." Pastiche and formal ambivalence are here the very conditions that enable the literary text to enter the public sphere as political act.

Given the meticulous attention Rushdie has always directed towards the critical role of the postcolonial artist-intellectual, and towards the function of writing, it is perhaps ironic that his most politically interventionist work to date should have been read by so many progressive critics in the West only as an exercise in cosmopolitan irony and detachment, the work, as Timothy Brennan puts it, of a "court satirist."[9] No such piety has clouded the discussion in India itself, where the novel has been discussed in explicitly political terms by antagonists and supporters alike, raising questions about secularism, class, citizenship, and the nature and role of the state—the most urgent and explosive constellation of issues facing Indian political life today.

The two earlier novels of Rushdie's trilogy, *Midnight's Children* and *Shame,* have most often been read as wide-ranging examinations and critiques of the modern nation-space designated by "India" and "Pakistan" respectively.[10] They portrayed an essentially *critical* role for the artist-intellectual vis-à-vis the national project. While alluding in authorial asides to the substantive questions of intellectual authenticity in the postcolonial world, the earlier novels nevertheless approached the question of the intellectual in terms that were primarily negative: they were concerned with the *failure* of the imaginative work of nation-building in two postcolonial countries.[11] In *The Satanic Verses,* a far more positive stand is taken in favor of the hybrid perspectives of postcolonial identity, a stand Rushdie had already elaborated at great length in essays and interviews.[12] Fredric Jameson has argued that the characteristic form of the "Third World text" is "the national allegory."[13] Without ignoring the ubiquitous complicities and connections between literature and the national, it must nevertheless be pointed out that this formulation addresses only one moment in the "worldliness" of the texts it takes as its objects, that it is unable to account fully for the *oppositional* thrust of the first two novels of Rushdie's trilogy, and that it falls far short of understanding the self-consciously supra-national concerns of this third book. The role of the intellectual, as it appears in Rushdie's writings, involves, I will argue, going beyond a mere "telling of the experience of the collectivity itself," to a posing of specific challenges, directed at historical fictions of community and representation.[14]

Before proceeding to the specific issues raised by the "Islamic" reception of the novel in India, I wish to take a brief detour and discuss the persistent theme of intellectuals and critique in Rushdie's writing, and the change and expansion of focus it has undergone over the course of the trilogy. There is, I suggest, progressively greater foregrounding of the author's persona in each subsequent novel, and greater identification of the author himself with the critical thrust of the work. The passage from *Midnight's Children* to *The Satanic Verses* also marks a shift away from what I shall call a politics of constituency, to what I have already spoken of as a politics of offense.

In *Midnight's Children,* the intellectual appears in the form of the narrator himself. Saleem Sinai, born at the moment of the country's emergence from colonial rule, is "mysteriously handcuffed" to the fate of the nation and endowed with mysterious powers of "seeing into the hearts and minds of men."[15] In order to fully grasp the relation of Saleem to the nation itself, we may begin by recalling that it is under the prophesy of Jawaharlal Nehru, framed and hanging on the wall, that the boy Saleem grows up: "You are the newest bearer of that ancient face of India," the Prime Minister's letter to the infant reads, "which is also eternally young. We shall be watching over your life with the closest attention; it will be, in a sense, the mirror of our own" (122). The shadow of Nehru, the totemic intellectual of Indian nationalism, hangs heavy over Saleem's life, and his attempts to discover and impose a "third principle" (248–249) beyond "the endless duality of masses-and-classes, capital-and-labour, them-and-us," on the other one thousand mysteriously gifted "midnight's children," are deeply informed by the pedagogic and mediating role that the intellectual-politician is meant to play within the narrative of Indian nationalism.[16]

Saleem's disintegrating body and unfulfilled life highlight not so much the failure as the impossibility of the national (liberal-democratic) project of turning colonial subjects into democratic citizens while simultaneously insisting on the leadership role of the anglicized elite. Saleem's anguished search in the Midnight Children's Conference—the organization of the supernaturally gifted individuals born within the first hour of independence from British rule—for a "third principle" is thwarted as each child becomes "distracted by his or her own life" and is swayed by the counter-arguments of Shiva, "midnight's darkest child," that "the world is not ideas, rich boy; the world is no place for dreamers or their dreams." And the adult Saleem, the artist-intellectual literally narrating the nation's history, is forced to conclude that "if there is a third principle, its name is childhood. But it dies; or rather, it is murdered."

It is the impossibility and fraud of this mediation or "third principle," so brutally revealed by the repression and tyranny of Indira Gandhi's Emergency Rule, that *Midnight's Children* confronts. It records the historical failure of the elite to "represent" the entire nation—in both the aesthetic-semiotic and political senses of the word. This record does have its allegorical moments: Saleem, raised in privilege, is actually the illegitimate son of the departing Englishman Methwold, and conceals this colonial patrimony from the Midnight Children's Conference, whose leadership he claims on the basis of superior ability and higher principles; Shiva, who is brought up in the street, and whose "birth-right" is denied him by Saleem, becomes his nemesis both within and outside the Conference and is ultimately his undoing; Padma, the earthy "dung goddess" at once fascinated by the urbane Saleem and frustrated by his inability to fulfill her desires, becomes his protector and collaborator in the composition of the autobiography that is also a history of the nation. But the allegory remains incomplete in the resistance of the novel to the very idea of the nation as produced within the "grand narrative" of India's liberation and modernization.[17] And to dislodge the authority of this narrative from *within,* to voice its blind-spots, absences and exclusions, becomes the primary task of that special child of midnight, the postcolonial intellectual.

Hence the series of inversions enacted in the novel. If "national time," as Benedict Anderson suggests, is linear, calendrical time, the time of *Midnight's Children* is cyclical, ritual, or, as Rushdie puts it, "pickled" time;[18] if the typical nationalist narrative proceeds from interior to exterior time and space, giving "hypnotic confirmation of the solidarity of a single community, embracing characters, author and readers,"[19] *Midnight's Children,* like the oral tale, "goes in great loops and circles back on itself, repeats earlier things, digresses,"[20] in order precisely to suggest a multiplicity of voices, interests, communities; and if the solitary nationalist hero moves "through a sociological landscape of a fixity that fuses the world inside the novel with the world outside,"[21] Saleem, this ironic and restless consciousness, his body wracked by the "rip tear crunch" of the nation's history, himself puts the veracity of his narrative in doubt, and raises questions about the authority of his class—the anglicized middle-class—as an interpretive community.

The critical consciousness that emerges in *Midnight's Children,* then, is double-edged: it is directed at both colonial culture and the myth of cultural authenticity and authority that replaced it. Frantz Fanon argued in "On National Culture" that "the native intellectual who wishes to create an authentic work of art" must overcome his assimilation in the culture of the colonizers as well as the temptation to articulate the immemorial "truth" of the nation ("we have the right to ask if this truth is in fact a reality"). He must come to inhabit, Fanon wrote, that "zone of occult instability" where the culture of a people is forged.[22] Deeply aware of its colonial and local-elite affiliations, *Midnight's Children* is at one level an account of the struggle to represent that instability.

While I have so far emphasized the negative moments of the novel's attitude towards the nation, it should be pointed out that this attitude is in the end quite ambivalent. Rushdie's frequent assertions to the effect that *Midnight's Children* was motivated by the desire to reclaim "that part of my life that was in danger of being lost," must not be read at the level of autobiographical memory alone.[23] For the account of the failure of the anglicized elite to dream-up the nation in its own image is accompanied by a lingering nostalgia for the social order envisioned in that dream, an order reflected in the graceful life of Methwold Estate.[24] This nostalgia has played no small part in creating for the novel an enthusiastic constituency within the very same social class whose self-proclaimed place in society it set out to criticize.

In *Shame,* while the critical relationship of the artist to the false certainties of (in this case, Pakistani) national culture is maintained, a formal change occurs that has the effect of increasing the stakes and intensifying the critique. The narrator, no longer a Saleem-like "character" in the novel, is repeatedly identified with the author himself. At various junctures, the "story" is interrupted by passages of varying length in which the author inserts himself into the narrative with commentary and with biographical information that even the relatively uninformed reader recognizes as referring to the author himself. And once again the question of critical authority is raised. By what authority, he imagines his Pakistani readers objecting, can the voluntarily exiled writer speak of Third-World realities?

> Outsider! Trespasser! You have no right to this subject! . . . I know: nobody ever arrested me. Nor are they ever likely to. Poacher! Pirate! We reject your authority. We know you, with your foreign language wrapped around you like a flag: speaking about us in your forked tongue, what can you tell but lies? (S: 23).[25]

To which the author-narrator at once replies: "Is history to be considered the property of the participants solely? In what courts are such claims staked, what boundary commissions map out the territories? Can only the dead speak?" (23).

This sudden appearance of the author between the reader and the plot of the novel, aside from insisting on the right to critique, *personalizes* the novel's critical intention, adding a confrontational tone that was not present in *Midnight's Children*. It also marks a shift away from the residual nostalgia for the nation that was still present in that novel. The combined effect is a weaker sense of identification with a constituency within the "community" (Pakistan) that is the object of the novel's representation.

In *The Satanic Verses* this personalization is given a new turn, for one of the forms in which the author now "appears" is that of Salman the Persian, a minor character with respect to the novel as a whole, but pivotal in the Jahilia sequences that are at the center of the Islamic controversy.[26] This "identification" of the author with the Prophet Mahound's scribe, responsible for secretly emending and polluting the word of God, is carried out in a number of ways. Aside from the common name Salman—"Persian" in early Islamic culture was simply synonymous with "non-Arab Muslim"—and the common writer's vocation, a number of textual markers facilitate this identification. Salman's account to Baal of his loss of faith and fall from Mahound's grace, for instance, shifts suddenly from the third person to the first, from "Salman complained to Baal," to "*I* began to get a bad smell in my nose" (365).[27] The effect of course is to associate Salman the author with the doubt, apostasy, and treachery of Salman the scribe. It is this insistence on personalizing the novel's intervention, reinforced by the tone and substance of Rushdie's reactions early in the controversy, that placed him outside the pale of discussion and disputation as far as his critics are concerned. It also made it nearly impossible for the novel to be *publicly* identified within the context of contemporary political and cultural life in the Muslim world. The shift away from a politics of constituency, in other words, is complete.

Each of the two novels that have followed *Midnight's Children* represents, then, an intensification of political engagement at the same time that it marks a shift away from what might be called a politics of constituency: *Shame* in comparison with *Midnight's Children,* and *The Satanic Verses* in comparison with *Shame,* seem less and less concerned with addressing actual audiences in South Asia with whom they might be able to declare a commonality of purpose and position. This is not to say that such constituencies do not exist. If anything, the (traditionally conceived) audience for these novels within the Islamic world is larger than most outsiders suspect. I am simply arguing that the novels go beyond these possibilities, in order to enact what I have called a politics of displacement and offense, transgressing universally enforced norms of literary representation and public discussion—from state-enforced censorship in Pakistan to the political and cultural taboos of contemporary "Islamic" culture—with such force and to such an extent that some aspects at least of the official culture are thrown into question. In the transgressive politics of *The Satanic Verses* vis-à-vis "Islam," this process has reached its climax.

It is worth recalling at this juncture that the offending passages are contained mostly within two chapters—"Jahilia" and "Return to Jahilia"—that add up to less than seventy-five pages in this rather large book. There are, broadly speaking, three areas that, in terms of content, constitute the novel's most transgressive moments. The first, suggested by the title itself, is the incident of the verses that were revealed to Mahound in response to the Jahilian Grandee's offer of peace if three of the Jahilian goddesses were accepted as minor deities by the new religion; the verses sanctioning this arrangement were renounced by Mahound as the work of Satan once the Grandee's wife Hind had withdrawn her husband's offer of peace (123). The second is the incident involving Salman, already discussed above, in which the scribe, beginning to lose faith in the Prophet, tests the latter by altering the verses as they are dictated to him; Mahound fails to notice the emendations when the verses are read back to him for confirmation (367–368). The third concerns the Jahilian whorehouse named The Curtain or *Hijab*—the Arabic word is now used widely in the Islamic world for the shoulder-length scarf that has come to be equated, in varying cultural contexts, with the required Islamic headdress for women—whose prostitutes take on the names of Mahound's wives (which happen to be the names of the historical Muhammad's wives as well) in order to heighten the excitement and pleasure of their customers (376–392).

While the first two sequences put in question the infallibility of the revelation—in the first case by problematizing the mode of transmission of the word of God, and in the second by suggesting the addition and emendation of passages by a human—the last personalizes the offence by playing irreverently with figures held in deep reverence by believers. It is these three moments that have most often been extracted from the novel for quotation and transmission and have acquired a sort of iconic value in the mass politics in which it has become embroiled.[28] Syed Shahabuddin, the Indian opposition member of Parliament who led the successful campaign for the banning of the book in India, castigated Rushdie's novel on precisely these points, in an open letter which deserves a closer look, and to which I will shortly return:

> The very title of your book is suggestively derogatory. In the eyes of the believer the Koran is the word of God, and you plead innocence of the possible Muslim reaction. You depict the Prophet whose name the practicing Muslim recites five times a day, whom he loves, whom he considers the model for mankind, as an impostor and you expect us to applaud you? You have had the

nerve to situate the wives of the Prophet, whom we Muslims regard as the mothers of the community, in a brothel, and you expect the Muslims to praise the power of your imagination?[29]

Similarly, Shabbir Akhtar, the animus behind the Bradford-based campaign for a banning of the book in Britain, characterized the novel as "a calculated attempt to vilify and slander the Prophet of Islam."[30] It portrays Muhammad, he argued, as "an unscrupulous politician . . . the book he claims to bring from God is really just a confused catalogue of trivial rules about sexual activity and excretion . . . his household is portrayed in pornographic scenes in a brothel incongruously called 'The Veil'—the symbol of female modesty and chastity in the Islamic ethical outlook."[31] And beyond the mere content of the offending passages, Akhtar pointed to the tone, "the idiom and the temper" of the novel, which are "uniformly supercilious and dismissive," and seem "calculated to shock and humiliate Muslim sensibilities."[32]

It is difficult to convey the transgressive force of the offending passages in the political atmosphere of much of the Islamic world in the 1980s and 1990s, but especially in Muslim South Asia. The decade after the Iranian Revolution saw the rise to political center-stage of political groupings that had previously been of marginal significance at best. The various fundamentalist guerilla organizations in Afghanistan that fought the Soviets and the Afghan communists,[33] the Hizbollah among the Shiites of Lebanon and Hamas in the occupied Palestinian territories, the Jamaat-i-Islami in Pakistan under the Army's patronage,[34] such figures as Shahabuddin and the Imam Bukhari of Delhi's Jaama Mosque in India,[35] and organizations such as the Bradford Council of Mosques in Britain,[36] have been able to command influence and attention far beyond the numerical strength of their followings. (And as the on-going trauma in Algeria has shown, this influence is capable of turning itself into electoral strength, with devastating results.) The centerpiece of this new political culture is of course "Islam," the sign at once of a return to an authentic past and of passage out of neocolonial structures of domination towards a more empowering future.

The change even from the 1970s has been so marked and so sudden that Eqbal Ahmed has spoken of an on-going "crisis" of Islamic society:

> Thus, as in all religious communities, there is a repository of millennial traditions in Islam that tend to surface most forcefully in times of crisis, collective stress, and anomie. Times have rarely been as bad or as stressful for the Muslim peoples as they are now. Hence, all the contrasting symptoms associated with deep crises of politics and society—rise of religious fundamentalism, radical and revolutionary mobilization, spontaneous uprisings and disoriented quietism —characterize Muslim politics today.[37]

First the traumas of colonial rule and then economic "modernization" under postcolonial regimes, have caused, Ahmed argues, "the erosion of economic, social, and political relationships which had been the bases of traditional Muslim order for more than a thousand years."³⁸ Secular politics of various hues—Kemalist modernization, Nasserite pan-Arabism, Bhutto's *awami* populism—failed, in the decades since decolonization, either to generate sustained political and economic independence from the West, or to acquire hegemonic force within civil society, producing an atmosphere, beginning in the 1970s, that has proven favorable to the rise of fundamentalist, neototalitarian movements across the Islamic world.³⁹

Very broadly speaking, the public discourse of Islamic fundamentalism has produced two distinct but related critiques of the contemporary state of affairs in Islamic societies. And while the two typically occur as moments of the same argument against the status quo, they need to be separated for the purpose of analysis. We may speak of the first of these as an essentially *cultural* critique, directed at cultural forms and practices which come to be marked within the discourse as "modern," "western," "foreign"; in short, as un-Islamic. The range of such practices is, of course, enormous, from habits of eating and dressing to the operation of educational and juridical institutions; but the one area of social life where the cultural critique has come to rest with particular force, and with particularly disastrous consequences, is that of gender and sexuality. The fundamentalist obsession with female "chastity"—the segregation of the sexes, the veiling of women, the minimizing (if not elimination) of women's presence in public life—is well known. These concerns find room, as Fatima Mernissi has pointed out, in the radical split within the "individual between what one does, confronted by rapid, totally uncontrolled changes in daily life, and the discourse about an unchangeable religious tradition that one feels psychologically compelled to elaborate in order to keep a minimal sense of identity."⁴⁰ Claims about the *literal* truth of the Koran therefore become the means of insisting upon the possibility of an unmediated reconstruction, in modern times, of the original, "righteous" community. And the "chastity" of women, in the over-coded form outlined above, comes to signify the minimal condition for the desired return to a state of cultural purity and authenticity.⁴¹

The other, directly *political* moment in fundamentalism's critique of society is directed at neocolonial structures of domination and exploitation, and the ("secular") national elites that function as comprador classes within those structures. It is able, for this purpose, to draw upon collective memories and traditions of resistance to colonialism, which are framed very often in terms of a historical struggle between Islam and the Christian West. (The truth value of these political claims is not the *primary* concern here. But it should of course be noted that there *is* a history of conversation and collaboration between fundamentalist groupings and imperialist interests, as witnessed by the CIA's decade long sponsoring of the Afghan fundamentalist guerrillas and Iran's "contragate" dealings with Israel and the US.) As I have already noted, these two assertions—claims about cultural and political authenticity, respectively—typically occur in conflated form in fundamentalist argumentation. Hence secular and "modernizing" tendencies in society—from the securing of legal rights for women, to demands for the protection and strengthening of democratic rights, including freedom of expression—are represented as signs of westernization, and hence of neocolonial bondage. Furthermore, the protracted history of struggle and out and out conflict between the secular left and the machinery of the postcolonial state is either erased entirely or at best seen as being of minimal importance. In speaking of Rushdie as an apostate from Islam, for instance, Akhtar is able to make the following astonishing equation: "There are therefore countless Rushdies in the House of Islam. The Shah of Iran and his supporters were, to a man, atheists blindly imitating Western patterns of conduct."[42]

And the accusation of *gharbzadegi* or "West-contamination" is of course the broad brush with which the pro-Khomeini, populist segment of the Irani clergy painted the whole range of its opponents, including liberals, communists, and Islamic radicals who especially had played a leading role in the movement against the monarchy, as it sought to eliminate them and consolidate its own hold over the course of the Revolution within months of the fall of the Shah.[43]

Despite this relative discursive stability, fundamentalism has proven notoriously difficult for the secular left to identify and critically engage. Apart from a recurrent failure of will on the part of the left, too often unable to see its position in Muslim society as anything but anomalous, this has resulted from the very nature of fundamentalist discourse itself. With its *universalizing* language of "Islamic" authenticity, fundamentalism has been able to make alliances with, appropriate and mobilize sectors of society whose religious life and traditions have themselves been the object of vigorous critique in fundamentalist theology. Thus, the contemporary sense of social crisis, the erosion of popular cultural traditions and social practices under the impact of uneven urbanization, industrialization, and consumerization, are easily construed as threats to "Islamic" culture and polity, and the desire for the recovery of that disappearing life displaced onto the fundamentalist slogan for the reconstruction of the original, "righteous" community of seventh century Islam.

It should be made explicitly clear that in no sense am I portraying fundamentalism as a *return* to pre-modern social, cultural, and political forms. On the whole it would be accurate to say that fundamentalism in fact critiques and rejects most of these "traditional" forms, seeing them as violations of the principles of the "righteous" community inaugurated by Muhammad and his early followers at Medina. (Khomeini even went so far as to claim that revolutionary Iran had surpassed even the Prophet's society in the implementation of true Islam "in all spheres of life, particularly in the material and the spiritual spheres."[44]) Not to see this is also to miss the crucial point that what fundamentalism represents is precisely a struggle over the cultural artifacts of modernity—nationhood, citizenship, representative government, the forms of anti-imperialist and revolutionary struggle, the terms and institutions of the public sphere—and who gets to *define* them and in what terms. The first two years of the Irani Revolution—which saw a protracted struggle between the populist mullahs on the one hand, and liberals, Marxists and the Islamic radical Mojahedin on the other—are an object lesson in this process of gaining control of, and redefining, the institutions of modern public life.[45] It is in this context that "the West" (and the taint of association with it) becomes a site for negative contestation, as both the historical source of these cultural artifacts and the chief impediment to their acquisition and development.

My purpose in outlining the salient features of the public discourse of fundamentalism—and it will be clear that my concern is with its popular constructions of "Islam," and not with fundamentalist theological discourse—is not to suggest the existence of a monolithic religio-political movement around the Islamic world. The aim here is to sketch out that discursive unity which allows similar fundamentalist arguments to be formulated in very different political and cultural contexts. The self-representation of fundamentalism in terms of "Islamic" cultural authenticity and anti-imperialist political purity is such a constant. So is the insistence on a rationalist-literalist reading of the Koran as a basis for the transformation of society. (Hence the opposition of fundamentalism to the enormous range of forms—including saint worship, the disciplines of the Sufis, the numerous traditions of mystical union with the divine around the Islamic world—in which Islam has been lived and practiced by the great majority of Muslims over the centuries.[46]) The diversity of actual fundamentalist groups around the world—as indexed by the kinds of alliances (and enemies) they make in particular historical situations, the political strategies they employ, and even the theological systems to which they ascribe—is actually quite staggering. More importantly, the range of political contexts in which one or more elements of this discourse of "Islam" have in recent years been mobilized, by fringe groups and state structures alike, is also enormous.

In Pakistan during the 1980s, for instance, "Islamization" became the means of consolidation of the Army's hold on power, a process carried out with the active participation of, among others, sections of the land-owning class, the bureaucracy, industrial and commercial bourgeoisies, and the small but influential Jamaat-i-Islami.[47] The term refers in principle to reform of public institutions such as the judicial and financial systems in accordance with the requirements of traditional Islamic law or *shari'a*. However, the full range of its discursive functions reaches far beyond that institutional focus, and rests on an identification of the interests of "Islam" with the state, and until his death in 1988, with the person of Zia in particular.

Despite its self-proclaimed role of citadel of South Asian Islam, however, Pakistan was slow to react to the publication of *The Satanic Verses*. The first country to ban it, within weeks of its publication in Britain in the early Fall of

1988, was Rushdie's native India. There the book became victim to an ongoing and bloody struggle between Hindu fundamentalist and Muslim groups over a sixteenth century mosque in Ayodhya in northern India, claimed by the Hindu groups to have been built by a lieutenant of the first Mughal emperor Babar on the site of the temple marking the birthplace of the Lord God Rama. The Babri Masjid-Rama Janamabhoomi conflict, which had already taken scores of lives, was threatening to explode out of control:[48] the Babri Masjid Coordinating Committee, consisting of notable Muslim politicians and clerics, with Shahabuddin as one of its leading figures, had promised a huge march to Ayodhya to underline Muslim claims to the site. Hindu groups had promised an equal show of force, and widespread bloodshed was expected. The Congress government of Rajiv Gandhi was having discussions with the Muslim leaders, negotiating to have them cancel their proposed march. On October 5th the Government announced its ban; on the 12th Shahabuddin announced that the march had been indefinitely postponed. Despite official denials from both sides, it is difficult not to see a connection.[49]

Rushdie at once denounced the decision in somewhat breathless and vituperative terms, suggesting that Rajiv Gandhi had come out "looking not only philistine and antidemocratic but opportunistic" as well.[50] The reply to Rushdie's harangue came from Shahabuddin, in the open letter published in *The Times of India* of October 13 which I have already quoted from above. The thrust of Shahabuddin's critique is that the novel is in fact an act of cultural imperialism—"literary colonialism," he calls it—coming as it does from the West, "which has not yet laid the ghost of the crusades [sic] to rest, but given it a new cultural wrapping." It is Rushdie's willingness to "vend his Islam wares in the West," Shahabuddin argues, that "explains why writers like [him] are so wanted and pampered" there. India would stand up against this act of cultural violation, and not cringe in the face of accusations of loss of expressive freedoms from Rushdie's "British champions and advisors."[51]

But despite the fact that it is actually addressed to Rushdie, much of Shahabuddin's response is an engagement with what he identifies as the "Anglicized elite" and "liberal establishment" of the country. He excoriates them for not having thrown off the psychological fetters of colonialism, as witnessed by their undignified and unconcealed pleasure at the fact that "a book by a writer of Indian origin [has been] nominated, sorry, shortlisted, for the highest literary award in the *Vilayat* [that is, Britain] by the sahibs themselves." But what is interesting here is that Shahabuddin defines the Muslims of India as distinct from, and in *opposition* to, the national intelligentsia: "Even more shocking and saddening at the same time is the communication gap between the Muslim community and the so-called intelligentsia. There is no mental rapport, no instantaneous recognition of pain, no spontaneous sharing of anguish . . . It's unbelievable that what pains one section gives pleasure to the other."[52]

This strange distinction is due in part, of course, to the majority/minority dynamics of the Indian nation-state, and the marginal, though "protected," place of the Muslims within it. But it also articulates with the wider discursive formation I have been attempting to describe. For "Muslim" and "Islam" here are semantic spaces that exclude the experience of secular intellectual life, and Shahabudddin's statement is at one with Akhtar's declaration that "given that the Koran is the book which defines the authentically Muslim outlook, there is no choice in the matter. Anyone who fails to be offended by Rushdie's book *ipso facto* ceases to be a Muslim."[53]

One of the more astonishing features of the Rushdie affair is the fact of its truly international dimensions, encompassing as it does political contexts as diverse as post-Zia Pakistan, the "communal" problem in India, and the politics of Asian immigration in Great Britain. And public responses by Muslims to the publication of this book, written by a writer of Indian origin naturalized and living in Britain, have been registered not only in Britain, India, and Pakistan, but in places as diverse and as remote from the scene of the infraction as South Africa, (then) Soviet Central Asia, and Indonesia, with attacks on individuals associated with translations of the novel in such places as Japan and Scandinavia. What this range allows us to see is that it has become possible today to speak of an "Islamic" public sphere, incorporating elements of the public life of a large and diverse set of Muslim communities, ranging from nation-states in the Third World to ethnic minorities across the globe. Increased access to the international media, either directly or filtered through the regional and national media, continuing links between migrants and their parent communities, and increasing cooperation and coordination between agencies of the state and between religio-political groups in different parts of the world, have all led to the transmission of information at unprecedented levels and with amazing speed. Public discussion of the place and meaning of Islam in contemporary life has therefore become surprisingly pan-Islamic in scope. What the response to the publication of the novel has also made clear is that this discussion is dominated by the literalist and universalizing discourse of fundamentalism.

It is the stability of this public sphere, in which resistance to neototalitarian movements and discourses is marginalized, deemed anti-Islamic and often brutally suppressed, that *The Satanic Verses* disturbs. The concept of "public sphere" as defining the institutions of modern society owes its elaboration, of course, to the work of Jürgen Habermas. For Habermas the concept of the public sphere is tied to an ideal of a space for "rational-critical debate" in which "access is guaranteed to all citizens"[54] and which is characterized by a co-incidence of the narrow interests of those who come to be defined as citizens and the "general interest" of society.[55] I use the term in a significantly different sense. My use of it points, first of all, to the processes of selection and transfiguration through which something gets to be constituted and disseminated as an object of dispute and discussion within this public sphere. On the one hand, low levels of literacy in the Third World, and on the other a generally high measure of access to electronic media and means of information transmission—radio, television, cinema, audio and video tape technology, public address systems, fax machines, and the internet—produce conditions of reception in direct contradiction with the requirements of most genres of (both indigenous and metropolitan) high literary production, a question to which I will shortly return. Secondly, I wish to point precisely to the enforced exclusions—in this case women, peasants and workers, dissident activists, artists and intellectuals—on which this public sphere is based.

But of more immediate concern for us at this point are the discursive constraints I have tried to evoke, which regulate discussions of "Islam" and its meaning and place in contemporary society. By questioning the infallible divinity of the Revelation, by refusing to accept the required code of strict reverence when speaking of the Prophet and his close circle of relatives and companions, and, more generally, by secularizing (and hence profaning) the sacred tropology of Islam in insisting upon its appropriation for the purposes of fiction, the novel threw into doubt the discursive edifice within which "Islam" has been publicly produced in recent years.[56] What this destabilization made at least momentarily possible is the expansion of the discussion about Islam in the contemporary world, the insertion of other voices into this public sphere, and greater and more coherent resistance to the discourse of fundamentalism within it. It is in this sense that the politics the novel enacts is not one of constituency, but of displacement and offense. Critics who place the novel only or primarily within the metropolitan context, ignore this mode of the novel's self-insertion into the politics of contemporary Islam.[57]

It would be dangerous and naive, however, to see the novel as embodying an unambiguously anti-religious view-point, for that, of course, is precisely the view of its fundamentalist critics. As Sara Suleri has convincingly shown, the Western liberal appropriation of the embattled author as "one of us" does not "acknowledge the strong possibility that Rushdie's latest novel epitomizes the profound cultural fidelity represented by specific acts of religious betrayal."[58] "Rushdie performs," she argues, "a curious act of faith: he chooses disloyalty in order to dramatize his continuing obsession with the metaphors that Islam makes available to a postcolonial sensibility."[59] For the effect of this disloyalty is not to replace belief with the final certitude of disbelief. It is, rather, to posit doubt as "the opposite of faith," (92) as the inevitable corollary of faith, or, as Suleri puts it, as "the very historicity of belief."[60]

The thematics of doubt appear repeatedly in the Jahilia sequences and are most successfully figured as the dissolution or overlapping of subjectivities. Thus, in the process of "listening" for the divine revelation concerning the three pagan goddesses, Mahound finds himself first reversing positions with Gibreel, and then becoming indistinguishable from him, so that it is no longer "possible to say which of us is dreaming the other" (110). Furthermore, Rushdie makes it clear that, in insisting upon doubt as a constitutive modality of human experience, what he is opposing is any conception of belief that denies its materiality, placing it outside the realm of human effort and will:

> Angels are easily pacified; turn them into instruments and they'll play your harpy tune. Human beings are tougher nuts, can doubt anything, even the evidence of their eyes. Of behind-their-own eyes. Of what, as they sink heavy-lidded, transpires behind closed peepers . . . angels, they don't have much in the way of a will. To will is to disagree; not to submit; to dissent. (92–93)

"Doubt" therefore becomes in *The Satanic Verses* a sign of resistance to the fundamentalist hijacking of Islam, a means of prying open, even if ever so slightly, the seamless whole regarding which the only public choice offered the contemporary Muslim is submission or disbelief. When Rushdie speaks of his sustained respect for the religious mind, this must be taken not only seriously, but as the very basis of his novel's complex engagement with the culture and politics of contemporary Islam.

Since the beginning of the controversy, Rushdie's Islamic critics have argued that the enormous literary machinery within which these relatively short passages occur—their framing as the hallucinations of a man going mad, their only partial and fantasticated use of places, events, and persons significant in the narratives of Islam, their relatively minor place within the "plot" of the novel, traditionally conceived—do not in any way modify or condition the directness of the attack. Within weeks of the publication of the book in Britain, Shahabuddin warned Rushdie in his open letter that "you cannot take shelter behind the plea that after all it is a single dream sequence in a piece of fiction." And, responding to Rushdie's charge that "some of us have condemned you without a hearing and asked for a banning without reading the book," he replied: "Yes, I have not read it, nor do I intend to. I do not have to wade through a filthy drain to know what filth is. My first inadvertent step would tell me what I have stepped into. For me, the synopsis, the review, the excerpts, the opinions of those who had read it and your own gloatings were enough."[61]

Such sentiments were in fact voiced repeatedly in the course of the controversy. Akhtar, for instance, wrote of the offending chapters as "Rushdie's attempt to rewrite chronologically the history of early Islam . . . (and to) proffer an alternative biography of Muhammad, his wives and companions."[62] It is, in other words, on a realist *and* fragmented reading that the militant opposition to the novel has insisted from the start. An understanding of this insistence therefore requires critical rethinking of the relationship between reception and form.

The question of form in Rushdie's novels can be approached in a number of ways. In the following pages, I will sketch out three related issues that may be subsumed under the rubric of parody and pastiche: The manner in which an important aspect of the novels' critical self-consciousness—their awareness of colonial-metropolitan affiliations—is worked out on the level of form; the correspondence between the novel's form and its pastiche-like reception within the "Islamic" public sphere; and the fact that the formal ambivalence of pastiche becomes in *The Satanic Verses* an enabling condition for this political intervention.

In a series of essays on the functions of pastiche in Latin American fiction, Jean Franco has argued that the notion of pastiche "needs the notion of originality as counter-point" and is therefore a natural corollary of the exhaustion of modernism's "search for originality."[63] For the same reason, pastiche is also a corollary of the decline of the "high" narrative of the (postcolonial) nation's cultural originality. For the purpose of this discussion, I suggest the following working definition: pastiche is hybridity or melange, but it is also imitation and citation. It is not merely the seemingly random juxtaposition of different discourses; it is also a repetition of something that went before. More specifically, it ironically enunciates the signs of the colonizer in order to subvert their meanings. Against Jameson's stricture regarding the sharp contrast between (postmodern) pastiche and (modernist) parody—"Pastiche . . . is a neutral practice of . . . mimicry, without any of parody's ulterior motives"[64]—it is my argument that parody and pastiche comprise in Rushdie's novels two aspects of the same formal intention, marking the texts' hesitation with notions of originality and purity, on the one hand, and their self-critical sense of affiliation, on the other. Parody thus provides ironic distance as a means of expressing a simultaneous sense of continuity and discontinuity with the (colonial) past, offering "a workable and effective stance toward the [latter] in its paradoxical strategy of repetition as a source of freedom."[65]

Gayatri Spivak has spoken of postcolonial claims to nationhood, democracy, and social and economic justice as "catechreses," the assigning of new and unfamiliar values to the "concept-metaphors" of metropolitan culture.[66] In *The Satanic Verses,* postcolonial culture incorporates such acts of citation, of repetition "with a difference." In the hybrid identities of the postcolonial world, in these shifting, unsettled perspectives, it is repeatedly suggested, may be found a metaphor for the modern world. Rushdie is unapologetic about an ambivalent "insider/outsider" status, a "historically validated eclecticism," as Zeeny puts it to Saladin (52). To borrow, in *The Satanic Verses,* is therefore also to appropriate and renew.

Already, in *Midnight's Children,* Rushdie showed an anxious but ironic awareness of that novel's metropolitan affiliations. The opening of Rushdie's novel, as that of Forster's novel of India, centers around a Dr. Aziz. (And the name of another character in the novel, Wee Willie Winkie, recalls a story by Kipling.) But whereas Forster's novel begins with Aziz anxiously protecting the sanctity of a mosque from imagined desecration by a European—he thinks Mrs. Moore is wearing shoes in the place of worship—Rushdie's Aziz has an experience during the act of praying that leaves "a hole inside him" and takes him away permanently from religious faith. The Midnight Children's Conference (MCC) is also an allusion, to both the Marylebone Cricket Club and the "Mayapore Chatterjee Club" to which the anglicized Indian Hari Kumar in Paul Scott's *The Jewel in the Crown* is laughingly said to belong.[67] As Brennan has pointed out, "Rushdie even mimics Scott's method of introducing the novel's defining themes in a painting's iconography."[68] In Scott's case, the painting referred to in the title shows an Indian prince presenting a bejeweled crown to Victoria, the classic tributary exchange between a colonial subject and his foreign ruler; in *Midnight's Children,* it is a picture of the young Raleigh seated at the feet of "an old, gnarled net-mending sailor . . . whose right arm, fully extended, stretched out towards a watery horizon," and in fact *westwards* towards the Arabian Sea visible from the window of Saleem's room, in which it is hung (122). This scene of colonial conquest with its inviting gesture, ominously echoed in Mary Pereira's lullaby, "anything you want to be, you can be," becomes for the child Saleem a source of horror and anguish. At the end of his life, in the final, unstoppable passage of the novel, he hears once again that refrain, with the role it promises for the national elite molded in the image of the colonial rulers, and says: "I hear lies being spoken in the night, anything you want to be you kin be, the greatest of all lies" (445).

In the case of *The Satanic Verses,* "pastiche" comes to refer at the most general level to the novel's formal equivocation between genres and styles, between realism, magical realism, the fantastic, the historical novel, reportage, allegory, autobiography. The question here, first of all, is the old Adornian problem, which reemerges with a vengeance in poststructuralist theory, of the appropriateness of form to the object of representation. Pastiche, in this context, is the textual correlate of a hybrid external reality, the presence/reflection within the text of the Third World's "uneasy and unfinished relationship to modernity."[69] But, in fact, the question of repeating the colonial text acquires in *The Satanic Verses* an even greater significance. As many of its Islamist critics have pointed out, the Jahilia chapters employ motifs, imagery, emphases, and phrasing—ranging from the use of the medieval derogatory "Mahound" to a fascination with the sex life of the Prophet—that have a well-known pedigree in the discourses of orientalism.[70] And the fact that the protagonist of Rushdie's novel is called Saladin, and Mahound is merely the figment of a demented mind, recalls Dante's preference for the historical Saladin over "Mahometo" in the *Inferno.* In *The Satanic Verses,* Rushdie himself addresses the question of repeating the orientalist sign:

His name: a dream name, changed by the vision. Pronounced correctly, it means he-for-whom-thanks-should-be-given, but he won't answer to that here ... Here he is neither Mahomet nor MoeHammered; has adopted, instead, the demon-tag the farangis hung around his neck. To turn insults into strengths, whigs, tories, Blacks all chose to wear with pride the names they were given in scorn; likewise, our mountain-climbing, prophet-motivated solitary is to be the medieval baby-frightener, the Devil's synonym: Mahound. (93)

But the repetition here goes beyond the mere inversion of an orientalist hierarchy. For, by simply *accepting* the colonizer's words, even if with the intention of standing them on their head, that is, by inserting the polluting colonial sign within the space of the authentic and divine, the novel enacts another, *formal* transgression within the discursive field of contemporary "Islam," calling into question the assumption of purity vis-à-vis colonial-metropolitan culture upon which the former is based.

Pastiche therefore becomes a means of appropriating and rewriting the colonial text—novel of Empire, orientalist motif, narrative of adventure and conquest—for contemporary purposes, within a global situation that might simultaneously be termed post- and neocolonial. The rewriting of the metropolitan text is itself, in other words, a double-edged activity: on the one hand, it extracts from the latter a new knowledge of (colonized) self and (colonizing) other, precisely by problematizing that radical alterity; on the other, it uses it to question the authoritative discourses of public culture within the periphery. The scene of colonial conquest and the iconic presence of the novel of Empire therefore make possible in *Midnight's Children* a severe critique of the cultural and material privileges of the national(ist) elite; and the orientalist term of abuse, hurled down this time by an "insider," challenges in *The Satanic Verses* the premises of authoritarian Islamic theocracy. The fitful, fragmented, and "doubt-ridden" narrative of *The Satanic Verses* must therefore be read as the writing of a *supplement*—in Derrida's double sense of an addition as well as a voicing of the silences and suppressions of the original—to the totalizing narratives of contemporary "Islam." It is, to borrow a phrase once again from Jean Franco, an act of "substitution that undermines all essentialisms."[71]

The second sense of "pastiche" I want to address relates to the novel's reception. I have already suggested that the failure of progressive critics to identify with the novel's anti-fundamentalist "Islamic" politics results in part from outmoded notions of reception. There is now a need for a sustained effort to theorize the kinds of conditions of reception I have tried to evoke, under which a text, after a process of fragmentation and selection, becomes consumed within already existing cultural and political discourses, and becomes an object of debate, dispute, and discussion within different but often overlapping public spheres. As Arjun Appadurai has argued, the "globalization of culture is not the same as its homogenization."[72] Much of the confusion caused in the West by the Islamic reaction to the book is due precisely to this failure of perception: the political life of *The Satanic Verses* in the Islamic world cannot be contained within the rubric of "novel." The same text that has been acclaimed in the West as a major experiment in that genre (and rejected by many as a failed experiment) is "read" in very different ways in what I have called the Islamic public sphere.

It might be useful in this context to quickly check the facts of the early stages of the anti-Rushdie campaign in Britain, as described in a *Sunday Times* report of February 9, 1989:

> Aslam Ejaz, of the Islamic Foundation in Madras, [had] already written to Faiyazuddin Ahmad, a friend in Leicester, telling him about the impending ban in India. A similar campaign, wrote Ejaz, should be mounted in Britain, which still remained largely oblivious to the blasphemous nature of the book.... Ahmad, who came to Britain from India five years ago, is public relations director of the Islamic Foundation in Leicester. His actions, as much as anything, were to spark the row in Britain.... He sent out a secretary to buy the novel for £12.95 at a local bookshop. The offending passages were photocopied and immediately sent on October 3 to the dozen or so leading Islamic organizations in Britain. Four days later copies were despatched to the 45 embassies in Britain of the member countries of the Organization of Islamic Conference (OIC), including Iran.[73]

This process then repeated itself in several directions, leading to the petitioning of various British officials for banning the book, the soliciting of assistance from Muslim governments and the OIC, and greater coordination between the various organizations in Britain itself. In India extracts from the book were not widely available even after the actual ban, but the Hindu fundamentalist Bharatiya Janata Party announced plans for publishing passages in Hindi translation in its official newspaper. (I have been unable to determine whether these plans were carried out.) The dissemination of the novel in India—through written and verbal commentary, and general rumor and hearsay—therefore involved an even greater degree of fragmentation and transformation. And in Pakistan the novel and its purported offense against Islam have received greatest publicity in the form of fantasticated representation in the cinema: The popular Punjabi and Urdu film "International Guerrillas" tells the story of the men of a Pakistani family who have taken an oath to avenge the blasphemous act by assassinating Rushdie, here portrayed as the scotch-guzzling, woman-molesting agent of an international Zionist conspiracy to destabilize Pakistan. In the final scene of the film, the defeated brothers (who had appeared in an earlier scene in Batman costumes), nailed by Rushdie and his allies to wooden crosses, pray to God for intervention. Help descends from the heavens in the form of three copies of the Koran, which then strike Rushdie down with what looks like a laser beam. The only reference to the *content* of the novel anywhere in the film is a suggestion that it calls the Prophet's wives prostitutes.[74]

What is of greatest interest in this reception of *The Satanic Verses* in the Islamic world is the text's own provocation of the manner in which it has been consumed. In the conversation with Günter Grass that I have already quoted from, Rushdie himself makes an attempt to relate the two, usually separate questions of form and reception. I will quote the passage in full:

> In India the thing I've taken most from . . . is the oral narration. Because it is a country of still largely illiterate people . . . the power and the vitality still remain in the oral story-telling tradition. And what's interesting about these stories is that they command huge audiences, the best story tellers, with literally hundreds of thousands of people. . . . It's a very eclectic form, and of course is not at all linear. . . . And it seems to be formlessness. . . . Now, it occurred to me to ask the opposite question. Let us assume, for the sake of argument, that this is not formlessness but that this is a form which after all is many thousand of years old and has adopted this shape for good reasons. Now, if so, what could those reasons be? It struck me the answer is very simple, which is that the story teller has the problem of holding the audience. . . . And suddenly this suggested to me that what we were being told was [that] this very gymnastic form, this very convoluted, complicated form was in fact the reason why people were listening.[75]

While I do not think that Rushdie's account of the relationship of his work to orality should be taken literally, it is nevertheless interesting that he should have formulated the problem in this way during the period that *The Satanic Verses* was in the works. For it allows us to think through the manner in which "readers" in the Islamic world have been "listening" to the novel's transgressions. The novel's pastiche-like structure—the situating of different discourses in juxtaposed, textually marked sections, the playful rewriting of well-known and easily recognizable episodes from the narratives of Islam, the enactment of these Islamic transgressions within brief, self-contained passages—corresponds to the selection, extraction, and the immediate, almost totemic identification of textual episodes with bits of Islamic lore, that have characterized the novel's reception in the Islamic world. In linking form with reception, I am not, of course, making an argument about authorial intention. What I am suggesting is that there is, in "the Rushdie affair," a coincidence of the (political) imperative of "holding the audience," textual form, and the dynamics of mass communication in the contemporary postcolonial world.

Finally, the novel's formal ambivalence also has more fundamental implications for its political life in the public sphere of contemporary "Islam." As we have seen, the Islamic opposition has insisted throughout on a reading that takes the offending passages literally, as a recklessly revisionist account of the birth of Islam, a rewriting of narratives held sacred by every practicing Muslim. Rushdie, on the other hand, has insisted that the novel is "fiction" and "fantasy," and cannot be read as "history."[76] It is the fact that the novel equivocates formally between these possibilities that allows it a positive political role in the postcolonial world. Rushdie's demand to be read "fantastically" is, in this context, a demand for expressive freedom. The "Islamic" response to this demand is basically the following: "*Despite* the machinery of freedom you have erected, and beyond its ingenuity and splendor, we can see what the novel is *really* about." The opposition and struggle are not between the prerogatives of Literature (Fiction) and Faith. The kind of cultural autonomy sought by *The Satanic Verses* must not be confused with the claims that are made on behalf of "autonomous art."[77] On the contrary, the conflict is about a particular *kind* of writing and its ineradicable *connection* with reality, and the social and cultural goals for which it can (and has) been mobilized. Rushdie and the fundamentalists understand each other only too well. For what the novel represents is an attempt to give "freedom"—not some abstract, universal freedom, but rather the concrete freedom to write outside and against the totalizing discourses of contemporary "Islam"—a literary form.

Discussions of Rushdie and *The Satanic Verses* have been conducted, understandably, in explicitly polemical terms, in the somewhat stark language of "for" or "against." It has been an aim of this essay to at least partially disengage itself from this discourse, in order to distinguish more clearly between the cultural politics highlighted by the "affair" and the person of the author himself. The point is to make it possible for us as critics on the left to identify those elements of this cultural politics of the novel's political intervention in the "Islamic" public sphere which we may consider politically useful, despite the obvious problems posed by what Brennan has quite correctly identified as Rushdie's "complicity . . . with power."[78] (Khomeini's *fatwa* may be read as an attempt to make this complicity unequivocal, a fact Rushdie himself seems not to have understood.) And we should not be deterred from this task by Rushdie's rather clumsy experiments, through the language of "conversion," with the meaning of Muslim "community."

The situation of secular left intellectuals in many parts of the postcolonial world today is characterized by a problematizing of the category of the "popular" in a manner that bears chilling comparison to the predicament of the German left intelligentsia in the 1930s. To recognize the class-marked nature of "secular" political and cultural claims in much of the Third World is one thing; to then fail to distinguish between *official* secularism and *oppositional* ones, and to reduce secularism as such to the ideological reflex of the indigenous national bourgeoisie—as in Brennan's declaration that "the banner of 'secularism' has for more than a century been the standard of a Westernized elite"—and leave the matter at that, is quite another.[79] Such critiques of postcolonial secularism do not acknowledge the participation (or at least acquiescence) of sections of the local elites (and of metropolitan interests) in the production of "Islam" and the rise of fundamentalist groups and parties in South Asia and across the Muslim world. While clearly needing to rethink its relationship to popular religious practices and to engage in new ways with progressive Islamic groups, the secular left cannot and must not pretend to be anything but that—secular. For us as critics located in the West to reject the politics of secularism in the Third World wholesale because they might not be *spontaneously* produced within the domain of subaltern political and cultural life would not be so different, after all, from condemning the demands for reproductive rights in the US, or for artistic freedom from official control, as the reflex of a "cultural elite" alienated from the values of society at large.[80]

The importance of the cultural-political intervention in the public sphere of contemporary "Islam" that Rushdie's novel represents is therefore that it highlights the fact that the fight is far from over. The magnitude of the agony and anxiety it generated was in part a reflection of the fact that it made palpable, however fleetingly, the manner in which "Islam" has been produced in recent years. The left must not fail to take advantage of the consequences of this intervention, even as it distances itself from Rushdie's visibly growing comfort in the corridors of metropolitan power.

Notes

1. Gayatri Spivak, "Reading *The Satanic Verses*," *Public Culture* 2, no. 1 (Fall 1989): 79.
2. I am grateful to Homi Bhabha for suggesting the use of this term in the context of *The Satanic Verses*.
3. For a discussion of the necessity (and simultaneous difficulty) of balancing the critique of Western orientalist discourse with one directed at the authoritarian politics of the contemporary Islamic world, see Eqbal Ahmed, "Islam and Politics," in *The Pakistan Experience,* ed. Asghar Khan (Lahore: Vanguard, 1985).
4. Ervand Abrahamian, "Khomeini: Fundamentalist or Populist?" *New Left Review* 186 (March/April 1991).
5. See, especially, Timothy Brennan, *Salman Rushdie and the* Third World: *Myths of the Nation* (London: St. Martin's Press, 1989), chapter 6; For a far more nuanced reading of the cultural politics of the Rushdie affair, but one nevertheless limited to the politics of South Asian immigration in Britain, see Talal Asad, "Ethnography, Literature, and Politics: Some Readings and Uses of Salman Rushdie's *The Satanic Verses*," *Cultural Anthropology* 5, no. 6 (August 1990): 239–269.
6. For a collection of Western reactions to the Rushdie affair, see *The Rushdie File,* ed. Lisa Appignanesi and Sara Maitland (Syracuse: Syracuse University Press, 1990), henceforth *File.* It should be said that Rushdie has himself leveled this charge against his opponents. See, for instance, his open letter to Rajiv Gandhi, written in response to the banning in India, reprinted in *File,* 34.

7. See Dahl's February 28, 1989 letter to the London *Times*, in *File*, 200. For Le Carré, see "A Book Not Worth the Bloodshed," *Manchester Guardian Weekly*, January 28, 1990: 26–27.

8. See Fredric Jameson, "Third-World Literature in the Era of Multinational Capitalism," *Social Text* 15 (Fall 1986). I am indebted to Jean Franco's discussion of pastiche in "The Nation as Imagined Community," in *The New Historicism*, ed. H. A. Veeser (New York: Routledge, 1989) and "Pastiche in Contemporary Latin American Literature," *Studies in 20th Century Literature* 14, no. 1 (Winter 1990).

9. Brennan, *Salman Rushdie*, 164. See also Asad, "Ethnography," and David Caute, "Prophet Motive," *New Statesman*, February 16, 1990: 18–19.

10. See Timothy Brennan, "India, Nationalism, and Other Failures," *South Atlantic Quarterly* 87, no. 1 (Winter 1988) and Nasser Hussain, "Hyphenated Identity: Nationalistic Discourse, History, and the Anxiety of Criticism in Salman Rushdie's *Shame*," *Qui Parle* 3, no. 2 (Fall 1989).

11. See Benedict Anderson, *Imagined Communities: Reflections on the Origin and Spread of Nationalism* (London: Verso, 1983).

12. See, for instance, "Author from Three Countries," *New York Times Review of Books*, November 13, 1983: 3, 22–23.

13. Jameson, "Third-World Literature."

14. Jameson, "Third-World Literature," 85.

15. All page references are to the 1981 Jonathan Cape edition.

16. For the paradigmatic dramatization of this theme of intellectual mediation, see Nehru, "Bharat Mata," *The Discovery of India* (New Delhi: Oxford University Press, 1989), 60–61. A thorough and brilliant discussion of this theme in Nehruvian thought is to be found in Partha Chatterjee, *Nationalist Thought and the Colonial World: A Derivative Discourse?* (London: Zed, 1986).

17. See Chatterjee, *Nationalist Thought*, 30: "even as (nationalism) challenged the colonial claim to political domination, it also accepted the very intellectual premises of 'modernity' on which colonial domination was based."

18. Anderson, *Imagined Communities*, 30–33.

19. Anderson, *Imagined Communities*, 33.

20. Rushdie, in conversation with Günter Grass, "Writing for a Future," in *Voices: Writers and Politics*, ed. Bill Bourne, Udi Eichler, David Herman (Nottingham: Spokesman, 1987), 58.

21. Anderson, *Imagined Communities*, 35.

22. Frantz Fanon, "On National Culture," in *The Wretched of the Earth* (New York: Grove Press, 1979), 225–227.

23. Rushdie, "Writing," 53.

24. For similar contradictory moments in Latin American fiction, see Jean Franco's introduction to the issue "Contemporary Latin American fin de siècle," *Studies in 20th Century Literature*, 14, no. 1 (Winter 1990): 6.

25. All page references are to the 1983 Knopf edition.

26. The other autobiographical trace in the Jahilia dream sequences is of course the poet Baal. And there are obvious autobiographical moments in Saladin Chamcha as well.

27. Emphasis added. All references are to the 1988 Viking edition.

28. The passages about the exiled Imam, obviously based on Khomeini and the Irani revolution, have not played any significant role in the public controversy. What role they might have played in the decision to issue the *fatwa*, however, is not known.

29. Syed Shahabuddin, "You did this with satanic forethought, Mr. Rushdie," *Times of India*, October 13, 1988; quoted in *File*, 39.

30. Shabbir Akhtar, *Be Careful with Muhammad! The Salman Rushdie Affair* (London: Bellew, 1989), 1.

31. Akhtar, *Be Careful,* 4.
32. Akhtar, *Be Careful,* 6, 12.
33. See Eqbal Ahmed and Richard Barnet, "Afghanistan," *New Yorker,* April 11, 1988, and Raja Anwar, *The Tragedy of Afghanistan: A First-Hand Account* (London: Verso, 1988).
34. For the Jamaat's activities around the issue of women, see Khawar Mumtaz and Farida Shaheed, *Women of Pakistan: One Step Forward, Two Steps Back?* (Lahore: Vanguard, 1987).
35. See the special issue on "Communalism: Dangerous Dimensions," *India Today,* October 31, 1989.
36. See the work by Akhtar, *Be Careful,* and "The Case for Religious Fundamentalism," *The Guardian,* February 27, 1989, in *File,* 227–231.
37. Ahmed, "Islam," p. 19.
38. Ahmed, "Islam," p. 27.
39. For a discussion of the consequences of the Gulf War for the fortunes of fundamentalism, see Eqbal Ahmed's introduction to *Beyond the Storm: A Gulf Crisis Reader,* ed. Phyllis Bennis and Michel Moushabek (New York: Olive Branch Press, 1991).
40. Fatima Mernissi, *Beyond the Veil: Male-Female Dynamics in Modern Muslim Society,* revised edition (Bloomington: University of Indiana Press, 1987), ix–x.
41. The literature on "women and Islam" in the modern world is of course enormous, but a large amount of it is guided by ahistorical and excessively textual notions of Islam. For a critique of such tendencies in diverse writings on Muslim women, see Marnia Lazreg, "Feminism and Difference: The Perils of Writing as a Woman on Women in Algeria," *Feminist Issues* 14, no. 1 (Spring 1988): 81–107. For a set of regional studies that carefully and self-consciously avoid the pitfalls of essentialism by focusing on the *state* as the locus for determinations of notions of gender, see *Women, Islam, and the State,* ed. Deniz Kandiyoti (Philadelphia: Temple University Press, 1991). Also see Nayereh Tohidi, "Gender and Islamic Fundamentalism: Feminist Politics in Iran," in *Third World Women and the Politics of Feminism,* ed. Chandra Talpade Mohanty, et al. (Bloomington: Indiana University Press, 1991), 251–267.
42. Akhtar, *Be Careful,* 89.
43. See Ervand Abrahamian, *Radical Islam: The Iranian Mojahedin* (London: I. B. Taurus, 1989), especially chapter 2.
44. Quoted in Abrahamian, "Khomeini," 103.
45. See Abrahamian, *Radical Islam,* and Michael M. Fischer, *Iran: From Religious Dispute to Revolution* (Cambridge: Harvard University Press, 1980), especially chapter 6 and the epilogue.
46. It should be noted that the Shiite fundamentalism of the Irani clergy is a partial exception to this, for reasons that lie within Shiism's own status as unorthodox opposition to mainstream, Sunni Islam.
47. See Ziaul Haque, "Islamization of Society in Pakistan," in Khan, *Pakistan Experience,* 114–126.
48. Since the writing of these words, the issue has of course achieved international notoriety, following the destruction of the mosque by a throng of Hindu fundamentalist "volunteers" on December 6, 1992.
49. For a somewhat more detailed account, see my "In the Realm of the Censors," *Voice Literary Supplement,* March 1989, 13.
50. Rushdie, "Open Letter," *File,* 36.
51. Shahabuddin, "Satanic Forethought," *File,* 37–41.
52. Shahabuddin, "Satanic Forethought," 37.
53. Akhtar, "Fundamentalism," *File,* 228.
54. See Habermas, "The Public Sphere," *New German Critique,* Fall 1974, 49.
55. Habermas, *The Structural Transformation of the Public Sphere: An Inquiry into a Category of Bourgeois Society* (Cambridge, Mass.: MIT Press, 1991), 88.

56. For a brilliant discussion of the complex dynamic of loyalty and betrayal in this act of appropriation, see Sara Suleri, "Contraband Histories: Salman Rushdie and the Embodiment of Blasphemy," *The Yale Review,* 78, no. 4 (Summer 1989).

57. Such is the case with Brennan's sense that *all* aspects of Rushdie's art and politics are to be explained by his membership in a group he (Brennan) terms "Third-World cosmopolitans" (*Salman Rushdie,* pp. viii–ix): "those writers Western reviewers seemed to be choosing as the interpreters and authentic public voices of the Third World—writers who, in a sense, allowed a flirtation with change that ensured continuity, a familiar strangeness, a trauma by inches." For a far more nuanced critique of Rushdie's novelistic intervention, see Asad, "Ethnography, Literature, and Politics."

58. Suleri, "Contraband Histories," 605.

59. Suleri, "Contraband Histories," 606–607.

60. Suleri, "Contraband Histories," 617.

61. Shahabuddin, "Satanic Forethought," 39. The Islamic Society of North America also decried the novel as a "blatant assault on Islam and the Prophet," *File,* 174. And Dr. H. Morsi, Director of the Islamic Cultural Center of Chicago, declared that there was "no doubt that the book . . . slanders the Prophet in particular and the religion of Islam in general," *File,* 177.

62. Akhtar, *Be Careful,* 4.

63. Franco, "Pastiche," 95; also see Fredric Jameson, "The Shining," *Social Text* 4 (Fall 1981), 114.

64. Fredric Jameson, "Postmodernism, or the Cultural Logic of Late Capitalism," *New Left Review,* no. 146: 65.

65. Linda Hutcheon, "Modern Parody and Bakhtin," in *Rethinking Bakhtin: Extensions and Challenges,* ed. Gary Morson and Caryl Emerson (Evanston: Northwestern University Press, 1989) 41.

66. Gayatri Chakravorty Spivak, "Poststructuralism, Marginality, Postcoloniality and Value," in *Literary Theory Today,* ed. Peter Collier, et al. (Ithaca: Cornell University Press, 1990), 229.

67. Brennan, *Salman Rushdie,* 82.

68. Brennan, *Salman Rushdie,* 82.

69. Franco, "Nation," 211.

70. See Shahabuddin, "Satanic Forethought," in *File,* 39, and Akhtar, "Fundamentalism," in *File,* 228.

71. See Jean Franco's discussion of Silviano Santiago's *Em Liberdade* in "Pastiche," 102–104.

72. Arjun Appadurai, "Disjuncture and Difference in the Global Cultural Economy," *Public Culture* 2, no. 2 (Spring 1990), 16.

73. See *File,* 44–46.

74. Steve Coll, "Salman Rushdie, Blueprint for a Bad Guy," *The Washington Post,* June 25, 1990.

75. Rushdie, "Writing," 58–59.

76. Rushdie put it thus in his open letter to Rajiv Gandhi: "The section of the book in question (and let's remember that the book isn't actually about Islam, but about migration, metamorphosis, divided selves, love, death, London and Bombay) deals with a prophet who is not called Muhammad living in a highly fantasticated city—made of sand, it dissolves when water falls upon it—in which he is surrounded by fictional followers, one of whom happens to bear my own first name. Moreover, this entire sequence happens in a dream, the fictional dream of a fictional character, an Indian movie star, and one who is losing his mind, at that. *How much further from history could one get?*" (*File,* 35–36, emphasis added.) See also the interview with *India Today,* September 15, 1988, *File,* 32. However, he has also suggested that the book itself "metamorphoses all the time" (*File,* 7).

77. In criticizing what appeared to be Rushdie's "embrace" of Islam in late 1990, Sara Suleri suggested that he is a "naive reader" of his own novels ("Wither Rushdie?" *Transition* 51: 212). A reading of Rushdie's post-*fatwa* pronouncements on the place of art and literature in society will confirm this verdict. See, for instance, "Is Nothing Sacred?," *Imaginary Homelands: Essays and Criticism 1981–1991* (London: Granta, Viking, 1991), 415–429. For a completely different account, written in 1984, see "Outside the Whale," *Imaginary Homelands,* 87–101.

78. Brennan, "Rushdie, Islam, and Postcolonial Criticism," *Social Text* 31/32 (1992): 275.

79. Brennan, *Salman Rushdie,* 144.

80. Andrew Rosenthal, "Quayle Attacks a 'Cultural Elite,' Saying It Mocks Nation's Values," *The New York Times,* Wednesday, June 10, 1992, 1.

Rushdie's *Dastan-e-Dilruba:*
The Satanic Verses as Rushdie's Love Letter to Islam

Feroza Jussawalla

Meheruban likhoon
ya dilruba likhoon
hyran hoon
ke apke khat me
kya likhoon

Ye mera prempatr padh kar
ke tum naraz na hona
ke tum meri zindagi ho
ke tum meri bandagi ho

[Should I address you as respected one
Should I address you as beloved one
I am so distraught
about how
I should address you

When you read my love letter
You should not be disappointed
Because you are my life
and you are my "life's work"]
—Popular Hindi film song from Raj Kapoor's *Sangam* (1964) [my translation]

Salman Rushdie has been classified as a postcolonial[1] writer whose fiction depicts the hybrid nature of postcolonials in their migrations and movements, their merging and mixing. Rushdie has variously been called a "Third World Cosmopolitan" (Brennan, *Salman Rushdie* viii), a "metropolitan intellectual," and "a hybrid" but most often a "postcolonial," because of his "birth" as a

Reprinted from *Diacritics* 26, no. 1 (Spring 1996): 50–73.

"Midnight's child"—a child born as India was gaining independence at midnight on 14 August 1947[2]—his subsequent education in England, and the making of his home in metropolitan London. Such a perspective is Eurocentric and does not provide complete answers to Rushdie's complex works or the complicated response to his work. For the very hybridity that Rushdie manifests results from his being not only a "post-British" colonial but also a "post-Mughal" colonial.

The British were not the only colonizers of India. In fact, Indian historians have traditionally identified several waves of colonization. Journalists Larry Collins and Dominique Lapierre best summarize the two major waves of colonization as follows:

> Hinduism itself had been brought to India by the Indo-European hordes descending from the North to wrest the subcontinent from its ancient Dravidian inhabitants.... The faith of the Prophet had come much later, after the cohorts of Genghis Khan and Tamurlane had battered their way down the Khyber Pass to weaken the Hindus' hold on the great Gangetic Plain. For two centuries, the Moslem Mogul emperors had imposed their sumptuous and implacable rule over most of India, spreading in the wake of their martial legions the message of Allah, the One, the Merciful. (*Freedom at Midnight* 36)

While the British were actually occupying India, post-Mughal colonialism in the form of Persian poetry, literature, and the general "sumptuousness" of its art and architecture held sway. The Persian language begot Urdu, often described by linguists as a "camp language" of the Muslim invaders of the Subcontinent. However, Persian, Arabic, and Hindi had come together to create a new language for the poetry, literature, arts, and in general the "high culture" of today's Indian Muslims. Jawaharlal Nehru, in his definitive history of India entitled *Discovery of India,* wrote,

> The Mughals were outsiders and strangers to India and yet they fitted into Indian structure with remarkable speed and began the Indo-Mughal period.... Their dynasties became completely Indianized with their roots in India, looking upon India as their homeland, and the rest of the world as foreign. (236)

> A synthesis worked itself out: new styles of architecture arose; food and clothing changed; and life was affected and varied in many other ways.... The Persian language became the official court language and many Persian words crept into popular use. (237)

Persian was the lingua franca of the incoming Muslims from AD 1193 onward, and Persian literature became the favored literature of India for approximately five centuries (Ali 3–4).

It is in this tradition of post-Mughal Urdu high culture that Rushdie grew up. In a 1983 interview with Michael Kaufman, Rushdie said,

> My grandfather, my father's father, was a good Urdu poet. My father is not a writer but he's a very literary and literate man, a student of both Arabic and Persian Literature and of Western Literature. At Cambridge he was quite scholarly. So I grew up in an atmosphere of books. And both my parents, in their different ways, were very gifted storytellers.
>
> My mother, in common with most Eastern women and perhaps even women of the West, was the keeper of the family stories. . . . From my father I got more conventional fairy tales. He always claimed he was making them up, but in fact I think he was drawing quite heavily on the great storehouse of the Arabian Nights. He would tell us these stories in serial form, kind of Scheharazade episodes, but death was not the issue, just sleep. (Kaufman 22)

Thus it is that Rushdie's "imaginary homelands" lie beyond colonial Britain and contemporary India in the history to which he claims he is handcuffed (*Midnight's Children* 1). They lie with his fathers and forefathers, the migrants who created Mughal India. Rushdie's tradition, together with British and European modernism, is that of Persian poetry and storytelling incorporating wordplay—a tradition so effectively recreated in *Midnight's Children*. Writing about *Midnight's Children*, Rushdie said,

> When the book is discussed in the West, it seems to get discussed almost entirely in terms of a certain string of writers who always get hung around its neck like a kind of garland, which is, you know, García Márquez, Günther Grass, Rabelais, Laurence Sterne, Cervantes, Gogol, etc. So I thought that instead of talking about all that *I'd try to talk about its Eastern literary ancestors and the sense in which it derives out of an Indian tradition which, to my mind, is much more important than this aforesaid list.* And I suppose the main thing to talk about is the use of techniques derived from the oral narrative. It is really impossible to overstress the fact that the oral narrative is the most important literary form in India. ("*Midnight's Children* and *Shame*" 4–6; my emphasis)

To his British education and metropolitan interests, then, Rushdie urges us to add these indigenous literary qualities. His postmodernity of style—characterized by wordplay, a flashback style of narration, and "magical realism"—is usually ascribed to his Western influences, as though characteristics most identified with postcolonial writing had no counterparts in world literature before the twentieth century.[3]

So, while Rushdie clarifies for us his Eastern literary ancestors, in " 'In God We Trust' " he tells us how religion shapes the form of his literary output:

> As for religion, my work, much of which has been concerned with India and Pakistan, has made it essential for me to confront the issue of religious faith. Even the form of my writing was affected. If one is to attempt honestly to describe reality as it is experienced by religious people, for whom God is no

symbol but an everyday fact, then the conventions of what is called realism are quite inadequate. The rationalism of that form comes to seem like a judgement upon, an invalidation of, the religious faith of the characters being described. A form must be created which allows the miraculous and the mundane to co-exist at the same level—as the same order of event. (376)

The religious influence directly impacted on the form of his writing, bringing traditionally Muslim—and, in *The Satanic Verses,* specifically Islamic—narratives, such as those concerned with the writing of the Qur'an, to the forefront of his creativity. The story of Salman, the scribe, leaving in the "Satanic Verses" is a specifically Islamic tale told in all Muslim cultures. Without the religious need, he would not have had to turn to his Middle Eastern literary ancestors. The practice of Islam on the Subcontinent also becomes the content of his literary output. For this reason Rushdie wants us to understand his Indian-Muslim background, which shows how secular Muslims lived and practiced Islam in India:

> I was brought up in an Indian Muslim household, but while both my parents were believers neither was insistent or doctrinaire. Two or three times a year, at the big Eid festivals, I would wake up to find new clothes at the foot of my bed, dress and go with my father to the great prayer-maidan outside the Friday Mosque in Bombay, and rise and fall with the multitude, mumbling my way through the uncomprehended Arabic much as Catholic children do—or used to do—with Latin. (" 'In God We Trust' " 376–77)

Much of this background shapes, as Rushdie says in this essay, "the characters being described," so that the practice of Islam in India becomes not just a religious and literary influence but the content itself—a content that, if one is not aware of the context, can easily be misinterpreted.[4]

Therefore, facts of Mughal-Islamic religion, history, culture, and literature as they were syncretized in India are important for more than a simple exegesis of *The Satanic Verses*. They are important in understanding Salman Rushdie's current dilemma and in pointing to new directions for theoretical interpretations of cross-cultural "hybrid" writers from the Indian Subcontinent.

Rushdie is the victim not only of the condition of postmodernity, where meaning is wrenched from the author's hands to rest in the hands of readers like the Ayatollah Khomeini, but of the indeterminacy of meaning outside certain cultural contexts. For instance, in looking at *The Satanic Verses* as manifesting an Islamic narrative form, we also have to consider that this form is from an Indo-Islamic tradition that is not as fundamentalist as some Islamic traditions—like those of the Persian or Arab Shiites—that did not get mixed and merged with the Indian soil.[5] India's Islam is that of *khawali* (bawdy oral narrative) and of *baed-bazi* (debate) through the recitation of poetry, an Islam merged with Hinduism, as of the poet Kabir, an Islam whose presumptions might seem more blasphemous to the undiluted strain. Of Rushdie's use of Urdu *ghazal* (lyrical love poetry) in *The Satanic Verses,* Sara Suleri writes, "it links Rushdie to a highly wrought tradition in which a recurrent trope is the rejection of Islam for some new object of epistemological and erotic devotion" (609). In fact, in the Indo-Mughal tradition, love for one's religion, whether Hindu or Muslim, is expressed as love for a beloved, both in lyric poetry and longer oral narratives, which is not only why the *dastan-e-dilruba* (a love song for a beloved) is an appropriate metaphor for *The Satanic Verses* but, as I will show in the latter half of the essay, the form of the *dastan,* a long prose narrative delivered as a complaint to the beloved, is the form or the genre of *The Satanic Verses.* Continuing with this metaphor of the beloved, I would say that it is not the "rejection of Islam"—the beloved—for "ironized submission to the alterities" (Suleri 609) that Rushdie represents as much as love for the Islam—the religion—of the subcontinental soil, where it flourished under the Mughals and came into question at the end of Mughal dominance, where it was and is practiced in an atmosphere of mixing and merging.

While such a hybridized Islam as that of the Mughals of India might seem to embody the metropolitanism of the West, despite its long tradition of satire and humor, in today's fundamentalist climate it does not. Because Rushdie was working within an Islamic tradition that does not conform to the particular strain as practiced by the late Ayatollah Khomeini, his work drew the *fatwa* from Iran. Rushdie, then, became a victim of cross-cultural (mis)understanding, on the one hand because the tradition he is writing out of is foreign to the majority of the Islamic societies of the Middle East, and on the other because he is writing out of an indigenous tradition that is not fully understood through Western constructs alone.

Hence it is important to locate Rushdie within the high Muslim culture of India and its Mughal/Muslim/Indian traditions to understand why he would not have fully understood the import of his narrative in an increasingly fundamentalist environment. Conversely, seeing *The Satanic Verses* as an exercise in European postmodernity by a hybrid metropolitan intellectual fails to show how deeply rooted it is in Muslim cultural and religious traditions. Seeing *The Satanic Verses,* then, as a post-Mughal Islamic colonial consciousness, rather than simply as a post-British colonial consciousness helps to understand the cross-cultural conflict in which the novel and its author are trapped. By no means, however, would my interpretation absolve the writer of his "sins" in Islamic eyes. Rushdie dwells in the land of his own creation—Peccavistan—"I have sinned!" In *Shame,* Rushdie changes Pakistan (Pak(holy)istan(land)) to Peccavistan, a pun on the British governor's coded telegram to London when he had conquered Sind—Peccavi, "I have sinned."

Rushdie has written extensively, in various parts of his work from *Midnight's Children* to *Imaginary Homelands,* not only that an Islamic religious sensibility is central to his work but that the Muslims in their traditional "Mughalness" are central to India's history. In the introduction to *Imaginary*

Homelands, Rushdie talks about attending an "Indo-Anglian" writers' conference in London, where he objected to "some participants' desire to describe Indian culture—which I had always thought of as a rich mixture of traditions—in exclusive, and excluding, Hindu terms" (2). Rushdie felt that he was being told that he wasn't "really Indian." When Rushdie questioned one academic from the floor,

> the professor smiled benignly and allowed that of course India contained many diverse traditions—including Buddhists, Christians and "Mughals." This characterization of Muslim culture was more than merely peculiar. It was a technique of alienation. For if Muslims were "Mughals," then they were foreign invaders, and Indian Muslim culture was both imperialist and inauthentic. At the time we made light of the gibe, *but it stayed with me, pricking at me like a thorn.* (2, my emphasis)

Obviously, Rushdie felt then and more so in *The Satanic Verses* that it was important to assert the centrality of Indian Muslims and of Muslim culture in India. From the above quotation, it would seem that Rushdie is "the marginal voice" of "minority discourse" (because the Muslims are a minority in India), as Homi Bhabha posits ("DissemiNation" 301). But this is not so. Situating and locating Rushdie and his characters within their actual temporal history and culture rather than speculating about their "zone of occult instability" (Fanon's phrase, qtd. in Bhabha, "DissemiNation" 303) show that Rushdie is rooted in a majority and dominant culture—the Mughal Muslim culture of India. In so doing, one realizes that the histories created by a postcolonial writer such as Rushdie are not simply those of anti-European colonial struggle but rather, as Fanon has so aptly put it in *Black Skin, White Masks,* of the desire to become like the dominant colonizer. In Rushdie, the desire to appropriate both the British and the Mughal colonizers' sensibilities is acute; but he leans more heavily toward what he sees as Muslim high culture, what he calls "Indian Muslim Culture."[6] Even today, in India there is a strong desire to be assimilated into "Indian Muslim high culture" because such belonging is seen as being khandani, or "upper class." It has society's stamp of approval.

Sara Suleri, in her essay "Contraband Histories: Salman Rushdie and the Embodiment of Blasphemy," nods toward Rushdie's Muslim roots but writes them off as "the structure of anachronism" (606) as she gets caught up in the paradigm of European postcoloniality. She writes, "Rushdie has written a deeply Islamic book . . . but the imperative of its narrative simultaneously allows for a devotional return to the structure of anachronism, enabling Rushdie to extend . . . his engagement with both cultural self-definition and Islamic historiography" (606). But she concludes, "Rushdie performs a curious act of faith: he chooses disloyalty in order to dramatize his continuing obsession with the metaphors that Islam makes available to a postcolonial sensibility" (606–07). Rushdie was not choosing disloyalty. He himself answers this charge in "Why I Have Embraced Islam." Writing of his character Gibreel, who is the embodiment of the postcolonial sensibility and the parables from the Qur'an that he draws on, Rushdie writes, "*The Satanic Verses* was never intended as an insult . . . the story of Gibreel is a parable of how a man can be destroyed by the loss of faith" ("Why I Have Embraced Islam" 431). In creating the portrait of a man destroyed by his loss of faith, Rushdie is pointing to ways in which postcolonials can reclaim their religion—Islam. In fact, here again, Rushdie provides us with clarification: "such offence has been taken against my work when it was not intended—when dispute was intended, and dissent, and even, at times, satire, and criticism of intolerance and the like, but not the thing of which I'm . . . accused" ("In Good Faith" 413). Dissent, dispute, criticism—this is the reformist agenda Rushdie was proceeding from, not blasphemy. Rushdie is here constantly reaffirming his intent. To understand Rushdie, one has to understand that he is not disloyal to Islam but that he is an Indian "Mughal postcolonial"—in the tradition of Indian Muslims as described by Nehru: "An Indian Moslem is considered an Indian in Turkey or Arabia or Iran or any other country where Islam is dominant" (50). He is not a Muslim first but an Indian.[7]

Rushdie's representation of Islam in *The Satanic Verses* is conditioned by this tradition of adapting the religion to Indian ways. And though Muslims are a minority group in India today, they were up to 1947 the dominant cultural influence and in many ways continue to be so. Hence, Rushdie is really not writing "histories of marginality," as Bhabha has called his work. If he is indulging in postcolonial self-fashioning, he is fashioning himself into the post-Islamic Muslim high culture of literature, poetry, mysticism, and even the secularism that leads to the fragmenting of Islam into peculiarly Indianized versions like those of the Khodjas and Bohras. Again, Rushdie explains to his readers that Islam in India at least is not a monolithic whole: "any examination of the facts will demonstrate the rifts, the lack of homogeneity and unity, characteristic of present-day Islam" (" 'In God We Trust' " 383). There are many forms of Islam in India that are reformist in their practice of Islam but by no means sectarian,[8] as the word is usually understood in the West. Even Rushdie turns to the late Prime Minister Nehru to explain his Muslim secularism: "To be an Indian of my generation was also to be convinced of the vital importance of Jawaharlal Nehru's vision of a secular India" ("In Good Faith" 404). So that those of us who grew up with Nehru's dictum of "Hindu-Mussalman bhai-bhai" (Hindu-Muslim brother-brother) grew up also with the sense of many Hindu and Muslim sects among whom different religious practices flourished secularly. This is Rushdie's Islam. In this context, questioning of the Prophet, elevating alternate prophets and saints like Ali is completely natural, as is the desire to reform Islam, as expressed by such deeply religious nineteenth-century Indian-Islamic poets as Hali. Neither they nor Rushdie anticipated the fundamentalists' response to their work as blasphemy.

Therefore, it is wrong to say as Suleri does that "Rushdie was acutely conscious of *The Satanic Verses* as blasphemy" (606). Suleri extends this to say that where Rushdie creates deracinated characters he is committing cultural heresy and that those moments are equally blasphemous moments. Homi Bhabha extends this even further to say, "Blasphemy goes beyond the severance of tradition and replaces its claim to a purity of origins with a poetics of relocation and reinscription" (Bhabha, *Location* 225). Both cultural critics show a lack of contextual knowledge of how squarely *The Satanic Verses* fits into the traditions of Islam in India—the only Islam that Rushdie knew. Rushdie's review of V. S. Naipaul's *Among the Believers* published in 1981 shows Rushdie's secular Muslim attitude in his impassioned defense of Islam in Iran—an Islam he really didn't know. Naively, Rushdie wrote of Naipaul's book: "The trouble is that it's a highly selective truth, a novelist's truth masquerading as objective reality. Take Iran: no hint in these pages that in the new Islam there is a good deal more than Khomeinism, or that the mullocracy's hold on the people is actually very fragile" ("Naipaul among the Believers" 374). The irony of this statement cannot fail to escape us today. This is not someone expecting in a few years to be condemned to death for "blasphemy" by the people he thinks are his own people. His is not therefore a poetics of relocation and transcription. And it is interesting to note that Rushdie does know "his people." The fact that Rushdie is still alive shows "the fragile hold of the mullocracy."

Therefore, because of the context from which he was functioning, that of the Persian and Indian Islamic writers of the last four centuries, Rushdie would not have thought of himself as consciously blaspheming but rather would have seen himself as doing the Muslim community a favor by urging the re-examination, "dissent, dispute and criticism" which are possible for Islam in India and now in England.

This claim bears some examination. Islam in India has historically been "secularized" in ways in which it has never been secularized and reformed anywhere else. This "tradition" of reforming or secularizing Islam, which has become synonymous with the practice of Islam in India, goes back to the Mughal Emperor Akbar (1556–1606). Akbar was the first of the Muslim emperors to intermarry a Hindu woman. Though Islamic proselytization flourished under Akbar, he was discontented with the practice of Islam and sought to create a new religion, drawing on the best of all religions. This was called *din-i Ilahi* (Divine Faith) and was established in 1581. Akbar meant distinctly to get beyond "the sectarian Islamic law" (Wolpert 132). For instance, he forbade cow slaughter by Muslims in his effort to bring together Islam and Hinduism, making it an offense against Divine Faith. It is ironic that the Islamic war cry "Allahu Akbar" generates from Akbar's court, where it meant not only "God is great" but "Akbar is God" and was the motto of Akbar's court's reform of Islam (Wolpert 132). Today it is the call to jihad. It is generally accepted in Indian history that the period of stability and the establishment of Islam in India under Akbar occurred because of his openness to mixing and merging with the Hindus. He was even able to quash the rising of the mullahs of Jaunpur in 1581. But as soon as fundamentalist sectarianism reared its ugly head under Aurangzeb (1658–1707), the Muslim foothold slipped, and the British seized their opportunity. An anonymous letter sent to Aurangzeb said, "If your Majesty places any faith in those books by distinction called divine, you will be there instructed that God is the God of all mankind, not the God of Mussalmans alone" (Wolpert 160; Sarkar 3: 34).

While Akbar's was an emperor's effort to reform Islam, there had been several previous efforts, the most famous that of the poet Kabir (1440–1518). While many Hindus converted to Islam to escape the caste system, Kabir, a poor Muslim weaver, chose to follow the Hindu guru Ramananda and to write poetry to Allah in the Hindu tradition of *bhakti*, devotional poetry in which God is addressed as a lover. The history of Islam in India is the history of the syncretism of Islam and Hinduism (Wolpert 120). Even today, all over India there are shrines to Islamic mystics and saints—whether they be of Khwaja Sahib Chisty (said to have come to India in the twelfth century AD) or Saint Ayesha (whose pilgrimage Rushdie describes in *The Satanic Verses*)—who are worshipped as though they were Hindu gods, with flowers, coconuts, money offerings, and so forth. Hence the practice of Islam in India up until the new fundamentalism of today has meant living the secularized Muslim culture.

The subcontinental Indian emigrés to Britain carry with them their notion of a secularized Islam but also adherence to the faith and its beliefs without making fundamentalist public protestations. It is in this effort that Rushdie's work connects with the earlier Indian Muslim reformists. The most recent example of the subcontinental reformist attitude is embodied in Hanif Kureishi's short story "My Son, the Fanatic" and in *The Black Album,* where Kureishi seems to be criticizing the mullahs for "reading vegetables and burning books." Western critics such as Timothy Brennan who are insistent upon metropolitanizing the emigrés' response do not understand Rushdie's Indian Islamic roots. Brennan writes, "Rushdie, however, is hardly Islamic in any hard sense, although he has certain emotional attachments to Sufism as *Grimus* and *Shame* both show. That reading of his work (as Islamic, expressing Islamic alienation from Hindu India) nevertheless reminds us that his intended audience is a Western one, where the full range of his satire's targets (and he leaves no one out) can be appreciated naively without sectarianism but also without fear of loss" (*Salman Rushdie* 109).[9] In fact, the groundwork for misreading *The Satanic Verses* had already been laid by the "metropolitanizing" of *Midnight's Children* and by its established interpretation as a postcolonial's satire of his "motherland" and the subsequent libel suit brought against Rushdie by Mrs. Gandhi.

Misinterpretation of Rushdie's work results from forcing him into the paradigm of the metropolitan, marginal postcolonial: in doing so he is forced into a "subaltern space" which Rushdie does not occupy and has not occupied even during his "hiding." It is not a subaltern who defied Mrs. Gandhi or to this day the late Ayatollah Khomeini. If it is, he is carrying off a major mutiny! Homi Bhabha writes, "The postcolonial space is now 'supplementary' to the metropolitan centre; it stands in a subaltern adjunct relation that doesn't aggrandise the presence of the west but redraws its frontiers" ("DissemiNation" 318). Rushdie's project is to redraw his frontiers backward from the West and its metropolitan space, to expand into his Islamic history in a liberatory gesture rather than a "counterhegemonic" gesture.

It is perhaps the portrayal of Rushdie's work as counterhegemonic that was possibly misinterpreted by the Islamic community and the Ayatollah as being counter to "their hegemony" which resulted in the extreme reaction to *The Satanic Verses*. Can one conjecture that had the *New York Times Magazine* of 29 January 1989 not created the brouhaha over the Muslim letters of protest and the few book burnings of Bradford that the controversy over *The Satanic Verses* would have ended there and not attracted the attention of the Ayatollah Khomeini, who then issued his fatwa on 14 February 1989? The West chose to portray the work as a huge "counterhegemonic" revolutionary free speech issue from a "marginalized subaltern" accompanied by dramatic portraits of immigrant Muslims (the very marginalized peoples who actually occupy subaltern spaces in the West and whose cause Rushdie was supposed to be championing) burning the book. Rushdie touring Brick Lane with Gerald Marzorati in his Saab was described as alienated from those inhabitants of Brick Lane who had brought along too much excess baggage, "their old selves, old traditions" (Marzorati 44). Rushdie is portrayed as distancing himself from the newly transplanted Islamic culture of the immigrants in Britain:

> Basically, Islamic culture is the one in which I grew up—I know it well. Its narratives are my narratives. But their Islamic culture is something new and dangerous. You have a situation where a handful of extremists are defining Islam and what makes it even sadder for me is that they are simply feeding the Western stereotype: the backward, cruel, rigid Muslim, burning books and threatening to kill the blasphemer. (Marzorati 47)

Thus, the Western press misrepresented Rushdie's counterhegemonic discourse as counter to the hegemony of Islamic fundamentalism rather than of European stereotypes. The work and its academic, intellectual contexts were unfortunately (re)contextualized and (re)defined on a different map.

Similarly, Gayatri Spivak has attempted to categorize Rushdie and *The Satanic Verses* as postcolonial based on her characterization of postcoloniality as (1) dislodging every metropolitan definition and (2) reinscribing and rerouting history. The theme of *The Satanic Verses* she sees as that of the postcolonial divided between two identities, migrant and national ("Reading *The Satanic Verses*" 79). But are these in fact the characteristics of postcoloniality? I would like to venture again that this is a rather narrow, Eurocentric view of postcoloniality, as it sees all colonization as stemming from Europe and in that it sees an individual like Rushdie as the effect of post-European colonization. Rushdie is the European metropolitan intellectual who does not dislodge metropolitan definitions but instead reinscribes them into his roots and his history, which are post- yet another colonization—Muslim colonization.

In contemporary academic criticism, the two main characters of *The Satanic Verses,* Gibreel Farishta and Salahuddin Chamcha, are seen as the essence of post-European coloniality—as hybrid migrants. But migration and hybridization are not just conditions of recent postcoloniality. They are in Rushdie's work metaphors for the Prophet, who himself was a migrant who took shelter in exile. Rushdie parallels their migration with Mohammed's emigration to Yathrib, where in exile he rethinks his sense of identity. Both these characters do so too as they find that their liberation from the monstrous states they have grown into (and here Rushdie literally depicts them as monsters), from their doubts and their distance from their faith, can be gained only through their own people, the family that owns the Shandaar cafe, actually the family with another Islamic metaphor, the family of Hind Sufayan. Though the Sufayans had originally been opposed to Mohammed, through a series of treaties, Abu Sufayan himself, a powerful campaign organizer, remained neutral in the battle against Medina. Mohammed had granted complete immunity to any Medinans who took shelter in the Sufayan's home. Thus it is that Rushdie's character, the contemporary *mohajir* (immigrant), Saladin Chamcha, takes shelter in the Sufayan home and is liberated only through them. Rushdie is in fact saying that liberation from this "subaltern" status can only be achieved by turning to one's roots and one's religious/national group/family.

Thus, Gibreel Farishta and Salahuddin Chamcha reject their categorization as half-breed bowler-hatted Englishmen and stretch backward into their Islamic history which they reclaim in a celebration of their heritage—a celebration that has been misunderstood largely by contemporary critics such as Homi Bhabha, who classifies these fictional characters and their real-world counterparts as subalterns in a marginalized space. It is this interpretation of the work that those who actually occupy the marginal spaces in metropolitan London—the Muslims of Bradford and Brick Lane—have been deceived by. They have been led by all the Western press's interpretations, which are largely dependent on academic interpretations, to see Rushdie's fictional characters as caricatures of themselves. They therefore attempt to reject this caricature of themselves as violently as they can through book burnings and so on.

Hanif Kureishi's *Black Album* (1995) is a portrait of the way in which the "Cockney Asians" came to believe that "the book" ought to be burned. The East London Asians, already feeling embattled by British racism, by the

British National Party, then began to feel that "He insulted us all—the prophet, the prophet's wives, his whole family" (140). The young man who has never read the book but heard about it is named Muhammed Shahabuddin, after Syed Shababuddin, who started the original movement to ban *The Satanic Verses*. The book is burned in the name of "the standard argument about the crimes committed by whites against blacks and Asians in the name of freedom" (187). Ironically also, the Muslim students at the college where "the book is burned" discover that their Cultural Studies professor Dee Dee Osgood, who they believe is in solidarity with them, betrays them by sending for the police when they burn the book. Kureishi's student characters interestingly express their bewilderment over "postmodernist truth." "She is against authority yet tried to have us arrested," they say. Or again, "She believes in equality, all right, but only if we forget that we are different. . . . If we assert our individuality, we are inferior because we believe foolishness." "And today she has prevented us from free expression. Isn't that racist censorship, Shahid?" (190–91). Kureishi is showing very clearly here that contemporary academic interpretations led the Asian students at "the college" to see themselves as subalterns and therefore to feel further embattled when Rushdie supposedly satirized "the Asians" and their religion.

Therefore, I would like to posit that had Rushdie's characters in *The Satanic Verses* not been depicted by contemporary criticism and consequently the book reviewers and so on, as though they had walked out of a Magritte painting with green apples for faces, and had this interpretation not been presented widely, the outcome of the Rushdie affair would have been different. In selling Rushdie's book to an audience interested in postcoloniality and postmodernity, the advance publicity and reviews misdirected the audience and consequently misshaped the response. What for instance was the purpose of portraying Rushdie in the pose of "Fiction's Embattled Infidel" haughty against a background of graffiti (see Marzorati)? Was it simply a misdirected guess that such a gesture would sell more books among the politically correct of the US? Or was it simply that the intellectuals who surrounded Rushdie, his agents and reviewers, being so much a part of the climate of postmodernity, postcoloniality, and hybridity, misdirected their notion of resistance, attacking not the hegemony of recent colonizers but those already feeling embattled, the Islamic immigrants and the Islamic nations?

Gibreel Farishta and Saladin Chamcha need to be seen not only as homoerotic (Suleri 606) Bombay-talkie Englishmen and metropolitan migrants but also as characters looking backward at a liberatory history of Islamic struggle with affection (*dilruba*) and respect (*meheruban*). Explaining Islam with affection and respect was Rushdie's *bandagi*, or "binding life's work," or original purpose, which seems to have been perverted in the heady atmosphere of the condition of postmodernity only to be returned to in "Why I Have Embraced Islam."

Rushdie's complex relationship with Islam, it must be remembered, is colored by his being Indian. It is interesting that in *Midnight's Children* he has identified himself in part with his narrator Saleem Sinai ("Author from Three Countries" 23) and with the whole Indian generation that had come to be called *Midnight's Children.* Pakistan and India both obtained their independence at midnight, a time chosen by astrologers for India. Hence Midnight's Children make up the generation of Indians and Pakistanis born after independence was granted to India at midnight of 14 August 1947: "The first pangs hit her just as hundreds of miles away, M. A. Jinnah announced the midnight birth of a Muslim nation (Pakistan was created twenty-four hours before India)" (*Midnight's Children* 111). New citizens were born in both countries immediately after those midnight hours. These were of course the first citizens of a new nation. Of the moment of his birth, the first baby born in independent India, Saleem Sinai waxes lyrical:

> and this year—there was an extra festival on the calendar, a new myth to celebrate, because a nation which had never previously existed was about to win its freedom, catapulting us into a world which, although it had five thousand years of history, although it had invented the game of chess and traded with Middle Kingdom Egypt, was nevertheless quite imaginary; into a mythical land, a country which would never exist except by the efforts of a phenomenal collective will—except in a dream we all agreed to dream; it was a mass fantasy shared in varying degrees by Bengali and Punjabi, Madrasi and Jat and would periodically need the sanctification and renewal which can only be provided by rituals of blood. India, the new myth—a collective fiction in which anything was possible. . . .
> I have been, in my time, the living proof of the fabulous nature of the collective dream. (*Midnight's Children* 111)

Being intensely Indian therefore also means being intensely disparate. The characters that Rushdie creates both in *Midnight's Children* and in *The Satanic Verses* are proof of the collective hybridization of many colonialisms and many cultures, which makes for the divided loyalties and the irreverence that characterizes their hybridity. Yet Rushdie, like Ahmed Sinai, his fictional father in *Midnight's Children,* claims his heritage thus: "Mughal blood, as a matter of fact." "Wrong side of the blanket, of course; but Mughal certainly" (*Midnight's Children* 109). And while the Mughal and the Islamic are emphasized, a further complication is the factor of being Kashmiri, because the Kashmiris themselves felt pulled between Islamic Pakistan and Hindu India. Tai, the fictional boatman that Rushdie created in his short story "The Prophet's Hair," dies in *Midnight's Children* in 1947 when he walks to Chhamb (37) to stand before the two opposing forces to cry, "Kashmir for the Kashmiris," and is shot. Similarly, Rushdie seems to defend his fictional and nonfictional heritage: "Thirty-two years before the transfer of power, my grandfather bumped his nose against Kashmiri earth. . . . On that day, my inheritance began to form—the blue of Kashmiri sky which dripped into my grandfather's eyes" (*Midnight's Children* 106). The two heritages are immediately established—the Islamic "immigrant" bumping against the Indian earth by virtue of genuflection. Later, he tells us his grandfather had a permanent bruise on his forehead from praying. The image is repeated in *Shame:* "Who bore upon his forehead the gatta or permanent bruise which revealed him to be a religious fanatic who pressed brow to prayer mat on at least five occasions per diem, and probably the sixth, optional time as well" (*Shame* 38). So you have the Islamic and the Indian merging immediately. Saleem Sinai says of his family, and this could be Rushdie himself: "we throw our lot in with India, but the alienness of blue eyes remains" (107). So as these Muslims are beginning to see themselves as Indian, the distancing from Islam begins.

What becomes the prophetic foretelling of the project of *The Satanic Verses* is the telltale idea "And my father's dream of rearranging the Quran has its place" (*Midnight's Children* 108). *The Satanic Verses* should have been no surprise to those who studied *Midnight's Children,* in which Rushdie gives us many hints that he is about to embark on a reformist retelling of the history of Islam, but particularly what it meant to Indians. Again, Rushdie says of his fictional father, Ahmed Sinai:

> perhaps he wished that . . . he had had the strength to pursue his original ambition, the rearrangement of the Quran in accurately chronological order. (He once told me: "When Muhammed prophesied, people wrote down what he said on palm leaves, which were kept any old how in a box. After he died, Abubakr and the others tried to remember the correct sequence, but they didn't have very good memories." Another wrong turning: instead of rewriting a sacred book, my father lurked in a ruin awaiting demons. It's no wonder he wasn't happy. . . .) (*Midnight's Children* 82)

And so it is that Rushdie undertakes the rewriting of a sacred book not to target and satirize, not to create a counterhegemonic discourse, but to correct a wrong out of the love for his religion and his forefathers. Unfortunately, due to misinterpretation, he finds himself "lurking in the ruins awaiting demons."

This idea of retelling the story of Islam was the project of the many Indian Islamic groups—such as the Ismailis, the Aga Khanis, the Khodjas, and Bohra—predominant among the Muslim community in India, particularly in Bombay, where Salman Rushdie, Saleem Sinai, Gibreel Farishta, and Salahuddin Chamcha all originate. Their effect on Islam was a secularizing or broadening one, since many of them as converts to Islam from Hinduism brought their traditions and in a sense "Hinduized" Indian Islam. Each of these sects chose their favorite martyr and recreated the story of the Prophet to make their martyrs, in Hindu fashion, saints.

For instance, Major Zulfikar is the son-in-law in the Sinai family in *Midnight's Children*. Rushdie writes, "Zulfikar is a famous name amongst Muslims. It was the name of the two-pronged sword carried by Ali, the nephew of the Prophet Muhammed. It was a weapon such as the world had never seen" (*Midnight's Children* 61). Ali married Mohammed's daughter Fatima, was greatly trusted by the Prophet, and "was the intermediary between him and the discontented" (Gibb and Kramers 30). Ali often protected Mohammed. According to the Sunnis, Ali is only the transmitter of the law. But for the Shiites, Ali is "the friend of God," the true Saint, while Mohammed is only the nabi, or the prophet of God (Gibb and Kramers 31). Therefore, while it is true that Rushdie's death sentence for blasphemy was issued by the Shiite Ayatollahs, it is also almost natural that Rushdie embodies the irreverence toward Mohammed the Prophet himself. After all, he was raised among and surrounded by the Indianized Shiite sects, for whom Ali is more important than Mohammed. Among the Indian Shiites, Ali is treated almost like any other Indian saint, with shrines and flowers and stories of the martyrdom, all of which would be idolatrous and strictly forbidden by Islamic law. V. S. Naipaul in *Among the Believers* talks about visiting Sind: "Sind was full of the shrines of Muslim saints. Islam had long ago taken over the old holy places of Buddhists and Hindus; but memories of old religious attitudes adhered, and Islamic purists didn't always approve of the mystical or ascetic or near-idolatrous practices of some of these places" (*Among the Believers* 143). There is therefore a fair amount of confusion of doctrine and practice, which makes for the Indians' and Pakistanis' distance from a strictly followed Islam and makes the current politicized Islamicization so foreign to ordinary middle-class Muslims in these countries. Whenever Adam Aziz, the patriarch in *Midnight's Children*, doubts or breaks away from practice, his wife rails against him for being godless: "Who had spent his life offending God Whatsitsname and on whose head was this a judgement?" (*Midnight's Children* 61). And Adam Aziz says, "I started off as a Kashmiri and not much of a Muslim. Then I got a bruise on my chest that turned me into an Indian. I'm still not much of a Muslim" (*Midnight's Children* 40).

In similar fashion, post-Mughal colonials expressed their love for the colonizer's culture by adopting the literature and the cultural practices. This is best described by Salman Rushdie in *Shame*, the work that comes between the establishing of the post-Mughal colonial's identity in *Midnight's Children* and the challenging and reinscribing of the Islamic colonizer's culture in *The Satanic Verses*. In *Shame*, we see the education of the author as embodied in his fictional counterpart Omar Khayyam Shakil:

> by the time he left "Nishapur" he had learned classical Arabic and Persian; also Latin, French and German; all with the aid of leather-bound dictionaries and the unused texts of his grandfather's deceptive vanity.... Illuminated manu-

scripts of the poetry of Ghalib; volumes of letters written by Mughal emperors to their sons, the Burton translation of the *Alflaylahwalaylah* (*1001 Nights* or *Arabian Nights*) and the travels of Ibn Batuta and the *Qissa* or tales of the legendary Hatim Tai. . . . And one day the three mothers sent a servant into the study to remove from their lives an exquisitely carved walnut screen on which was portrayed the mythical circular mountain of Qaf, complete with thirty birds playing God thereupon the flight of the bird parliament revealed to Omar Khayyam a little bookcase stuffed with volumes on the theory and practice of hypnosis: Sanskrit mantras, compendiums of the lore of the Persian magi. . . . (*Shame* 28–29, my emphasis)

All of these elements make up the culture of post-Mughal Islam in India. The love for the *Arabian Nights* and the *qissa* and mystical Sufi Islam all merge with Sanskrit mantras. And they go into the making of Rushdie's work—particularly *The Satanic Verses*. The *qissa*, or tales of legendary adventure, particularly as developed in the form called the *dastan*, become the dominant form of *The Satanic Verses*, which is therefore less of a novel and more of a *qissa*. *Qissa* is a very particular form, somewhat like an oral picaresque using a "legendary" hero, and should not be translated simply as "story." A *dastan* is a loosely constructed prose "epic," a long-winded story that goes on and on. In the appendix to *Haroun and the Sea of Stories,* Rushdie translates *kahani* simply as "story" but not *qissa*. All three are separate forms of the genre of prose storytelling. Even before *The Satanic Verses,* Rushdie defined his form as follows:

An Oral narrative does not go from the beginning to the middle to the end of the story. It goes in great swoops, it goes in spirals or in loops, it every so often reiterates something that happened earlier to remind you, and then takes you off again, sometimes summarizes itself, it frequently digresses off into something that the story-teller appears just to have thought of, then it comes back to the main thrust of the narrative. Sometimes it steps sideways and tells you about another, related story which is like the story that he's been telling you, and then it goes back to the main story. Sometimes there are Chinese boxes where there is a story inside a story inside a story inside a story, then they all come back, you see, so it's a very bizarre and pyrotechnical shape. ("*Midnight's Children* and *Shame*" 7)

With this evidence behind us, I would like to venture that the *qissa* of *The Satanic Verses* is created in the form of the *dastan-e-dilruba,* a love story created for the beloved, as in Scheherazade's thousand and one stories, precisely because the form manifests: (1) Rushdie's postcolonial love for Muslim high culture;[10] (2) Rushdie's Indianized Muslim's secular attitude toward Islam; and (3) the project of rearranging the Qur'an. In doing so, Rushdie's postcolonial experiences must be placed squarely in a post-Islamic colonial heritage. He is in the tradition of poets like Farid ud-din Attar, the Sufi who created *The Conference of the Birds* (1177), which refutes the idea of a God outside the individual,[11] or Firdausi Tusi, or the narrator of the *Arabian Nights*.

Rushdie is also in the long tradition of Indian Islamic writers who both criticized Islam and yet were deeply part of the post-Mughal literary/religious tradition: Ghalib and his student Altaf Husain Hali, Bahadur Shah Zafar,[12] and Dagh. They lived in nineteenth-century British India, but for them it was almost as though the British were a relief; they took over governing of the country, freeing the Muslim princes to play chess, recite poetry, and generally indulge in what Rushdie in *Haroun and the Sea of Stories* calls "guppa maro," telling tall tales. Laurel Steele notes, "While Sir Saiyid was visiting England (1870) and attempting at home to arouse Islamic India through essays modelled on those of Addison and Steele, the poet Dagh was reciting his verses in a wealthy court and leading a life comparable to that of a literary figure of the seventeenth century" (1). Under the influence of Sir Saiyyid Ahmed[13] and his return from England, these poets were more preoccupied with satirizing and reforming Islam in India. Altaf Husain Hali's work Musaddas is very similar to *The Satanic Verses* in that it traces the rise and fall of Islam and he too was debunked. But there is a more significant parallel. Musaddas examines the Muslim failure in the 1857 mutiny as a result of Muslim degeneration and expresses shame at what pre-1857 Islam had become in Lucknow. Rushdie seems to be doing the same thing in *The Satanic Verses,* as he examines the degeneration of Indian-British Muslims. Both works urge changes in their contemporary Islamic society. Both writers were chastised. Similarly, in criticizing the *mohajir* Muslims, that is, the immigrants to England, Rushdie's purpose could be seen as being very similar to that of the fundamentalist Muslims. He is telling them to reaffirm their Islamic sensibility and reject the condition of Europeanization which leads to the degeneration of character, as in Gibreel Farishta. Like Hali, Rushdie uses the martyrdom as a metaphor for present-day griefs. This in itself is the form of the traditional *marsiyah* (elegy).

Amir Hamza, the narrator and principal character of the Dastan-e-Hamza, a much older work, is criticized for his policy of conversion by the sword.[14] Even Amir Hamza complains to the hazrat, or master, "O Hazrat! Killing and killing my two arms have grown weak" (Pritchett 14). This was a complaint against Islam's refusal to accept any other religion and meant through satire and humor to ask for changes in such policies.

It was, however, the Angare group, four upper-class Muslim short story writers in the 1930s, who found thugs with daggers waiting for them because they portrayed not just the Prophet but Allah himself as a sexual being (Coppola 58). Coppola quotes from Sajjad Zaheer's story:

> A prophet found escape through migration. No one knew what the poor prophet did on this occasion. Women had also made his life hell. Then what

am I? . . . How can a poor, weak person bear the burden of this trust on his shoulders? And I know what will happen on Judgement Day. These same women will create turmoil there too, will show such coquetry and will wink in such a way that poor Allah himself will start to scratch his beard. (Coppola 58)

Now this is with full knowledge of the Qur'anic verse: "Those who speak ill of Allah and his apostle shall be cursed by Allah in this life and in the life to come" (sura 33, verse 57). Yet to banter like this had also become a tradition. This is very much like what Rushdie has created rather extensively in *The Satanic Verses*. It has the same sense of humor rather than satire. Sajjad Zaheer also showed that the Prophet had various encounters with women. It is, however, true that Rushdie embellishes this sort of humor and extends it unendingly, weaving it into the present-day characters' lives. Perhaps the mullahs found this offensive, but this is exactly what characterizes the Urdu/Persian dastan. Daniel Pipes, in *The Rushdie Affair,* details other Persian poets who criticized Islam and were censored though not threatened. The Indian Urdu writers, however, establish Rushdie squarely in the post-Mughal colonial literary tradition, and it is their form, particularly Hali's form of the *dastan,* that Rushdie picks up on in his search for the "new form" in which everyday religiosity is treated in an everyday manner.

A *dastan* in Urdu and Persian literature is simply a long-winded stream-of-consciousness tale that incorporates many related and sometimes loosely strung-together frame tales and assorted humorous anecdotes—like the Chinese boxes. Frances W. Pritchett tells us, "Professional narrators demonstrated their fluency, virtuosity and power to hold an audience by prolonging the *dastan:* a longer *dastan* narration, like a longer tight-rope walk, was inherently superior to a shorter one" (4). In Urdu someone wishing to say that a person is creating a long-winded "cock and bull" story would say "Are bap! voh *dastan* laga raha hay!" *Dastans,* while embodying humor, particularly slapstick humor, often have tragic results, in that a beloved cannot be had or the beloved is disappointed or a kingdom is lost, and so forth. A dastan-e-dilruba is a story created for a beloved that tells of a beloved who cannot be had.

The *dastan* is essentially Persian. The stories of the *Arabian Nights* are Arabic in tradition. While the Arabic counterpart of *dastan* is *qissa,* and it is *qissas* that make up the *Arabian Nights,* the words have different implications. The *dastan* is long-winded, tedious; it is in the nature of a complaint. When a woman has her menstrual period, she has her *dastan* in colloquial language. The implication is therefore of a burden. *Qissa* is suspenseful, shorter, full of excitement—but if you have a long night to fill, to enchant a beloved, you need more than a *qissa;* you need a *dastan.*

Ralph Russel, a Reader in Urdu at the School of Oriental and African Studies in London, defines *dastan* as follows: "Urdu prose narrative cycles of medieval Islamic romance, which assumed their present form perhaps in the

18th century and were transmitted orally by professional reciters until in the second half of the nineteenth century they were written down at their dictation" (qtd. in Pritchett 43). But William L. Hanaway, Jr., further defines the characteristics of the *dastan,* which are all explicit in *The Satanic Verses.*

> The action covering a broad geographical area including most of the world known to the medieval geographers, takes place in an indefinite time, generally said to be long in the past. The storyteller's geography is shaky at best. It is not unusual for the hero to march his army from Persia to China, from there to Arabia and India, and finally back to Byzantium. Space is highly compressed and seldom are we given details of the journey; in the same manner, time is generally foreshortened. We never know how long these journeys take; time is clearly defined only when some event, such as a battle, is presented in great detail. (141)

I believe that the *dastan-e-dilruba* is the perfect metaphor for Rushdie's *Satanic Verses.* It was a story he created for a beloved, his religion, which he could not "have," because of both his ambivalent postcolonial relationship and his Indianized secular Muslim attitudes, a beloved who was going to be disappointed by the tale and yet for whom and out of his love for whom he creates the particular *dastan.*

As we have already seen at the beginning of this paper, the Islamic storytelling background that Rushdie claimed in interviews, essays, and in his previous fiction makes him partial to Islamic narrative forms. Even in *The Satanic Verses,* Saladin Chamcha, visiting his father, finds "A ten volume set of the Arabian Nights which was being slowly devoured by mildew and bookworm . . ." (36). The *Arabian Nights* is present in every work he writes. In *Haroun and the Sea of Stories,* he even sees himself as evolving into a version of Haroun-al-Rashid. Ironically, "Rushdie" simply means "diminutive Rashid" or "son-of-Rashid." Is Rushdie then a son of Haroun-al-Rashid of the *Arabian Nights*? The answer is a resounding yes. The stories and the tales of the *Arabian Nights* seem to flow through his veins and flow out of the "tap" of stories, as is witnessed by the layer upon layer of stories of the Prophet's life and adventures Rushdie tells in *The Satanic Verses.* Unfortunately, he finds himself as a storyteller who is in the land of *gupchup,* quiet (censorship), ready to be made *khatm shud,* finished. And though there is humor, the tediousness of the complaint in Rushdie's *dastan* (*The Satanic Verses*) is probably what the Iranian mullahs found so burdensome. It belabors over and over again the Prophet's faults.

What is interesting to see is that as Rushdie delivers his *dastan* he is fairly and squarely in Islamic tradition and delivering his complaint like Firdausi Tusi when denied the proper remuneration for writing the *Shahnameh.* Both conveyed their complaint via a literary work. And as has already been noted, a more recent counterpart to Rushdie is the late nineteenth-century

Urdu poet Hali, whose *dastan* was written to criticize the shape and form Islam had taken. In fact, what is said of Hali's *Musaddas* is true of *The Satanic Verses:* "It traces the rise and fall of Islam, beginning with preMuslim Arabia, talking about the prophet, the Arab triumph and then the gradual decline" (Steele 13). Like Hali, Rushdie in *The Satanic Verses* seemed to be warning that if Islam in its contemporary decadence, especially in the migration to Britain, didn't take stock of itself, "Neither you nor your friends will be saved. If the boat sinks all will be drowned" (Hali, qtd. in Steele 14). In fact, this was Hali's message to the *mohajir,* or migrant Persian Muslims in India. Rushdie, aware as all literary Indian Muslims are of the tradition of Ghalib, Hali, and Mir therefore follows in their footsteps, both echoing the complaint and using the form. In fact, this is what Rushdie has already told us: that through his character Gibreel, he meant to show the importance of retaining faith. What happens to a religion when it is preoccupied with stricture and not with faith? Farishta and Chamcha had begun what the Reverend Mother in *Midnight's Children* criticized—eating pork, educating the children into disbelief and greater secularism, and so forth. When Adam Aziz throws out the *maulvi,* the religious tutor to the children, because he taught the children intolerance, he is chastised by his wife, and this exchange takes place:

> "He was teaching them to hate, wife. He tells them to hate Hindus and Buddhists and Jains and such, and who knows what other vegetarians. Will you have hateful children, woman?"
> "Will you have godless ones? Reverend Mother envisages the legions of the Archangel Gabriel descending at night to carry her heathen brood to hell."
> (*Midnight's Children* 43)

For Rushdie, retaining one's Islamic sensibility is just as important as being secular and open-minded. It is important to have the mullah educate the children but not to fill them with hate. The reformist agenda has always been to make Islam more tolerant, less "hate-filled" and less practice-oriented.

Following the characteristics of a traditional *dastan* in *The Satanic Verses,* Rushdie gives us detailed catalogues of the sins of those who are becoming infidels:

> He got out of the limousine at the Taj hotel and without looking left or right went directly into the great dining-room with its buffet table groaning under the weight of forbidden foods, and he loaded his plate with all of it, . . . he began to eat as fast as possible, stuffing the dead pigs into his face so rapidly that bacon rashers hung out of the sides of his mouth.
> During his illness he had spent every minute of consciousness calling upon God, every second of every minute. Ya Allah whose servant lies bleeding do not abandon me now after watching over me so long. (*Satanic Verses* 30)

> But when Gibreel regained his strength, it became clear that he had changed, and to a startling degree, because he had lost his faith. (29)

Here again Rushdie is questioning simply the rigor of practice. In " 'In God We Trust' " he talks about losing faith and immediately thereafter eating a ham sandwich (377). Is faith simply a matter of not eating ham? Has Islam, then, become simply a matter of practice and of bargaining with God? It is this superfluity that Rushdie is questioning and seeking to reform.

Like Hali, though, he was speaking out of a love of Islam, seeking reforms that would reinstill faith in the practitioners. One of the features of the *dastan-e-dilruba* is that the *dilruba*, or sweetheart, is *naraz*, or disappointed, by the *dastan*. And the effect of *The Satanic Verses* was in fact to cause such a disappointment among those wooed—the Muslims; this only causes the narrator of the dastan to hold his dilruba in greater reverence, and she becomes *meheruban*, the revered. The *dastan-e-dilruba* is so named not only because through the tale the narrator wishes to win his beloved but also because the tale itself reflects the pursuit of a beloved. In Rushdie's *Satanic Verses* Gibreel Farishta is and remains in pursuit of the elusive Rekha Merchant, who, despite her suicide, appears to him frequently on magic carpets. She is interestingly very much like the Meccan goddesses that Mohammed intended to worship, which caused him to utter the "Satanic Verses" which he had to retract.

All three of Rushdie's novels follow the *dastan* pattern. Space and geography are compacted in *Midnight's Children,* as Saleem Sinai moves all around the continent. In *Shame* he moves all over Pakistan and Afghanistan with a narrator coming to visit from England. In *The Satanic Verses,* this feature is much enhanced, of course, not only by the sudden arrival, via the explosion of an Air India flight, of Gibreel and Saladin Chamcha in England but by the sudden switches in time into the Arabia of the Prophet Mohammed. Though the other two novels had compacted geography in that form, *The Satanic Verses* perhaps most exaggerates the movement of the narrative from India to England to the Arabia of Mohammed to England, and so forth. Seldom are we given details of time and space but are left to figure out the various Sufayans and whether Hind is the wife of the contemporary cafe owner or the wife of the Prophet. Then there is the necessary battle over Farishta's monsterlike state, and he is transformed into a human again after the battle of wax statues in a discotheque.

Two characteristics of the *dastan* are predominant in Rushdie's work: (1) the form of the narration; (2) the use of the magical/supernatural or fabulous. As we have already seen, both of these characteristics are usually assigned to the condition of his post-British coloniality and his subsequent interest in postmodernism. But as we have also seen, they are predominantly rooted in Rushdie's post-Mughal consciousness. Traditionally, the *dastan,* as it was narrated in Persia and later brought to India by the late Mughal emperors (particularly Jehangir, who had his own storyteller), was an oral narrative form. As it turned into an Urdu literary form, its orality was emphasized even more, because Urdu was the language of the illiterate people whereas Persian was the language of the literati of high culture. It wasn't until the late nineteenth century that the Indian entrepreneur Nawal Kishore thought of publishing the orally transmitted *dastans*. So they retain(ed) the characteristics of oral transmission. However, William Hanaway makes a distinction that is particularly applicable to *Midnight's Children* and *The Satanic Verses:*

> The stories begin at the beginning and proceed in a fairly straight line to the end. There are, with one minor exception in *Samak-i-Ayyar*, no flashbacks. The stories are never begun *in medias res* or work backwards and forward as they are in Modern Literature. The open-endedness and flexibility of the form result in a lack of internal cohesion. The integrated progression of the modern plot is absent. In its place we find a loose stringing together of episodes which in their lack of organic connection seem at times almost random. (142)

While Gibreel Farishta and Saladin Chamcha's fall can be construed as an *in medias res* beginning, the story of both those characters does begin there, and their story unfolds almost in an episodic, picaresque fashion. While Rushdie does give us glimpses of their childhood, the story of their immigration as also the story of the Prophet's immigration progresses from beginning to end. In fact, the beginning of *The Satanic Verses* is very similar to that of *Midnight's Children*. It is almost as though there is an *ayah* (maidservant) telling a little boy the story of Gibreel and Saladin. "Baba, if you want to get *born again*" (3, my emphasis), she seems to say, listen to this story. "It was so and it was not so." The "born again" metaphor is interesting. Is Rushdie applying to Islam a metaphor from contemporary America? From his long discussion in " 'In God We Trust' " (387–92) of "born again" Christianity in America, it would seem so.

From there we go to the story of the Prophet Mohammed. This is not a flashback, but a story within a story, a frame tale. The narrative voice is like that of the *ayah* Padma in *Midnight's Children,* who says, "Once upon a time it was so and not so as the old stories say" (35). There is therefore no attention to "structural matters," as Hanaway calls such strategies as pacing, the laying out of climaxes or the setting up of flashbacks. Rushdie, like the *dastan* narrators of yore, brings these together in loosely knit episodic form, a rambling story always going forward. Hanaway also writes, "Much of the length of the *Dastan* comes from exhaustive catalogues of people and places as also from elaborate plays on words and multiple repetition" (142).

What Frances Pritchett says of the classical Urdu *dastan,* the *Dastan-e Amir Hamza,* is true of Rushdie's work: "The language is rhythmic, repetitive, almost hypnotic, and gives the narrator's vision a dream-like power and authority" (6). Pritchett adds, "The classical Urdu dastan became so inconceivably long and so elaborately fantastic that it exhausted its own possibilities" (6). With Rushdie's novels, the fantastic is often attributed to postmodernism. But it is in looking at the form of the *dastan* that one finally understands the origins of Rushdie's fantastic and what he calls "fantabulous." *Dastans* are peopled by "paris," usually fairies or winged creatures. The hundreds of yellow butterflies that clothe the visionary Ayesha in *The Satanic Verses,* which have been attributed to García Márquez's yellow butterflies, are characteristic of this supernatural element. Ayesha herself may be considered a "pari"—Mohammed had always called his favorite wife an "angel." There are magically animated puppets—Saladin Chamcha turns into one, as does his penis, and like a true *dastan* hero he lives in a world full of "marvellous events—mysterious inexplicable and magical" (Pritchett 9). Ironically, much of this is controlled by black magic, which in the eyes of a good Muslim is always evil. Saladin thinks the Welsh policemen who captured him practiced some black magic, and English black magic causes the migrant *mohajir* to sprout horns and turn into an evil character. Here Rushdie develops a post-European colonialization metaphor: he seems expressly to disapprove of the postcolonial who turns European. He is asserting that transmogrification into the foreign culture is dangerous, which in itself can be taken as a call to retain one's religious and cultural identity.

Moreover, it is those who are rooted in their own culture who provide deliverance for Saladin Chamcha. Therefore the clever spies and secret agents, the *ayyar,* so vital to the *dastan* hero are, in *The Satanic Verses,* the Indians and Muslims of Bradford and Brick Lane like Mishal and Hind Sufayan, who eventually transform the *dastan* hero Saladin from a cross-cultural monstrosity in suit and tie and bowler hat with long penis into a human being. Read in this way the fantastic, one of the characteristics of the *dastan,* is meant to be liberatory for the Muslims of Bradford and Brick Lane. This does not mean that Rushdie is satirizing these Muslim immigrants as "fantastic and unbelievable," as the Western press had made it seem he had. He is simply deploying one of the techniques of his chosen genre. *Dastan* narrators make "so much use of marvellous events that in a sense such events lose their marvellousness and become the 'normal' " (Pritchett 11). And, in showing how the fantastic has become normal, Rushdie meant not to be criticizing the uprooted Muslims but urging them both into secularizing reform of strictures and into greater "faith," as Hali and Sir Sayed Ahmed Khan meant to in the nineteenth century. In fact, it was Sir Sayed Ahmed's travel to England that turned him deeper toward Islam, yet he brought back a sense of British secularism and was able to merge the two.

Islam has not been a stranger to criticism or satire. While panegyric was part of *maqamas* (eloquence), so was *hija* (satire), a form that came to the

Islamic poets from the pre-Mohammedan meccans. When the Persian poet Firdausi Tusi was paid only in silver for the *Shahnameh,* the complaint he registered through satire was rewarded by the gold he should have received. A complaint or a satire was not always punished. Like a modern-day Hali, Rushdie genuinely meant his satire to be reformist, not a target satire but a satire that was actually delivered out of love for his religion, fraught as it is with contemporary cross-cultural problems not only in Bradford and Brick Lane but in international diplomacy and policy. The use of the *dastan* is "the ancient Arab story-tellers' formula," which Rushdie tells us in his essay "In Good Faith" he had used in *The Satanic Verses* (409).

What I hope will emerge from this analysis is a recognition of the need for new ways of looking at literatures from around the world in English. Specifically, localized interpretations that study the history and the context of the texts need to be created by perhaps an intermediary interpretive community—one that can study a work in the specific locale in which it is situated and provide such clues to an understanding of the work that can be picked up and used by academic and intellectual communities across disciplinary and interest boundaries. Timothy Brennan writes, "the nation-centered origins of literary studies distorts the coverage of the vast realm of experience arising from imperial contacts" ("National Longing" 61). Indeed, I hope I have shown that instead it provides deeper understanding of the work and of various "imperial contacts." It can also be argued that claiming that only those who know the localized contexts can find meaning in a work is lapsing into essentialist universals or ghettoizing the work. I hope I have convincingly argued for the failure of the current Eurocentric theories' approach to *The Satanic Verses*. The African-American critic Barbara Christian has pointed to the failure of the contemporary "race for theory" in approaching Afro-American and West Indian literature. But she rejects the challenge to provide alternatives, dismissing them as "harassment" to "invent wholescale theories regardless of the complexity of the literature we study" (39). On the contrary, I believe that it is important to develop alternatives such as nation-centered and context-based criticism which can in turn provide important insights into imperial contacts, particularly those contacts often ignored because of a lack of historical or contextual knowledge. Claiming such a position is not an antitheory argument but one that shows how theory can be complemented.

Therefore, to dismiss "cosmopolitan commentators on the third world who offer an inside view of formerly submerged peoples for target reading publics" (Brennan, "National Longing" 63) is merely a defensive gesture. I would say that any critic in order to establish his or her ethos has a responsibility to inform himself/herself about every aspect of the work's history, its literature, and its metaphoric import before offering theorizations about the work. In doing so, one can cut across essentialist boundaries that say that only an "insider" can provide the key to understanding a work or that only a reader informed in particular theories can read appropriately. In this sense, therefore, we need to return responsibility and accessibility to literary criticism. Literary studies per se have a long history of allowing texts to be approached by all who would come to study them thoroughly. If an "insider" critic can facilitate a text's accessibility, then his/her work should be used to understand the work better because such interpretations can lead to newer and more "catholic" understanding—the sort that can lead to current discussions of lifting the *fatwa* (see Reid). Postmodern indeterminacy can, as has been shown here, result in dangerous misinterpretation when authority is wrested from both the author and his/her cultural location.

Notes

1. The question of the term postcolonial and of the label postcolonial literature is increasingly problematic. Literatures in English from ex-British colonies are of course the direct result of the British colonialism that taught "English" to the colonials. But Urdu literatures and Sanskrit literatures are also the direct result of colonialism. Contemporary "postcolonial writers" espoused English as their medium of creative expression just as their forefathers had espoused Sanskrit or Persian. Raja Rao points out in his preface to *Kanthapura* that both Sanskrit and Persian were colonizers' languages and that Indians absorbed them and created a vast body of literature in each of these languages.

Do R. K. Narayan, V. S. Naipaul, and Rushdie all share a blanket "postcoloniality"? Rushdie himself has rejected these labels in his essay " 'Commonwealth Literature' Does Not Exist," at times quite sarcastically: "As for myself, I don't think it is always necessary to take up the anti-colonial—or is it post-colonial?—cudgels against English" (64).

2. Midnight was chosen by the late Prime Minister Nehru as the astrologically auspicious hour for India to obtain independence from the British. *Midnight's Children,* the title of Rushdie's second book, indicates the generation of Indians who were born in independent India. Rushdie's actual date of birth is 19 June 1947.

3. Rushdie's "magical realism" is born of the new form created to allow "the miraculous and the mundane to co-exist" (" 'In God We Trust' " 376). Much discussion has focused on "the form" of *The Satanic Verses.* Homi Bhabha, relying on Yunus Samad's reading of blasphemy, argues that Rushdie, by "casting his revisionary narrative in the form of the novel— largely unknown to traditional Islamic literature . . . violates the poetic license granted to critics" (*Location of Culture* 226). Of the postcolonial writer's use of the novel form, Timothy Brennan writes that "the constraints are real" and refers to the "crippling subaltern status implied by having to follow an imaginative form of another and oppressive culture" ("National Longing" 58). But Rushdie is not trying to write in the form of the novel. These (mis)representations make it all the more important to see the Indo-Mughal form Rushdie is working in.

4. " 'In God We Trust' " tells us how Rushdie had to change the form of his writing to accommodate the reality that religion is not a "symbol" but a daily magical component in the lives of the characters he is creating. More importantly, he says, "perhaps I write, in part, to fill up that emptied God-chamber with other dreams" (" 'In God We Trust' " 377). Rushdie without the usual nuancing and hedging tells us that he is his characters. Of the role of the author, he writes, "we can dream versions of ourselves, new selves for old. . . . We live in our pictures, our ideas. I mean this literally. We first construct pictures of the world and then we step inside the frames. We come to equate the picture with the world" (377–78). Now all of this is very problematic in terms of contemporary theorizing about the author and his/her intentionality.

In a previous essay on *The Satanic Verses,* "Resurrecting the Prophet," I had claimed, "Rushdie has become a victim not of the Muslim world so much as of the indeterminacy which is the condition of post-modernism, whereby authority has been completely wrested from the author and in his absence has been placed in the hands of warring factions of readers" (107). Rushdie, who seems never to have meant to relinquish authority over his text, stepped in after the *fatwa,* Prufrocklike, to say, "That is not it at all, That is not what I meant, at all." In "Why I Have Embraced Islam," Rushdie writes of his intention: "For over two years I have been trying to explain that *The Satanic Verses* was never intended as an insult" (431). He elaborates that the "insults" occur as "portraits of . . . disintegration." In fact, these religious figures are simply manifestations of the author. He adds that "*The Satanic Verses* itself, with its portrait of the conflict between the material and spiritual worlds, is a mirror of the conflict *within myself*" (430, my emphasis). So it is that despite our understanding about the role of the author and his/her intentionality, Rushdie not only attempts to maintain control over his text but infuses his characters with his "visions" or injects himself into his creations. Even as *The Moor's Last Sigh* went to press, there was rumor and speculation about Rushdie's intentions. With this publication event and in making his first "unguarded" public appearance in *The Times*/Dillon's Debate in Westminister Central Hall on 7 September 1995, Rushdie again attempted to assert not only his intentions but that "the author is not dead."

5. Islam's growth in the Indian soil was very different from the roots it lay down in Africa, for instance. The Somali writer Nuruddin Farah, who has also lived in India, describes his context in *Interviews with Writers of the Post-colonial World:* "The reason why Islam appears to be more relentless is twofold. One is that for everything Muslims do, they resort to the holy book, from which they seek divine approval. The second is that Islamic societies have not been secularized (in Africa) in the same way as Christian societies have been" (56).

6. "Islamic high culture," characterized by ornateness in architecture, for example, and Indian Muslim culture are alike not only because of the sumptuousness and richness of their poetry, art, clothing, and food but because of their intense religiosity even in their secularism. Daily discourse for instance is punctuated with words like *inshallah* (God willing), *marshah allah* (God forbid), and *l'illhauallah* (praise God). *Purdah,* along with other Qur'anic laws, is practiced in the most secular of households, those perfectly willing to educate their daughters, mingle with Hindus, and so forth. The distinction Rushdie himself makes is useful here: Islam in India and Pakistan is represented by a secular Muslim culture quintessentially embodied for instance in Zulfikar Ali Bhutto or even in a Muhammad Ali Jinnah, Western-educated, married to a Parsi woman, and so on. What Rushdie calls "Islamization" is "a means of shoring up . . . unpopular regime(s)" in the name of religion ("Naipaul among the Believers" 374). Rushdie adds, "Terrible things are being done today in the name of Islam" (375). When Karsten Prager of *Time* asked Rushdie why he had "embraced Islam," Rushdie said, "I believe there needs to be a secular way of being a Muslim. There are plenty of people in the Muslim world who feel exactly like that—an identity with culture and values—but who are not believers in the theology. That was what I was trying to say, or I would've said it if anybody had listened hard enough. But immediately I was called either a traitor to my own cause or a hypocrite" (Prager 50).

7. In the ongoing Hindu-Muslim debate, the Global Hindu Electronic Network quotes from Shri Padgaonkar's "Men in Dark Times": "there has emerged in the world Islamic community a European Islam, an Arab Islam, an Iranian Islam, an Indonesian Islam and so on. Indeed it is Indian Islam which has the greatest potential to emerge as a model where faith and culture and nationalism form a harmonious continuum" (GHEN, World Wide Web: 25 Nov. 1995).

8. Sect, as defined by the eleventh edition of the Encyclopaedia Britannica (1910–11), gives us an insight into how that term can be used to label the various Hindu and Muslim religious groups and how it is applied by scholars of Indian religions: "Sect, a body of persons holding distinctive or separate doctrines or opinions, especially in matters of religion; thus

there are various sects among the Jews, the Mahommedans, and the Buddhists, etc. In the Christian Church, it has usually a hostile or depreciatory sense and is applied like 'sectary,' to all religious bodies outside the one to which the user of the term belongs." Rushdie writes in "Why I Have Embraced Islam" that "most Indian Muslims affirm the value of the secular principle" (430).

9. Brennan here seems to be using Islamic in the Middle Eastern scholars' sense, in a more narrowly religious way than it is used in India. This could contribute to his misunderstanding of Rushdie's audience. Certainly, Indian Muslims would understand, though perhaps not all would fully appreciate, the full range of Rushdie's satire. In the sense in which I am showing Rushdie as deeply rooted in Muslim culture, there is a definite alienation from Hindu India. In *Midnight's Children,* the patriarch is described as having the blue eyes typical of Kashmiri Muslims. Jammu-Kashmir is the only state in predominantly Hindu India with a Muslim majority and hence the move toward Kashmiri separatism. Brennan, unaware of such contextual facts, guesses from the earlier work that Rushdie is not Islamic, although the later *Satanic Verses* shows Rushdie as deeply knowledgeable about Islamic history and theology.

10. It is true that the *Arabian Nights* would not be considered "high culture" in the Middle East, as they were popular, oral folk tales. However, when Muslim culture came into India as a colonizing force, all things Muslim became "culture" to be aspired to. It is interesting to note that the project of the first Mughal emperor, Babar, was very similar to that of T. B. Macaulay's famous 1832 memorandum introducing English to India as a means of civilizing the natives. Babar too looked around him and found the Indians uncultured despite thousands of years of art and civilization. Here is what he wrote: "Hindustan is a country that has few pleasures to recommend it. The people are not handsome. They have no idea of the charms of friendly society, of frankly mixing together, or of familiar intercourse. They have no genius, no comprehension of mind, no politeness of manner, no kindness or fellow-feeling, no ingenuity or mechanical invention in planning or executing their handicraft works, no skill or knowledge in design or architecture; they have no horses, no good flesh, no grapes or musk-melons, no good fruits, no ice or cold water, no good food or bread in their bazars, no baths or colleges, no candles, no torches, not a candlestick" (qtd. in Schimmel and Welch 14).

11. He refers to this in "Why I Have Embraced Islam" (430).

12. Bahadur Shah Zafar is the archetype of the Indo-Mughal Muslim degenerate who, preoccupied with drink, chess, and religious devotion, lost the Mughal Empire totally. The British sought to use him after the Mutiny of 1857 to reassert a central power in Delhi, especially since the Mutiny centered on a Muslim issue, the supposed use of pig fat to grease the Enfield rifles.

13. Sir Sayyid Ahmed Khan (1817–98) founded the Anglo-Oriental College at Aligarh (now Aligarh Muslim University).

14. Apparently, during a hunting expedition of 1564, Akbar asked to listen to the story of Amir Hamza, "whose character was based upon the mistaken unification of two personages of the same name, an uncle of the Prophet and a popular Iranian hero from Sistan. The fantastic stories perfectly suited the rough-and-tumble atmosphere of the dynamic young emperor's court from about 1566 until 1580" (Schimmel and Welch 43). Akbar had 2–1/2-by-2-foot paintings done of this *dastan.* It seems to have perfectly suited his secularizing project. "The text was intended to be read aloud from the back while the illustrations were held up to an audience" (42). It is interesting to note that the British edition of *The Satanic Verses* has part of a Persian miniature drawn from another such *dastan* of Rustum on the cover.

Works Cited

Ali, Ahmed, ed. *The Golden Tradition.* New York: Columbia UP, 1973.
Attar, Farid ud-din. *The Conference of the Birds.* Trans. Afkham Darbandi and Dick Davis. Harmondsworth: Penguin, 1984.

Bhabha, Homi K. "DissemiNation: Time, Narrative, and the Margins of the Modern Nation." *Nation and Narration.* Ed. Homi K. Bhabha. London: Routledge, 1990. 291–322.
———. *The Location of Culture.* New York: Routledge, 1994.
Brennan, Timothy. "The National Longing for Form." *Nation and Narration.* Ed. Homi K. Bhabha. London: Routledge, 1990. 44–70.
———. *Salman Rushdie and the Third World: Myths of the Nation.* New York: St. Martin's, 1989.
Christian, Barbara. "The Race for Theory." JanMohamed and Lloyd 37–49.
Collins, Larry, and Dominique Lapierre. *Freedom at Midnight.* New York: Simon and Schuster, 1975.
Coppola, Carlo. "The Angare Group: The Enfants Terribles of Urdu Literature." *Annual of Urdu Studies* 1 (1981): 57–69.
Dictionary of Oriental Literatures. New York: Basic, 1974.
Fanon, Frantz. *Black Skin, White Masks.* 1952. Trans. Charles Lam Markham. New York: Grove, 1967.
Gibb, H. A. R., and J. H. Kramers, eds. *Shorter Encyclopaedia of Islam.* Ithaca: Cornell UP, 1961.
Hali, Altaf Husain. *Musaddas-e-Hali.* Karachi: Peermahomed Ebrahim Trust, 1975.
Hanaway, William L., Jr. "Persian Popular Romances." *Review of National Literatures* 2 (Spring 1971): 139–60.
JanMohamed, Abdul R., and David Lloyd, eds. *The Nature and Context of Minority Discourse.* New York: Oxford UP, 1990.
Jussawalla, Feroza. "Resurrecting the Prophet: The Case of Salman, the Otherwise." *Public Culture* 2 (Fall 1989): 106–17.
Jussawalla, Feroza, and Reed Dasenbrock. *Interviews with Writers of the Postcolonial World.* Jackson: UP of Mississippi, 1992.
Kapoor, Raj, dir. *Sangam.* RK Studios, 1964.
Kaufman, Michael T. "Author from Three Countries." *New York Times Book Review* 13 Nov. 1983: 3, 22–23.
Kureishi, Hanif. *The Black Album.* London: Faber and Faber, 1995.
———. "My Son, the Fanatic." *New Yorker* 25 March 1994: 92–96.
Marzorati, Gerald. "Salman Rushdie: Fiction's Embattled Infidel." *New York Times Magazine* 29 Jan. 1989: 24–27, 44–49, 100.
Naipaul, V. S. *Among the Believers: An Islamic Journey.* New York: Knopf, 1981.
Nehru, Jawaharlal. *The Discovery of India.* 1946. London: Meridian, 1956.
Prager, Karsten. "Free Speech Is Life Itself." *Time* 23 December 1991: 50.
Pritchett, Frances W. *Marvellous Encounters: Folk Romance in Urdu and Hindi.* Riverdale, MD: Riverdale, 1985.
Rao, Raja. *Kanthapura.* 1938. New York: New Directions, 1963.
Reid, Calvin. "Iran Contradictory on Rushdie Threat." *Publisher's Weekly* 29 May 1995: 34.
Rushdie, Salman. " 'Commonwealth Literature' Does Not Exist." *Imaginary Homelands* 61–70.
———. *Haroun and the Sea of Stories.* London: Granta, 1990.
———. *Imaginary Homelands: Essays and Criticism, 1981–1991.* London: Granta, 1991.
———. " 'In God We Trust.' " *Imaginary Homelands* 376–92.
———. "In Good Faith." *Imaginary Homelands* 393–414.
———. Introduction. *Imaginary Homelands* 1–6.
———. *Midnight's Children.* New York: Knopf, 1981.
———. "*Midnight's Children* and *Shame.*" *Kunapipi* 8 (1985): 3–8.
———. *The Moor's Last Sigh.* London: Jonathan Cape, 1995.
———. "Naipaul among the Believers." *Imaginary Homelands* 373–75.
———. "The Prophet's Hair." *East, West.* London: Vintage, 1995.
———. *The Satanic Verses.* London: Viking, 1988.
———. *Shame.* New York: Knopf, 1983.
———. "Why I Have Embraced Islam." *Imaginary Homelands* 430–32.
Sarkar, Jadunath. *History of Aurangzeb.* Calcutta: Sarkar, 1952.

Schimmel, Annemarie, and Stuart Cary Welch. *Anvari's Divan: A Pocket Book for Akbar.* New York: Metropolitan Museum of Art, 1983.

Spivak, Gayatri Chakravorty. "Reading *The Satanic Verses.*" *Public Culture* 2.1 (1989): 79–99.

Steele, Laurel. "Hali and His Muqaddamah: The Creation of a Literary Attitude in Nineteenth-Century India." *Annual of Urdu Studies* 1 (1981): 1–55.

Suleri, Sara. "Contraband Histories: Salman Rushdie and the Embodiment of Blasphemy." *Yale Review* 78.4 (1989): 604–24.

Wolpert, Stanley. *A New History of India.* New York: Oxford UP, 1977.

The Cultural Politics of Rushdie Criticism: All or Nothing

Timothy Brennan

On December 14, 1991, after two unexpected public appearances, Salman Rushdie emerged from hiding briefly at Columbia University's School of Journalism to announce a strategy with two components: first, to pressure Western heads of state to help him win a reprieve from his death sentence, and second, to launch the paperback edition of *The Satanic Verses*. "*The Satanic Verses*," he wrote, "must be freely available and easily affordable, if only because if it is not *read and studied,* then these years will have no meaning."[1]

This dramatic appeal to reading will prompt my own appeal to reading later in this piece. Obsessed in his essays with the state, Rushdie had written a novel that, by all accounts, had become a matter of state, a condition that conspired against reading. What catapulted the novel into a matter of state, moreover, were charges that relied on the public presumption of inadequacy in two types of reading communities. The first was an ostensibly *mis*reading (or more often, *non*reading) community of naive Islamic faithful—the ones who had had, it was said, the audacity to burn the book without reading it, without even being capable of savoring the joys of an ironic literary knowledge. The second—in a much more localized and second-stage set of commentaries— was a supposedly ill-informed community of critics from the metropole who sought to comment on the affair without personally knowing Islam or the Islamic world. The first had been exposed mercilessly by a peremptory and powerful caste of reviewers in mainstream publications.[2] The second had been challenged by a proliferation of documentary clarifications by Muslim scholars in Europe and the Middle East. At the same time both had been the target of a third type of criticism authoritatively offered by scholars, many of South Asian origin, writing in a climate of postcolonial theory in the American and British universities. The "nativism" of the first was held up for scorn under the aegis of a Western pluralism, whereas the *Western* nativism of the second had been rebuked by a postcoloniality immune, in its own eyes, to nativism. It is as an amendment to those views that I offer mine here.

This essay was written specifically for this volume and is published for the first time by permission of the author.

What are the stakes of such a point? Over whom or what is this war of interpretations struggling? As a whole, the critical reception of Rushdie's work has been partial, although in uneven ways. A middlebrow, public-sphere commentary has jostled with an MLA journal–oriented expertise, with the former scandalously uninterested in the latter's knowledge, and the latter eager for the former's notoriety but unable to gauge the ideological consequences of the former's prior setting of the Rushdian stage. Unaccustomed to entering debates over reading under the klieg lights, as it were, of a *literature of state,* professional literary critics often conflated distinct issues—on the one hand, the viability of cultural criticism to foreign policy, and on the other, the Eurocentric gaffes of high-profile commentators whose notoriety (rather than their knowledge either of Rushdie's novels or of his precise cultural setting) had been their entry card into the debate.

One was dealing, then, with an unfamiliar set of interpretive problems. In Rushdie, the critic had to address a reputation so large—and so "now"—that the traditional luxury of working in separate critical spheres was not only in danger of confusing both but (as I have just suggested) was actually denied or finessed by the hermeneutic specialist seeking to break out of his or her academic confinement in a uniquely receptive commercial atmosphere. This was the case not despite but because the Rushdie "affair" demonstrated the impoverished view the public had of cultural criticism itself. Never before had a mass-market novel elicited official commentary from the likes of James Baker and Geoffrey Howe. And yet what the affair demanded, cultural criticism was best equipped to provide: for example, insights into problems of cultural translation raised when fiction crosses borders; the way that book markets structure international tastes and create literary celebrities; the different status that the written word enjoys in different societies; the actual traditions of secular literature within Islamic societies as well as how that literature had previously engaged with the sacred writings of Islam; and, importantly (perhaps most importantly), the problem of affiliation—the problem of how, in fact, to take Rushdie as a writer from India while being, in his own words, a writer also in and of England, a writer working on behalf of "democracy" but hostile to democracy's colonial interventions.

I. The Setting: History and Form

Rushdie first became an "important" author at a specific political conjuncture that needs to be repeated to be remembered. The "affair" and its aftermath are otherwise unintelligible. Despite the schematic nature of the forthcoming account, I want to sketch that conjuncture at the risk of understatement or omission, since the more detailed and site-specific reading I offer later depends on it. Rushdie, it should be recalled, first emerged as an author of renown only two years after the government of Margaret Thatcher assumed power in a period of renewed U.S.

imperial ascendancy that expressed itself in an emphatic riposte to a surge of anticolonial insurrections marking the final moment of the immediate post-Vietnam era (Nicaragua, the Philippines, Iran, El Salvador). The gradual weakening of those anticolonial movements and, in all but one case, their defeat coincided with the growth of his career against a backdrop of neoliberal triumphalism. As the official public sphere rang with endorsements for ending the welfare state, the new "Cold War" (in Fred Halliday's phrase) was being carried out with a messianic vigilance, ending finally in the fall of the Soviet Union in 1991 as a result of President Reagan's successful program of supply-side military spending.[3] Meanwhile, a correlative movement of posthumanistic thought in the universities and in the arts effectively disabled critical opposition to these developments, announcing itself through a self-contradictory (but coldly efficient) claim that "representation"—in both its organizational and semiotic senses—was a form of tyranny. Rushdie entered this prolonged liminal moment in a decidedly antinomian posture. His entire career, including the subjects and styles of his fiction, has been indelibly marked by a traditionalist defense of political and epistemological values against the public stream. A partisan of the Sandinistas, an ill-tempered enemy of Thatcher's new entrepreneurialism, and an unapologetic debunker of discursive theory, he set out to champion a brand of Left-Labor humanism bent on rehabilitating conscience in a frankly uncivil society.

Although the patterns of this transformation had been seen before (its history, in some ways, punctuates the entire postwar period), the important shift between 1980 and 1991 had been a grafting of traditional Cold War hostilities onto various "nationalisms," a meeting, as it were, of the enemies of the Anglo-American imperial self.[4] The decisive theoretical issues surrounding identity in the academy as well as the prompting to an almost involuntary nativism of focus in the field of postcolonial studies were both caught up in this shift and expressed it as a contradiction—that is, as a position hostile to an oddly universalized and abstract "nationalism" that failed to acknowledge its own congruency with official American policy toward insurgent movements of political independence, and as a position that drew energy from a renewed focus on alien ethnic and national specificities. For the shift produced a complex and self-defeating set of corollaries in which cultural critics, insufficiently attentive to the merging of diverse critical communities, found themselves. Given the success of Iran and the decline of the Soviet sphere, nationalisms in Africa, Eastern Europe, and elsewhere devolved from the classical anticolonial model associated with the era of Bandung—the model later of the nonaligned nations, with broadly social democratic and critically "Western" sympathies found recently, for example, in Nicaraguan socialism. Disenfranchised from a coherent political alternative following the fall of the socialist sphere, these nationalisms increasingly took on the shape of primarily religious, ethnic, or anti-Western movements. The political had become civilizational.

It is precisely in this shift that the complexities of Rushdean interpretation arrive, and where the ambiguity and self-contradictoriness of the "nativist" readings reside. To resolve it, however, means to read much more than the famous "affair" or its proximate cause, *The Satanic Verses,* and so I will turn my attention now to aspects of Rushdie's career as a whole: exactly what is wanting in much of the helpful work prompted by his now global fame.

In spite of that aim, it is the affair, finally, that exacerbated the conflict within Rushdie's brand of social democratic and civil intervention, one that mobilized the *literary* on behalf of public decency and civil rights while situating itself securely within a framework of free debate that no nativism (including the West's) would allow him. The surprising unanimity of the public portrait of Rushdie as the displaced "Indian" of Muslim parentage, the renegade from color and country, is remarkable. Nor is it in broad outline inaccurate, except contextually, which has made that portrait tendentious. It extends, at any rate, from the *Times* of London to the Bradford mullahs and a good deal of postcolonial criticism, although naturally the valence of that renegacy is utterly opposed, particularly between the first two groups. The third (postcolonial criticism) takes a more complicated position that borrows from the others, a position in defense of authorial freedom, desirous of inclusion in a broadly accessible Western public sphere but wearing the mantle of filiative authenticity. All for their own reasons quashed this other view—the one Rushdie tirelessly projected for himself, which had to do with an affiliation rather than a filiation: the venerable, new, proudly old-fashioned defender of the novel as a form, of the beneficent state, of tolerant public opinion, and of ethnic cross-dressing.[5]

Rushdie generally has been foreshortened by the "affair." As Martin Amis memorably put it, he had "vanished into the front page." For those who had been following his career closely throughout the 1980s, *The Satanic Verses* appeared very differently before the events of 1989 than it did afterward. I first read *The Satanic Verses,* in early 1988 on the couch of a friend in the form of a slightly faded typescript on which Rushdie had penciled in corrections. The book's publication in England was still some months off, so the future was unpredictable and unknowable. Many of the expected gestures—the same humor, above all the same satirical targets—could be found there in what clearly amounted at the time to nothing more than the third arm of a trilogy he had begun in *Midnight's Children,* continued in *Shame,* and was now bringing to completion. There was nothing essentially new—no added virulence, no obvious change in tone, no special provocations. The savaging of Islam was dramatically evident in the earlier novels, particularly in *Shame* with its sustained parody of the Qur'an, which was compared there to the rantings of the Pakistani military. The difference was that the parody was not, as in *The Satanic Verses,* found in a book whose very title gave the jest away and whose author had now attained a visibility *within* England that allowed the parody to be picked over by an avid international readership.

It was not, then, some newfound status as reprobate Muslim that caused the avalanche of protest and recrimination to fall; rather, it was a peculiar *combination* (one that a "nativist" reading explicitly denies): namely, the novel's England-centeredness—which is not to say its Englishness—along, and in equal measure with, the author's celebrity status. Religious apostasy may have been the proximate cause, but as in other sectoralist conflicts the struggle was, as always, over rights, labor, and land. As perceived by the book's detractors, Rushdie's crime was the combined product of notoriety and an insider status that could effectively translate itself in Anglo-American surroundings and do so in a context of palpable contempt for an immigrant community of believers in an era, as Syed Shahabuddin put it, of the "new Crusades." He had, in the view of Shahabuddin, "peddled his Islam wares in the West." Following the fatwa Muslim scholars seeking to explain what was outrageous in the book focused on his distance from the working-class Muslims and Hindus he typically wrote about—above all in England (and British Muslims were the first to burn the book publicly). What, for example, do we make of the fact that among them he was often referred to, with deliberate cruelty, as "Simon Rushton"? Postcolonial theory has at times alluded to the significance of these associations and the part they played in the ensuing controversy, but it has not emphasized them, for the view controverts their basic premise. After all, those who were arguably closest to Islamic knowledge and to the domestic complexities of religious politics in the subcontinent saw Rushdie not as too Muslim to be understood by the culturally illiterate Western critic but rather as too Western to recognize his own insiderism as a form of false advertising. They were exposing the luxury of a critique fully consonant with a British intellectual common sense and challenging a highly rewarded author in an atmosphere of heightening rancor toward the laboring faithful, who lived in British exile, were misunderstood, and were now laughed at by one considered to be (if not actually being) their own—only one example of the confusion of reading communities at work in the book's reception.

But the post-fatwa Rushdie was a Rushdie robbed of his resources, even (as we will soon see) by himself. He could not be seen but through the veil of filiation. One has to struggle to remember how inappropriate such a delimiting is for a writer who in review after review had spoken on behalf of his own multiple identities and national fealties. And it looked past his elaboration, in essay after essay, of politics—of imperialism as a grand theme worthy of our century's greatest writers but as yet unexploited by them. He had always been drawn compulsively to those, as he wrote of Graham Greene, who have a "total addiction to everything about [their] time." As the affair opened a door between the uneventful reveries of literature and consequential public events, critics found themselves plucked into the light. While a generation of award-winning prose stylists scurried into the refuges of minimalist novels of gloomy contemplation, Rushdie bushwhacked his way into a different clearing. He helped recall for modern Britain what it had forgotten was there in Blake, Swift, and Orwell: big-theme Politics, the clash of states, the dramas of national heroism and betrayal, the perfidies and hypocrisies of a race-driven world system of empire, creating a festering sprawl of Babbitts, Bumbles, and Sebastian Flytes on the home front, living off the colossal spoils of colonial pillage. *Midnight's Children* exploded this literature of constipation and threw open the doors to an entire generation of younger novelists for whom empire, race, immigration, and religious fundamentalism had been the basic food.

Picking up on the mood, Tariq Ali had complained about the reception in London circles of Abdelrahman Munif's powerful five-volume novel, *Cities of Salt:* "The novel went unnoticed on the London literary scene. Naturally, the critics were preoccupied with slender, wistful accounts of middle-class life in New York. A short, light-weight, but clever book about a man warming his baby's feeding bottle was the rage at the time. Let me be blunt. Munif's work is worth much more than most of the junk being turned out by publishing houses."[6] And so it was with Rushdie, only that Rushdie drove home his point fully 10 years before Ali, when almost no one thought in these terms, and did so with the great exclamation point of a novel—a 500-page epic that realigned English literature, making it more rife with possibilities, more uproarious, more carnivalesque, less European—but above all, more "Political" in the grand sense of that word, where history became a time-honored burr in the flesh of the imagination, taking us back to the fictive musings over sweeping movements of social change.

It is not just some lack of imagination that moves me to give an account of Rushdie that might be seen as purely sociological. It's rather a calculated sacrifice, and a conjunctural necessity demanded by the "affair"—although not an unwelcome one if only because readers begin in this way to approach the heart of his project and the ideological aspect of his aesthetic achievement. Like his politics, the formal stakes of his writing have yet to be commented on adequately. They are lost in the battle of nativisms that jump, on the one hand, to facile comparisons between Rushdie and Lawrence Sterne or Günter Grass and, on the other, to claims under categories with more MLA appeal in an atmosphere of liberatory essentialism. These latter speak of a Rushdie who is not at all based on Western authors but is interpretable exclusively through genres like the oral tale or the *ghazal*.[7] These readings stamp a specious authority on an always very partial ethnic identification. They employ a threatening cultural specificity locked within an experiential "science" of the East in a mode of temporary amnesia toward both Rushdie's actual writing and his emphatic statements about what that writing contains.

Rushdie alludes, no doubt, to such genres and incorporates their formal aspects. I made the case in 1988, for example, that Rushdie's most fully realized and densely crafted novel, *Shame,* is a deliberate contestation at the level of form between the Qur'an that it parodies and the oral tale that it seeks to emulate, in which the plebeian and gender-inflected vitality of the latter is set against the scriptural certitude—the frozen orality—of the former. What has to be remembered, though, is that *Shame* is among Rushdie's most derivative novels in the sense that every aspect of its plot and situation is taken scene by scene from *One Hundred Years of Solitude*. It is only the most obvious moment where Rushdie's potent intervention into the book markets can be seen for what it gloriously is: a systematic reapplication of the lessons of the Latin American boom to the Anglo-imperial world. The Americas were the source of the ideology of *mestizaje* that became hybridity in the hands of belated Anglo-Americanized exiles from the British colonies, and that Rushdie captured in a new context as a "contemporary" phenomenon—the migrant sensibility—that had been the staple of a specifically American (above all, Latin American) discourse for two centuries. Neither Rushdie nor the "postcolonial" critic likes to have this pointed out, but it is in that particular school that Rushdie apprenticed—a point, by definition, friendly to the migrancy he elaborates.

More important, Rushdie makes no sustained attempt to work *within* the genres of Holy Book or oral legend except as a commentary on them (for example, the role in *Shame* of the Qur'an and Bariamma's familial tales, respectively). He uses them metafictionally, in other words, and this use significantly alters their function in the context of a programmatic affiliation—in *Shame*'s case, the "oral tale" involves a point about women's domestic resistance to a male military elite. The flexing of the muscle of cultural capital that is seen in presentations of Rushdie as a mistranslated Muslim working in classical Oriental genres ignores his life. Let us recall a few important facts readily available from the public record. A child of popular culture, Rushdie grew up surrounded by Bollywood and American comic books. In his own words, he was the joint product of *The Arabian Nights* and Enid Blyton. As part of what he described as a "very Anglophile and Anglocentric" youth, his father hired a painter to decorate the walls of his nursery with animal characters from Disney films. He has stated that his most decisive single influence was *The Wizard of Oz,* the subject of his brief and brilliant study for the British Film Institute. Almost all of these early inspirations, moreover, appear again in *Haroun and the Sea of Stories*—Flash Gordon's rockets to the moon; Alice in Wonderland; the voyages of Sinbad; the heroic double lives of Clark Kent/Superman and Bruce Wayne/Batman; the riches of Ali Baba; and the colorful substitute home, people with talking animals and forbidden cities of (once again) *The Wizard of Oz*. Many of the professional influences of his more mature years were also woven into that novel's fabric, with echoes of James Bond's *Dr. No,* the medievally tinged science fictions of Italo Calvino, the "bwana" adventure films of Steven Spielberg, and Satyajit Ray's spectacularly popular children's film about two bumbling bumpkins (*Goopy Gyne Bagha Byne*), whose names are given to the novel's two talking fish.

The secularized irreverence was in no way innocent of religious intent, on the other hand, even if Rushdie's romance with Sufism was insufficient to brand him, without many levels of irony, as a Muslim critiquing Islam from within. Having lived, like *The Satanic Verses'* Gibreel Farishta, "a childhood of blasphemy," he would as a child mimic the art of Arabic calligraphers by drawing the name Allah so that it resembled the figure of a naked woman. Then came the years at Rugby, later King's College, Cambridge, where he took up his first serious study of Islamic civilization and later still, discovered his romance with film—especially Michelangelo Antonioni, Akiro Kurosawa, and Satyajit Ray—followed by his ventures into acting at the Oval and Kennington in the play *Viet Rock,* where, sporting long hair and a beard, he roamed London's counterculture, living his last college summer above a famous mod boutique on King's Road. Graduating in 1968, he declared, "I ceased to be a conservative under the influence of Vietnam war and dope." During his short sojourn in Karachi, where he had planned to move after his parents' relocation there, he adapted Edward Albee's *The Zoo Story* for the country's government-operated television station. He ran afoul of the censors, however, for including the word *pork* in the script, and the magazine feature he then wrote on his first impressions of Pakistan was censored as well. In 1969, he returned to England in disgust and, apart from short visits abroad, never left again.

His relationship to Islam in *The Satanic Verses* is impossible, then, to separate from a literary and civic project fed by the *soixante huitard* sympathies of a differently, but not uniquely, situated metropolitan. The third-worldist passions of that ethos had for him a more immediate register. He knew it personally, but what he knew was part of a reservoir of experiences drawn from a world whose literary associations were stuck in an older British "novel of empire"—a slightly staid discourse of MCCs, gin toddies, barrack-room ballads, and stiff upper lips desperately out of character with the epic-fantastic that emerged in the international book markets following Vietnam in the intervening 1970s—the years of his novelistic apprenticeship. The frustration of having a story that needed to be retold in an idiom appropriate to the time made *Midnight's Children* possible. And it led to a series of motifs of secularization operating at the level of form as much as of theme—the elements that, once the field of the "affair" has been cleared, will bring us back to his writing. So even here, one need not be sociological alone but can return with pleasure to the issues of form. Recall what these formal characteristics have been: his use of the political cartoon, for example, as distinct from what it often resembles and has often been confused with: pastiche. Rushdie's fiction (as he suggests in the metafictional asides in *Midnight's Children*) is current-events collage, articles clipped from a newspaper. One wants to talk more about the seamless edge between his journalism and his novels, or rather, the journalism *of* his novels, their reliance on the logic of the headlines, and the subordination of character to the allegorical logic of news commentary.

We are dealing, in other words, with a metafictional compendium that unlike many of its contemporary counterparts—*pace* Kum Kum Sangari—was resolutely nonpostmodern.[8] Rushdie's discovery of the world of the heart, of intimacy and conversation, is surprisingly evident and unapologetic in the 1990s. He found this intimacy first, after all, in the closing passages of *The Satanic Verses* in his portrayal of Chamcha's planting of a tree at his father's death—a fictional farewell to his real-life father, whose then-recent passing is memorialized there. Little has been said about this. One could easily argue that the significance of *The Moor's Last Sigh* is its attempt to extend that intimacy over the course of a novel via portraits of sexuality—in Rushdie's mind, for well or ill, a feminized strategy taken from the great women novelists of the nineteenth century: "It's funny how books, the classics, order you to reread them when you are preparing for a novel. I've been rereading *Wuthering Heights*. Before that, *Jane Eyre* . . . [t]hese characters possessed by personal feeling." Having surprised himself by the power of the closing scene of *The Satanic Verses*, he set out to sustain it: "I've got to write about sex. . . . [T]here is very little sex in my novels, very little stuff at all about the deep emotions. . . . [O]ne of the things I have failed to do . . . is write about strong feeling, cathartic emotion, obsession."[9]

If it is form that needs addressing, it is the following that matters: his calculated use of loan words (much richer and more natural than those in Kipling or Mulk Raj Anand), his angry wit (the most brilliant of his authorial gifts and the secret of his stature), and his cinematic sense (cinema so often *in* his novels, but also *of* them in the fast-cutting, blurry close-ups and the melodrama). Apart from these is this premier fact of his placard-prose, his two-dimensionality of character rescued from boredom by the multidimensionality of his political intelligence and frames of reference. It is an *intellectual* fiction whose aesthetic pleasures lie at the level of the phrase and of the idea, an aspect that has led to many misunderstandings given the literary presuppostions of a public criticism still operating under the "end of ideology." Thus *New York Times* reviewer Christopher Lehmann-Haupt's comment that Rushdie is "unreadable. . . . He couldn't write a sentence if his life depended on it."[10]

Rushdie set out to recover the political in literature. Weak in plot and character, he was strong in satire and in the presentation of suppressed history. And this is what should be talked about—not the exaggerations that come from overreading, in which allusions become illusions and wainscoting a foundation stone: Rushdie, the heir of Muhammad Iqbal in the land of the Angrezi *Dummkopfs*. The cultural politics of the Rushdie "affair," then, might at least consider the costs it demanded of his critique of empire, which screeched to a halt under the pressures of his own contradictory analysis of the forces poised against it. The affair was significant because it caught him, for a time, overtaken by events.

II. FIGHTING AND FORGETTING: THE AFFAIR'S FALLOUT

"These years," Rushdie writes in his Columbia speech. What, in fact, were the events that conspired to bring the traditionally Cold War and anti-Islamic discourses into a potent, and silencing, combination? As a prominent reviewer in high-profile magazines on both sides of the Atlantic, Rushdie had had reason to assume that the publication of *The Satanic Verses* on September 26, 1988, would be met with acute interest, if not open admiration. Indeed, the reception began that way, although there were early danger signs. Even before September, Khushwant Singh—Viking/Penguin's editorial consultant in India—advised against publication, warning that the novel's blasphemous parodies of the Prophet Muhammad would cause trouble. In an unfortunate interview for *India Today* on September 15, Rushdie unwittingly alerted the Muslim community to the book's offensive contents by declaring that his target was religious fanaticism. When the government of India banned the book on October 5, the measure only brought into realization what had earlier been promised. For in the initial months after publication, Viking had been deluged with calls and letters demanding the book's withdrawal, along with a petition containing hundreds of thousands of names. The first of many mass protests against the book took place in London on December 10, followed by demonstrations in every major British city with a sizable Muslim population. As the book proceeded to be banned by all of the officially Islamic countries, many other countries joined the ban, including Sri Lanka, South Africa, Kenya, Thailand, Tanzania, Indonesia, Singapore, Venezuela, and Poland.

Meanwhile, the demonstrations abroad had turned deadly. Ten were killed protesting outside the United States embassy in Islamabad, 5 in Kashmir, 13 in Bombay; hundreds more were injured in Dhaka, Bangladesh. As legal and public relations maneuvers in both camps continued—with Rushdie writing an open letter of complaint to Rajiv Gandhi and solicitors of England's Action Committee on Islamic Affairs trying to quash the book by having England's antiquated blasphemy laws apply to Islam as well as Christianity—events took a turn that rendered both actions moot. On February 14, 1989, the Ayatollah Khomeini's fatwa aired on Radio Teheran. Such activity had not died down immediately before Rushdie's Columbia appearance. Thirty-seven had just died in a hotel in Turkey in an apparent attempt to kill Aziz Nesin, *The Satanic Verses'* Turkish translator; in May of 1992, Jamia Millia Islamia, a university in India, was forced to shut its doors when its administrator, Mashirul Hasan, denounced the ban on the novel; a few months later, Britain expelled three Iranians suspected of plotting to assassinate Rushdie, and Hotoshi Igarishi, the Japanese translator, had just been stabbed to death.

What I am arguing is that the decisive issue of the "affair"—when one adopts, as here, an approach to the career as a whole—is the interpretive impasse arising from Rushdie's insistence on publishing the paperback edition when its appearance amounted to death, deportation, and suppression on an international scale. A warmly social democratic public persona came in conflict with a liberal apotheosis of the "literary" in the context of a Western triumphalism. And the insistence by certain critics on cultural particulars in a bid for authoritative reading stifled the issues to which Rushdie's career had been geared: the role of the "literary" in the public sphere and its capacity for liberalizing a climate of intolerance. For that reason, criticism needed to explore more fully where the interpretive impasse arose and how it played itself out in the public arena.

Rushdie's struggle to have others see *The Satanic Verses* as a matter of state won ground in May of 1993 when British prime minister John Major agreed to meet with the author and be photographed. Rushdie had, one remembers, made the point of such a strategy clear in his Columbia declaration when he equated his own travail to that of "the Western hostages in Lebanon and the British businessmen imprisoned in Iran and Iraq." The enticements and threats that had finally freed the hostages should, he argued, now be used on his behalf.

As the location of the clearly desperate author and the Western heads of state began to coalesce over a site occupied by ambiguous United States embassy personnel in Lebanon and unnamed British businessmen, the mere symbolism of *The Satanic Verses* as secular irreverence began to assume the garments of state in a more brutish, more solemnly literal form. Mamoun Fandy's April 13, 1992, article for the *Christian Science Monitor* found reason to hope that "Egypt's burgeoning movement towards free thought and civilized debate might become a bulwark against fanaticism throughout the Arab world" on the very grounds that an Egyptian newspaper had printed Rushdie's Columbia speech. An article like this—and there were many—exemplifies some of the politics of Rushdian representation. For even tauter ligatures between book and event existed in the *Boston Globe*'s report of January 19, 1992, that high-placed government spokespersons feared that British Muslims, now two million strong, were becoming a "state within a state" over the heated controversy of *The Satanic Verses*.

In the great fear of Islam, it was unclear what exactly constituted "pressure" to free Rushdie—particularly pressure of the type that freed the American hostages in Lebanon. Was it deportation? There had been, one remembers, allegations at the time of transnational plots involving Iran in Lebanon, HAMAS in the occupied territories, and Egyptian revolutionaries in the World Trade Center bombings. How can this representation of *The Satanic Verses* as a matter of state be set apart finally from the act of a Western power broker, flexing muscle on behalf of a beleaguered, justifiably frightened author? This question had been raised in another way by Cynthia Ozick's odious essay in the *New Yorker*, in which Ozick postulated that Rushdie's emergence at a writer's conference in Paris occasioned a prolix meditation on the genetic sadism and boorishness of Islamic culture.[11]

However bungled in some ways was the parody of Muhammad in *The Satanic Verses,* Rushdie's outlook has always been a world apart from that, but it was difficult to remember this, not least because Rushdie had. As much as *The Satanic Verses* had confused (in Agha Shahid Ali's words) "condemning fundamentalism with simply provoking it," it could only be after Rushdie's new strategy of state pressure that he would make the claim (as he did at Columbia) that the West finds "martyr-burning ... improbable"—a claim made, it should be remembered, not long after the incendiary events in Waco, Texas.[12] Nor would he have been likely to suggest that a "progressive, irreverent, sceptical, argumentative, playful and unafraid culture" can exist nowhere but in the lands of President Clinton and Prime Minister Major; nor would he have written of "mobs marching down distant boulevards baying for my blood" with its animal imagery ("baying") and its fear-inducing term *mob.* The point is not to reprimand Rushdie for using the resources at his command, only to note how the affair had dislodged him from his earlier views.

There are, in that sense, two kinds of points the decree and its aftermath should probably have raised but did not. One occurs in a helpful and often overlooked essay by Ali Mazrui in which he concedes that the language among defenders of the fatwa who speak of "Rushdie's pornographic betrayal of ancestry" or his "treasonous" writing does not for the most part apply in the West to religious apostasy.[13] However, he points out accurately that this very language and attitude is typically applied in the West to the religion of state. On the matter of censorship, one could then point simply to cases such as Britain's unapologetic silencing of IRA "terrorists" (or indeed, anyone even remotely connected to the IRA) or its suppression of Peter Wright's informative *Spycatcher*—examples that could be easily expanded to cases involving Muslims (as well as Arabs generally) in both the United States and Britain. One might counter that although censorship was at issue there, one was talking in Rushdie's case of something more than that: a decree of death. But here too the Western religion of state has had its many fatwas, openly admitted and conducted with the same campaigning righteousness as that of the Iranian government—for example, the discriminate bombing runs in Libya to eliminate Muammar Qaddafi, the assassination attempts on Fidel Castro, and the bombing and strafing of crowded Somali neighborhoods in order to murder Colonel Mohammed Farah Aidid: only some of the better-known consequences of the late- and post–Cold War shift to targeting oppressive "nationalisms."

Rushdie's second strategy—a *Satanic Verses* readily available to be "read and studied"—reproached the first and did so simply because the hugely neglected political center of the novel is a solidly social democratic demolition of Thatcherite Britain, its fatuous advertisements for a new middle class, its adventurist war in the Falklands, and its increasing police brutality and immigrant exclusionism. This is the reading the novel for the most part has not had. The indelicacy of criticizing an author who has been condemned to death was justified if only because *The Satanic Verses* had almost from the start been a matter of state and was instrumental in mobilizing dubious forces on several sides of a multiple divide. Why was Rushdie unable to follow through on what should have been to him an obvious conclusion?

Fred Halliday, in the *New Statesman and Society,* gave voice to some of those "dubious forces" when he furiously regaled "the condescending rubbish produced . . . to justify attempts to silence Rushdie in the name of . . . 'understanding' the Third World"—a point repeated, in a similar register, within postcolonial theory by Aamir Mufti.[14] Halliday's intemperance was palpable and part of a familial intemperance shared in the affair by Christopher Hitchens, Faye Weldon, and others. To Halliday, critics of Rushdie (among them Germaine Greer, John Berger, and Tariq Ali) were "a gaggle of windbags, fair-weather democrats and ignoramuses, unable to grasp the broader issues at stake, or besotted with some personal or parochial obsession of their own." They were "closet hooligans," "self-appointed censors," "back-seat heroes," "casual xenophobes."[15]

Surely something rawly seminal in the critique of Rushdie has set off this cascade of defensive peevishness. Could it have been, as Berger argued, that in *The Satanic Verses* there were "colonial prejudices"; that the battle for freedom of expression was not unalloyed by other, often countermanding considerations, like the dignity and physical safety of "mobs on distant boulevards" who were dying in street demonstrations as long as the book's print run in India continued; or that the issue of human rights did not always point its finger at the Islamic world? None of the reading communities, although for incommensurable reasons, was able to point out that the striking thing about Arabic fiction now available in the West was how consistently it failed to live up to the charges typically made against the culture of Arabic peoples: its mistreatment of women as the third-world horror of "traditional" societies, belying the extended studies of sexual politics in actual Arabic fiction, whose point of entry is often the troubling image and reality of male sexual privilege.[16]

As a professor at the London School of Economics and an author of rightfully acclaimed books on Iran and Pakistan, Halliday did not try to fortify his position with reference to his own specialist knowledge. This discretion, however, was not matched by other writers, especially within the academy, of whom some of the following comments were typical. Srinivas Aravamudan spoke of the "inside joke" of the number 420 in the novel, as well as the novel's generally "untranslated and untranslatable colloquialisms, allusions, and sprinklings of choice Hindi epithets."[17] Feroza Jussawala spoke of the "insider perspective of Rushdie's style," the "filmi slang," the "satire of Hobson Jobson."[18] Similar comments appeared widely in the journals where a territorial dispute over the valuable backlands of Rushdie's fiction had led to an exaggeration of difference to throw a specialist knowledge into bold relief. The point here, again, is not that these references to Islamic history or Indian popular culture are unimportant or universally accessible, only that a much more important darkness blankets this text than the ones created by missing allusions to Amitabh Bachchan, the historical source of the Titlipur Ayesha, or the fact that the word *jahilia* means ignorance. The collection of insider references a reader needs to grasp *The Satanic Verses* is not large. More important, these references are dwarfed in importance by the novel's larger need to ground the reader in the look and sound of a diasporic London.

What is this important darkness? It is of two very different types that cut across one another. First is that the Rushdie the fatwa kidnapped—the one it really did silence and subvert—is the Rushdie whose *Satanic Verses* was in conflict with a Western democracy of black mariahs and imperialist longings for the exotic (the meaning of the Rosa Diamond episode set in Argentina, an allegory of the Falklands War); or the commercial jingles operating as background to the activities of the National Front—all in a perfect symmetry with an accompanying attack (but only accompanying and parallel) on the antidemocratic thrust of the religion of the mullahs. Much of *that Satanic Verses* has been forgotten, even (in his case, perhaps understandably) by Rushdie himself. The failed parody of Islam is importantly a twofold failure, it must be said, at once too obscure and too anxiously aware of its own ambivalence toward the very people he wanted to, but could not, identify with.

The Rushdie of the early and mid-1980s is really the one lost in the uproar and in need of recovery. In 1983, Rushdie had declared himself an enemy of "nanny-Britain, straight-laced Victoria-reborn Britain, class ridden know-your-place Britain, thin-lipped jingoist Britain," which led him to say honorable things he could not, for tactical reasons, repeat when the affair broke out because he found himself relying on the British state for his bodily protection.[19] In the following passage from an essay of that time, he pretends to describe a fictional character whose name he borrows, characteristically, from a Rod Stewart song:

> A Tory Prime Minister, Maggie May, gets elected on the basis of her promises to cut direct taxation and to get the country back to work ("Labour isn't working"). During the next four years she increases direct taxation and contrives to add almost two million people to the dole queues. And she throws in all sorts of extra goodies: a fifth of the country's manufacturing industry lies in ruins, and (although she claims repeatedly to have vanquished the monster Inflation) she presides over the largest increase in prices of any British Prime Minister. The country's housing programme grinds to a halt; schools and hospitals are closed; the Nationality Act robs Britons of their 900 year old right to citizenship by virtue of birth; ... money is poured into the police force, and as a result notifiable crimes rise by 28%.[20] (*Imaginary Homelands*, 159)

The sustained fury of the passage, with its statistical overkill, leaves no doubt about how deeply these images remained with him. They play an enormous role in *The Satanic Verses* and, *mutatis mutandis,* provide the logic of his pre-Bharatiya Janata Party (BJP) satire of Indian entrepreneurialism and Zionism in *The Moor's Last Sigh.*[21]

A crucial reading community not typically a part of the public clamor has missed this book, or turned it into its own chapters 2 and 6—the Jahilia episodes, where a specialist knowledge has a far greater field of play. If *The Satanic Verses* really had been "read and studied," what would one have found? In terms both of narrative structure and sheer weight of pages, *The Satanic Verses* is principally about immigrant London; it is, as I have written elsewhere, an "immigrant theodicy," secular in its bearings, flamboyantly syncretic rather than strictly Muslim, however one wishes to deem the Muslim treatments in it. Like most of his novels, for example, he casts his Muslim characters with intentional inappropriateness as Hindus experiencing (and reflecting on) reincarnation, *the* central image of this novel. As such, it is important to ask what aims that portrayal of immigrant London sought to achieve, and on whose behalf it labored.

As an immigrant theodicy, *The Satanic Verses* sets forth a cast of characters continually exchanging their identities, merging with their others like the shifting sands of Jahilia, the immigrants' natural home. Exactly parallel to the coupling of Saleem and Shiva in *Midnight's Children,* or Iskander and Raza in *Shame,* Gibreel Farishta and Saladin Chamcha are the two that make one in Rushdie's world—the dialogue that, in a moment of fictional revelation, becomes the single mock Qur'anic "recital" of Rushdie alone as an internally divided author. To portray Rushdie, the author needed the dangerous, brilliant, famous, and unstable Gibreel as well as the unadventurous, proper, and toadying Chamcha—two aspects of the same self, a self that immigration as an almost spiritual state has made insecure, volatile, subject to revision, renewal, and self-redefinition. In the much-misunderstood dream structure of the novel, then, Ayesha the favored wife of Muhammad is also "Ayesha" the child prostitute, Ayesha as Allie Cone (Gibreel's lover), and Ayesha the fanatical Muslim girl who leads the people of Titlipur on a parody of Gandhi's march to the salt sea (another example of the Muslim *as* the Hindu in Rushdie's fiction).

One could repeat this process for most of the characters in the book. Farishta is Muhammad, the Archangel Gibreel, Shaitan, the real-life Hindi film star Amitabh Bachchan, and Azraeel, the exterminating angel. Played out this way to evoke the great dreamer Farishta's tortured mental life, there is, of course, also an implicit argument about the patterning of history here, seen to be as repetitive as the designs on the border of a work of Islamic calligraphy, which is perhaps why the dreams of Farishta themselves are at once the ravings of a paranoid schizophrenic, the calculated parodies of an immigrant trying to defend himself, memories of scenes from the sets of filmi "theologicals" that Farishta had directed while in India, Brahma's dream of the universe, and a Qur'anic revelation.

The postcolonial critic who speaks, as Feroza Jussawalla has, for example, of "indeterminacy of meaning outside certain cultural contexts" are absolutely right, of course, provided one remembers that these indeterminacies are not always ethnic, linguistic, or national—in a word, civilizational.[22] They are also positional. In that sense, the point cannot be only the elaborate Islamic troping or the domestic Indian popular cultural allusions—both so organizationally central to the story Rushdie was striving to tell in his overt bid at a kind of crossover modernism of a nonindigenous type—but the often overlooked conditions of Rushdie's training. It was, after all, the result of a highly individual mixture of childhood memories, adolescent and early adult accretions gained from his occasional visits home, and a deliberate (and belated) course of study carried out at Cambridge, in which the significance of Islam arrived to him (as it has for Indian and non-Indian students alike) via books. This is an important biographical detail: Rushdie's knowledge of Islam in *The Satanic Verses* was largely taken from his Cambridge essays. And yet this fact has been ignored.

To continue this sort of point, one might concede that it is not inaccurate to suggest that *The Satanic Verses* is a "love song" for an Islam that flourished in the Mughal period, although it is important not to overread this fact as dictating the overall structure of the novel.[23] As I have shown elsewhere, the Islamic thematics of the novel are working less in the service of specific literary forms (the Urdu *ghazal* or, in Jussawalla's terms, the *dastan*) than in a calculatedly irreverent reappropriation of Sufism, whose role in Rushdie's generically mixed narrative is free floating and multidirectional, aimed at a variety of targets—among them, the unquestioning devotees of the "Book" (in this novel, the Qur'an and the Bible), religious revivalism on the subcontinent, and the very contemporary (that is, not originally Mughal) phenomenon of a politically insurgent Islamic clerisy, above all in Iran and Pakistan.[24] To say that *The Satanic Verses* is not a novel so much as a misunderstood narrative convention drawn from the classical Muslim canon is to say too much and to ignore Rushdie's consistent (and appropriately superficial) employment throughout his fiction of "disposable" genres from a variety of traditions—although learning those traditions, and studying them independently of Rushdie's fiction, is, of course, paramount in any informed interpretation.

This line of argument fudges an important fact. As anyone familiar with contemporary India knows, the romance with the Mughal period is a standard one both at home and in the diaspora and is continually fed by the golden age of the Hindi cinema (particularly from the 1950s) whose frequent Mughal settings provide a ready-mind repertoire of courtly splendor and aesthetic grandeur in the arts of painting, dance, song, and food. It is much more reasonable to believe that the filmic sources of Bollywood, rather than a private attachment to Mughal form, were his inspirations. A certain edifice of firsthand experience is here coupled with a paralyzing challenge summoned by foreign language and broad specialist categories without regard to the contexts in which Rushdie actually used them. The proud nostalgia for the Mughal legacy in secular India also fuels Rushdie's writing, of course, even extravagantly so, but there is little mystery in it, nor does it require a native attachment, even if these shadings are missed in the (usually journalistic) readings of Rushdie as a sort of Günter Grass manqué.

Indeed, Rushdie carefully explains these references in his own essays—a characteristic act of self-interpretation that is, if not a guarantee of accessibility, at least a mild rejoinder to the critic who insists on the untranslatability of cultural dissonances while quoting Western scholars (Stanley Wolpert, H. A. R. Gibb, Laurel Steele, and others) as their own authorities. We have no more than assertions to tell us precisely why critics from India in the American and British academies are not, after all, "Western," nor why critics who are not originally from South Asia must—by genetic fate apparently—"metropolitanize" their subject. Civilization displants position, and so it ceases to matter what individual critics actually know about Sufism, the Qur'an, the politics and personalities of postwar London, *mestizaje,* or the *Shahnameh,* the medieval Persian epic that provides one of the models for Rushdie's early novel, *Grimus.*

The point, I imagine, is whether more is at stake here than might at first appear—more than just an unworthy struggle over critical territory, the planting of one or another national (or personal) flag in authorial terrain. For the point—at least my point—is not to finesse locality, or diasporic experience, or the impasse of a missed cultural context but precisely to underline what the "nativist" reading ostensibly stands for: namely, the importance of informing oneself about every aspect of a work's history, its literature, and its metaphoric import before offering theorizations about it.

A surprising number of otherwise informed readings have simply not done so, and yet they have ventured forth with remarkable energy in the name of a civilizational contest heightened by the specific conjunctures I outlined at the beginning of this essay. They are the fruit of a period of renewed self-definition in an era of imperial resurgence fed by a diasporic professionalization. Filiation steps in as a substitute for a more civic and less parochial critique of an empire sequestered, and immobilized, by a continuing Cold War criticism.

Thus the narrowing of focus in the nativist reading of *The Satanic Verses*—the failure to appreciate, for example, the parallels in that novel to the Padma subplot of *Midnight's Children.* Again, those who have closely *read* Rushdie's novels see in that subplot a key to what follows. It theorizes Rushdie-Saleem's anxiety about his own ambivalence toward the "people," a self-critique in which he casts himself as a protégé of the savvy, lower-class figure Padma, who keeps interrupting him by saying he is too intellectual, too skeptical, too out of touch. The subplot parallels an aspect of *The Satanic*

Verses but only in a cloaked way in the antagonism and friendship of Salman al-Farisi and Baal the satirist. If Rushdie had made a point about the adaptability of immigrants, and their tendency to try on identities to "turn insults into strengths," there is an aspect to the writing of these sections that is presented as a strength but which should in all justice be viewed as an insult. It was by many Muslim readers of the book.

Remember that Baal in the novel is a court hireling contracted by the Jahilian Grandee to satirize the village poor. His job is to practice on behalf of the state the "art of metrical slander." It is a key moment in the novel. When the story arrives at his portrayal of the resistance of the black communities of Britain, we are introduced to their comically overweight leader, Uhura Simba (named after Tarzan's elephant?), and the fatuous deejay toaster Pinkwallah, the white black man—both vicious send-ups of British dub poetry and the sorts of popular resistance represented by Linton Kwesi Johnson, Darcus Howe, and other figures recognizable to postwar British, especially Left, readers.[25] These portraits are combined with an almost unreadably condescending passage on the Afro-British communities, an Orpheus and Eurydice parody in "Black speech," involving two lovers who work in the London underground. One wonders why the first protests against the novel did not come from the black communities. It seems particularly depressing that one of the characters—Uriah Mosley—would be given the same surname as Oswald Mosley, the 1930s leader of British fascism.

From the perspective of the metropolis, there is a good deal of overlap, after all, between black people, working-class people, and the Islamic faithful. The village poor that the Jahilian Grandee first wants Baal to satirize are the water carrier Khalid, a Persian named Salman, and the black slave Bilal—the riffraff who become the Grandee's targets because they are early converts to Islam. The scene evokes a psychological truth, for Islam in the mind of many Western commentators is a religion of Semites of Arab extraction, Persians with dark eyebrows, laborers from the Punjab, and sub-Saharan blacks—the kind of people who, long before the Ayatollah posted his bounty, were demonstrating in Bradford, Detroit, and Karachi. What is Rushdie doing satirizing such people through his persona, Baal? Why is the historical Salman al-Farisi, Rushdie's namesake, the only original convert who flees, fearing the tyranny of the people defended by Islam (the former underdogs) once they have assumed power? Contrast this to his explicit statements about the novel in which he lays out clearly the position he thought he was taking toward Islam in the parody of the novel, one whose revisionist take on contemporary Islam was precisely to emphasize its originally progressive content as a looking back to a pre-Meccan (rather than pre-Islamic) culture codified in the word *nomad:*

> Muhammad, an orphan himself at an early age, was in an excellent position to appreciate the way in which Meccan culture failed to care for the weak as duti-

fully as the nomads would have. . . . The people on whom Muhammad's word made the strongest impression were the poor, the people of the bazaar, the lower classes of Meccan society—precisely those people who know that they would have been better off under the old nomadic system. [Islam was in part] a subversive, radical movement (*Imaginary Homelands*, 384).

To say that Rushdie in the actual performance of the novel displayed distance from ordinary people is to make the point Berger made glancingly when he referred rather unfairly to the novel's "arrogance"—a point that has either been savagely attacked (as by Halliday) or (more commonly) overwhelmed by the antagonists of the other reading communities I mentioned—most of all the "naive" Muslim believers, the supposed *non*readers.

In the academy, Sara Suleri combines the two genres by dismissing the fundamentalist rabble's "failure of cultural imagination to countenance representation" at the same time that she underscores the inadequacies of noninsider readings of the book—an underscoring dramatized by a presumptuous "open letter" to Rushdie at the close of one essay, replete with topical references to "the hill-station of Nathia Gali, which you may know."[26] She refers to a 1990 Pakistani film entitled *International Guerrillas*, which others have commented on as well—a film that stages the affair for the purpose of allowing its audience to witness Allah's righteous killing of Rushdie by the movie's end. But the film's content exemplifies the weakness of her reading. For having set up her argument to explore a formal paradox—namely, that the Pakistani faithful, seeking to censor *The Satanic Verses*, are here in effect publicizing it—she abdicates the opportunity of answering a more interesting and difficult question related to her theme of "representation." As depicted in the film poster, Rushdie wears a high-collared shirt, slicked-back hair, and sunglasses—a potent image, indeed, of "Simon Rushton." The issue, then, might be: what exactly in this representation suggests what the Pakistani (or more broadly Muslim) masses detest in Salman Rushdie? Aren't we missing the opportunity here of exploring meaning outside the stalemates of the conflict among religious hermeneuts, since this is a work, after all, of popular culture? It is this failure to imagine the desires and angers of ordinary people that links this brand of Rushdie criticism to Rushdie's own fiction, which has dealt with working-class life warmly and compassionately but always in a comic register. His accompanying political motif—evident in his comment from *Shame* that the people, like Robespierre, "distrust fun"—has blended with these comic portraits in the most unfortunate way and have much to do with the explosive anger that the affair produced. That reaction took only those critics by surprise who had overlooked his earlier condescensions.

On April 1, 1992, in the *Los Angeles Times*, Carlos Fuentes added finally another dimension to the acts of reading and misreading *The Satanic Verses*. He wrote that "Rushdie is the first victim of a religious atavism which filled the ideological void left by the end of the Cold War." This is a dodgy statement and, one could argue, exactly the opposite of the case, since what is called "religious atavism" here did not arise suddenly after 1989 with the triumph of Perestroika to fill a void. It was instead, of course, the Western states that latched onto the neotraditionalism of Islamic movements as the major obstacle to globalization following the openings created by the fall of the Soviet Union. Nevertheless, Fuentes forces us to ask clearly what *The Satanic Verses* has to do with the Cold War. That, I think, is a fertile question that could open up more interesting ways of reading *The Satanic Verses*. How has the criticism of what one might call the *Granta* Left facilitated the climate of globalism? The record is mixed.

The Satanic Verses has to be applauded for diagnosing one of the key processes of this emergent globalism in Thatcherite Britain's rough displacing of traditional societies within domestic Britain and its creation of a new command economy whose latest features can be seen in the GATT accords. Nevertheless, much of Rushdie's writing, although pre-Perestroika, had been proleptic. It was fully a part of Perestroika's fervent hopes and frames of reference as evidenced, for example, in his satire of the "magicians ghetto" in *Midnight's Children,* aiming its humorous wrath at older but still viable forms of resistance both to the current free-market open-door policy of the Indian government and what has since arisen in the form of the party of Hindu revivalism, the Bharatiya Janata Party (BJP)—the great enemy of *The Moor's Last Sigh,* which forces of the Hindu right in Bombay attempted to suppress in exactly the manner *The Satanic Verses* had been before.[27] In one of the best of his postfatwa responses in 1990, Rushdie wrote:

> The point of view from which I have, all my life, attempted this process of literary renewal is the result not of the self-hating deracinated Uncle-Tomism of which some have accused me, but precisely of my determination to create a literary language and literary forms in which the experience of formerly colonized, still-disadvantaged peoples might find full expression.

This is completely true. The angry protesters from within the community of nonliterary Islam forget that Rushdie has little in common with those who indulge in scares over the civilizational threat of the "Islamic terrorist." But the unhappy trajectory of debate over *The Satanic Verses* has also greatly strengthened the uncritical belief in Western freedom, which, although real and appreciable, comes always at the cost of a more global unfreedom to others. Close reading demands that we remember that.

Notes

1. Salman Rushdie, "One Thousand Days in a Balloon," *New York Times* 12 December 1991, B-8; my emphasis.

2. Their claims were, however, largely untrue. The detailed readings of *The Satanic Verses* by ardent Muslims were numerous. See, for example, M. M. Ahsan and A. R. Kidwal, eds., *Sacrilege versus Civility: Muslim Perspectives on the "The Satanic Verses" Affair* (Leicester, England: Islamic Foundation, 1991); Shabbir Akhtar, *Be Careful with Muhammad!: The Salman Rushdie Affair* (London: Bellew, 1989); Munawar Ahmad Anees, *The Kiss of Judas: Affairs of a Brown Sahib* (Kuala Lampur, Malaysia: Quill, 1989); Mohammad T. Mehdi, *Islam and Intolerance: Reply to Salman Rushdie* (New York: World Press, 1989); and Mutaharunnisa Omer, *The Holy Prophet and the Satanic Slander* (Madras, India: The Women's Islamic Social and Educational Service Trust, 1989).

3. Fred Halliday, *The Third World and the End of the Cold War* (Madison, Wisc.: University of Wisconsin, 1993).

4. George Orwell's seminal essay of 1945, "Notes on Nationalism," is one of those places. See my discussion in *At Home in the World: Cosmopolitanism Now* (Cambridge, Mass.: Harvard University Press, 1997), 141–44. Among its many contemporary counterparts is Samuel Huntington, *The Clash of Civilizations and the Remaking of World Order* (New York: Touchstone, 1997).

5. Rushdie's defense of the novel has always formed one of his principal political interventions, and it overlaps explicitly with his critique of the neoliberal state and his defense of immigrant rights. It has also dovetailed with his awareness of the Cold War context of his own writing, evident above all in his romance with Eastern and Middle European novelists and intellectuals, whom he has frequently reviewed (i.e., Günter Grass, Andrei Sakharov, Siegfried Lenz).

6. Tariq Ali, "Abdelrahman Munif's *Cities of Salt*," *Marxism Today* (1991).

7. This is not to say that Rushdie did not often complain of the ignorance of Western reviewers toward his subcontinental literary inspirations. If in "Is Nothing Sacred?" Rushdie recalled that the "surrealism and modernism and Marx" of his upbringing complemented rather nicely the change and flux inherent in Hinduism, with its multiple gods, it was another way of saying that the critics' free use of the label "postmodern" for his fiction was the result of their poverty of references. His metafictional games had their sources less in French theory than in the "Mimic Me Truth" narrative of the 1940s British Indian novelist G. V. Desani, the spiraling digressions of the Storyteller of Baroda, or indeed Bollywood itself.

8. Kumkum Sangari, "The Politics of the Possible," *Cultural Critique* 7 (1989): 157–86.

9. Salman Rushdie with Geraldine Brooks, "Salman Rushdie: My Lunch with a Condemned Man," *The New Republic* 207, no. 5 (27 July 1992): 22–25.

10. Christopher Lehmann-Haupt, telephone interview by the author, July 1995.

11. Cynthia Ozick, "Rushdie in the Louvre," *New Yorker* (13 December 1993): 69–79.

12. Agha Shahid Ali, "A Secular Muslim's Response: *The Satanic Verses* by Salman Rushdie," *Yale Journal of Criticism* 4, no. 1 (Fall 1990): 296.

13. Ali Mazrui, "Is *The Satanic Verses* a Satanic Novel?: Moral Dilemmas of the Rushdie Affair," *Michigan Quarterly Review* 28, no. 3 (Summer 1989): 347–71.

14. Fred Halliday, "The Fundamental Lesson of the *Fatwa*," *New Statesman and Society* (12 February 1993): 17; Aamir Mufti, "*The Satanic Verses* and the Cultural Politics of Islam," *Social Text* 31/32 (1992): 277.

15. Halliday was not alone. Several other essays condemned Rushdie's fair-weather friends with a similar virulence. See, for example, Geoffrey Wheatcroft, "The Friends of Salman Rushdie," *Atlantic Monthly* (March 1994): 22–43.

16. See, for example, Nawal El-Saadawi, *Woman at Point Zero,* trans. Sherif Hetata (London: Zed, 1983); Hanan al-Shaykh, *Women of Sand and Myrrh,* trans. Catherine Cobham (London: Quartet, 1989); Etel Adnan, *Sitt Marie Rose: A Novel,* trans. Georgina Kleege (Sausalito, Calif.: Post-Apollo, 1982); Andrée Chedid, *The Return to Beirut* (1985; reprint, London: Serpents Tail, 1989); Assia Djebar, *Women of Algiers in Their Apartment* (1980; reprint, Charlottesville: University Press of Virginia, 1992); Naguib Mahfouz, *Palace Walk,* trans. William

M. Hutchins and Olive E. Kenny (1956; reprint, New York: Doubleday, 1989); Tayeb Salih, *Season of Migration to the North*, trans. Denys Johnson-Davis (London: Heinemann, 1969); Tahar Ben Jelloun, *L'enfant de sable* (Paris: Éditions de Seuil, 1985).

17. Srinivas Aravamudan, " 'Being God's Postman Is No Fun, Yaar': Salman Rushdie's *The Satanic Verses*," *Diacritics* 19, no. 2 (1989): 7.

18. Feroza Jussawalla, "Post-Joycean/Sub-Joycean: The Reverses of Mr. Rushdie's Tricks in *The Satanic Verses*," in *New Indian Novel in English: A Study of the 1980s*, ed. Viney Kirpal (New Delhi: Allied, 1990).

19. Salman Rushdie, *Imaginary Homelands: Essays and Criticism, 1981–1991* (London: Granta, 1991), 161; hereafter cited in the text as *Imaginary Homelands*.

20. The essay was written in 1983.

21. See my reading of the novel in "Salman Rushdie," in *British Writers IV*, ed. George Stade (New York: Scribners, 1997).

22. Feroza Jussawalla, "Rushdie's *Dastan-E-Dilruba*: The Satanic Verses as Rushdie's Love Letter to Islam," *Diacritics* 26, no. 1 (1996) : 50–73 (reprinted in this volume). She is at her most ahistorical when she quotes, without proviso, Rushdie's "Why I Have Embraced Islam" to substantiate her peculiar argument that Rushdie is alienated from Hindu India. His essay was conjunctural, defensive, and later embarrassing to him. He repudiated it.

23. Ibid., 50. Her blunt claim that *The Satanic Verses* is not a novel—indeed, that Rushdie does not write "novels"—is a spectacular case of the excesses of nativist reading. Evidence to the contrary does not deter her. See, for example, Rushdie's "In Defense of the Novel, Yet Again," *New Yorker* 72, no. 17 (24 June 1996): 48–54; "A Dangerous Art Form," *Third World Book Review* 1 (1984): 3–5; "Fact, Faith, and Fiction," *Far Eastern Economic Review* 143, no. 9 (2 March 1989).

24. Timothy Brennan, "Pitting Levity against Gravity," in *A Practical Reader in Post-Colonial Theory and English Literature,* ed. Peter Childs (Edinburgh, Scotland: Edinburgh University Press, 1998).

25. See Rushdie's critique of this sort of resistance in his review of the Black Audio Film Collective's documentary *Handsworth Songs* in *Imaginary Homelands*.

26. Sara Suleri, "Whither Rushdie?," *Transition* 51 (1991): 198–221.

27. Hindus in India were incensed by the novel's parody of Bal Thackeray, the leader of an ultraright Hindu revivalist party, Shiv Sena. Maharashtra State considered banning the novel, but the attempt was repelled by India's supreme court in February of 1996.

An Invitation to Indian Postmodernity: Rushdie's English Vernacular as Situated Cultural Hybridity

BISHNUPRIYA GHOSH

Ever since the beginnings of a critical conversation on the "New Indian novel," critics have focused on the links between English (as the language of power and privilege in contemporary India) and the modernist homogenizing projects of nation making. Salman Rushdie—whose *Midnight's Children* often marks the genus of the New Indian novel and whose *Satanic Verses* brought to light a series of conflicts in both residual and emergent East-West/Third World–First World interactions—remains at the heart of many of these conversations. While drawing our attention to a new Indian literary luminary, Arundhati Roy, James Wood notes in the *New Yorker* (December 1997) that Rushdie "is central to the new power of Indian fiction in English, so dominating that he has gobbled up his predecessors, who now seem like clouds to his sun."[1] Given Rushdie's prominence in the Indian English writing scene, postcolonial critics have been forced to consider some key questions raised by his oeuvre: does he embody a spurious mode of postmodernism that dissolves indigenous Indian cultural specificities in the name of hybridity and sampling? Or is Rushdie invested in giving language to a nation (in the modernist sense), despite his avowed antifoundationalism?

My analysis seeks to locate Rushdie as a certain kind of Indian postmodern who, while not offering resistance to the West in a structural sense, certainly interrogates its continuing reduction of heterogeneous Indian experiences to an umbrella description—"postcolonial India." Perhaps Rushdie may be seen to move away from the category of the postcolonial as *the* organizing cultural experience for Indians at the close of the twentieth century. I will focus on Rushdie's culturally specific use of a hybrid English, arguing for his transformation of the language of global capital into a new kind of Indian *vernacular*. This vernacular can be decoded only with recourse to *situated* or contextual knowledges—historical, popular cultural, linguistic, and so

---

This essay was written specifically for this volume and is published for the first time by permission of the author.

forth—as it is inextricably harnessed to its space of enunciation.[2] Examining primarily his last major work, *The Moor's Last Sigh* (1995), I will suggest that Rushdie's English vernacular records a new vision of India, a global-local postmodern nation whose set of cultural references no longer constitutes a stable and homogenous national register.

Rushdie's use of English as a vernacular provides us with an example of a situated cultural hybridity that disallows Western appropriations of the postcolonial into discourses of postmodernity, a concern that has been energetically voiced by postcolonial critics in the 1990s. In this essay I will explicate Rushdie's manipulation of a situated cultural hybridity by exploring the possibilities of an English vernacular: a localized or regionalized urban (Bombayite) use of English that, far from being the antithesis to the vernacular, lives in memory of it. My characterization of particular English usages *as* Indian vernaculars circumvents the political aporias that surface in most critical discussions of postcolonial Indian literatures, impasses that result from the seemingly unbridged oppositions between the Indian literature in English and 18 vernacular or *bhasha* literatures.

In the final analysis, I insist on culture-specific readings of postcolonial texts in view of the postmodern-postcolonial problematics just mentioned. Ever since Kwame Appiah's (1991) invocation of the "post" in postcolonial as a theoretical space-clearing gesture, the emptying out of the postcolonial by the discourses and practices of postmodernity has been a critical issue in postcolonial studies.[3] Vijay Mishra and Bob Hodge, among others, suggest that the postmodern emerges as a Western strategy of absorbing, organizing, and consuming all "othernesses" ("native," "ethnic," "non-Western") that once signaled the fall of modernist epistemologies.[4] The postcolonial actually *precedes* the postmodern, but functioning within a global cultural economy—a bazaar for non-Western artifacts—the category panders to the needs of that global market, producing ever more reified versions of "other" worlds.[5] Others, such as Kumkum Sangari, Meenakshi Mukherjee, Geeta Kapur, Stephen Slemon, and George Yúdice, insist on reading the postcolonial in context of civil spheres completely saturated with mass electronic reproduction, originating in the first world and harnessed to the logics of transnational capital.[6] Critics' fear of internal and external cultural imperialism energizes a perusal of the *kinds* of postmodernism experienced in different cultural realms. Kumkum Sangari points out how Western theorists of postmodern styles and techniques have cannibalized postcolonial cultures, using them as examples of Euro-American postmodernism. For instance, she argues, Gárcia Márquez's magic realism should not be read simply as a "formal literary reflex" but as a "strategy of living" in a Latin American milieu that is hybrid, syncretic, and operating in simultaneous time; in other words, nonmimetic or marvelous perceptions are ways of seeing the world and therefore are not the same as the *anti*mimetism of Western postmodernism. Sangari's analysis points us to the historical specificity of emergent postcolonial postmodernisms, and this is precisely my claim for Rushdie's use of a *situated* cultural hybridity.[7] My main contention here is that the act of reading Rushdie's culturally resonant prose with close attention to contextual knowledges constitutes a postcolonial praxis of resistance, because the insistence on culture-specific knowledge ensures that non-Western contexts are not simply reified and reframed within Western epistemological paradigms.

THE LANGUAGE DEBATE: CULTURAL AUTHENTICITY VERSUS HYBRIDITY

Gauri Viswanathan's seminal work on the role of English education in the colonies, *Masks of Conquest,* extensively analyzes the Gramscian axiom of cultural domination by consent: that English literature under the British raj was particularly instrumental in transforming the native subject as "actor in history" to the "reflective subject of literature."[8] Postcolonials fear that English continues to enact such violence in neocolonial settings. In many postindependent colonies, English continues to be the lingua franca; especially in countries such as Nigeria, India, Pakistan, Ghana, and others where there is no other single indigenous national language, there has been a tendency to use the metropolitan language in education and administration. English was, and remains, the language of nation makers—of constitutions, of laws, of bureaucracy.[9] In India to a large extent, and certainly in most British African postcolonies, higher education has remained "firmly rooted to its English curriculum and orientation"; in such scenarios, most research and publication in college- and university-level education is in English, resulting in an exodus of intellectuals and technical personnel to metropolitan areas of the developed countries.[10]

Given this linguistic hegemony, which some see as the basis of epistemic violence, postcolonial critics have been vociferous in interrogating the material and cultural dynamics specific to English usages. For as Vijay Mishra and Bob Hodge remind us in their excellent analysis of postcolonialism, refusing the language of the colonizer enacts "the withdrawal of subjectivity [that] hits at the core of the Enlightenment project, the civilizing values of modernity which the colonized (a V. S. Naipaul for instance) sees as imperialism's positive, reconstructive and basically humane face" (278). They argue for the possibility of a new Indian *lebenswelt* where the indigenous languages would again show signs of resurgence: "In jettisoning the almost auratic status given to the English language, the new reckoning with an imperial language both changes the form of the language itself and marginalizes it politically: the Shiv Sena uses Marathi, the Sikh militants Punjabi, and so on" (279). Such a characterization marks the two poles of the debate: the mimic men of power who use English are pitched against the communities that, engaged in political struggle, deploy their vernaculars.[11]

The language debates that polarize English and the Indian vernaculars first emerge within the modernist trajectories of nation making in the 1920s and 1930s. Gandhi's *Hind Swaraj* (1909), asserting the need to valorize indigenous literatures and establish a nation-language, inspired groups of vernacular writers who protested against the "foreign tongue." In 1933, surveying Indian verse in English, Latika Basu concludes: "As long as the vernaculars in India are . . . alive it should be the aim of Indians to develop them, for writing in a foreign tongue can serve no useful purpose."[12] On the other side of the issue, others such as Raja Rao embarked on disciplining an "alien" tongue. The battle continued into the 1950s and 1960s, with the English poet P. Lal commenting in 1966: "The real writer in English not only thinks, but makes love in English. English is at the tips of his senses."[13] Reacting to Lal, the Bengali author Jyotirmoy Datta proclaimed English to be a "dead" language in postcolonial India, a vehicle for information, not ideas and feelings. But by the 1970s, Indian writing in English became a recognizable form: 10 excellent books of English poetry and the publication of *Midnight's Children* in 1981 propelled Indian English into international recognition.[14] These modernist polemics of doubling and othering in the language debates have dominated the critical conversation on the Indian novel in English.

This notion is, of course, not particular to the Indian critical context; rather, the reckoning between authentic vernaculars and hybridized tongues/foreign languages is as old as the field of postcolonial studies. Ngugi's famed *Decolonising the Mind* established the radical position that African writers should write in the African languages. The basis of this Afrocentric view of language is Ngugi's philosophy of language as a lived relation to the world, a labor process that sustains relations between people. In such a view, English, as an elite language of privilege spoken by the urban few, further entrenches and continues the uneven and violent hegemonic social relations of colonialism in a neocolonial setting.[15]

Ngugi's influential Afrocentric notion of language was hotly contested by other African writers and critics. Chinua Achebe, for instance, while marking a clear disjuncture between the African world and the English language, insists that the African writer must write the "universal" English that, nevertheless, must carry "his peculiar experience."[16] In a polemic against an Afrocentric critical theory, Wole Soyinka argues for "selective eclecticism," which should be the "right of every productive being," whether scientist or artist; Ogun, in Soyinka's words, is "today's god of precision technology; of oil rigs and space rockets," not merely a "benighted rustic cowering at the 'iron bird.' "[17]

The African debate on English provides leeway into my emerging argument on English as a vernacular in postmodern India of the eighties and nineties. For the first 50 years of the Indian novel in English (1930–1980), novelists have relied on standard British English for their models of language, now and then self-consciously and cautiously departing from the norm (G. V. Desani's satiric romp through the entrails of babu English in *All About H. Hatterr* [1948] being a marked exception). In the eighties and nineties, writers in English have twisted, pulled, broken, and played with the language that Arundhati Roy claims as "mine";[18] they draw on their own vernaculars to sustain a fused disjunctive hybrid language—a "situated hybridity"—that expresses their relation to the world. The new English is not a wrenching away from the mother tongue and an "indigenous" experience of India; rather, the writers' specific material relation to the global-local world, to the nation, and to their locales can find expression only in such innovative usages.

The contestation between authenticities and hybridities in language and thought is best characterized as a modernist gesture that situates English very differently from the kind of "situated hybridity" that I perceive in the new Indian English vernacular; I draw my observations from Homi Bhabha's more postmodern reading of hybridity as an enunciative act. In a recent volume dedicated to exploring cultural hybridities, Pnina Werbner argues for the need to move beyond the heuristic gains of modernist hybridity theory best exemplified in Levi Strauss's evocation of the ambiguous and equivocal tricksters or in Victor Turner's celebration of the "anti-structural properties" of liminality and hybrid sacra.[19] According to these theorists, hybrids are identifiable products (monstrosities, taboo breakers, etc.) that gain a critical self-reflexivity *within* a society. In the same collection, Jonathan Friedman presents a similar view on modern and postmodern cosmopolitans who valorize hybridity. The modernists "knew the larger world, understood cultural variation," but were primarily rationalists and universalists.[20] Achebe's sense of Nigerian English as a variant in a "universal" systematized language, and Soyinka's sense of identifiable "eclectic" instances of hybridity within linguistic and cultural systems, fit the modernist model. All of the African theorists discussed previously also present a sense of a larger reality—variously presented as the African experience, worldview, social/material relation to the world—that language fails to capture completely. In the Indian context, Raja Rao's introductory remarks in *Kanthapura* present a similar sense of disjuncture between world and text: one has to convey "in a language that is not one's own" the "spirit that is one's own."[21] British English is still the standard, for Rao comments exuberantly on the "colourful" Irish and American dialects.

Werbner stresses the need to move beyond old modernist insights in our postmodern, postcolonial, late capitalist era, citing Homi Bhabha's work as an example of such a gesture. Bhabha differentiates between "cultural diversity" that recognizes "pre-given cultural contents and customs" and "cultural difference" that focuses on "the problem of ambivalence" in cultural authority.[22] In the first instance, hybridity involves the recognition of two (usually) dichotomous cultural givens: for instance, the Yoruba and the English, or the authentic Indian tradition or spirit and the imported English text/resonance. Here both cultural contents are consumed as products, as we see in the discourses of multiculturalism. The oppositions between "English" and "indigenous" or "vernacular" languages, without attention to the leakage of the one into the other, smack of such modernist dichotomizations. Cultural difference, on the other hand, reveals "the place of utterance—the institutional strategy whereby self-other (modern-tradition, European-native) is produced," a "third space of enunciation" that makes visible the context and the moment and does not produce stable hybrids. Each hybrid is a process that surfaces with the interplay of discursive and institutional forces; one does not gain a critical perspective on the world (in classic modernist fashion) but resists essentialisms through interruptive enunciation. Postmodern hybridity, then, must be understood as an act whose enunciative space and context becomes the locus of inquiry. Situated and contextual knowledges, of the sort that Mishra and Hodge argue can be found only when the postcolonial critic delves into vernacular and popular/folk cultures, become central to analyzing the enunciative spaces of the new localized English usage, exemplified here in Rushdie's language.

This emphasis on the location of English vernaculars in India, a necessary step for reading Rushdie, is precisely what separates his linguistic and cultural projects from his acknowledged predecessor—G. V. Desani's more modernist Joycean experiments in *All About H. Hatterr*. This bildungsroman of a grotesque autodidact who builds up a vocabulary with the aid of an English dictionary and a French and Latin primer combines "colloquialisms of Calcutta and London, Shakespearean archaisms, bazaar whinings, quack spiels, references to the Hindu pantheon, the jargon of Hindu litigation . . ."[23] Desani's self-reflexive parody that in Bhabha's words "distends the space between self and other" through exaggeration is nevertheless conveyed to us as a failed rhetorical act by the author who was well versed in the British oratorical tradition. The sense of the world Hatterr cannot capture through his "rigmarole" English, the protagonist's social and cultural alienation through language, and the centrality of the colonial as it doubles back to see its distorted image are all modernist gestures that end in a political aporia. One needs little knowledge of Indian locales and contexts to understand the parody. Thus, even though Desani's work seems to exemplify Bhabha's notion of mimicry and parody as resistance, it does not fit my extension of Bhabha's theorization of hybridity. For the postcolonial critic who seeks to find momentary locations for English vernaculars, the current writers offer contextually *situated* writing that loses its muscle when displaced from the vernacular registers and specific cultural matrices. Desani's work provides an example of an earlier modernist project of créolisation in which the colonial tongue and its purity are still the centerpiece of all creative endeavors: Hatterr ostentatiously strains "[your] goodly godly tongue" (35).

Salman Rushdie's Situated Hybridity in *The Moor's Last Sigh*

While *Midnight's Children* is organized around the formation and evolution of a nation—thereby placing the postcolonial as the defining experience for India—in *The Moor's Last Sigh,* Rushdie seems to move away from issues of nation and colony to problems of representation (for Indian communities, both locally organized and stretching in global linkages across nations). *The Moor* is preceded by another work that is strongly marked by extensive linguistic experimentations: *Haroun and the Sea of Stories* (1991), a work that Rushdie wrote for his son—the fulfillment of a promise that proved to be the only thing that "brought [me] back to writing" after the *Satanic Verses* debacle.[24]

In a persuasive essay on *Haroun,* Suchismita Sen focuses on "Rushdie's use of the South Asian variety of English," a language that "evokes a lost childhood for Rushdie and for many of his generation."[25] Characterizing *Haroun* as Rushdie's *Wizard of Oz,*[26] Sen presents several ways in which Rushdie creates an identifiable Indian English (I would argue an urban English reminiscent of Bombay Hindi):

> Despite political opposition from non-Hindi-speaking regions to the language policy, the Bombay film industry has quite successfully spread Hindi to the farthest reaches of the subcontinent. Resistance to Hindi nonetheless remains strong in many parts of the country. As a result of the ambiguous position of Hindi, a typically South Asian variant of English has developed that is highly Indianized in incorporating speech patterns from not only Hindi but also other Indian languages. (660)

A self-professed Bombay cinema lover, Rushdie presents in his English one example of this Indianized variant, albeit—and here I part company from Sen's umbrella term "South Asian"—one of Bombay. Rushdie himself, when commenting on the transcription of his memory of Bombay of the 1950s and 1960s, asserts: "I found myself remembering . . . whole passages of *Bombay* dialogue verbatim"[27] (italics mine). What becomes clear in both *Haroun* and *The Moor* is that only linguistic analysis—of English and the vernaculars— proves adequate for full comprehension of Rushdie's prose. As Ngugi notes, language *is* culture; it carries with it the weight of contextual knowledge, resonances, and nuances that demands close attention to the locale of origin. In fact, the task of the audience is one of decoding the culture-specific material that reverberates within even standard usages of English. "Drive like hell and you will get there," for example, involves not just syntactical gymnastics; to understand the meaning of the passage within *Haroun* requires knowledge of its citation in the Indian context, its enunciative space.

Rushdie describes his process of encoding as illustrative of his migrant condition: "The very word *metaphor,* with its roots in the Greek words for *bear-*

ing across, describes a sort of migration, the migration of ideas into images. Migrants—borne-across humans—are metaphorical beings in their very essence" (*Imaginary Homelands,* 278). His English is thus palimpsestic, the image of one language and culture mapped over another. But to read adequately, then, requires a certain kind of audience, a qualification that opens the work to the possibilities of mistranslation. In Harveen Sachdev Mann's reading of Rushdie's project in *The Satanic Verses,* this is precisely what happened: "migrants remain the primal translated and translating beings" whose multivalent language leaves an opening for potential misinterpretation.[28] Homi Bhabha, who reads *The Satanic Verses* as a book *about* generic cultural translation, points out that in the attempt "to mediate between different cultures, languages and societies, there is always the threat of mistranslation, confusion and fear."[29] Rushdie, a self-acknowledged metropolitan man ("But the fact is that I am a boy who spent his life in gigantic rotting cities. They define me. I know very well that London and Bombay have much more in common with each other than either have with the hinterlands behind them"[30]), aims his translations to an urban bourgeois audience; his blind spot, highlighted in *The Satanic Verses* controversy, was his failure to imagine another audience for his work—the lower-middle-class Muslims of Brick Lane.

These questions of translation and audience are central to the notion of situated hybridity that I use to describe Rushdie's Bombay English. I would argue that Rushdie's own umbrella of a "metropolitan audience" needs to be further honed to an Indian urban audience that would "get" many of the nuances, insider resonances, citations, and other culture-specific material that energize Rushdie's prose. As a heuristic I have divided this culture-specific material into four categories: (1) speech patterns: recognizable colloquialisms, street slang, idiomatic speech, and the like, which draw on several oral registers and the syntax of the Indian vernaculars; (2) simulacric/popular cultural resonances: meanings drawn from context-specific or local collective memories; (3) recoded material: cultural signs from one locale reinterpreted and inserted into another; and (4) citations: "iterable" phrases that require specific cultural and political knowledges. While in the fairy-tale world of *Haroun* this material is deployed to evoke a lost world more fully, in politically astute texts such as *The Moor's Last Sigh,* culture-specific knowledge contains critical insights lost to a more generalized reading. For example, the truck and bus citation in *Haroun* merely flavors Alifbay for nostalgic purposes, but the Nargis reference (which I will explicate in detail) in *The Moor's Last Sigh* enacts a political critique that can be easily missed. Mann argues that Rushdie translates most of the "Eastern" cultural signs for his Western audience (e.g., concepts such as *kathaputhli* or *padyatra*) but fails to do the same with his Western material (e.g., Nietzsche, Red Riding Hood, Punch and Judy). I disagree with this argument because popular cultural signs from the East are *not* always translated (as Vijay Mishra's elaboration of the *Shri 420* subtext of *The*

Satanic Verses shows); the examples Mann seizes on are typically those classical (aesthetic, literary, philosophical) terms an Orientalist scholar would identify as necessary for translation.

I characterize *The Moor's Last Sigh* as the most postmodern of Rushdie's fictions because the central concerns of the novel are a nation's/world's romance with its representation: cinema, painting, popular visual culture, and folklore are at issue, held accountable for political and cultural imaginaries. If there is a community envisaged, it is a group of minority communities, always in danger of being steamrollered by the (Hindu) majority. A family saga of what Rushdie names "our far from ordinary clan" (Portuguese, Jewish, Catholics, and others) unfolds, not allegorically (as in the case of *Midnight's Children*), but it dovetails into the history of the nation.[31]

The narrator's mother, as the figure of the artist, constantly faces the key problem in the novel, which is the problem of representing this "clan" and its "real" stories: "our deepest mysteries usually ended up oils-on-canvas" (13). The central character, the Moor who gives birth to the narrative ("I sigh therefore I am, and I am always short of breath, inadequate to my task"), is finally imprisoned and expelled from his country. His fate is represented in a lost painting—*The Moor's Last Sigh* (which is a kitsch cover for a painting of Aurora, the mother)—of the Sultan Boadbil's expulsion from Granada. Moorist Spain and its moment of disintegration become a mirror for another moment of collapse: the possible decomposition of the Nehruvian secular pluralist India that Aurora bequeaths to her son as "Moloristan." It is no accident that the Moor, who has Jewish and Moorish blood, is a perfect composite of Europe's historical Others. European expulsions and exclusions become the shroud through which we gain a glimpse of India's current political climate. With the rising religious fundamentalisms (and *Hindutva* is Rushdie's primary target here), all plurality and hybridity—all *otherness*—is cleansed from Indian soil through violence. The culminating chapters of the novel record the Bombay bomb blasts:

> Bombay was central: had always been. Just as the financial "Catholic Kings" had besieged Granada and awaited the Alhambra fall, so now barbarism was standing at our gates.... We were both bombers and the bombs. The explosions were our own evil—no need to look for foreign explanations, though there was and is evil beyond our frontiers and within. (372–73)

Responding to the threat of communalism, Salman Rushdie comments in "In Good Faith":

> To be an Indian of my generation was also to be convinced of the vital importance of Jawaharlal Nehru's vision of secular India. Secularism, for India, is simply not a point of view; it is a question of survival. If what Indians call 'communalism,' sectarian religious politics, were allowed to take control of the polity, the results would be too horrifying to imagine....

To be a Bombayite (and afterwards a Londoner) was also to fall in love with the metropolis. The city as a reality and as metaphor is at the heart of all my work. "The modern city," says a character in *The Satanic Verses,* "is the locus classicus of incompatible realities." Well that turned out to be true. "As long as they pass in the night, it's not so bad. But if they meet! It's uranium and plutonium, each makes the other decompose, boom." (*Imaginary Homelands,* 404)

Here, of course, Rushdie is speaking of his own predicament in the face of Islamic fundamentalism; but these observations on sectarian violence and its result in disintegrating the secular urban polity find fictitious rendition in *The Moor's Last Sigh.*

In this novel Rushdie is careful to hide his critique of sectarianism under the central narrative of an artist's tussle with representation. Like the palimpsestic painting of Sultan Boadbil, Bombay's "incompatible realities" exist layer upon layer (as do Rushdie's own hidden critiques): "The city itself, perhaps the whole country, was a palimpsest, Under World beneath Over World, black market beneath white" (184). Palimpsests, with their layered plurality, are the basis of India's "survival." This is most evident when the Hindu fundamentalists "belittle the culture of Indian Islam that lay palimpsest-fashion over the face of Mother India" (299); their claim for the real (essential) India beneath all pluralities found its most virulent manifestation in the tearing down of the Babri Mosque in 1992. For Rushdie this "realness" is an invented essentialism, a claim to origins that Indian history makes impossible; thus, as in *Midnight's Children,* the protagonist's ethnic and religious heritage in *The Moor's Last Sigh* is not only mixed and untraceable but is also obfuscated by lies, stories, and myths. *The Moor's Last Sigh* records the coming of Ram (*local* religious/communal interests taking precedence over national concerns) and RAM (*global* cannibalism represented by a character from *Midnight's Children,* Adam Sinai, of the big "satellite dish-like" ears), both of whom destroy the secularist Nehruvian India.

Aurora in *The Moor's Last Sigh* is at once representative of Mother India—in direct opposition to Nargis's Hindu mythic rendition in the film *Mother India*—and her best historian ("she had put history on the walls," we are told). She is the epic fabulist painter, who takes on a task similar to the narrator in *Midnight's Children,* depicting reality juxtaposed with the imagined (or the "possible," in Sangari's terms). Most eloquent among her paintings of the clan/country is the protean sea-city, Mooristan (land of the Moor/country of *mórs* or peacocks, the national bird of India/place of *amor,* mother-son love):

"Place where worlds collide, flow in and out of one another, and washofy away. Place where an air-man can drowno in water, or else grow gills; where a water-creature can get drunk, but also chokeofy, on air. One universe, one dimension, one country, one dream, bumpo'ing into another, or being under or on top of. Call it Palimpstine. And above it all, in the palace, you." (226)

Annually, and symbolically, Aurora challenges Bombay's most celebrated Hindu Ganapati festival by dancing a pagan elephant dance on the cliffs. She has an erotic relationship with her son, the Moor—one that is duplicated in the cinematic popular imaginary by the Nargis–Sunil Dutt coupling—but the witticism that the "entire country has a mother-son problem" is to be taken seriously: Rushdie suggests that the mother-son symbiosis depicts the central political imaginary of the Indian nation, reaffirmed by cinema and popular culture. What this relationship omits is the real source of power: the father figure. In an increasingly paternalistic India of fundamentalist resurgences and urban mafia, the hidden godfather looms to destroy the political sutures on the imaginary that held the Indian nation together. By bringing these issues of imagination, narration, representation, the social responsibilities of the artist and the historian, to the forefront, Rushdie creates a novel about a *national culture*—its ramparts, possibilities, failures, and evolution—rather than a nation.

The language to narrate adequately this morphing, layered, globally penetrated locale that is Bombay can be only a culturally resonant vernacular, a hybrid Bombay English. Perhaps the easiest markers to identify are speech patterns that deviate from standard written English. Hindi and Urdu syntax molds conversations: "[W]here is the air to breathe?" says one character, instead of the more standard "Where is there any air to breathe?" (23). General Hindi phraseology—"hate me, don't me but," references to "my good-wife," idiomatic expressions such as "wallow-pallow" or "art-shart"—litters the speech of various characters, while specific accents heard among Goan Christians and Anglo-Indians are mouthed by the narrator's family: "shutofy" or "washofy," for instance, are recognizable constructions that mean "will shut up" or "will wash away/out." There are in *The Moor's Last Sigh* very detailed renditions of the English used by particular classes or groups for very definite purposes and in specific contexts. For example, the English of Adam Sinai (renamed and reclaimed as Adam Zogoiby), the representative of the globally oriented corporate managerial class (the "babu" English of the 1990s, in some respects) and the Westernized Bombay sophisticate, is parodied when he attempts to please or impress, a feat that the part jealous, weary narrator characterizes as "a positive tizzy of social-climbing panic":

> Should we go Polynesian at the Oberoi Outrigger? No, no, it was only a buffet luncheon, and one did so appreciate a little fawning. Maybe just a bite at the Taj Sea Lounge? But, on second thoughts, too many old buffers reliving fading glories. How about the Sorryno? Close to home, and a nice view, but darling, how to tolerate that old *groucho* of a proprietor? A quick businesslike in-and-out at an Irani joint—Bombay AI or Pyrke's at Flora Fountain? No, we need less noise, and to talk properly one must be able to *linger*. Chinese, then?—Yes, *impossible* to choose between the Nanking and the Kamling. The Village? All that fake-rustic themeing, baby: *so* passé. (353)

The ease with which Adam drops the ritzy names of the social spaces of rich Bombayites, and the *manner* of his delivery—*the* Nanking versus *an* Irani joint that is ethnically cool but not unique—bespeaks his community. The verbal accentuations on "linger," "impossible," and "passé" imitate the speech rhythms of a type of corporate sophisticate, while the "baby" and "darling" seem to float up from Bombay's glossy magazines and gossip columns, a large part of the city's film-industry–based mass culture.

These community parlances can be understood only when placed in Bhabha's "third space," the performative locus of enunciation outside of which the accents, references, and nuances have little significance. But accented speech is not restricted only to the characters. Sometimes the narrator's humor, disdain, or anguish can be located by decoding specific cultural signs that acquire meaning in relation to each other. For example, the spice factory that belongs to the narrator's family is administered by a "trinity of controllers" whose names are Mr. Elaichipillai Kalonjee, Mr. V. S. Mirchandalchini, and Mr. Karipattam Tejpattam. Any reader familiar with Indian spices will easily catch the silliness in naming the spice factory officers after popular spices such as cardamom (*elaichi*), red chili pepper (*mirch*), cinnamon (*dalchini*), and bay leaves (*tejpatta*) and lesser-known, sometimes region-specific spices such as *karipatta* and *kalonjee*. But more difficult to catch is the regional flavors added to these "names," Sanskritized to sound pompous or officious: the "pattam" in the last name, for instance, marks this gentleman as a South Indian, while the "pillai" and "kalonjee" have definite Parsi connotations. In a cosmopolitan city like Bombay, it is very probable that people from all over India should find work, a fact that becomes a grievance manipulated by politicians of the Hindu right who want to reclaim Maharasthra for the Marathis. The business, family, friends, and artistic community gathered at Malabar Hill—Aurora's little India—are gathered from the heterogeneous India, the India of ethnic, regional, and religious pluralities. The narrator's humorous labeling of the "trinity," therefore, carries a political edge that adds to the plea for secularism made in the novel.

If Rushdie refuses to translate such "Indian" material for his Western audience, he does the same for Western references—and I don't mean globally produced cultural signs but references recognizable to very particular readerships. For instance, Dr. Zeeny Vakil, art critic/doctor and the chief spokesperson for cross-cultural translations in *The Satanic Verses,* in which her book entitled *The Only Good Indian* mounts an attack on authenticity and essentialism, reappears as an art historian once more in *The Moor's Last Sigh.* In the latter, she is the mouthpiece for hybridity as she writes critical works reminiscent of Homi Bhabha—*Imperso-Nation and Dis/Semi/nation: Dialogics of Eclecticism and Interrogations of Authenticity in A.Z.* The title is, of course, Rushdie's parody (note the excessive use of slashes between words) of poststructuralist theory ranging from Barthes to Bhabha. This kind of information might not be readily available to a nonacademic general readership in the Indian metropoles or, arguably, even in Western contexts.

Rushdie's seasoned rampage of what Arjun Appadurai has called the "cultural warehouses" of the postmodern era creates a network of cross-cultural references in the text. He draws cultural signs that exist as simulacric signifiers dislocated from their original context or use, signifiers that would be part of the popular culture and memory of Bombayites. Images or ideas are simply inserted in the prose without explanation or further elucidation, creating an extraordinarily dense and resonant prose. The range of these references is impressive: Hollywood film knowledge (in a city obsessed with commercial film industries) coupled with Indian preferences (the popularity of Audrey Hepburn as a feminine icon) are juxtaposed when "Minnie" (the Moor's sister who becomes a nun) appears at the door looking like "Audrey Hepburn" (211); a mafia boss in a Hindi film is referred to the "godfather, the dada of dadas" (168), "godfather" citing Hollywood and "dada" an Indian colloquialism connoting neighborhood goon ("dada" of the realm); the well-known Indian disdain of Nehru's compulsive speech making finds expression in the name of a dog, "jaw-jaw Jawaharlal," a national-level in-joke; Miltonic phrases soar just as easily when the Moor sees himself "hurled from the garden" (5); Buñuel is implicitly cited when we are told of Vasco Miranda's "spiced-up rehash of the European surrealists" in the latter's short film *Kutta Kashmir Ka,* "a 'Kashmiri'—rather than Andalusian—'Dog' " (148).

More difficult to fully excavate are the cultural signs that Rushdie recodes to fit his Bombay milieu. Take, for example, the character named Jimmy Cashondeliveri, a country-and-eastern singer who marries one of the Moor's sisters. The Moor's mafioso black-marketeer father, Abraham Zogoiby, undercuts the "great [industrial] houses" that previously had their grip on Bombay's and, to a large extent, the nation's financial nerve: "[I]n the mid-Fifties, he made his spectacular takeover of the House of Cashondeliveri," the name part-parodically denoting a Parsi ethnicity (181). Abraham Zogoiby's ousting of the "old Parsi" business networks heralds a new globally oriented financial era and power center for Bombay that, in turn, dislocates one of the "great clan's weakling scions," Jamshedjee Jamibhoy Lifebhoy Cashondeliveri—Jimmy Cash for short. The narrator wryly notes that the irresponsible Jimmy Cash was only too happy to sell his "birthright," "ill-equipped" as he is to shoulder the responsibilities of the business. The decline of old business houses slowly replaced by new corporate and underground structures has an instant resonance with the Parsi name; the name Jamshedjee, in its turn, resonates with that of one of the greatest industrialists (from arguably the most prominent industrial house) in India—Jamshedjee Tata. In this half of the equation, Rushdie draws on contextual knowledge of Bombay's (and India's) history and communities. But in the other half of this quick and dirty portrait, Rushdie borrows just as easily from Western popular cultural references. The fictitious character Jamibhoy Cashondeliveri takes on a stage name that echoes the famed Johnny Cash of country-and-western music, when he starts on a career of country-and-eastern music in none other than Nashville, Tennessee. The carefree, partially on-the-road and at-home-in-the-world image of the country-and-western singer—"yodelling rhinestone cowboys," according to our caustic narrator—acquires a recoded value when it becomes a signifier for this uprooted and economically fallen Parsi boy's angst. The signification of displacement through the country-and-western singer image provides a clear instance of the recoding of contextual knowledge that, of course, depends on one's familiarity with *both* Western (here, American) and Indian culture and history.

To this Jimmy Cash episode is added another unexplained reference drawn from Indian mass culture that perhaps only film buffs would notice. Ina, the sister who marries Jimmy Cash, begins to sing with him on tour: "She, who had become a legend by remaining silent, now opened her mouth and sang," and took the stage name "Gooddy." *Gooddy* is a film starring the actress Jaya Bhaduri, who married the Indian megastar Amitabh Bachchan; the Indian public have often criticized Bachchan for not allowing Bhaduri to reenter the film industry after their marriage. This restriction—which some read as a mark of possessiveness and as an antiquated gender ideology—was anticipated by a film entitled *Abhimann,* in which the two starred together as husband and wife; the husband mistreats the wife, who outclasses him as a singer. After a miscarriage, the wife loses her voice—becomes "silent"—until forgiveness and reconciliation ensue in the end. Ina's stage name, Gooddy, in *The Moor's Last Sigh,* recalls Jaya Bhaduri's memorable screen role (in *Abhimann*) of breaking the silence and bursting into song. At the same time, given the Bachchan-Badhuri contretemps in real life, our attention is drawn to the reality effect of film narratives—a point that Rushdie is at pains to make in this novel. Since Jaya Bhaduri retired early from Bollywood, she remains frozen in cultural memory as young, lovable, and girlish, all qualities that endeared the character Gooddy to the audience when the film came out. These valences all have a bearing on Ina's character and fate in *The Moor's Last Sigh*. Rushdie not only plays with the idea of a cultural memory and the feedback effect of the media in symbolic ways that are clearly identifiable but he nuances the references in a manner that shows just how familiar he was and is with Bombay's culture, gossip, and local stories.

While Rushdie sometimes recodes and inserts cultural signifiers from the world over to tell the story of the Indian context, at other times he depends almost entirely on the reader's knowledge of the Bombay milieu—an act of vernacular resistance that prevents his work from being sold merely as a global commodity disengaged from the milieu of which it speaks. In the evocation of lame pirate Long John Silver from Robert Louis Stevenson's adventure fiction *Treasure Island,* in the one-legged character Lambijan Chandiwala (whose name translates into Long John Silverfellow, as Rushdie explains), we are offered an instance of a Western signifier reinterpreted for the Indian context; yet the particularities of Lambajan's role and function in the novel are completely dependent on our comprehension of Hindi slang, Bombay's indigenous religious festivals, and the myth making of the local Hindu fundamentalists. Lambajan, referred to as "our personal pirate" by Aurora, who furnishes the former with a parrot to make her Westernized myth complete, is the gatekeeper for the Zogoiby family. As gatekeeper he guards the "treasure" Aurora, who embodies secular pluralistic India, the India of magic and palimpsests. Stevenson's adventure, colonial fiction, is woven into the fabric of Indian storytelling; the narrative of search, betrayal, and loss is recoded to fit the young Moor boy's imaginative Indian landscape, for the Moor will pursue that lost treasure, Aurora, and immortalize her until his (asthmatic) last breath.

While this Western allusion provides one key to reading Lambajan, the complex weave of Bombay references can be further decoded by the vigilant reader. Lambajan exerts a fascination for the adolescent Moor, for he tells legendary tales of an older India. The Elephanta caves, renowned for ancient cave paintings, are Lambajan's other treasure island:

> "Once in that place there were elephant kings, baba," he confided. "Why do you think-so god Ganesha is popular in Bombay City? It is because in the days before men there were elephants sitting on thrones and arguing philosophy, and it was the monkeys who were their servants. It is said that when men first came to Elephanta Island in the days after the elephants' fall they found statues of mammoths higher than the Qutub Minar in Delhi, and they were so afraid that they smashed up the whole lot." (127–28)

That this other world, a mythic India, threatened men who knew the Qutub Minar indicates that Lambajan is speaking of a precolonial (perhaps Hindu) India. Bombay's indigenous Hindu traditions derive from this earlier time, but the monuments ("statues of mammoths") that testify to that mythic Hindu past are effaced by the Muslim conquerors. Here the narrative about Ramjanmabhoomi (the birthplace of Ram where the Muslim Babri Masjid once stood) in the contemporary Hindu right's political imaginary is shown up for precisely what it is: a tall tale. For Lambajan is the myth maker whose precious tales are stolen, reappropriated, by the Hindu right to attack the Muslim conquests of India. This assumed knowledge of all-Indian cultural politics is then given a local twist, for Lambajan gives us an interesting detail: the "monkeys" are "servants" of the elephants. Northern Indian Hindu fundamentalist traditions often celebrate the monkey-god, Hanuman, who fought for Ram in the epic *Ramayana,* while Bombay's most popular Hindu festival invokes Ganesha, the elephant-god. Lambajan is therefore claiming a Hindu fundamentalist harnessing of traditions specific to Bombay. To this complex fabric is added the relationship of Aurora and Lambajan's parrot,

Totah, who screams "Peesay—saféd—hathi!"—a verbal echo of Stevenson's "pieces of eight," which Aurora fails to teach the recalcitrant Totah; "peesay—saféd—hathi" translates as "mashed white elephants," perhaps indicating Totah's cultural memory of the death of elephants and the smashed monuments on Elephanta Island.

More interesting is that Aurora, while dancing on the cliffs during the Ganapati festival, plunges to her death screaming "mashed white elephants" (127). The suggestion here is that Aurora understands the "stupid" parrot's cultural memory at the moment of her own death—the memory of a lost time, a secular/magical India that she has both represented and valorized in her art. Equally pertinent to this nexus of meaning is Totah's reluctance to learn the Anglo version of "pieces of eight" and his Hindization of the line; while this could be a reference to a pre-Anglicized India, it also resonates with the Shiv Sena's Hindu fundamentalist rejection of English as the language of political struggle. That Totah's words can signify a Hindu fundamentalist cultural agenda points to the Hindu right's renarrativization and appropriation of a precolonial past. Finally, Totah's line becomes prophetic when pagan, secular, magical India (Aurora) is "mashed" by the power of a newly designed elephant, the organized Hindu majority (87). Communalism will end the Moor's world and text, but until then this "yarn" becomes Rushdie's lament for the old secular India, imagined and constructed in the colonial past. Once again, Rushdie's palimpsestine swings at the religious right can be identified only when the reader can decode and recode cultural meanings specific to his regional milieu.

Another set of long and involved recodings is drawn from the world of Indian art and painting; although impossible to recount here, these are fairly important in a novel about artists, their relationships to their work, and the role of representation in the political life of a nation. The various stages in Aurora's career as a painter—realism, abstract art, folk murals—roughly follow developments in the history of Indian painting.[32] The exhibition, distribution, and consumption of Aurora's art is also taken up as an issue since mass, folk, and popular and high art designations come under Rushdie's perusal in their varying roles of creating viable national representations. As Abraham Zogoiby—the man with a finger on the pulse of Bombay's underworld—scornfully notes: " 'You art-wallahs.' . . . 'Always so certain of your impact. Since when do the masses come to such shows?' " (131). In reading Rushdie's excursions into the Indian art world, one encounters the last category of cultural specificity: citations that, when taken out of their original context and inserted into another, begin to function as critical commentaries on Indian public spheres.

Clearly, aside from the political critiques, one of the projects of *The Moor's Last Sigh* is to explore the extent to which the artist bears some degree of *responsibility* in generating political imaginaries and symbolic products that stimulate vibrant public debates and discussions; for without critical counterpoints, majority rule—the flap-eared herd—simply extinguishes all democratic possibilities. The involved citations in *The Moor's Last Sigh* create a conversation/argument about national art, culture, and politics, particularly the relationships between mass, folk, popular, and high cultures. Mass-produced cultural forms that mediate dominant ideologies—for instance, the Hindu mythifications in *Mother India*—are definitely dangerous when they are the *only* representations of the nation. Ashish Nandy's characterizations of the various categories of postindependent Indian national culture are particularly useful in understanding Rushdie's complicated argument about bourgeois art that, for Rushdie, bears the responsibility for maintaining a critical democracy.[33] Nandy differentiates between "folk" culture as artisan, nonmodern cultures and "mass" culture referring to urban mass-produced forms that serve dominant ideologies and political interests—a culture that imitates western/"universal" mass culture and rejects middle-class, highbrow links to classical culture. "Popular" culture, in this scenario, is the creative output of the *haut bourgeois* or the urban middle-class who have enormous "economic muscle" and a "huge pool of professional skills" (196); this class—exemplified by a Tagore, or a Satyajit Ray, or an Amrita Sher Gil—"mediates" classical traditions and the old colonial culture for the more "low-brow" mass cultural realm; Nandy pithily sums up the distinction between mass and popular as the differences between "calendar art" and the art of "Ravi Verma." Popular culture, in its accessibility and historical vanguardist political status, can offer alternatives to mass culture while partially funneling and diffusing the complexities of high art.

Aurora, who paints lively pan-Indian murals (and styles herself as Ravi Verma in the Chipkali paintings), is the bourgeois artist from a business family with political connections. She is deeply critical of commercial Bombay movies: her bitchy interchange with Nargis, the actress who plays Mother India in the film of the same name and later (in her career) becomes a member of parliament, marks her dislike for those who serve dominant political interests. An acknowledgment of Bombay's Hindi film industry as the factory for the nation's major cultural and political imaginaries is integral to any discussion of Indian cultural politics. Cinema is also—as the overdetermined rivalry between Aurora and Nargis indicates—painting's visual other. Aurora's tumultuous life-filled murals invoke the active visual language of cinema rather than the more traditional histories of painting. Her competition, Nargis—"mother" and "India"—is brought into the text much later when Aurora weighs her ability to represent India, struggling with the trend set by her realist predecessors:

> The great Bengali film director Sukumar Sen, Aurora's friend and, of all her contemporaries, perhaps her only artistic equal, was the best of these realists, and in a series of haunting, humane films brought to Indian cinema—Indian cinema, that raddled old tart!—a fusion of heart and mind that went a long

way towards justifying his aesthetic. Yet these realist movies were never popular—in a moment of bitter irony attacked by Nargis, Mother India herself, for their Westernised élitism—and Vasco (openly) and Aurora (secretly) preferred the series of films for children in which Sen let his fantasy rip, in which fish talked, carpets flew and young boys dreamed of previous incarnations in fortresses of gold. (173)

I would argue that the citation of Nargis's remark about "Sukumar Sen" is the cornerstone for understanding Rushdie's larger argument about national culture in this passage. To begin with, the film director here is, of course, Satyajit Ray, who is best known for his realistic *Apu Trilogy,* films that remain defining moments for Indian "art cinema." Ray was also well loved in Bengal for his role as author of children's fiction written in the vernacular, a role in which he was no longer the elite artist but a popular writer whose stories informed every childhood. Ray's fabulous films, the ones that Aurora "secretly" liked, such as *Goopi Gyne, Bagha Byne* (in which carpets fly), and *Sonar Khella* (in which young boys dream of previous incarnations), are based on his own stories written for children and young adults. These films remain less known outside of Bengal mostly because of their culture-specific humor, depictions of familial relationships, and prototypical local characters; therefore these films are constructed in a cinematic vernacular that reaches few universal registers.[34] Perhaps it is this vernacularism that attracts Aurora, who yearns to harness popular representations; she is drawn to particularities that make up the myriad Mooristan that is her India rather than universal stories. Moreover, in her vision, India is hyperbole and excess and thus best captured in fantastic and epic dimensions. The name "Sukumar Sen" is also no accident, for it sutures two other popular cultural figures in Bengal: Ray's father, Sukumar Ray, most famous as a poet of nonsense verse, and the other great Bengali director (often regarded as Ray's antithesis), Mrinal Sen, whose politicized "art cinema" continues to mediate popular Bengali Marxist sentiments.[35] Aurora's "equal," then, constitutes a composite of three luminaries who greatly influenced, even fashioned, the Bengali cultural imaginary; her evocation of this composite marks her desire to influence the cultural imaginary of her own community.

The comment on Nargis in this passage refers to a now infamous remark made by the actress that Ray's films should not be considered the best of Indian cinema, as their realism exhibited and exposed India's poverty to the world.[36] The "bitter irony" of Nargis's nationalistic prescription inheres in the fact that Ray's films put Indian cinema on par with Western art cinema, acquiring critical acclaim for his country. Aurora's reinvocation of Nargis functions as a certain kind of self-fashioning: she remains the artist who paints with a commitment and passion unadulterated by political agendas (the politics of global markets and the nation's images exchanged there).

The specific speech patterns, cultural resonances, recodage, and citationality of Rushdie's prose require contextual knowledge without which much of the political critique is effaced.[37] Rushdie's English, in which "pieces of eight" become the politically relevant "peesay—saféd—hathi," is bent and nuanced to carry a local, urban, and specific cultural and political memory. When one has to research actively every context-specific reference, the novel becomes a prodigious text, leading to standard response in the Western press, such as James Wood's dismissive description of *The Moor's Last Sigh* as "a little sickening" in the *Guardian* (September 1995).[38] This emphasis on contextual knowledges solicits the question of how to read Rushdie: do we read him for his highly patterned literary and philosophical allusions? Or do we read him as a down-to-earth critic of his localized milieu through the manipulation of cultural and political resonances in his prose? The second characterization remains partly hidden within the sophisticated folds of the first, perhaps an intentional strategy for a man whose project was once read as too unequivocal.

Modernist Aporias, Postmodern Vernaculars

Midnight's Children, critically hailed as the progenitor of the New Indian novel in English, features the multivalent English that is characteristic of the vernacular English languages that I examine here. Rushdie has been touted as the Indian postmodern, but I would argue that he is a cusp figure in the evolution of the New Indian novel. Certainly his vision is a modernist one, tied to a clear world-text divide[39] and to a linguistic project. In a PBS interview on 14 August 1997, he spoke of India as a fount of inspiration, a "cornucopia," the "horn of plenty" whose "inexhaustible" abundance cannot ever be absorbed by a set of narratives. In spite of realizing the possibility of failure, Rushdie professes to take on "the whole damn thing,"[40] an attempt that is aptly captured in Kumkum Sangari's description of *Midnight's Children:* "Running aground on the shoals of parody and allegory, he scarcely uses his freedom as a professed fabulist. The totalizing potential of his chosen form cohabits uneasily with the modernist epistemology of a fragment, the specific perspectivism of the bourgeois subject."[41] It is the uneasiness of form that moves Rushdie into the realm of the postmodern. Even while he vacillates between the modern and postmodern in terms of form and vision, Rushdie's use of language has been consistently postmodern—a situated hybrid English that escapes all "purity" or universality. Rushdie claims new ground for Indian English in his early essay " 'Commonwealth Literature' Does Not Exist": "What seems to be happening is that those people who were once colonized by the language are now rapidly remaking it, domesticating it, becoming more and more relaxed about they way they use it—assisted by the English language's enormous flexibility and size, they are carving out large territories for themselves within its frontiers" (*Imaginary Homelands,* 64).

It is disappointing, then, that the writer who engages with global-local India with vigor, if not ferocity, should claim in his introductory piece in the *New Yorker:*

> This [the ironic conclusion] is it: The prose writing—both fiction and non-fiction—created in this period by Indian writers working in English is proving to be a stronger and more important body of work than most of what has been produced in the eighteen "recognized" languages of India, the so-called Indian "vernacular languages," during the same time; and, indeed, this new and still burgeoning "Indo-Anglian" literature represents perhaps the most valuable contribution India has yet made to the world of books.[42]

Again the unbridgeable gap: the "Indo-Anglian" versus the vernacular traditions. The reactionary edge to this piece becomes evident when one looks back at Rushdie's earlier balanced defense of Indian literatures in " 'Commonwealth Literature' ": "It is worth saying that major work is being done in India in many languages other than English; yet . . . the Indo-Anglians seize all the limelight" (69). In fact, in this earlier piece, Rushdie acknowledges the logical problems of positioning English in opposition to the vernaculars for three reasons: he points to the fact that English as a foreign tongue has resonance for the older generation of Indo-Anglians, the children of independent India using it as "an Indian language" (64); that the friction over languages in India has more to do with the debate of Hindi versus other Indian languages than with a conflict over English; and that Mulk Raj Anand and other writers writing from India probably have more in common with vernacular writers than a diasporic *litterateur* like himself. In light of these assertions, the *New Yorker* essay is quite a volte-face—perhaps the result of Rushdie's self-professed vulnerability to critics, especially postcolonial critics who had taken him to task for becoming the signifier of free speech after the *Satanic Verses* controversy. Rushdie's awareness of his critics finds voice in the latter piece: "There is a whiff of political correctness about them: the ironic proposition that India's best writing since independence may have been done in the language of the imperialists is simply too much for some folks to bear. It ought not to be true, and so must not be permitted" (54). Here Rushdie cleverly clears his critical ground, for to be up in arms about Indian vernacular literatures and their merit can now easily be shrugged off as simply chauvinistic. It is precisely the gesture toward authenticity—the modernist reclaiming of India-in-the-vernacular—that Rushdie hopes to foreclose by his delight over such a postmodern "ironic" suggestion. Yet his own logic of contestation between "English" and the "vernaculars" smacks of a similar closed modernist paradigm leading to, as I have suggested, critical and aesthetic aporias. And of course, predictably, his comments caused much furor in India, as Arundhati Roy reported in a recent interview; even though she falls into the literary set privileged by Rushdie, she marked her distance from his evaluations by labeling them as "unnecessary."[43]

Even in a quick read through the article, the reader can easily pick up the revealing aside that marks Rushdie's own limited—perhaps even impoverished—reading in the Indian vernacular literatures: "Admittedly, I did my reading in English, and there has long been a genuine problem of translation in India" (52). So the "contribution" is only to the *English-speaking* "world of books," a recognition that reiterates the bourgeois worldview of the metropolitan colonized. The "canon" of vernacular writers that Rushdie lists as important—and in the PBS interview he makes the distinction between "serious" writers with "linguistic projects" (another modernist touch) versus other writers—includes mostly older writers or translated writers in the vernacular traditions.

Perhaps the stringency of Rushdie's claims in the *New Yorker* piece stems from his reaction to critical discourse on the Indian novel in English that has often valorized the vernacular literatures for their "authentic" depictions of India. Meenakshi Mukherjee, a veteran critic of the Indian novel in English, observes that there seems always to be an "anxiety of Indianess" in the novel in English, a sensibility not integral to prose fiction in the Indian vernaculars (the *bhasha* novels). Writers in English always create a unified imaginative topos out of Indian heterogeneity, while *bhasha* writers are more tuned to local and regional specificities. Thus Malgudi in R. K. Narayan's work is pan-Indian, eternal and immutable, Kanthapura an allegory and legend. But Lohri, in Mahasweta Devi's Bengali story "Rudali," is geopolitically located at the precise intersection of Chotanagpur-Ranchi, Palamau and Sargiya, and this is "not a gratuitous piece of information" (2608). In Indian English texts, Mukherjee notes a "greater pull toward a homogenisation of reality" and a "certain flattening out of the complicated and conflicting contours" (2608). Perhaps, she concludes, English has fewer registers than the vernaculars that draw on folktales, films, riddles, nonsense verse, nursery rhymes, slogans, and street-corner culture. Moreover, the novel in English must be read in terms of the nation-building project; the writers attempt to create a "field of unified meanings and symbols" connected with national life.[44]

It is certainly true that English continues to be the language of power and privilege in India. But I would argue that the cultural anxiety that Mukherjee locates in the Indian novel in English, the essentializing and homogenizing gestures she reads there, describe the genre between 1930 and 1980—a time span that corresponds to the Nehruvian vision of a modern progressive India when there was a dire need to establish common national registers and field of communication. R. K. Narayan, Mulk Raj Anand, Raja Rao, Kamala Markandaya, and Anita Desai all fit Mukherjee's paradigm. In post-Emergency postmodern India, the new novelists do not even attempt to capture the whole Indian reality. Arundhati Roy, whose recent novel *The God of Small Things* (1997) has received international critical acclaim, insists that her subject is the "practice of everyday life"—for instance, she devotes a whole chapter to the experience of being caught at a traffic light.[45] Unlike Rushdie, hers is not a "linguistic project": "You can't just say, 'This language is more important.' Why should that be? There is no one language that can claim to represent all of India, but there are stories. . . . If no one else, at least writers must believe that they govern language."[46]

Roy claims to dream in English, and her novel intersperses English with untranslated Malayalam, an idiomatic mix that has—to return to Mukherjee—a very specific regional location in India. This insistence on vernacular English languages that we see in the New Indian novel, then, finally overcomes the political aporia generated by the modernist oppositions of English and the vernaculars: a failure to imagine an adequate medium of expression for a diverse nation that escapes both vernacular (because of its regional locus) and English (because of its history and global status) depictions. One hopes that Rushdie, a writer whose energetic and vibrant use of English galvanized a new beginning for Indian writing in English, will take heart from this new generation, that he will move away from defensive stances and critical aporias to claim his place in an emergent tradition of Indian vernaculars.

Notes

1. James Wood, "An Indelicate Balance," *New Republic* 29 (December 1997): 32.
2. Homi Bhabha explicates the "third space of enunciation" most clearly in his essay "The Commitment to Theory," in *Location of Cultures* (New York: Routledge, 1994), 19–39. As I will explain later in this essay, he is referring to the "performance" of hybridity that circumvents the identification of stable hybrids.
3. Kwame Appiah, "Is the Post- in Postmodernism the Post- in Postcolonial?" *Critical Inquiry* 17, no. 2 (1991): 41–72.
4. Vijay Mishra and Bob Hodge, "What Is Post-Colonialism?," *Textual Practice* 5, no. 3 (1991): 399–414.
5. Deepika Bahri, Anne McClintock, Ella Shohat, Arif Dirlik (1994), Gayatri Spivak (1991), and others are unified in their commitment to rescuing the category "postcolonial" from becoming a historical abstraction that overlooks contemporary power axes. The "postcolonial" skews temporality by encapsulating everything that came before the colonial period into the blandly utopian "precolonial"; only artifacts that contain whiffs of colonial contamination are subject to avid scrutiny. See Deepika Bahri, "Coming to Terms with the 'Postcolonial,'" in *Between the Lines: South Asians and Postcoloniality,* ed. Deepika Bahri and Mary Vasudeva (Philadelphia: Temple University Press, 1996), 137–66; Anne McClintock, "The Angel of Progress: The Pitfalls of the Term 'Post-Colonial,' " *Social Text* 31–32 (1992): 84–98; Ella Shohat, "Notes on the Post-Colonial," *Social Text* 31–32 (1992): 99–113; Arif Dirlik, "The Postcolonial Aura: Third-World Criticism in the Age of Global Capitalism," *Critical Inquiry* 20 (Winter 1994): 328–56; Gayatri Spivak, *Outside in the Teaching Machine* (New York: Routledge, 1993).
6. A critical evaluation of this perceived globalization that has created new political and cultural terrains has been central to any analysis of postmodernism. In the case of India, a

globalized media interpenetrating the (so far) state-run Doordarshan (television) beams messages of conspicuous consumption to remote villages, and people in the survival sector dream of washing machines and microwaves. Meenakshi Mukherjee, in "The Anxiety of Indianess: Our Novels in English," *Economic and Political Weekly* (27 November 1993):2607–11, notes that there is a cultural amnesia generated by the infiltration of STAR TV, MTV, and CNN into homes, obliterating local and regional cultures unless they are brought back as "planned authenticities" or the "exportable ethnic." For a further analysis of global interpenetration in the Indian context, see Bishnupriya Ghosh and Bhaskar Sarkar, "Diaspora and Postmodern Fecundity," *Communicare* 16, no. 1 (June 1997): 19–48.

7. Kumkum Sangari, "The Politics of the Possible," *Cultural Critique* (Fall 1987): 157–86.

8. Gauri Viswanathan, *Masks of Conquest: Literary Study and British Rule in India* (New York: Columbia University Press, 1989), 437. Terry Eagleton, in *Literary Theory: An Introduction* (Minneapolis: University of Minnesota Press, 1983), made a similar argument about the political use of English literature by showing how the discipline was deployed to tame and sublimate the "philistine" commercial middle classes of Victorian industrial England.

9. Simon During, in "Waiting for the Post: Some Relations between Modernity, Colonization, and Writing," in *Past the Last Post: Theorizing Post-Colonialism and Post-Modernism*, ed. Ian Adams and Helen Tiffin (Calgary, Canada: University of Calgary Press, 1990), 23–45, makes an interesting point about India's entry into the English linguistic realm. He argues that the use of secular print languages in the discourses of nation spelled the inevitable death of nation, as the nation-signifier became simulacric and transmittable and transferable across nations. Diasporic communities that parley these signifiers are the first signs of postmodern nationhood; the use of English in the Indian context carries with it a similar "death" in transmitting India to many elsewheres.

10. For more on third world–first world relations of publishing, distribution, academic, and critical contexts see Philip Altbach, "Education and NeoColonialism," *Teacher's College Record* 72, no. 1 (May 1971): 454.

11. Hodge and Mishra suggest vernacular use as an oppositional strategy. This is a common proposition made even by critics like Meenakshi Mukherjee, most of whose work has been on the Indian novel in English; Mukherjee asks us to "interrogate the loss of the mother tongue" in our perusal of Indian use of English.

12. Quoted in Aparna Dharwadkar and Vinay Dharwadkar, "Language, Identity, and Nation in Postcolonial Indian Literature," in *English Postcoloniality: Literatures from around the World*, ed. Radhika Moharam and Gita Rajan (Westport, Conn.: Greenwood Press, 1996), 89–106.

13. Ibid., 92.

14. Ibid., 93.

15. Having abandoned English after 1978 for his mother tongue, Gikuyu, Ngugi wa Thiong'o, in *Decolonising the Mind: The Politics of Language in African Literature* (London: James Currey, 1986), emphasizes the need for a "language of struggle, of transformation in our societies." All page references here refer to the excerpt reprinted in *Colonial Discourse, Postcolonial Theory*, ed. Laura Chrisman and Patrick Williams (New York: Routledge, 1994), 435–55.

16. Chinua Achebe, "The African Writer in English," in *Colonial Discourse, Postcolonial Theory*, 430.

17. Wole Soyinka, "Neo-Tarzanism: The Poetics of Pseudo-Tradition," in *Art, Dialogue, and Outrage: Essays on Literature and Culture* (New York: Pantheon, 1994), 293–305.

18. Arundhati Roy, interview on PBS that also featured Rushdie, 14 August 1997.

19. Pnina Werbner, "Introduction: The Dialectics of Cultural Hybridity," in *Debating Cultural Hybridities: Multi-Cultural Identities and the Politics of Anti-Racism*, ed. Pnina Werbner and Tariq Modood (London: Zed Books, 1997). In defining modernist conceptions of hybridity, Werbner refers specifically to Claude Lévi-Strauss, *Structural Anthropology*, trans. C. Porter (Lon-

don: Harvester Wheatsheaf, 1963), and Victor Turner, *The Forest of Symbols: Aspects of Ndembu Ritual* (Ithaca, N.Y.: Cornell University Press, 1967) and *Dramas, Fields, Metaphors: Symbolic Action in Human Society* (Ithaca, N.Y.: Cornell University Press, 1974). Besides Bhabha, another major theorist of hybridity whose work has some bearing on the question of modernist and postmodernist hybridities is Robert Young, *Colonial Desire: Hybridity in Theory, Culture, and Race* (London: Routledge, 1995).

20. Jonathan Friedman, "Global Crises, the Struggle for Cultural Identity, and Intellectual Pork-barrelling," in Werbner ed. (1997): 71.

21. Raja Rao, foreword to *Kanthapura* (Bombay: New Directions, 1963).

22. See Bhabha, "The Commitment to Theory" and other essays in which he has addressed this question (such as "The Other Question" and "Signs Taken for Wonders") in *Location of Cultures*.

23. Editor's introduction to G. V. Desani, *All About H. Hatterr* (1948; reprint, London: Mcpherson & Company Publishers, 1970). All citations of Desani refer to the 1970 edition. Desani, according to Rushdie (see Rushdie, "The Empire Writes Back with Vengeance," the *Times* (London), 3 July 1983), "showed how English could be bent and kneaded until it spoke in an authentically Indian voice"; he further claims Hatterr to be "the first great stroke of the decolonizing pen." As will become clear later, I part company with Rushdie's modernist characterizations of the hybrid and the authentic indicated in this comment.

24. See interview in "Keeping Up with Salman," *New York Times Book Review* (28 March 1991): 33.

25. Suchismita Sen, "Memory, Language, and Society in Salman Rushdie's *Haroun*," *Contemporary Literature* 36, no. 4 (1995): 654–75; quote is from p. 655.

26. Here Sen is literally quoting Rushdie on *Haroun*. In a small booklet published by the British Film Institute, Rushdie describes how this film affected his career: "When I first saw *The Wizard of Oz* it made a writer of me. Many years later, I began to devise the yarn that eventually became *Haroun and the Sea of Stories,* and felt strongly that if I could strike the right note it should be possible to write the tale in such a way as to make it of interest to adults as well as children; or, to use the phrase beloved of blurbists, to 'children from seven to seventy' " (qtd. in Sen, 662).

27. Salman Rushdie, *Imaginary Homelands: Essays and Criticisms, 1981–1991* (London: Granta Books, 1991), 11; hereafter cited in the text as *Imaginary Homelands*.

28. Harveen Sachdev Mann, " 'Being borne across': Translation and Salman Rushdie's *The Satanic Verses*," *Criticism* 37 (Spring 1995): 281–308.

29. Mann, 288. Bhabha addresses this question of translation and audience in "Culture's In-between," *Artforum* 32 (September 1993): 167–68.

30. "Keeping Up with Salman," 32.

31. Salman Rushdie, *The Moor's Last Sigh* (New York: Pantheon Books, 1995); hereafter cited in the text as *The Moor*.

32. Note that the cover for the 1995 hardback edition (Pantheon Books) carries a cave painting, possibly drawn from the Ajanta caves, a clue to the central subjects of the work.

33. Ashish Nandy, "An Intelligent Critic's Guide to Indian Cinema," in *The Savage Freud and Other Essays on Possible and Retrievable Selves* (Princeton, N.J.: Princeton University Press, 1995), 196–236.

34. Some clues to Rushdie's situating of Ray and "art cinema" can be found in his essay on Satyajit Ray in *Imaginary Homelands*. There he mentions Ray's "fabulous" films that were not successful outside of India—"they failed to attract the plaudits accorded to his more realist films" (111).

35. In the same essay on Ray alluded to in note 34, Rushdie remarks on his own fascination (doubling Aurora in *The Moor's Last Sigh*) for Ray's vein of fantasy: "Ray came from a family of fantasists, creators of nonsense verse and fabulous hybrid animals," a reference to Sen, 111.

36. In the essay on Ray, Rushdie actually quotes the Nargis interview in which she complains of Ray's ambition for awards, leading to his presenting to the West an image of India that they already had—an "abject" India (108–9). When the interviewer asks her what characterizes the "modern" India that she would rather have on-screen, she replies vaguely, "[D]ams . . ."; this last comment is sardonically produced verbatim in an earlier reference to Nargis in *The Moor's Last Sigh*. Rushdie goes on to comment on the Nargis-Ray interchange as a clash between the old intellectual traditions of Calcutta and the brash urban mass culture of that "bitch-city," Bombay.

37. S. Aravamudan's analysis of the 420 motif in *The Satanic Verses* shows how Rushdie deploys that reference to effect a critique of Islam; Aravamudan, "Salman Rushdie's *The Satanic Verses*," *Diacritics* 19, no. 2 (Summer 1989): 3–20.

38. James Wood, "Tales from the Lost City," *Guardian* 8 September 1995, 5.

39. Salman Rushdie, "Outside the Whale," *Granta* 11 (1984): 125–38.

40. Rushdie further explains himself: "Anyway, I'm a boy from a big country, and there's a part of me that's always hankering for a big country around me, not a small island" ("Keeping Up with Salman," 29.

41. Sangari, 264.

42. Salman Rushdie, "Damme, this is the Oriental scene for you!," *New Yorker* (23 June 1997): 50.

43. Adrienne Johnson, "India Ink" [interview with Arundhati Roy], *Los Angeles Times,* 19 August 1997, E3–4.

44. Mukherjee cites Aijaz Ahmad's analyses in *In Theory: Classes, Nations, Literatures* (London: Verso, 1992); Ahmad argues that English is the language of bourgeois civility and literary sophistication. In such a scenario, the recuperation of the local and traditional becomes, for Mukherjee, the "exportable ethnic" cannibalized by a globalized language of capital. She acknowledges the language debate, pleading for critical attention to the Indian novel in English in a backhanded way: if English instigates the loss of the mother tongue, then we should interrogate the reasons for and the terms of that loss—not throw out the baby with the bathwater. Interestingly enough, she dismisses an attempt on the part of a literary magazine in the vernacular—*Desh*—to praise the new Indian writing in English as a certain chauvinism: since many of the new writers in English are Bengali, *Desh,* the magazine of the Bengali literary establishment, valorizes this new writing, forgetting old enmities.

45. Johnson, E3.

46. Ibid., E4.

The Moor's Last Sigh and India's National Bourgeoisie: Reading Rushdie through Frantz Fanon

Farhad B. Idris

Like Salman Rushdie's other novels about India, *The Moor's Last Sigh* offers a narrative that maneuvers in and out of the country's political history. *The Moor's Last Sigh,* in fact, does more—it has a lot to say about the economy of postcolonial India; no less significant is its critique of India's culture, especially the film industry. The characters in this work represent the different spheres of national life that combine to make contemporary India. Their destiny thus parallels India's as a nation, which in turn becomes the sum and consequence of their action. The future they create for India derives from a paradigm of conduct that Frantz Fanon outlines in his discussion of the national bourgeoisie in *The Wretched of the Earth.* Although Fanon's focus is on decolonizing African nations, his analysis applies well to decolonized India, particularly to its bourgeois capitalists who grow intensely active after India's independence. It is true that India, with its more developed commerce, industry, and infrastructure, does not fully resemble a newly independent African nation. Still, Fanon's observation that the national bourgeoisie plays a detrimental role in the development of a decolonized country can be seen also in India. Reading Rushdie's novel in light of Fanon's study of the ills a decolonized country is prone to thus helps explain some of the complex causes of India's failure to realize the potential independence promised decades ago.

Events in *The Moor's Last Sigh* center on the rise and fall of the Zogoiby family. Members of a Jewish community who emigrated to India from Spain way back in late fifteenth century, the Zogoibys fell on hard times over the centuries but have begun to thrive phenomenally in the wake of India's decolonization. Abraham Zogoiby plays his cards right and becomes the owner of a lucrative spice business soon before independence by marrying the heiress of a century-old spice trading house in Cochin. Ambitious and aggres-

---

This essay was written specifically for this volume and is published for the first time by permission of the author.

sive, Abraham multiplies his wealth many times over in decolonized India by shrewd speculation, ruthless elimination of all rivals, and a series of criminal financial dealings. Especially when read through Fanon, Abraham can be seen as representative of the rising class of bourgeois capitalists in postcolonial India. Indeed, Rushdie implies that many of India's postindependence plights can be attributed directly to this class.

In Abraham, Rushdie portrays the ultimate decolonized bourgeois who stops at nothing, brooks no opposition, in his effort to realize his ambition, the end of which is nothing short of being "God in Paradise . . . *YHWH. I am that I am*" (author's emphasis).[1] In 1945, Abraham moves from Cochin, the old imperial trade point founded by the Portuguese, to Bombay, the hub of modern commercial activity in India, because he is aware that the center of business is about to shift upon decolonization.[2] Built by the British, Bombay too has its imperial past, but unlike Cochin, it is quick to adapt to the demands of the new bourgeois economy, a process that in fact has started well before independence. Abraham uses his Jewish link to gain an audience with one of the few men who control all business in this city of opportunity and learns, to his dismay, that though " '[t]he country may be about to become free, . . . Bombay is a closed town' " (180). The old bourgeoisie who have been serving the imperial power oppose his entry to their club, but Abraham not only invades it, he rules a sizable portion of it about 15 years later.

This meteoric rise of Abraham as the financial overlord of Bombay occurs from his prior understanding of the shapes decolonized India's politics and economy are likely to assume. He expends considerable time and effort to comprehend the economic situation that will arise in the wake of British departure. Aware that he is operating in a vacuum and competing against declining powers, he sets out to learn the weaknesses of his rivals. His takeover of the House of Cashondeliveri, a financial institution with extensive and diversified holdings, succeeds because he knows that "the old Parsi family at its heart was in a state of terminal decline" (181). The transition of power from imperial era to more modern bourgeois times signals a shift, indicating that India is finally making an attempt at bourgeoisification, that a new force is emerging in the nation.[3]

Unlike the European bourgeoisie, however, the new postcolonial bourgeois class comes to power not through a long process of economic, political, and cultural revolution but through a process of mimicry and replacement in which the Indian bourgeoisie have been carefully prepared to step into the shoes of their colonial predecessors. The situation is typical of the process of decolonization, as Fanon explains:

> The national middle class which takes over power at the end of a colonial regime is an underdeveloped middle class. It has practically no economic power, and in any case it is in no way commensurate with the bourgeoisie of the mother country which it hopes to replace.[4]

Granted, Abraham does exhibit a flair for industrial entrepreneurship, suggesting that he likes to compete with the West. One product that he officially manufactures is "Baby Softo," a talcum powder. He takes great pride in his work and describes the product's marketability in patriotic terms, "characterising India as the one Third World Economy capable of rivaling the First World in its sophistication and growth, without necessarily becoming enslaved by the almighty US dollar" (183). But the seemingly promising business turns out to be merely a front for covert drug shipments, whose origin and destination remain unknown; it is a smuggling operation on a huge scale whose details Abraham guards as one of his deepest and most closely held secrets. The genuine innovation typical of the bourgeoisie during their revolutionary rise to power in Europe is completely missing in what Abraham does, which vindicates Fanon's assertion that "In underdeveloped countries . . . no true bourgeoisie exists; there is only a sort of little greedy caste, avid and voracious, with the mind of a huckster. . . . [I]t becomes not even the replica of Europe, but its caricature" (*WE,* 175).

Within a few years after India's independence, Abraham has amassed wealth no other can match by hiding his shady, sinister dealings behind legitimate business operations. Like the Baby Softo endeavor, most of his businesses are just facades for his unlawful moneymaking activities. Abraham's key to success is his ability to bribe his way through all barriers of law. Indeed, despite all his criminal doings, he remains beyond the reach of all legal arms of the government because he is privy to one secret not known to many: that corruption can foil all legal impediments in the new nation. And it is a secret he knows too well because he has foreknowledge of the society that is about to emerge in decolonized India. Vasco Miranda, a family friend who becomes the Zogoibys' worst enemy at the end of the novel, articulates this situation for Abraham in a drunken outburst. On the night of independence, threatened by rising Hindu fundamentalism, Vasco pours out his view of India in the coming years to "Mr. Big Businessman Abie":

> "Let me give you a tip. Only one power in this damn country is strong enough to stand up against those gods and it isn't blankety blank sockular specialism [secular socialism]. It isn't blankety blank Pundit Nehru and his blankety blank protection-of-minorities Congress watch-wallahs. You know what it is? I'll tell you what it is. Corruption. You get me? Bribery." (166)

He also adds that to Abraham, the way to success in India is no secret: " 'Abie-ji being such a bleddy big shot, of course, he knows it all. Such a bleddy big grandmother sucking so many bleddy big eggs' " (167).

Fanon warns us that the bourgeoisie of a freshly decolonized nation are likely to be prey to such corruption, partly because they lack the energy and know-how to revamp the country's economy. Given this inability to develop initiative and infrastructure, the postcolonial bourgeoisie are likely to devote themselves to a variety of questionable activities, ranging from serving as mere compradors for Western capital to outright crime. He points out that "neither financiers nor industrial magnets are to be found within this national middle class. The national bourgeoisie of underdeveloped countries is not engaged in production, nor in invention, nor building, nor labor; it is completely canalized into activities of the intermediary type" (*WE,* 149–50).

Several businesses that Abraham runs belong, in fact, to a category worse than "the intermediate type," though on the surface they appear productive as well as inventive, dealing with building and employing labor. These businesses are governed by what Abraham calls "the principles of invisibility, those hidden laws of nature that could not be overturned by the visible laws of men" (185–86). "The principles of invisibility," which depend on corruption—on " 'V. Miranda's definition of democracy: one man one bribe' " (167)—allow Abraham to do with impunity what he has to do to further his business interests. As a beginner in the game, Abraham does not possess any lawful source of finance; hence he devises an intricate money-laundering scheme, so "invisible funds could find their way through a series of invisible bank accounts and end up, clean as a whistle, in the account of a friend" (186). The site of his construction project in Bombay is in the Reclamation area of the city, a location where the authority wants to regulate the size of buildings to relieve living congestion in an overcrowded city, as it is planning to build instead another city center on the mainland (185). Abraham devises ingenious ways to frustrate the government scheme, so the "continued invisibility of the dream city across the waters" would be to his advantage as greater demand of housing would enable him to sell the high-rise buildings he has raised in the Reclamation zone in contravention to city regulations (186).

But the supreme application of the principles of invisibility occurs when Abraham has his invisible city built by an invisible workforce. Brainchild of a local politician whose influence in the Municipal Corporation Abraham uses in his many projects, this invisible workforce is generated by an official city policy that dictates that the existence of any residents of Bombay who have settled there subsequent to the last city census is simply ignored. By regarding these residents as nonexistent, or at best essentially as illegal immigrants in a city of their own country, the city is able to disavow all responsibility for their housing or welfare (186). Abraham, by employing this nonpeople in his various construction projects, appears to be a savior—that is, he succeeds in hiding his ruthless capitalist fangs when he appears to them as a lifesaving benefactor, paying them minimal salaries but at least providing them with a means of subsistence, however marginal. In the meantime, since his employees do not officially exist, he is able to avoid any and all regulations regarding the pay and treatment of his workers, responsibility for their health and safety, and the like.

The government's failure to protect these people testifies to the failure of the nationalist dream to create if not equal wealth, at least equal opportunities for all. Indeed, the government is not able to ensure even that all of its citizens will be regarded as human beings. Moreover, the event demonstrates more than India's failure to establish a just society for all. It suggests that divisive forces based on regionalism and class are striking at the heart of the union. Certainly, independence to many in India meant more than political independence; to those in dire want it meant a chance at economic uplift. Wealth, on the other hand, remained and grew only in a select group, who in their characteristic nationalist bourgeois way refused to share the pie with the rest. Rushdie, in fact, notes the tendency of private capital in postcolonial India to be concentrated increasingly in the hands of fewer and fewer large conglomerates, including not only Abraham's fictional da Gama-Zogoiby C-50 Corporation but also several well-known nonfictional businesses and financial institutions on his list (180).

As is typical in the postcolonial situation, the cause of this glaring inequality in different segments of the nation can be dated back to the colonial period, which, Fanon rightly indicates, favored the growth of infrastructure in selected locations, such as the cities.[5] Occasioned by independence, the promise of a better future draws many from the poverty-stricken villages to the cities where they find that employment and amenities are not for them. The bourgeoisie here are self-serving with an overtness unmatched in Europe. Fanon notes that though the principle does not translate into actual practice, especially when it comes to treating the other races, "[European] bourgeois ideology . . . is the proclamation of an essential equality between men" (163). However, in decolonized nations, the bourgeoisie, in their haste to profit from the new opportunities opened to them by the departure of their former colonial masters, do not even bother to pay lip service to the Enlightenment principle of equality.[6]

In the Marxist terms Fanon adopts, Bombay's invisible workers would be similar to the *lumpenproletariat* of decolonized African nations, the landless peasants and the displaced workers, who "leave the country districts[,] . . . rush toward the towns, crowd into tin-shack settlements, and try to make their way into the ports and cities founded by colonial dominion" (*WE*, 111). This teeming mass of humanity "circle tirelessly around different towns, hoping that one day or another they will be allowed inside" (*WE*, 129). But perceived as an intrusion and a threat, they are denied all city conveniences (as the policy of the Bombay municipality Rushdie refers to ensures). Despised by the property owners, whose interest all city policies must reckon with, as they are the ones who elect city officials, these "hopeless dregs of humanity, all who turn in circles between suicide and madness," turn to petty crimes and are severely punished when the law gets hold of them (*WE*, 130).

There is, however, a difference between Rushdie and Fanon in their understanding of the possible role of the "invisible work-force" or the *lumpen-*

proletariat in a decolonized nation. Fanon describes them as "the most revolutionary forces of a colonized people," thus suggesting that they do possess a kind of revolutionary energy (129).[7] The vast majority of Rushdie's "invisible work-force" officially does not exist, thus becoming a nonentity that is unlikely to possess the powerful revolutionary potential that Fanon sees in the African *lumpenproletariat*. But Rushdie, in his novel, refers to another class of people who are politically active, a class that perhaps grows out of the *lumpenproletariat* and climbs one notch higher on the scale. These are characters such as Lambajan Chandiwala, Chhaggan, Sammy Hazaré—all hatchet men of Raman Fielding, the Hindu fundamentalist political leader. Fielding recruits them from among those who survive on odd jobs in the city. Manipulated by his fundamentalist rhetoric, they are capable only of destructive violence, a habit that does not change even when they break free of his control.[8]

When Fanon examines the leaders and political parties in decolonized nations, many of his findings resemble the politics of India in postindependence years that *The Moor's Last Sigh* depicts. Fanon notes that the concept of nationhood, however central it might be to the drive for independence, tends to crumble after the event as sectarian sentiments set in. Ethnic minorities are often subject to violent attacks, and religious fanaticism is fueled by unscrupulous politicians. Fanon observes, "From nationalism we have passed to ultra-nationalism, to chauvinism, and finally to racism" (*WE*, 156).[9] Critical of the very notion of nationalism, calling it a "vague formula," Fanon shows that it ceases to be an all-embracing cohesive force on decolonization: "African unity takes off the mask, and crumbles into regionalism inside the hollow shell of nationality itself" (*WE*, 159). Part of the legacy of a colonial economy that promoted unequal growth in the colony and left its indelible stamp on colonial politics, hostilities along regional, racial, and religious lines break out after independence as those who live in "more prosperous regions realize their good luck . . . refusing to feed the others" (*WE*, 159). Political parties no longer represent the common people, who often play a reactionary role and become a tool of oppression for those in power against them.[10] For many, the party is a vehicle for "private advancement" (*WE*, 171); some of those who assume its leadership are thugs; as Fanon remarks, "[T]he party in certain districts is organized like a gang, with the toughest person in it as its head" (*WE*, 184).

Rushdie's account of Raman Fielding's rise as the leader of Mumbai's Axis (MA) follows a pattern well probed by Fanon.[11] Advocating regionalism, fomenting fundamentalism, and threatening all non-Hindu minorities, MA is indeed "organized like a gang" and thrives in an atmosphere of fear and violence. Informed by a bizarre mixture of Anglophilia, regionalism, and Hindu revivalism, Fielding, Rushdie explains, is the son of a "cricket-mad father" whose words of entreaty to be in the game, *"just one fielding,"* earned him the sobriquet in cricket circles (230). His son, Raman Fielding, chose not to be a cricketer but saw in the game's short history in the subcontinent enough "inter-community rivalry," especially machinations by the Parsis and Muslims to keep the Hindus out of it (231). He is also aware that a famous English novelist had the same name and uses the fact to underscore his father's cultural sophistication, claiming that he was "an educated, cultured, literary man, an internationalist, who had taken the name 'Fielding' as a genuflection to the author of *Tom Jones*" (232).[12] The political manifesto of MA, a one-man show, is best summed up by Rushdie's description of Fielding:

> He was against unions, in favour of breaking strikes, against working women, in favour of sati, against poverty and in favour of wealth. He was against "immigrants" to the city, by which he meant all non-Marathi speakers, including those who had been born there, and in favour of its "natural residents." (298–99)

The creed is appealing both to the blue bloods and the working class of the nation; the party's cadre, however, is formed mostly from the latter. Consequently, Hindu fundamentalism, which promises the "eternal stability of caste" and the glory of "a golden age 'before the invasion' when good Hindu men and women could roam free," spreads like wildfire in the city of Bombay as well as in the state of Maharashtra (299).

It is a well-known fact that much of the religious strife India suffers today is a result of the British divide-and-rule policy that lasted for more than a century. Fanon, too, shows that the nationalist bourgeoisie, who cannot shake off colonial propaganda even after independence, derive their religious fanaticism from the rhetoric of colonialism; even upon decolonization, they continue to shape nationalism along religious and regional lines for their own political gain. This is why they revive exotic religious practices and demonize other communities. In Fanon's words, "minor confraternities, local religions, and maraboutic cults will show a new vitality and will once more take up their round of excommunications [of those not in their community]" (*WE*, 160).

Fielding's MA allies itself with other political parties of similar persuasion, creating what Rushdie describes as "that alphabet soup of authoritarians, BJP, RSS, VHP" (337). An aim of all these right-wing parties is a return to the days of Ram, to establish "Ram-Rajya" (kingdom of Ram; 337). One ritual they introduce is mass *puja*, or collective worship, which the left-leaning art connoisseur Zeeny Vakil finds absurd because it goes against the polytheism of Hinduism, attempting to impose a single practice on a fundamentally plural religion with a "thousand and one gods" (338).[13] Congregation as a large group allows these parties to launch their political agendas with religious fervor. Fanon witnesses the same trend in some African nations, explores its causes, and discovers that these parties hold mass meetings to demonstrate to themselves and to others a show of force because they lack the stability of established bourgeoisie (*WE*, 181). Indeed, to Fanon such politics "shows a certain anxiety to hide its real convictions, to sidetrack, and in short to set itself up as a popular face" (*WE,* 181). What Fanon reveals here is the fear underlying all fascist movements; and fascism, by its very nature, always turns a blind eye to all contradictions within itself. As Zeeny Vakil indicates, Hindu fundamentalism fails to resolve the paradox of turning a religion of multiplicity into one of unvaried singleness when it promotes collective worship. She rightly points out that the practice comes at a cost because Hinduism becomes a monologic discourse in that process, more so since to create its monolithic entity, it privileges *Ramayan* over all other sacred Hindu texts, such as the Gita and Puranas (338).

Hand in hand with religious fanaticism comes fascist xenophobia. Fanon identifies this phenomenon as a predictable continuation of the politics the national bourgeoisie inherited from colonial times. Having achieved their primary goal of replacing the "foreigners" with themselves, the postcolonial bourgeoisie desire no further political change; their rank-and-file supporters, many of whom occupy much lower rungs in wealth and position than their leaders, attempt to reenact the pattern by driving out minorities and assuming the vacated jobs and businesses themselves. Fanon is perspicacious to realize that "the 'small people' of the nation—taxi drivers, cake sellers, and boot blacks—will be equally quick to insist" on the departure of those minorities (158). It is no wonder that MA's extreme regionalism is popular among people like Lambajan and Sammy Hazaré, and that the party is "growing rapidly in popularity among the poor" (230).

As in the real world of postcolonial India, the Hindu fundamentalist movement Rushdie depicts finally culminates in the explosive event of the Babri Mosque demolition in Ayodha. Violent communal hostility erupts between Hindus and Muslims and engulfs the whole subcontinent, not India alone. "Both sides," Rushdie comments, "sacrifice their right to any shred of virtue; they are each other's plague" (365). Bomb attacks also rock the city of Bombay, killing Hindus and Muslims alike in the blaze. Rushdie makes it clear that the carnage cannot be attributed to any single group. Moraes, Abraham's son, who is acting as his instrument of revenge, kills Fielding in his palace, only to discover moments later as he is fleeing the scene that it is blowing up in smoke—the work of Sammy Hazaré, a renegade MA cadre. Hazaré also blows up the Cashondeliveri Tower, with himself, his assistant the dwarf Dhirendra, and presumably Abraham in it. As Moraes learns that his home has been blown up as well with all the domestics he grew up with, he gains an insight into the whole massacre, realizing that deeper forces of history are at work here, not just the visible players who enact the show: "Was it dead Fielding's revenge, or freelance Hazaré's, or was there some more profound movement in history, deeper down, where not even those of us who had spent so long in the Under World could see it?" (372).

That part of history that Moraes finds unfathomable is the product of the doings of his father, Abraham, of Raman Fielding and MA workers, of the

Muslim retributive forces—all of whom constitute the nation and cling to its bourgeois ideology. All these characters resonate with strong allegorical overtones, and Rushdie's novels as a whole constitute one of the best demonstrations of the argument by recent critics such as Fredric Jameson that third-world literature tends to employ allegorical modes of representation.[14] Perhaps the most powerful of such portraits in *The Moor's Last Sigh* is Moraes himself. In the drastic fragmentation of his personality at the end of his narrative, Rushdie illustrates the disintegration of the Indian nation as enacted by its own self-destructive citizens, as he did earlier in *Midnight's Children* with the disintegration of Saleem Sinai.[15] Rushdie not too subtly suggests that Moraes, in his splintered psyche, embodies the effect of the whole nation's wrongdoings by giving him more than one paternity. Other than the one he derives from Abraham, there is that of Nehru, the first prime minister of India (75–77). Moraes gives some credence to the likelihood of the latter—illustrious, though illegitimate—because his mother, Aurora, did visit Nehru exactly nine months before her son's birth. But this lineage is just a mere possibility, not conclusive proof. Moraes suffers from an age disorder that matures him at twice the normal rate, and the disease clearly suggests that he is Abraham's son because Abraham and Aurora made love exactly four and a half months before his birth and because the disease made him grow at double speed even in gestation. The truth is certainly known to Aurora (who, after all, knows how long she was pregnant), but Moraes has no access to her secrets and considers the possibility of his paternal link to Nehru when he reconstructs his mother's life, from the family cook's culinary records, prior to his birth (176–79).

What does Rushdie convey through all this? Perhaps he implies that Nehru's healthy vision of the nation, one of slow but steady socialist progress, was capitalized on by self-aggrandizing fortune hunters whose unchecked ambition and lawless profiteering sped up certain spheres of the economy, ailing it and creating inequality in the process.[16] Moraes thus represents the consequence of Abraham's unbridled rapacity; fittingly, he is endowed with remarkable height. Like the tall buildings Abraham raises with his invisible workforce, Moraes is "a skyscraper freed of all legal restraints, a one-man population explosion, a megalopolis, a shirt-ripping, button-popping hulk" (188). Earlier, in a similar passage, Moraes explains his disease in terms of the city he lives in, compares his own sped-up metabolism with the pace of life in a Bombay seeking to catch up with the modern world through high-tech innovation while failing to deal with the social problems that plague its slums (145).

In general, Fanon's findings about the ills of the bourgeois nation are very similar to Rushdie's. Fanon indicates that "since the bourgeoisie has not the economic means to ensure its domination and to throw a few crumbs to the rest of country . . . the country sinks all the more deeply into stagnation" (*WE*, 165). The bourgeoisie often raise skyscrapers, he astutely observes, to mask this state of stagnation and "regression" and to give themselves self-confidence: "to reassure itself and to give it something to boast about, the bourgeoisie can find nothing better to do than to erect grandiose buildings in the capital" (165). Thus, in Moraes's extraordinary height, Rushdie calls attention to a tendency in the third-world bourgeois society, unique not only in India but in other countries as well.

The other symptom of Moraes's disease, his aging at twice the normal pace, is more significant than his height, for it captures in a telling metaphor the predicament of modern India as a nation.[17] In Moraes's accelerated growth, Rushdie embodies, as one reviewer puts it, "the plight of a country forced to grow up too quickly,"[18] attaining decadence before its time.[19] Fanon, too, notes the decadence of the decolonized bourgeoisie and sees in this propensity signs of premature aging. As he remarks, "We need think that it [the decolonized bourgeoisie] is jumping ahead; it is in fact beginning at the end. *It is already senile before it has come to know the petulance, the fearlessness, or the will to succeed of youth*" (*WE,* 153; emphasis mine).[20]

Fanon also notices "a process of retrogression" in the path taken by the national bourgeoisie of African countries. Since they fail to evolve an all-inclusive national consciousness, and since they carry on the same oppression that characterized colonial occupation, surely they do not move forward, regressing instead to the rule of their former rulers. Indeed, in continuing the same exploitation, the same violence, and the same separatist politics, the bourgeoisie of decolonized countries perpetuate the old colonial system in a new garb.

Rushdie emphasizes that rule by the national bourgeoisie in a country such as India is still under the grip of imperialism continually through *The Moor's Last Sigh* by associating Abraham with spices, the commodity that first enticed his forefathers to India. Abraham and Aurora's first lovemaking, leading to his marriage with the prosperous heiress to a lucrative spice empire—what Rushdie calls "Pepper love"—takes place in a spice warehouse, on sacks of spices "in that foetid atmosphere heavy with the odours of cardamom and cumin" (90). Abraham's career as a spice trader suffers a setback when a series of shipments sink during World War II, "adding spice to the ocean-bed; and the C-50 condiment empire (and, who knows, perhaps also the heart of Empire itself, deprived of *peppery inspiration*) began to totter and sway" (110; emphasis mine). Part 2 of the book, which recounts Abraham's phenomenal rise as a business tycoon and a godfather of the Bombay underworld, is called "Malabar Masala" (Malabar spices), calling attention to the fact that all his activities after the independence reenact his earlier dealing with spices but are of a different kind. "The prime supplier of new young girls," Abraham runs his sophisticated prostitution ring by procuring prostitutes from the temple dancers of southern India: "Thus Abraham the spice merchant was able to use his widespread Southern connections to harvest a new crop" (183). When brought before the law, Abraham obtains a speedy acquittal by establishing that " 'he is a respectable gentleman in the pepper-and-spice business,' " that his " 'whole life has been spent in the spice trade' " (360). When the center of his kingdom, Cashondeliveri Tower, collapses in a bomb attack, spices fall "rat-a-tat on the roads and sidewalks like perfumed hail," for he "had always kept sacks of Cochin spices at hand," apparently for nostalgic reasons (375).

This continual association of Abraham with spices, even though little of his business actually deals with the commodity later in the book, underscores the colonial roots of his identity. After all, the early impetus to imperial movements in the coastal waters of the Indian subcontinent—for example, Vasco da Gama's "discovery" of India—came from spices. Pepper was the prime mover of this historical event of profound implication. Rushdie writes on the fourth page of his book, "[H]ad it not been for peppercorns, then what is ending now in East and West might never have begun. Pepper it was that brought Vasco da Gama's tall ships across the ocean."[21] Hence it is only appropriate that when Abraham's empire collapses, peppers and spices rain down on the surrounding roads and sidewalks.

Right before Abraham is about to strike the city of Bombay with a series of vengeful bomb attacks (evidently for its Hindu fundamentalism, but the carnage hits Hindus and Muslims alike), he places his son out of harm's way by sending him to Spain to recover his mother's paintings, stolen by Vasco. As Bombay burns, Moraes's plane is flying away from the city as it convulses in apocalyptic flames. Moraes is carrying a stuffed British bulldog called Jawaharlal, left to his father by his mother's uncle, who named it after Nehru out of spite for the nationalist leader (50). Abraham's reason for giving the stuffed dog to the departing Moraes is ostensibly to save a family heirloom. The stuffed Jawaharlal, on the other hand, emblematizes what the nationalist dream has become nearly four decades after independence. With Moraes thus departs the effigy of a dream; that dream, as articulated by his grandfather before independence, however, was founded on high idealism:

> *dawning of a new world . . . a free country . . . above religion because secular, above class because socialist, above caste because enlightened, above hatred because loving, above vengeance because forgiving, above tribe because unifying, above language because many-tongued, above colour because multi-coloured, above poverty because victorious over it, above ignorance because literate, above stupidity because brilliant, freedom . . . the freedom express, soon soon we will stand upon that platform and cheer the coming of the train.* (51; Rushdie's emphasis)

None of these promises has come true in the India that Moraes leaves behind. Indeed, the grim world that emerges from Moraes's tale is one Fanon would have found quite familiar had he lived to see it. He, perhaps, would have found it grimmer in many respects because it has realized so many of his worst fears about decolonized nations. According to Rushdie's treatment of nationalism in *The Moor's Last Sigh,* it is clear that violence and exploitation do not end after freedom from colonial masters. Decolonization thus becomes a relatively superficial shift that corresponds not to genuine liberation but merely to another phase in a system not unlike colonialism in its oppression of the disadvantaged and use of violence to enforce this oppression. Certainly Rushdie's India of the late eighties illustrates the culmination of a process that Fanon's African nations of the fifties and sixties were beginning to experience. Thus, despite the differences in genre and in the history of two colonial regions that they depict, *The Wretched of the Earth* and *The Moor's Last Sigh* treat similar mechanisms and phenomena. Fanon terms "the bourgeois phase in the history of underdeveloped countries . . . a completely useless phase" (*WE,* 176). This is so because he indicates that "nationalism is not a political doctrine, nor a program" and maintains that the alternative to "regression, or at best halts and uncertainties [is] a rapid step . . . taken from national consciousness to political and social consciousness" (*WE,* 203). Fanon also suggests ways to accomplish that goal, for example with a socialist economy (*WE,* 99) and with decentralized political parties in reach of the masses of even the remote areas of the country (*WE,* 185).

Rushdie, on the other hand, does not provide any means to defeat the vicious nexus of sectarian politics and economic inequality plaguing India in *The Moor's Last Sigh.* But the novel does not end on a note of absolute despair. As Moraes's plane is flying away from Bombay, he is thinking of Nadia Wadia, the woman to whom he was once betrothed, who apparently has survived Sammy Hazaré's violence. Moraes wishes he could give her hope for a better future: "Girl, get a grip, OK? The city will survive. New Towers will rise. Better days will come" (377). At the end of the novel, when he is bringing his grim tale to a close, having failed to retrieve his mother's paintings from Vasco and lying on a tombstone in a cemetery, Moraes does not entirely rule out hope. Delivered from this cheerless site, to which Moraes, now very old, has dragged himself, his narrative closes with the following words: "*I'll lay me down upon this graven stone, lay my head beneath these letters R I P {Rest in Peace}, and close my eyes, according to our family's old practice of falling asleep in times of trouble, and hope to awaken, renewed and joyful, into a better time*" (434; Rushdie's emphasis).

"Our family" here includes in a profound diasporic sweep not only personal ancestors but also the cultural and social forces they represent. They are embodied in

> the glory of the Moors, their triumphant masterpieces and their last redoubt. The Alhambra, Europe's red fort, sister to Delhi's and Agra's—*the palace of interlocking forms and secret wisdom, of pleasure-courts and water gardens, that monument to a lost possibility that nevertheless has gone on standing long after its conquerors have fallen.* (433; Rushdie's emphasis)

Evidently, Moraes here attempts to lessen the impact of the dark tale he has just told. Thus, though *The Moor's Last Sigh* attests to Rushdie's bleak vision of the reality of a postcolonial state, it also suggests the possibility of a better future.

The view that emerges of the decolonized nation from Moraes's rather subdued optimism can be best summed up with Rushdie's own view on a comment Gramsci makes in his *Prison Notebooks*, which, to underscore the repressive nature of the politics of the eighties, Rushdie quotes in his introduction to *Imaginary Homelands*. Gramsci says, "The crisis consists precisely in the fact that the old is dying and the new cannot be born; in this interregnum a great variety of morbid symptoms appear."[22] Referring to the remark, Rushdie observes that "*Homelands* is an incomplete, personal view of the interregnum of the 1980s, not all of whose symptoms . . . were morbid" (1). Written a few years after *Homelands* during his confinement after the fatwa—which itself should perhaps be understood in the light of Fanon's comments about postcolonial religious fanaticism—*The Moor's Last Sigh* offers the vision of a time not unlike the one at which Rushdie hints in that statement. Hence the book should not be seen as an expression of absolute despair. Just as the architects of history still proclaim their glory through the Alhamábra, Moraes the narrator knows as the book closes that after the current interregnum, informed by his "family's old practice of falling asleep in times of trouble," there lies "hope to awaken, renewed and joyful, into a better time" (434).

Notes

1. Salman Rushdie, *The Moor's Last Sigh* (New York: Pantheon, 1995), 336; hereafter cited in the text.
2. " 'Cochin is finished, anyway,' " he observes and explains. " 'From a strictly business point of view the move makes complete sense' " (119).
3. Despite the rule by a bourgeois capitalist power for nearly two centuries, colonial India, oddly enough, retained many feudal aristocratic characteristics. For a discussion of this phenomenon, see M. Keith Booker, *Colonial Power, Colonial Texts: India in the Modern British Novel* (Ann Arbor: University of Michigan Press, 1997), 23–30.
4. Frantz Fanon, *The Wretched of the Earth* (New York: Grove Press, 1963), 149–50; hereafter cited in the text as *WE*.
5. Fanon's analysis of this aspect of a decolonized country applies well to India. He says, "Certain countries which have benefitted by a large European settlement come to independence with houses and wide streets, and these tend to forget the poverty-stricken, starving hinterland" (100). Bombay and other major Indian cities were such European settlements enjoying prosperity while the rest of India suffered abject poverty.
6. Fanon also remarks that "In 1789, after the bourgeois revolution, the smallest French peasant benefited substantially from the upheaval. But it is a commonplace to observe and to say that in the majority of cases, for 95 percent of the population of underdeveloped countries, independence brings no immediate change" (75).

7. It might be observed that Fanon's position is quite unlike Marx's in relation to the *lumpenproletariat* of Europe. To Marx, they are unruly elements, concerned only with their own welfare and too politically underdeveloped to become an effective force for revolution.

8. Fanon is aware that the *lumpenproletariat,* weak in strength and lacking organization, can be exploited by the "oppressor" (colonial power) under certain circumstances (*WE,* 136–37). That is, there is no reason to assume that they cannot be on the wrong side.

9. He cites some specific examples, such as anti-Dahoman and anti-Voltaic demonstrations on the Ivory Coast and anti-Sudanese demonstrations in Senegal (*WE,* 156–57).

10. In fact, when it came to a real confrontation against even the colonial regime, nationalist parties generally shied away from the prospect, preaching "non-violence" instead (61). *The Moor's Last Sigh* relates such an incident; when a strike occurs among the naval sailors, Congress acts like "chamchas, toadies. . . . When the masses actually do rise up . . . the bosses turn tail. Brown bosses, white bosses, it was the same thing" (133).

11. Mumbai is named after Mumbadevi, "the mother goddess of Bombay . . . growing rapidly in popularity among the poor" (230). Mumbai is also the new name for Bombay.

12. Raman Fielding, also nicknamed "Mainduck" (frog), is modeled after Bal Thackeray, leader of the Shiv Sena Party, a militant Hindu fundamentalist organization. This caricature has led *The Moor's Last Sigh* to meet a fate reminiscent of its predecessor, *The Satanic Verses,* albeit on a much smaller scale. It didn't take Thackeray long to pronounce his fatwa on the book by forbidding bookstores in Bombay to carry it. See *Economist* (9 September 1995): 43.

13. Zeeny appears in Rushdie's earlier novel *The Satanic Verses;* Adam Braganza, the fast-talking young entrepreneur whose business acumen impresses Abraham and whom he adopts as his own son, on the other hand, is Shiva's son, raised by Saleem Sinai in *Midnight's Children.* Though no major protagonist of one appears in another, Rushdie clearly intends these books, including *The Moor's Last Sigh,* as a series of some sort, whose common motif is India's turbulent postcolonial political history.

14. Jameson identifies allegory as the distinctive feature of all third-world literature in "Third-World Literature in the Era of Multinational Capitalism," *Social Text* 15 (1986): 65–88. Though the remark has drawn severe protest from Aijaz Ahmad in his "Jameson's Rhetoric of Otherness and the 'National Allegory,' " in *In Theory: Classes, Nations, Literatures* (London: Verso, 1992), 95–122, it applies well to most of Rushdie's fiction. Michael Gorra describes Saleem Sinai in *Midnight's Children* as an "emblematic" protagonist; Gorra, *After Empire: Scott, Naipaul, Rushdie* (Chicago: University of Chicago Press, 1997), 120. Booker, on the other hand, sees Saleem "more as a postmodern parody of national allegory than national allegory proper"; Booker 1997, 139.

15. "We have chopped away our own legs, we engineered our own fall. And now we can only weep, at the last, for what we were too enfeebled, too corrupt, too little, too contemptible to defend" (372–73). Here Moraes places the blame of the carnage squarely on his own countrymen. Compare also Fanon's "A government or a party gets the people it deserves and sooner or later a people gets the government it deserves" (198).

16. I am aware that Nehru's paternity of Moraes would be a bastard one. Like some other instances of Rushdie's allegory, this one is not entirely free of ambiguity.

17. The correct medical term for the disease, according to one reviewer, is "Cockayne's syndrome." See Sara Maitland, "The Author Is Too Much with Us," *Commonweal* (22 February 1996): 22–23.

18. See Michiko Kakutani, "Rushdie of India: Serious, Crammed Yet Light," *New York Times,* 28 December 1995, C13, C20.

19. Rushdie is not alone in using the image of uncommon growth to indicate nationalist decadence. Ayi Kwei Armah has one suggesting decadence in decolonized Ghana, a child "born with all the features of a human baby, but within seven years it had completed the cycle from babyhood to infancy to youth, to maturity and old age, and in its seventh year it had died

a natural death." Armah, *The Beautiful Ones Are Not Yet Born* (London: Heinemann, 1969), 63. For a discussion on Armah's use of this metaphor from a Fanonian perspective, see M. Keith Booker, *The African Novel in English: An Introduction,* (Portsmouth, N.H.: Heinemann, 1998), 108–9.

20. On another occasion, Fanon calls the national bourgeoisie "afflicted with precocious senility" (172).

21. Occasioned by the spice trade, Rushdie firmly establishes the meeting, "called Discovery of India," as a rape: "[H]ow could we be discovered when we were not covered before . . . 'not so much sub-continent as sub-condiment.' . . . 'They came for the hot stuff, just like any man calling on a tart' " (4–5). However, whether colonial domination was a rape or a different encounter is a charged issue. For a discussion on this controversial topic, see Booker 1997, 121–28.

22. Salman Rushdie, *Imaginary Homelands: Essays and Criticism, 1981–1991* (London: Granta, 1991), 1.

"The Mirror of Us All": *Midnight's Children* and the Twentieth-Century Bildungsroman

Dubravka Juraga

Salman Rushdie's *Midnight's Children* narrates the growth and development of its rather idiosyncratic protagonist, the Indian Muslim Saleem Sinai, from his birth at midnight on August 15,1947, at the moment of Indian independence, through his childhood, and on into early adulthood. Actually, the narrative encompasses more than Sinai's own life; the first third of the book is set before his birth, describing the lives of two generations of his putative ancestors in British colonial India, thus setting the stage for Sinai's birth and for the birth of postcolonial India. The bulk of the novel then goes on to narrate, in Sinai's own words, his childhood in a well-to-do Muslim family and his various traumatic experiences within both the family circle and the larger community of India and Pakistan. To an extent, then, it is fair to characterize Rushdie's book as a bildungsroman, though the book clearly eschews any notion of purity, generic or otherwise. Thus Patricia Merivale identifies both Günter Grass's novel *The Tin Drum* (an obvious predecessor to Rushdie's novel) and *Midnight's Children* as "Bildungsromane—indeed, *Künstlerromane*—as well as genealogical allegorizing of historical and metatextual particularities."[1]

On the other hand, most critics have tended to discuss *Midnight's Children* as a sort of historical novel, and rightfully so.[2] Sinai's personal experiences mirror Indian history in an intentional and striking way. The novel is constructed in such a way that from its first paragraph, in which Sinai announces that he has been "handcuffed to history" so that his destinies were "indissolubly chained to those of my country," the novel leads the reader to see the history of Sinai's life as an allegory of the life of the Indian nation.[3] From the portentous moment of his birth, Sinai was "linked to history both literally and metaphorically, both actively and passively" connected to the world around him (*MC*, 285–86). The lives of Sinai and India remain con-

---

This essay was written specifically for this volume and is published for the first time by permission of the author.

nected to the very end of the book, set in the late 1970s, when his body, "the bomb in Bombay," appears about to explode into myriad individual "specks of dust" (about six hundred million—the number of Indians at the time of Sinai's writing) just as India itself is bursting and cracking at its seams (*MC*, 552).

On the other hand, the bildungsroman and the historical novel have much more in common than is immediately obvious. M. Keith Booker notes that for bourgeois historians, "the movement of history into the era of bourgeois hegemony was tantamount to the growth of an immature and youthful European feudal society into a mature and responsible adult capitalist society." As a result, the bourgeois bildungsroman and the bourgeois historical novel tell very much the same story, and "it is thus not really surprising that the greatest examples of either genre actually belong to both."[4] Still, reading *Midnight's Children* within the tradition of the bildungsroman may reveal different aspects of the novel than does reading it as a historical novel. After all, generic identification is not an innocent choice given the reminders of critics such as Mikhail Bakhtin and Fredric Jameson that generic conventions reflect specific ideological inclinations. This is especially the case with the bildungsroman, which bears particularly obvious ideological markers. The genre narrates the successful emergence of individuals into society: "the acculturation of a self—the integration of a particular 'I' into the general subjectivity of a community, and thus, finally into the universal subjectivity of humanity."[5] It thus centrally addresses the crucial issue of the relationship between the individual and society. In *The Way of the World*, an important study of the generic characteristics of the European bildungsroman, Franco Moretti argues that the rise to prominence of the genre (with its intense focus on youthful experience) in the late eighteenth and nineteenth centuries can be directly related to a sense of newness that was crucial to the European experience of modernity in these years.[6] In other words, the bildungsroman embodies the historical experience of a youthful European bourgeoisie newly risen to power in Europe, reflecting the concomitant notion that *"the biography of a young individual was the most meaningful viewpoint for the understanding and the evaluation of history."*[7] In this sense, Moretti's analysis is very much in accord with Barbara Foley's observation that the bildungsroman represents the "classic form" of the nineteenth-century European bourgeois novel.[8] Moretti does, however, do a bit more than Foley to historicize his account, describing not only the centrality of the bildungsroman to early-nineteenth-century European literary culture but also the rise of the genre in the late eighteenth century and the demise of the genre in the late nineteenth century. For Moretti, in fact, novels such as Flaubert's *Sentimental Education* and George Eliot's *Daniel Deronda* and *Felix Holt* reflect, though in different ways, the loss of a tension between youth and maturity that once made the bildungsroman the central bourgeois genre. In a historical model very similar to Georg Lukács's famous account of the rise and decline of the bourgeois historical novel during the same historical period, Moretti depicts the bildungsroman as a decadent genre well past its peak by the beginning of the twentieth century, no longer capable of achieving the heights reached by earlier practitioners such as the Goethe of *Wilhelm Meister.*

The bildungsroman's generic focus on the relationship between the private and the public, between the individual and society, is obviously of central importance in *Midnight's Children.* Meanwhile, the seemingly direct connection between the personal and the political that is the most striking characteristic of Rushdie's novel would seem to allow it to overcome the central historical development that, for Moretti, marks the demise of the bildungsroman as the central genre of European bourgeois literature. Indeed, in this sense, *Midnight's Children* at first appears to resemble the "classical" bildungsromans Moretti associates with late-eighteenth-century writers such as Goethe, in which the integration of the individual into society is particularly smooth and complete because that integration is pictured as a natural part of individual development rather than the end and defeat of individuation.

Here, Moretti seems to be pointing to the same aspects of Goethe's work Bakhtin discussed in his (now largely lost) study of the bildungsroman, which focuses on *Wilhelm Meister* as the quintessential expression of the genre's characteristic energies. For Bakhtin, Goethe's book is the most representative "novel of emergence," a specific form of the bildungsroman prominent in the late eighteenth century. These novels narrate the emergence of a new (bourgeois) man, which occurs simultaneously with the emergence of bourgeois nations throughout Europe. For Bakhtin, such a novel is no longer "a man's own private affair. He emerges *along with the world* and he reflects the historical emergence of the world itself. He is no longer within an epoch, but on the border between two epochs, at the transition point from one to the other. . . . He is forced to become a new, unprecedented type of human being."[9] In particular, Bakhtin notes, the representation of this new type of human being involves "an image of *man growing in national-historical time.*"[10]

Bakhtin's discussion of the rise of the new bourgeois individual in tandem with the new bourgeois national state seems to anticipate *Midnight's Children* in a striking way. On the other hand, one of the things Bakhtin admires most about Goethe's novels is their smooth sense of temporal progression, a characteristic that Rushdie's novel hardly shares. Indeed, the narrative structure of *Midnight's Children* seems almost intentionally designed to violate the kind of smooth temporal progression that is central not only to *Wilhelm Meister* but to the European bildungsroman as a whole. The general temporal movement of the text is forward through four generations, roughly beginning with the youth of Saleem's putative grandfather Aadam Aziz and continuing beyond the birth of Saleem's son Aadam Sinai. But much of the plot is driven by accident and coincidence rather than by logic and cause and effect. Numerous sudden twists and turns make the movement of the plot seem anything but logical and inevitable, and these changes in narrative direction often leave conflicts unresolved, plot strands hanging, and mysteries unsolved. Meanwhile, the general forward movement is disrupted by numerous ruptures, asides, and Shandean digressions. Saleem periodically postpones the forward movement of his narrative, going back to provide quick recaps of events previously narrated in the text. In addition, he not only employs frequent flashbacks to provide reminders of events that have come before but also provides previews of events that are yet to come through numerous flash-forwards. Finally, these flash-forwards resonate with the motif of prophecy that frequently occurs in *Midnight's Children,* a motif that combines with the strong thread of magic realism that runs through the text to provide a potential challenge to rationalist models of history.

Of course, one would expect Rushdie's work to differ from Goethe's, given the obvious fact that the birth of the postcolonial Indian state occurred under very different historical circumstances than did the birth of Germany, Britain, and other modern European nations. Indeed, both Moretti and Bakhtin see Goethe as a special writer largely because of the special nature of his historical context, a context no longer available to twentieth-century writers like Rushdie. On the other hand, despite (or perhaps because) of this decline in the bourgeois bildungsroman, the form has remained attractive to twentieth-century writers who have sought, either for aesthetic or political reasons (as if the two could ever really be separated), to undermine the tradition of bourgeois fiction. Thus the bildungsroman has been a favorite genre of modernist experimentalists such as James Joyce (for example, in *A Portrait of the Artist as a Young Man*) who seek to subvert the conventions of the bourgeois novel and thereby reveal (intentionally or not) its ideological underpinnings. In fact, Moretti himself elsewhere notes that the period between 1898 and 1914 saw a burst of activity in the production of bildungsromans, with works such as Joseph Conrad's *Youth,* Thomas Mann's *Tonio Kröger,* Robert Musil's *The Perplexities of Young Törless,* Robert Walser's *Jakob von Gunten,* Rainer Maria Rilke's *The Notebooks of Malte Laurids Brigge,* and Franz Kafka's *Amerika* (in addition to Joyce's *Portrait*) all being published or written during this period. However, Moretti labels such works "late bildungsromans" to differentiate them from their nineteenth-century predecessors, noting that they embody a new, more decentered sense of subjectivity than that typical of the nineteenth century ("Crisis 44"). And he sees this burst of activity as a final last cry of protest against the dissolution of the stable, autonomous bourgeois self in the light of the growing alienation and fragmentation of life under capitalism.[11]

If in these modernist novels the bildungsroman becomes a protest against the maiming of the subject under capitalism, then perhaps it comes as no surprise that the bildungsroman has also frequently been the genre of choice of overtly leftist writers who seek to challenge the hegemony of bourgeois ideology and aesthetics even more directly. Foley notes that the bildungsroman was the favorite form of American proletarian novelists during the 1930s.[12] One thinks, for example, of Mike Gold's *Jews without Money* (1930), often considered the founding text in the proletarian fiction movement that flourished, if ever so briefly, in the United States in the troubled decade of the 1930s. American leftist writers such as Agnes Smedley, Jack Conroy, Henry Roth, and James T. Farrell also produced important examples of the genre during the 1930s, though often blurring the boundary between the bildungsroman and autobiography. But this blurring itself is important; it is part of an effort to bridge the gap between the private and the public, the personal and the historical, that had by this time become central to life in bourgeois society.

A similar project was central to the literature of the Soviet Union as Soviet writers sought to contribute to the development of a new socialist cultural identity in the decades after the 1917 revolution. Drawing on the work of Evgeny Dobrenko[13] and Katerina Clark,[14] Lily Wiatrowski Phillips notes that in the typical socialist realist novel, "the individual comes to understand that his public and private roles are inseparable. . . . Any conflict that arises between the individual and society is resolved such that the impulses of individuals will reflect the best interests of society."[15] The bildungsroman is the ideal genre for the exploration of this project, and numerous Soviet bildungsromans were produced. Particularly important was a special form of documentary bildungsroman, based either on biographical or autobiographical material and closely following its real-life models. Nikolai Ostrovski's *How the Steel Was Tempered* (1932–1934) and Fyodor Gladkov's trilogy *A Tale of Childhood* (1949), *The Free Gang* (1950), and *Hard Times* (1954) are examples of autobiographical texts depicting the authors' own growth and maturation into a revolutionary commitment. Konstantin Fadeev's *The Young Guard* (1945) and Boris Polevoi's *The Story of a Real Man* (1946) are novels focused on the development of characters who undergo transformation together with their societies and simultaneously and harmoniously develop into committed and affirmative members of their society. In such novels, the protagonists do not mature and adapt well into the existing society. Instead, they develop into committed revolutionaries who are firmly opposed to the existing society, and who substantially contribute to the destruction of the existing society. Thus while one could say that the protagonists of these novels are as alienated from the official public life as the protagonists of bourgeois novels of the nineteenth century, the protagonists of the Soviet novels were able to chose a path that was not open to the protagonists of bourgeois novels: that of revolutionary struggle and eventual overthrow of an existing society they find as reprehensible as some of the bourgeois protagonists.[16]

If the bildungsroman offered to Soviet writers the perfect literary venue for the exploration of new socialist identities that escape the domination of the bourgeois past, this same generic potential has also made the bildungsroman a favorite genre of other "marginal" American writers, including women and African-Americans.[17] In the same way, postcolonial writers such as Kenya's Ngugi wa Thiong'o and Barbados's George Lamming, who have every reason to resent the bourgeois aesthetic tradition and all that goes with it, have often nevertheless chosen the bildungsroman as the form within which to explore new forms of cultural identity that go beyond the baleful experience of the colonial past. Indeed, there is a direct link between the use of the bildungsroman by postcolonial novelists and the earlier use of the genre by socialist realist novelists in the Soviet Union, the latter often providing important novels for the former in their effort to overcome the legacy of the bourgeois culture of the colonial powers of Europe.

There are, of course, fairly obvious reasons why the bildungsroman as a genre might appeal to all of these different kinds of writers. For one thing, however much the process might vary from one society to another, the incorporation into society is an experience common to individuals in all forms of human society. Various societies seek to express the experience of growing up and maturation through their own distinctive literary forms, from African initiation poems and narratives to Serbian folktales and western European novels. But the novel itself is now something like a "world genre," so that the bildungsroman becomes a potential mode of expression of the process of socialization in a variety of societies around the globe. Moreover, Moretti points out that the bildungsroman itself is a flexible genre that can take different forms in different situations. Thus the French bildungsroman, influenced by the radical legacy of the French Revolution and the ensuing decades of periodic coups and upheavals, often views the nineteenth-century status quo as extremely problematic, while the English bildungsroman, the genre of a much more firmly established bourgeoisie whose revolution was less radical and in any case occurred back in the seventeenth century, generally takes a much more conservative and affirmative stance toward the existing social and political order. Moreover, if, as Moretti claims, the bildungsroman is intensely caught up in the phenomenon of modernity, then it would seem to make sense that the genre would interest modernist writers who, though in sometimes very different ways, seem consistently convinced that big changes are afoot and that a new beauty, terrible or not, is on the verge of historical emergence. In a similar way, Moretti's delineation of the very problematic relationship between the bildungsroman of writers such as Stendhal and the bourgeois social order of nineteenth-century France suggests that the form has a great deal of potential for challenging bourgeois ideology in ways that might be of great interest to writers of the political left. Finally, the very alignment between individual desire and social demand that seems central to the resolution of the more conservative English bildungsroman suggests that the genre has a significant antibourgeois potential for postcolonial writers whose works often narrate the rise of new national societies from energies based on anticolonial resistance.

Various modern experiments in the bildungsroman are of relevance to *Midnight's Children.* For one thing, the setting of Rushdie's book is specifically postcolonial and the subject matter specifically deals with attempts to define postcolonial identities in an Indian nation informed by tremendous cultural diversity. The close connection between the individual and the historical that informs the socialist realist bildungsroman anticipates Rushdie's book as well, even though Rushdie's book shows little interest in the building of socialism, despite the centrality of socialist ideas to the thought of Nehru and to the official ideology of the new Indian state.[18] In a formal sense, meanwhile, *Midnight's Children,* with its emphasis on the fragmentation and consequent destabilization of Sinai's individual identity (and India's national identity), has a great deal in common with the modernist, or late, bildungsromans Moretti discusses, even if the ironic-parodic tone of Rushdie's text would seem to mark it as more postmodernist than modernist. Postcolonialism, socialism, and postmodernism, then, provide the principal contexts for the new developments in the evolution of the bildungsroman that have occurred in the twentieth century. They also provide the central frameworks within which to consider *Midnight's Children* as a bildungsroman.

Read as a postcolonial bildungsroman, Rushdie's book might be expected to have less in common with the "national-historical" bildungsromans Bakhtin associated with the work of Goethe than with the "national allegories" Jameson associated with Third-World literature as a whole in a now somewhat notorious essay.[19] The considerable controversy over Jameson's essay has arisen principally from his seemingly imperious attempt to specify "what all third-world cultural productions seem to have in common" and to argue that these common characteristics set Third-World texts distinctly apart from First-World ones. Most controversial of all is Jameson's sweeping claim that "all third-world texts are necessarily, I want to argue, allegorical, and in a very specific way: they are to be read as what I will call *national allegories,* even when, or perhaps I should say, particularly when their forms develop out of predominantly western machineries of representation, such as the novel" (Jameson's emphasis). In particular, Jameson argues that this allegory can function because Third-World societies still maintain a sense of community that provides a connection between public and private experience that has been entirely lost in the radically fragmented and thoroughly reified world of late capitalism. This connection provides the allegorical impulse behind Third-World texts, in which *"the story of the private individual destiny is always an allegory of the embattled situation of the public third-world culture and society"* (Jameson's emphasis).[20]

The all-encompassing nature of Jameson's model seems suspiciously similar to the Orientalist discourse famously described by Edward Said. Moreover, Jameson's model seems to reduce the history of Third-World societies to the phenomenon of colonialization and subsequent decolonization, much in the traditional mode of colonialist historiographies. It is thus not surprising that Jameson's essay has drawn criticism from so many readers.[21] Some of these critiques, especially Aijaz Ahmad's, are powerful, though Jameson's essay has also proven amazingly durable and now seems to be indispensable in discussions of nationalism in postcolonial literature. In any case, the fundamental goal of Jameson's essay—to urge First-World intellectuals to pay serious attention to Third-World literature—is in itself a laudable one. And it is a goal that has been accomplished largely in the decade since Jameson's essay was first published. Third-World literature in general is now a hot topic in American literary studies (much to the chagrin of conservative proponents of "traditional" culture such as William Bennett, whom Jameson specifically identifies as an antagonist in his essay). Rushdie has been a particularly hot topic; partly as a result of the controversy over *The Satanic Verses* and partly because of the growing canonicity of *Midnight's Children,* he now receives at least as much critical attention as any of his contemporaries in Britain or America.

At first glance, *Midnight's Children* would seem to epitomize Jameson's notion of national allegory. The 1,001 Children of Midnight, born at approximately the same moment as India's independence from Britain, seem to serve as allegorical representatives of the new state in a fairly transparent way, and Sinai plays a particularly obvious role as a stand-in for postcolonial Indian culture as a whole. Rushdie emphasizes the allegorical nature of his text quite explicitly, particularly by calling attention to Saleem's allegorical role. Saleem's very face, for example, appears to resemble a map of India, with his spectacularly huge nose (which also identifies him with the elephant-god Ganesh) representing the Deccan peninsula (*MC,* 277). Because of the timing of his birth, the infant Saleem receives a note from Nehru calling him the bearer of the "ancient face of India" and telling him that his life will be "in a sense, the mirror of our own" (*MC,* 143). On the other hand, that "in a sense" is a key qualifier, the significance of which Saleem himself later ponders: "How, in what terms, may the career of a single individual be said to impinge on the fate of a nation?" (*MC,* 285). Indeed, much of Saleem's narration represents an attempt to answer this question and thus to make sense of the apparently momentous relation between the history of India and his confused and fragmented personal biography. Sinai himself continually reminds us that his story is also the story of India, that "my private existence was symbolically at one with history" (*MC,* 286). And he describes himself as the bearer of the burden of Indian history and as the culmination of that history, the "sum total of everything that went before me" (*MC,* 457).

Saleem's status as a universal marker of Indian national identity is also indicated in his remarkable telepathic ability to share the thoughts and feelings of the others around him. Because of this power, he serves as a sort of human switchboard through which the other Children of Midnight can communicate. But his negative capability extends beyond the Midnight's Children's Conference, allowing him to empathize with members of all segments of India's complex, multilayered society: "I leaped into the heads of film stars and cricketers—I learned the truth behind the *Filmfare* gossip about the dancer Vyjayantimala, and I was at the crease with Polly Umrigar at the Brabourne Stadium; I was Lata Mangeshkar the playback singer and Bubu the clown at the circus behind Civil Lanes" (*MC,* 206). Saleem also "becomes" a range of figures that encompasses the great social and economic inequities of Indian society: he is a rich man ordering about serfs, a poor man starving in Orissa, a baby whose mother has run out of breast milk, a corrupt political campaigner, a Keralan peasant turning to communism. He even briefly occupies the minds of important government figures such as Prime Minister Nehru and State Chief Minister Morarji Desai.

On the other hand, as his initial handcuff metaphor shows, Sinai is hardly comfortable in his recognition of the fact that "I was inextricably entwined with my world" (*MC,* 286). For example, he sometimes feels that his close connection to the outside world poses a powerful threat to his own identity, which is always in danger of being dissolved amid the mass of alternative identities that he entertains through his close contact with others. Thus the young Sinai tries to convince himself that he is personally in control of the various events he witnesses through his telepathic powers, that he is, in fact, causing these events and thus driving Indian history rather than the other way around. Sinai compares this illusion to the "self-aggrandizement" of the artist who believes himself fully in control of the fictional worlds he creates.[22] Sinai's illusions of grandeur also serve as a commentary on Indian politics and on the failed hopes of figures such as Nehru that they would be able to engineer a glorious future for Indian society. Of course, Sinai's seeming megalomania also tends to undermine his claim to be an allegory of the Indian state, which thus begins to look like another aspect of his personal delusion. Meanwhile, combined with the ironic postmodern playfulness of Rushdie's text, Sinai's allegorical status may be a little *too* obvious. As M. Keith Booker has noted, referring directly to Jameson's essay, Sinai may be "more a postmodern parody of a national allegory than a national allegory proper.[23]

That *Midnight's Children* is not at all what Jameson has in mind when he proposes the notion of national allegory can perhaps best be illustrated through comparison to some of the texts that do match Jameson's description of the allegorical tendency of Third-World literature. For one thing, a quick look at Jameson's own central examples, including Ousmane Sembène's Senegalese novel *Xala* and the short stories of the Chinese writer Lu Hsun, shows that Jameson appears to have in mind something considerably more subtle than the overtly self-conscious allegorization that appears in *Midnight's Children.* Indeed, a look at these examples provides the best evidence that Jameson's essay is less simplistic than it first appears. For one thing, none of the examples Jameson cites deal specifically with the historical process of colonization and decolonization, though *Xala* certainly deals with the impact of neocolonialism on modern Senegal. Similarly, none of the texts Jameson discusses involve protagonists who are direct allegorizations of postcolonial national identity in the manner of Saleem Sinai, though characters such as Sembène's El Hadji or Lu Hsun's Ah Q are certainly the products of very specific historical processes.

A look at these examples shows that Jameson, in his notion of national allegory, really has in mind something very similar to the notion of "typicality" that Lukács (following Engels) associates with the characters of the great bourgeois realists (such as Scott and Balzac) of the early nineteenth century. Jameson himself insists elsewhere on the identification of "the typifying of characters as an essentially allegorical phenomenon," and interestingly, he does so within the context of a discussion of Balzac's *La Vielle Fille*, a text that bears remarkable thematic similarities to Sembène's *Xala*.[24] To a certain extent, then, what Jameson is really saying is that postcolonial novelists quite often follow Lukács's advice that early-nineteenth-century bourgeois realism provides the best models for twentieth-century writers who would seek to oppose bourgeois cultural hegemony. And while Jameson's description of the extent to which this phenomenon dominates Third-World literature may be an exaggeration (perhaps made consciously, for heuristic purposes), it is in many ways not at all surprising. Postcolonial novelists such as Nadine Gordimer have quite openly identified Lukács as a major influence on their work.[25] One might also note Neil Lazarus's argument concerning the relevance of Lukács's work to postcolonial literature, based on the fact that Lukács has a great deal in common with Frantz Fanon, especially as "the position he elaborated in the context of proletarian struggle in Europe in the 1910s and 1920s was analogous to that which Fanon would later come to formulate in the context of the national liberation struggle in Algeria."[26] Further, there are significant parallels in general between the project postcolonial writers pursued and that which socialist writers pursued in the Soviet Union.[27]

Reading Jameson's notion of national allegory through Lukács indicates that, among other things, the texts Jameson has in mind are primarily realist and therefore differ substantially from *Midnight's Children*. It is also worth pointing out that both Lu Hsun and Sembène are socialist writers who derive far more important energies from the Marxist tradition than from the traditional cultures of their respective Third World societies. None of the Third-World texts Jameson discusses are bildungsromans, but a look at postcolonial bildungsromans shows that they often match Jameson's description quite well. One might, for example, consider George Lamming's *In the Castle of My Skin* (1953), a largely autobiographical work based on Lamming's childhood and adolescence in Barbados.[28] However, the book moves beyond the personal dimension to establish an important dialogue with the history of Barbados and of the Caribbean. Although the book is essentially a bildungsroman, relating the growth and maturation of its protagonist, designated simply as

G., *In the Castle of My Skin,* as Lamming notes in his introduction, focuses on the "collective human substance" of the village in which G. lives, so that "community, not person, is the central character."²⁹ Thus, as Sandra Pouchet Paquet points out in her foreword, "G.'s individual predicament is always dissolving into the collective predicament of other village boys, and into the adult world of social and political relations of which the child has only partial awareness."³⁰

Lamming, however, is highly aware of these relations. He addresses in a sophisticated way a number of issues that would later become central to the field of postcolonial studies, focusing on the difficulty of establishing viable and stable individual or communal identities amid the fundamentally alienating context of colonialism. He does so through both content and form, detailing G.'s experience with and growing awareness of the impact of colonialism on the society around him in a mode that departs in many ways from the conventions of the Western bourgeois novel. The book derives important energies from Caribbean oral folk culture, representing the rhythms of popular life in Barbados while eschewing the focus on plot and individual characterization typical of the Western novel. In particular, Lamming seeks, through a variety of strategies, such as alternating between first-person and third-person narrative voices, to establish a connection between public and private experience of precisely the kind that has been obliterated in the bourgeois novel (and bourgeois society) since the middle of the nineteenth century. And Lamming seeks, throughout *In the Castle of My Skin,* to call attention to class and to avoid falling into the trap of obscuring the reality of class through a focus on race, although race is an obvious locus of colonial oppression. In his treatment of America, meanwhile, he warns that nominal independence from colonial rule does not necessarily mean liberation for the Third World but may, in fact, merely lead to the replacement of British political domination by American cultural and economic domination. For example, Lamming makes clear his understanding of the threat posed to the Caribbean by the spread of an American capitalist system that seems determined to devour everything in its path: "Sometimes the twilight darkens and threatens to obliterate all memory in the tidal wave of capitalist consumerism. America spreads itself like a plague everywhere, capturing the simplest appetite with the fastest foods and nameless fripperies the advertising industry instructs us are essential needs."³¹

Lamming was a major influence on Ngugi, one of the leading practitioners of the postcolonial bildungsroman. For example, Ngugi's *Devil on the Cross* (1980) is a bildungsroman that centrally concerns the education and development of the young woman Wariinga.³² Wariinga is clearly a typical character in that she is representative of the experience of many women in postcolonial Kenya, to the point that her story is specifically described in the text as that of "any girl in Nairobi." Meanwhile, her education is quite political in nature, involving lessons she learns about neocolonial capitalism from observing a

"Thieves' Competition" at which various members of Kenya's comprador bourgeoisie try to impress their Western bosses by describing their techniques for the exploitation of the people of Kenya. Wariinga also learns important lessons from mentor figures who are themselves typical characters, including the woman Wangari (closely associated with the Mau Mau guerrillas) and the worker Muturi (a former Mau Mau who is closely associated with the Kenyan trades union movement). Having learned these lessons (and in the meantime, having also been educated as a mechanical engineer), Wariinga understandably ends the book not by comfortably integrating into the existing order, as in the traditional British bildungsroman, but by becoming a revolutionary and taking up arms against the existing order.

Even so, Wariinga, unlike the radically individualistic rebels of the nineteenth-century French bildungsroman, does join a community at the end of *Devil on the Cross,* sharing her revolutionary fight with Wangari, Muturi, and other proponents of socialist revolution in Kenya. In short, her identity is verified and stabilized via the development of a firm proletarian class consciousness. The same might also be said for Rosa Burger, the protagonist of Gordimer's *Burger's Daughter* (1980), who survives a detour into bourgeois individualism and ends the book dedicated to the fight against apartheid in South Africa in the same leftist mode that her parents embraced. Hillela Capran, the central figure in Gordimer's *A Sport of Nature* (1988), experiences even more resolution in opposition to the society in which she grows up, ending the text by participating (in a scene that turns out to have been prescient) in a glorious public festival celebrating the fall of apartheid.

In an Indian context, one might point to an antibourgeois bildungsroman such as Mulk Raj Anand's *Coolie* (1936), whose protagonist, the lowly worker Munoo, dies at the end of the text but in the meantime has experiences (including work in a pickle factory) that make him a sort of allegory of working-class experience and that indicate the potential for socialism as a means to overcome the oppression and exploitation Munoo has experienced throughout his life. Jameson's notion of national allegory, however controversial, provides a perfectly useful conceptual framework within which to read these postcolonial bildungsromans, but the radical difference between the novels of Lamming, Ngugi, Gordimer, and Anand and those of Rushdie should be obvious. For one thing, Sinai, despite his bitter criticisms of Indira Gandhi and the Congress Party, takes no real action to oppose their rule. Nor does he propose any alternatives. Moreover, there are significant lacunae in Rushdie's perspective on modern Indian history, in particular the almost complete lack of coverage of the Gandhi-led Nationalist movement, the Indian trades union movement, and other anticolonial movements.[33] Indeed, India offers a long history of rebellion against British colonial rule, including the tens of thousands of Indian "Jiffs" who took up arms against the raj during World War II, offering potential images of heroic resistance that might serve the same function for radical Indian writers that the Mau Mau have long served for Ngugi.[34]

But Rushdie is not a radical writer, and there is little room for such movements in Rushdie's book because it focuses on Sinai, a perennial outsider who does not participate in any of them. Indeed, despite his self-proclaimed status as an allegory of India and despite his purported telepathic contact with individuals from all aspects of Indian society, Sinai never experiences any real sense of belonging to any group. He does not, for example, belong even to his own family, being neither the son of his putative father nor the father of his putative son. Read as a bildungsroman, Sinai's story is really the story of one failed effort after another to incorporate into some sort of viable community, whether it be his family, the Midnight Children's Conference, the Pakistani Army, or the Communist Party. Saleem, however, never feels at home anywhere, especially within the imagined community of the Indian nation, which he treats with disgust reminiscent of Naipaul's early writings on India, his vicious assaults on Indira Gandhi amounting to a declaration of his belief that the Indian populace is too naive, gullible, and primitive to be able to participate properly in a modern democracy. Obviously, then, Sinai does not represent the kind of close connection between individual and community Jameson associates with Third-World national allegories. On the contrary, he is far more reminiscent of the radically fragmented characters that Jameson elsewhere associates with the schizo-texts of postmodernism, the "cultural logic of late capitalism," a fact directly thematized in the text by Sinai's literal fragmentation.[35]

Such fragmentation might be expected, of course, in the postmodern bildungsroman, but the only "postcolonial" bildungsromans that resemble *Midnight's Children* in this sense are ones strongly influenced by postmodernism (or even by *Midnight's Children* itself). The best example is probably *The Gunny Sack* (1989), by M. G. Vassanji, which seems to have drawn upon *Midnight's Children* as a model.[36] Vassanji's book deals with the experiences of Indian Muslims who live in what eventually becomes postcolonial Tanzania and focuses particularly on its bildungsroman protagonist, Salim Juma Huseni, whose name could be read as a gesture toward Rushdie and whose private life is closely intertwined with and affected by the larger historical and political developments on the continent. One might also compare *Midnight's Children* with the novel *Maps* (1986) by the Somali writer Nuruddin Farah. This novel narrates the growth and maturation of the young protagonist Askar, who himself is a jumble of cultural identities that represent to a certain extent the cultural confusion of postcolonial Somalia. *The Gunny Sack* ends as Salim flees Tanzania, where he has never really fit in, and goes first to Portugal, then to America. At the close of *Maps,* Askar learns that his adopted mother, Misra, has been gruesomely murdered by members of the Somali Liberation Front, who suspect her of complicity with Ethiopian enemies in a recent conflict, leaving Askar, whose cultural identity is already hopelessly confused, with no firm anchor. Significantly, both of these novels display a number of the formal and thematic characteristics of postmodernism, and in neither of them does the protagonist show a strong sense of belonging to his national community—perhaps because Vassanji and Farah both (like Rushdie) live and write in a state of migrancy rather than in their native countries.

From this point of view, it is significant that many of the texts from world literature that most resemble Rushdie's work are not postcolonial texts per se but texts written in a postmodern mode by Russian emigré novelists during the last decades of the Soviet Union. For example, Vassily Aksyonov's novels *The Burn* (1980) and *Say Cheese!* (1989) closely resemble *Midnight's Children* in their formal structure and in the aesthetic criteria they enact.[37] These novels, like *Midnight's Children,* are ebullient Menippean satires bursting with encyclopedic knowledge and Rabelaisian imagery. *The Burn,* in particular, is a sort of postmodern bildungsroman whose protagonist fragments into several different alternative adult identities in the course of his development. Such parallels should not be surprising. Emigré Russian novelists also write in a state of migrancy, and they occupy much the same cultural position as Rushdie in the West, writing for Western audiences about their exotic homelands in ways that make Westerners feel comfortably superior. Meanwhile, the banning of texts by these Russian writers in the Soviet Union served to reassure the West of its moral superiority to the benighted Soviets, just as the condemnation of *The Satanic Verses* by Islamic fundamentalists verified, for Westerners, the savagery of the Muslim world in relation to the civilized Christian West.

Of all the novels of the Soviet diaspora, the one that most resembles *Midnight's Children* is probably Sasha Sokolov's *Astrophobia* (1989), a rollicking, carnivalesque saga that rewrites the history of the Soviet Union from the days of Catherine the Great into the twenty-first century and focuses especially on the Stalinist decades.[38] *Astrophobia* is also a bildungsroman that relates the life of protagonist Palisander Dahlberg, a character of truly gargantuan proportions (and a host of physical peculiarities), who is deeply involved in the history life of Russia and the Soviet Union. Huge, hairless, and capable of gargantuan sexual exploits, Dahlberg is the ultimate Kremlin insider. The grandson of the monk Rasputin and great-nephew of Stalin's notorious security chief, Lavrenty Beria, he is raised in the Kremlin by a Guardian Council that includes Stalin and other illustrious figures. The text was supposedly compiled by a biographer in the year 2757 A.D. from documents written by Dahlberg himself around the year 2044, though many claims made in the text lead the reader to suspect that Dahlberg (like Saleem Sinai) may be a less than reliable source of information, either because of his own dishonesty or because of his failing memory. Meanwhile, Dahlberg displays many characteristics that might be associated with postmodernism, including the almost total lack of any sense of time, which adds to his unreliability as a historian, causing him to mix up his chronology and conflate events from different eras.

Dahlberg's version of history is, if anything, even more distorted than Sinai's, and one could argue that Sokolov's text marks an additional step beyond Rushdie's into total postmodern distance from any real engagement with history. In this sense, it is also useful to compare Peter Carey's recent novel *The Unusual Life of Tristan Smith* (1995), whose eponymous character (and narrator) moves beyond the merely offbeat into the realm of the grotesque.[39] So ugly that his looks are likely to cause strangers to vomit, Tristan is repulsive even to the politically correct members of the agitprop theater troupe within which his actress mother raises him in the fictional Third-World land of Efica, a group of islands long under the colonial domination of the rich and powerful First-World nation Voorstand. Carey manages within this conceit to contrive a number of criticisms of the imperial machinations of global capitalism. Voorstand, for example, uses Efica as a dumping ground for chemical waste. But Carey's strongest satire is reserved for the glitzy, Disneyesque popular culture of Voorstand, with which Efica is constantly bombarded and toward which even Tristan feels an attraction. Late in the book he travels to Voorstand, where he encounters a nightmarish postmodern world of crime and simulacra that presumably serves as a biting critique of contemporary America. Unfortunately, Carey also enacts the unreal nature of life under capitalism in the form of his book, which is so thoroughly decked out with postmodern artifices of its own that it really has no ground on which to stand in its criticisms of the unreal nature of life under modern capitalism. In his choice of the abstract and fictional lands of Efica and Voorstand as the settings for his critique, Carey estranges his novel from material reality in a way that merely reinforces the phenomena he is attempting to criticize, while his choice of a monstrous hero may gesture toward the radical alienation of all postmodern subjects. Few of the subjects of global capitalism, however, will be able to appreciate the literary gimmickry of a text that only true aficionados of postmodern fiction are likely to enjoy or to see as subversive.

Midnight's Children is not so thoroughly postmodern as *Tristan Smith,* which might be another way of saying that there are at least vestiges of traditional Indian culture lurking somewhere in the margins of Rushdie's text. No one, not even Jameson, would want to argue that the postmodern homogenization of global culture has made all texts absolutely identical, whether they arise from India, the Soviet Union, or Australia. Obviously, it makes no sense to read *Midnight's Children* as a purely Indian work that can somehow serve as an authentic specimen of Indian culture, preserving that culture as in a museum so that First-World readers can view it at their pleasure to experience a certain nostalgia for forms of social experience no longer available in the West. But even in the realm of the postmodern, some cultural specificity remains, and it would equally make no sense to read *Midnight's Children* purely as a postmodern text without paying attention to the book's, and its author's, Indian background.

In this sense, one might want to suggest that Rushdie's book is modernist rather than postmodernist, given Jameson's argument that one of the key distinctions between modernist works and postmodernist ones is precisely that the former can still draw upon certain traditional energies that help to highlight their fundamental newness, while the latter are marked by a complete modernization in which the old is entirely swept away, leaving the concept of the "new" without any real meaning.[40] Ultimately, however, it is fruitless to quibble over categories in this way. *Midnight's Children,* read within the generic context of the bildungsroman, clearly has more in common with postmodernist texts than modernist ones, but in either case it has relatively little in common with the texts of writers such as Lamming and Ngugi, who are engaged in the construction of positive postcolonial cultural identities in ways that Rushdie clearly is not. *Midnight's Children* is in many ways and from many points of view a very fine novel, as its enthusiastic critical reception in the West shows. But it is hardly the Indian national epic that some readers have seemed to want it to be, and anyone who approaches the text seeking unadulterated knowledge about India does so at great peril.

This is not to say, however, that we can encompass the cultural specificity of *Midnight's Children* by a simple appeal to concepts, now fashionable in postcolonial studies, such as hybridity. By my reading, Rushdie's text is not an elaborate melting pot in which Eastern and Western cultures can mix and mingle as equals, producing something richer than either could alone. Far from suggesting the rich cultural hybridity that results from the colonial encounter, *Midnight's Children* reenacts the colonial encounter in ways that ultimately, if inadvertently, provide reminders that this "hybridity" was underwritten by a relationship of brute force, of domination and submission. Rushdie's text is a fundamentally Western one that has been elaborately tricked out with ornamentation derived from Indian culture. But these ornaments are thoroughly reified and act very much like the artificial images through which Flaubert's *Salammbô* presents, in the words of Lukács, "the alien and distant, incomprehensible but picturesque, decorative, grandiose, gorgeous, cruel and exotic world of Carthage."[41] Within the exotic and alien world of the reified India of his text, Rushdie presents us with the struggles of a protagonist who is thoroughly Western, whose fragmented psychic experience is that of a subject of late capitalism. In short, Rushdie is performing, in *Midnight's Children,* a sort of Westernization very similar to the "modernization" Lukács associates with *Salammbô* and other decadent historical novels, in which the past is not linked to the present as its prehistory but is used simply to provide an exotic locale for an essentially modern story. In *Midnight's Children,* India is not linked to the West as part of a hybrid, cosmopolitan global culture; it is merely a colorful stage setting on which Saleem Sinai can act out his thoroughly Western postmodern angst.

Notes

1. Patricia Merivale, "Saleem Fathered by Oskar: Intertextual Strategies in *Midnight's Children* and *The Tin Drum*," in *Reading Rushdie: Perspectives on the Fiction of Salman Rushdie*, ed. M. D. Fletcher (Amsterdam: Rodopi, 1994), 86.

2. See, for example, Uma Parameswaran, "Handcuffed to History: Salman Rushdie's Art," *Ariel* 14 (1983): 34–45; Neil ten Kortenaar, "*Midnight's Children* and the Allegory of History," *Ariel* 26, no. 2 (1995): 41–62; David Lipscomb, "Caught in a Strange Middle Ground: Contesting History in Salman Rushdie's *Midnight's Children*," *Diaspora* 1, no. 2 (1991): 163–88; Rustom Bharucha, "Rushdie's Whale," *The Massachusetts Review* 27 (1986): 221–37.

3. Salman Rushdie, *Midnight's Children* (New York: Penguin, 1981); hereafter cited in the text as *MC*.

4. M. Keith Booker, *Colonial Power/Colonial Texts: India in the Modern British Novel* (Ann Arbor: University of Michigan Press, 1997), 143.

5. Marc Redfield, *Phantom Formations: Aesthetic Ideology and the Bildungsroman* (Ithaca, N.Y.: Cornell University Press, 1996), 38.

6. Franco Moretti, *The Way of the World: The Bildungsroman in European Culture* (London: Verso, 1987).

7. Ibid., 227.

8. Barbara Foley, *Radical Representations: Politics and Form in U.S. Proletarian Fiction, 1929–1941*, (Durham, N.C.: Duke University Press, 1993), 321.

9. M. M. Bakhtin, "The *Bildungsroman* and Its Significance in the History of Realism (Toward a Historical Typology of the Novel)," in Bakhtin, *Speech Genres and Other Late Essays*, ed. Caryl Emerson and Michael Holquist, trans. Vern W. McGee (Austin: University of Texas Press, 1986), 10–59, 23.

10. Ibid., 25.

11. Franco Moretti, " 'A Useless Longing for Myself ': The Crisis of the European Bildungsroman, 1898–1914," in *Studies in Historical Change*, ed. Ralph Cohen (Charlottesville: University of Virginia Press, 1992), p. 59.

12. Foley, 323.

13. Evgeny Dobrenko, *The Making of the State Reader: Social and Aesthetic Contexts of the Reception of Soviet Literature*, trans. Jesse M. Savage. (Stanford, Calif.: Stanford University Press, 1997).

14. Katerina Clark, *The Soviet Novel: History as Ritual* (Chicago: University of Chicago Press, 1981).

15. Lily Wiatrowski Phillips, "W. E. B. Du Bois and Soviet Communism: *The Black Flame* as Socialist Realism," *The South Atlantic Quarterly* 94 (1995): 844, 837–64.

16. Of particular interest in this sense is Maxim Gorky's splendid novel *The Life of Klim Samgin*, whose eponymous protagonist is a bourgeois par excellence, living in late-nineteenth- and early-twentieth-century Russia (he dies symbolically at the precise moment of Lenin's arrival to St. Petersburg in 1917). Samgin belongs to the same bourgeois family as the protagonists of Musil's *Man without Qualities*, Mann's *Magic Mountain*, or Flaubert's *Sentimental Education*, except that Gorky's text offers a (socialist) alternative to the radical alienation these bourgeois protagonists suffered.

17. See, for example, Geta Leseur, *Ten Is the Age of Darkness: The Black Bildungsroman* (Columbia: University of Missouri Press, 1995); Gunilla Theander Kester, *Writing the Subject: Bildung and the African American Text* (New York: Peter Lang, 1995); Elizabeth Abel, Marianne Hirsch, and Elizabeth Langland, eds., *The Voyage In: Fictions of Female Development* (Hanover, N.H.: University Press of New England, 1983).

18. See M. Keith Booker's essay in this volume for an argument that *Midnight's Children* is in fact underwritten by an anticommunist subtext reminiscent of the Western propaganda of the Cold War.

19. Fredric Jameson, "Third World Literature in the Era of Multinational Capitalism," *Social Text* 15 (1986): 65–88.
20. Ibid., 69.
21. The first, and still the best, critique of Jameson's essay is that formulated by Aijaz Ahmad, originally published in *Social Text* and reprinted in Ahmad's *In Theory: Classes, Nations, Literatures* (London: Verso, 1992), 95–122.
22. Kathleen Flanagan notes that this motif in *Midnight's Children* also serves as a parody of the "great man" theory of history. See Kathleen Flanagan, "The Fragmented Self in Salman Rushdie's *Midnight's Children,*" *Commonwealth Novel in English* 5, no. 1 (1992): 43, 38–45.
23. Booker 1997, 139.
24. Fredric Jameson, *The Political Unconscious: Narrative as a Socially Symbolic Act* (Ithaca, N.Y.: Cornell University Press, 1981), 162.
25. On Gordimer and Lukács, see M. Keith Booker, *The African Novel in English: An Introduction* (Portsmouth, N.H.: Heinemann, 1998), 136–37.
26. Neil Lazarus, *Resistance in Postcolonial African Fiction* (New Haven, Conn.: Yale University Press, 1990), 16. Lazarus is particularly concerned with pursuing parallels between Lukács and Fanon within the context of his readings of the Ghanaian novelist Ayi Kwei Armah. For more on Armah, Lukács, and Fanon, see M. Keith Booker, "The Historical Novel in Ayi Kwei Armah and David Caute: African Literature, Socialist Literature, and the Bourgeois Cultural Tradition," *Critique* 38, no. 3 (1997): 235–48.
27. See M. Keith Booker and Dubravka Juraga, "The Reds and the Blacks: The Historical Novel in the Soviet Union and Postcolonial Africa," *Studies in the Novel* 29, no. 3 (1997): 274–96.
28. George Lamming, *In the Castle of My Skin* (1953; reprint, Ann Arbor: University of Michigan Press, 1991).
29. George Lamming, introduction to Lamming, *In the Castle of My Skin*, xxxvi.
30. Sandra Pouchet Paquet, foreword to Lamming, *In the Castle of My Skin*, xvi.
31. Lamming 1991, xlv–xlvi.
32. For more on *Devil on the Cross* as a bildungsroman, see Booker 1998, 173–77.
33. For more on the significance of these omissions, see M. Keith Booker's essay in this volume.
34. For a recent succinct account of the Indian "Jiffs" who fought with the Japanese against the British in World War II, see Amitav Ghosh, "India's Untold War of Independence," *New Yorker* (June 23 and 30 1997): 104–21.
35. Jameson's most important discussions of postmodernist culture to date appear in *Postmodernism, or, The Cultural Logic of Late Capitalism* (Durham, N.C.: Duke University Press, 1991). Additional comments concerning the fragmentation of the subject in postmodernism appear in the essay "Postmodernism and Consumer Society," in *The Anti-Aesthetic: Essays on Postmodern Culture*, ed. Hal Foster (Port Townsend, Wash.: Bay Press, 1983), 111–26.
36. M. G. Vassanji, *The Gunny Sack* (London: Heinemann, 1989). The relationship is emphasized on the cover of the novel, which calls the book "Africa's Answer to *Midnight's Children*."
37. Vassily Aksyonov, *The Burn,* trans. Misha Glenny (New York: Random House, 1985); *Say Cheese!,* trans. Antonina W. Bouis (New York: Random House, 1989).
38. Sasha Sokolov, *Astrophobia,* trans. Michael Henry Heim (New York: Grove and Weidenfeld, 1989). For more on Sokolov's text, see M. Keith Booker and Dubravka Juraga, *Bakhtin, Stalin, and Modern Russian Fiction: Carnival, Dialogism, and History* (Westport, Conn.: Greenwood Press, 1995).

39. Peter Carey, *The Unusual Life of Tristan Smith* (New York: Knopf, 1995). The Australian Carey is also a migrant writer in the West, who lives and works in New York City.

40. Jameson 1991, 311.

41. Georg Lukács, *The Historical Novel,* trans. Hannah Mitchell and Stanley Mitchell (Lincoln: University of Nebraska Press, 1983), 186.

"This Angrezi in which I am forced to write": On the Language of *Midnight's Children*

MICHAEL GORRA

I

Born into a rich Muslim family at midnight, August 15, 1947—the very instant of India's independence—Saleem Sinai grows up "handcuffed to history," believing that the words with which Nehru proclaimed the new nation's existence have been especially addressed to him (11).[1] Saleem too wants to "build the noble mansion of free India, where all her children may dwell" (116); for hasn't Nehru himself suggested, in a commemorative letter to "Dear Baby Saleem" that the boy's life will be "the mirror" of the nation's? (122). So a childhood accident to the fictional Saleem leads in Salman Rushdie's *Midnight's Children* (1981) to the historical 1957 language riots that ended with the partition of the state of Bombay. What happens to him, happens to his country; what happens to his country, happens to him.

Rushdie presents the novel as Saleem's autobiography: one the character has written while working, at the age of thirty, in a Bombay pickle factory, written as a defense against the disintegration of his own body, written in despair at the way his "life has been transmuted into grotesquery by the irruption into it of history" (57). The book's title has come in popular parlance to refer to that generation born around the time of Independence—Rushdie's own generation, and that of Rajiv Gandhi as well, a generation that has known only Indian and not colonial rule. Yet, though Rushdie surely intends that large meaning, in the novel itself the phrase applies only to the particular group that Saleem comes to embody, the 1001 children born in the first hour of India's independence, "seeds of a future which would genuinely differ from anything the world had seen," and all of whom have magical powers (193).

Saleem uses his own gift, that of telepathy, to form those children into a club, inviting them to join a nightly congregation in his mind. The Midnight's Children's Conference—the novel's central conceit—makes Saleem's

---

Adapted from Michael Gorra, *After Empire: Scott, Naipaul, Rushdie* (Chicago: University of Chicago Press, 1997) with the help of the author.

autobiography an attempt to enact belief in another sort of narrative, in that of the India that Gandhi and Nehru conceived as a democratic, secular, and pluralist state; a dream that found its political voice in the Indian National Congress (INC). Congress claimed to represent all Indians, and never abandoned that claim, even after the rise of Muhammed Ali Jinnah's Muslim League and the subsequent creation of Pakistan made the INC seem increasingly identified with Hinduism; even after Independence changed it from a resistance movement into a ruling party. And in evoking a similar congress, Rushdie attempts, with both the Midnight's Children's Conference (MCC) and with *Midnight's Children* itself, to provide a vision of the country he wants India to be: an attempt to imagine a unifying form for the subcontinent as a whole, from Kerala to Kashmir, from Bombay to the jungles of Bengal; a country that has indeed made a fresh start at the moment of independence, in which the differences between Hindu and Muslim and Sikh, brahmin and beggar, are contained within a single structure.

Yet in describing that vision, that community, the adult Saleem, at work in the pickle factory where he preserves his past in vinegar and spice, sees himself as suffering from a peculiarly "Indian disease . . . [an] urge to encapsulate the whole of reality" (75). What makes it a disease—and one to which novelists as well as Indians are peculiarly liable—is the impossibility of shaping such disparate materials into a coherent narrative; not just those of his own autobiography, but those of a partitioned and ever more fragmented India itself. And indeed Saleem's own family history is marked by a parodic version of that fragmentation. His maternal grandfather, a doctor, had wooed his wife through a hole in a "perforated sheet." She was in *purdah,* kept from the eyes of "strange men"; her father would only let him see that part of which she complained (24). He came to know her not as a whole, but through one, and she always remained for him "a badly-fitting collage of her severally inspected parts . . . partitioned woman. . . . Glued together by his imagination" (26). So when Saleem starts to despair over the possible incoherence of his story, he insists that his own body has begun to fall apart, that it's riven with actual cracks and fissures, even if no one but he can perceive them. Throughout the novel, in fact, Saleem will transform such psychological states into physical realities, insisting that "Reality can have metaphoric content," that he's speaking "the literal, by-the-hairs-of-my-mother's-head-truth" (197); and this is the source of the fantasy that so marks Rushdie's work as a whole.

Saleem's personal disintegration comes in the novel to stand as an emblem for that of the national collage as a whole, a country that looks whole on the map but that has, in the years since the novel's publication in particular, become increasingly divided from itself. In its most explicit form, however, the conflict between Nehru's noble mansion and the communal strife that characterizes Indian political life fills only a few of the novel's pages. Instead Rushdie embodies both India's extraordinary diversity and the concomitant centrifugal force of its national form in the very structure of Saleem's narrative itself. For like the eponymous narrator of Rushdie's beloved *Tristram Shandy,* Saleem can't resist interrupting his story to observe himself in the process of telling it—questioning his own reliability, noting his doctor's visits, wondering how the tale might go over with Padma, the illiterate factory worker, the Indian everywoman, who must and yet cannot be his audience. The novel seems itself a "badly-fitting collage," and in reading one even forgets the midnight's children for chapters at a time, and follows instead, now enchanted, now appalled, Saleem's thousand and one digressions from the main narrative of his life: odes to chutney; Tai the Kashmiri boatman, who for years refused to wash; the pyromania of Saleem's sister, the Brass Monkey; a father who offers to have his daughter's teeth pulled and replaced with gold, as a dowry; the atrocities of the Bangladesh war; the ghostwomen of the Sundarbans; mango-kissing in the Indian film industry; smuggling in the Rann of Kutch; Bombay billboards, snakecharmers, and bicycles.

II

The exuberance of Rushdie's style makes his chronicle of Saleem's growing despair more entertaining, more bearable and more hopeful, than it would otherwise be. The inventive fantasy of Saleem's disintegration provides an alternative to that disintegration itself, a gesture of imaginative freedom in an otherwise intractable world. That's most obviously a response to Pakistan's 1971 invasion of its own East Wing (now Bangladesh) and to the incipient totalitarianism of Indira Gandhi's 1975–77 "Emergency." But the playfulness of the novel's form also stands as an attempt to engage the ideologically defined discourses of both colonialism and its nationalist counterparts. Timothy Brennan has described Rushdie as the type of the "cosmopolitan" writer, those who either because of social class or emigration (both in Rushdie's case) are in "perpetual flight from a fixed national or ideological identity."[2] Cosmopolitan writers are at once anti-imperialist and yet suspicious of "radical decolonisation theory."[3] Instead they engage in what Brennan describes as the demythification of Third World nation-building, in a way that's sometimes held to confirm Western prejudices, showing that a new nation "can act as abominably as the British did."[4] In consequence, Brennan suggests, many Third World critics feel that such a writer isn't firmly on their side against a West that will use such work as an excuse for one form or another of neocolonialism; though, as Tariq Ali points out, *Midnight's Children* "says nothing that Indians or Pakistanis do not say to each other in private." [5]

Disagreements should be kept in the family, not aired in public—that is, in English. The charge of cosmopolitanism is one that Rushdie himself poses in *Shame* (1983), through a peremptory, italicized voice that dialogically interrupts and challenges his own narrative:

> Outsider! Trespasser! You have no right to this subject . . . I know: nobody ever arrested me. Nor are they ever likely to. Poacher! Pirate! We reject your authority. We know you, with your foreign language wrapped around you like a flag: speaking about us in your forked tongue, what can you tell but lies? I reply with more questions: Is history to be considered the property of the participants solely? In what courts are such claims staked, what boundary commissions map out the territories? (S, 23)

"Nobody ever arrested me"—this is sad irony in the aftermath of the *fatwa* that the Ayatollah Khomeini issued against *The Satanic Verses* (1988). To be cosmopolitan is, on this reading, to be inauthentic. Yet Rushdie's work as a whole can perhaps best be seen as an attempt to contest the terms on which such judgements get made. In *The Satanic Verses* he provisionally identifies the movie star Gibreel Farishta with the "good"—good because he constantly reaffirms his Indian origins, because he wishes to "remain . . . *continuous*—that is joined to and arising from his past . . . his is still a self which . . . we may describe as 'true.' " And Rushdie opposes Gibreel to Saladin Chamcha, "a creature of *selected* discontinuities," and one who therefore seems "false"—and not only in his capacity for evil (SV, 427). For Saladin's Anglophiliac mimicry of British norms has indeed made him a *chamcha,* the subcontinent's equivalent of an Oreo cookie; "Toadji" (SV, 58). Yet Rushdie no sooner establishes those identities than he undermines them: Gibreel has lost his Islamic faith, and Saladin makes peace with the father he's spurned. Saladin shows himself capable of self-sacrifice; Gibreel reveals a corresponding evil. And in blurring the distinctions between them, Rushdie clears a space for the cosmopolitan by challenging the very concept of cultural authenticity on which the assumption of Gibreel's "goodness" depends.

Midnight's Children explores a complicated set of questions about cultural identity and allegiance, about the relations between India and England, colony and metropolis. Those questions are difficult in themselves, but they're made especially so by the fact that Rushdie rarely poses them in explicit terms. He locates them instead in the ground of the novel's language itself, in what he describes as "this Angrezi in which I am forced to write," (S, 34) and in doing so demonstrates that to be Anglicized isn't to stop being Indian. With the exception of an obligatory scene at the Jallianwallah Bagh, *Midnight's Children* doesn't appear to deal with British colonialism in any great detail. In terms of plot it seems almost irrelevant. And yet the colonial background proves inescapable. All Saleem's schooling is in English. His family and friends live in a small cluster of hill-top houses built by the British, and indeed the cut-rate terms on which they've bought those houses from the Englishman William Methwold stipulate that they're forbidden to throw anything away. At first they protest about the budgies and the "half-empty pots of Bovril" the British have left behind them, but soon they start drinking cocktails, and "slip effortlessly into their imitation Oxford drawls" (98). For, in Frantz Fanon's terms, Saleem's family stands as the very model of a native bourgeoisie, happy to "take over the posts that the foreigner has vacated."[6] Or as Saleem himself will later joke, "The businessmen of India . . . [are] turning white" (176).

Their English hill-top allows these mimic men to insulate themselves from India's "stream of chanting humanity" (186). At school, for example, Saleem's two worst subjects are Marathi and Gujarati, Bombay's chief indigenous languages; in fact Rushdie suggests that the boy's ignorance of them is what touches off the language riots of 1957. For neither Saleem nor the India he embodies can simply repudiate the British past, however much they might want to. The novel hypothesizes that he is a changeling, the biological son not of the rich Muslim couple who raise him, but instead of the poor Hindu Vanita. Yet Saleem also claims that he is of mixed blood, that his actual father wasn't her street musician husband, but the Englishman Methwold. Just how he knows this remains unclear—Vanita dies in childbirth and Methwold has gone back to Britain, out of reach of Saleem's telepathy. His parentage remains conjectural. But Saleem's belief in his British blood shouldn't be seen as the chamcha's desire to be accepted as English; in fact Anglo-Indians have such a marginal social status that he's deeply embarrassed by it. His British ancestry functions, rather, as a trope for his hybrid cultural heritage, for the different forces that the novel suggests have shaped modern India. Because the novel's most important attempt to engage the discourse of colonialism is also its most obvious—one so obvious, so completely naturalized, that we almost miss it. *Midnight's Children* is written in English.

Or is it? In *The Satanic Verses* Rushdie introduces a character named Zeeny Vakil with this gloriously ramshackle sentence: "She was an art critic whose book on the confining myth of authenticity, that folkloristic straitjacket which she sought to replace by an ethic of historically validated eclecticism, for was not the entire national culture based on the principle of borrowing whatever clothes seemed to fit, Aryan, Mughal, British, take-the-best-and-leave-the-rest?—had created a predictable stink, especially because of its title." A maze of clauses, almost impossible to parse; a portmanteau stuffed to bursting, with question marks and dashes as luggage straps that barely hold it together. That interjection about the "folkloristic straitjacket," for example, is far more important than what surrounds it, in a way that almost makes the sentence feel as if it has wobbled out of control. A few lines later Zeeny wonders why there should be " 'a good right way of being a wog?' " (SV, 52). Her question points most obviously toward Rushdie's conception of the "national culture," in ways I'll describe below, and yet his style itself seems to ask something similar. Why should there be a good right way of writing an English sentence? Rushdie makes English prose an *omnium gatherum* of whatever seems to work, sprinkled with bits of Urdu, eclectic enough even to accommodate cliche, unbound by any grammatical straightjacket. The very structure of the sentence seems to open possibilities, to recut the borrowed clothes of English until they've become those of that new Indian language Angrezi. And while the sound of that new name onomatopoeically evokes the anger implicit in having to use a language "marred by the accumulated detritus of its owner's unrepented past" (S, 34), it also transforms that bitterness into laughter; the master's tongue appropriated for one's own subversive purposes.

Gauri Viswanathan has shown how the disciplinary study of English literature, in both India and in Britain itself, was a product of the Raj's attempt to provide a rigorously moral but not explicitly Christian education.[7] British literature came to be seen as the repository of the wisdom and values that it had been England's unique destiny to articulate, the values that Hari Kumar in Paul Scott's *Raj Quartet* has been trained to accept. And that literature was presented in the shape of a narrowly defined Great Tradition, a tradition that even now determines the curriculum of English education in India; Shakespeare and Milton themselves were held to have a civilizing mission. For post-Independence India, the English language and its literature stand as one of the structuring institutions—like the army, the civil service, and the capital in New Delhi—that the British left behind and that the current nation-state can never quite discard. Even the revisionary impulse of Rushdie's Angrezi depends on the existence of that inherited tradition. What else is his evocation of the midnight's children but a fantastic version of Rudyard Kipling's description of Kim's entry into the Grand Trunk Road, with its "new people and new sights at every stride—castes he knew and castes that were altogether out of his experience . . . ?"[8] English is the language in which Nehru announced the new country's very existence; the tongue through which it continues to present itself to the outside world. Yet it remains the first language only of the Anglo-Indians and of the tiny elite to which Saleem belongs; an elite who, as Saleem's linguistic hill-top suggests, have an attenuated relation to what he ironically if edgily describes as the country's "so-called teeming millions" (166).

There's no need to rehearse here the overall history of the English language in India. What concerns us is its literary use. In the preface to *Kanthapura* (1937), one of the seminal novels of the Independence movement, Raja Rao wrote that while English had become the language of India's "intellectual make-up," it wasn't the tongue of its "emotional make-up." And he called on the Indian writer to create a distinctive dialect in which "the tempo of Indian life . . . [would be] infused into our English expression even as the tempo of American or Irish life has gone into the making of theirs."[9] But how could that Indian English develop when the cardinal rule of one's schooling was to deny that "emotional make-up" by writing and speaking an English as close to British norms as possible? Not to do so was to invite condescension and contempt. And most Westernised Indians tried to avoid the derision attached to "Babu English," not by declaring their independence of British models, as did many African and Caribbean writers, but by demonstrating their mastery of the master's style. Yet in the end that Anglicization only underlined the fact that one was, in Homi Bhabha's words, *"almost the same but not quite . . . almost the same but not quite."*[10]

In practice spoken Indian English soon became what in 1951 Nirad C. Chaudhuri described as a "mixed language," marked by a heteroglossia in which words, phrases, and even syntactic structures from Indian languages played a role in English conversation.[11] "There is a language for books," as Anita Desai has written, "and a language for conversation, and the two are not the same—so we were taught in school and so we believed."[12] Some allowance in the writing of fiction might be made for words—often italicized, to mark their foreignness—that denote food, clothing, or religious beliefs. And of course many such words, like "bungalow," have long since entered British English itself and are enshrined in *Hobson-Jobson,* the famous 1886 glossary of Anglo-Indian vocabulary. Some allowance was made as well for the dialogue of characters who don't know English, like R. K. Narayan's Tamil speakers, whose speech is marked by the sentence structure of their mother tongue. But those are the exceptions that prove the rule; Narayan's narrative prose remains largely monoglot, without the colloquial bite that makes spoken Indian English so distinctive. For Indians, Chaudhuri argued, were "not as yet permitted to write" that mixed language. "No Indo-English equivalent of the Indo Persian Urdu has as yet made its appearance as a written language."[13]

That was not entirely true, for the first-person narration of G. V. Desani's *All About H. Hatterr* (1948) had indeed drawn on that spoken language. Insisting that "Life is contrast," above all the contrast between the narrator's "rigmarole English" and the "higher English poetical works of the Bard," Desani created a difficult linguistic hybrid, and as in *Midnight's Children,* his narrator's mixed blood serves as a metaphor for the heterogeneity of his style.[14] For although Anglicization can indeed make one a *chamcha*, condemned by history to ape the West, Desani showed how a deliberate mimicry can use the essentially ironic difference in sameness that characterizes Anglicization to upset conventional expectations, to make that mimicry parodic, carnivalizing it, using it to guy the colonizer, as an impressionist does the politicians he caricatures. Rushdie has praised the novel's use of Babu English—half parody, half revelation of its resourcefulness—as "the first great stroke of the decolonizing pen."[15] But it remained *sui generis* until his own invention of Angrezi, in Desai's words, "brought the spoken language off the street and onto the printed page, with such energy and electricity that . . . [India finally saw] the two tongues as one."[16]

" 'Proper London, bhai!' " Gibreel calls out as he falls toward earth on the first page of *The Satanic Verses.* " 'Here we come! . . . Out of thin air, baby.

Dharrraaammm! Wham, na? What an entrance, yaar. I swear: splat' " (SV, 3). "Yaar"—the favorite interjection of the English-language fan magazines that serve Bombay's Hindi film industry. And perhaps Rushdie's stylistic roots can be found there as much as in Desani, for popular journalism has been far more willing than "literature" to acknowledge the hybridity of spoken Indian English. "Ek dum," his characters say when they want something done at once; "funtoosh" when they feel washed-up; and neither word is italicized. The illiterate Padma asks Saleem about the purpose of all his " 'writing-shiting,' " and tells him to " 'Eat, na, food is spoiling.' " And while earlier novelists had used Hindi words for food, Rushdie overfills the plate; neighbors arrive "bearing rasgullas and gulab jamans" (155) and when he's sick Saleem's ayah promises him " 'chocolate cake . . . ladoos, pista-ki-lauz, meat samosas, kulfi. So thin you got, baba, the wind will blow you away' " (234).

And always there is the All-India Radio of the streets—its film music, its channa-wallah's calls, its curses and epithets and endearments and interjections. Toward the end of *Midnight's Children* a "vendor of notions" who's found robbing the dead on a battlefield in Bangladesh makes Saleem an offer for his lapis lazuli-encrusted spittoon, the one family heirloom Saleem has left: "Ho sir! Absolute master thing! Is silver? Is precious stone? You give; I give radio, camera, almost working order, my sir! Is a damn good deals, my friend. For one spittoon only, is damn fine. Ho yes. Ho yes, my sir, life must go on; trade must go on, my sir, not true?" (360). The wheedling contempt with which the peddler views his victim would be memorable in any language—and so would the skill with which Rushdie tosses this portrait off, this character who exists but for a page. Yet the brilliance of that characterization lies in the way the peddler's phrasing departs from British norms—the lack of a pronoun with the verb "is," the placement of "only" and the plural of "deal," above all the idea that the spittoon is an "Absolute master thing!" One laughs, not because the syntax seems wrong, but because its liberation from the rules of standard English creates a shameless energy that is at once monstrously inappropriate and yet absolutely right for a scene set on a field of corpses.

The inventive impurity of Rushdie's heteroglot style provides a challenge to the idea of proper English, the King's English, and therefore to British colonialism. Though it stands itself as the belated consequence of Macaulay's "Minute on Indian Education" it nevertheless subverts the Minute's assumption that educated Indians should be British in everything but blood. Instead it bends and twists and transforms the language, refashioning it to fit the experience of contemporary Indian life, in a way that allows one to be something other than a *chamcha* in using it. Yet if the hybridity of Angrezi marks the postcolonial "separation" of English from its "origins and essences," that same hybridity challenges any notion of the authentically Indian as well.[17] For Rushdie's account of Zeeny Vakil, one remembers, isn't a description of the English language itself, even though it provides a model of how to use it. No—it deals instead with a particular conception of India's "national culture."

Zeeny's rejection of "the confining myth of authenticity" in favor of an "historically validated eclecticism" seems so closely allied to the terms of Fanon's "On National Culture" as to suggest that Rushdie has taken that essay as a model. Fanon's account turns on what he describes as the desire of "native intellectuals to shrink away from that Western culture in which they all risk being swamped," and their consequent "search for a national culture which existed before the colonial era."[18] This has been especially true in Africa, where the novelist's task, in Chinua Achebe's words, has been to help his or her people "regain belief in itself" by showing them that the past "was not one long night of savagery from which the first Europeans . . . delivered them."[19] Yet because colonialism in Africa exploited its subject peoples not as "Angolan [or] Nigerian," but simply as "the Negro . . . a Savage," Fanon argues that on that continent the appeal to a precolonial culture is never conceived of in national terms; indeed the nations themselves are colonial creations.[20] Instead the appeal becomes a racial one. The Francophone concept of *negritude* stood as "the emotional if not the logical antithesis of the insult which the white man flung at humanity," for it posited the existence of an essential—an essentialist—African identity, whose mark could be seen throughout the Diaspora, in Angola and Alabama alike.[21]

In India the appeal to an essential or authentic identity at first appears to work in exactly the opposite way, for it's couched not in terms of what is larger than the nation, but in terms of what's smaller, of one's religious or linguistic or caste affiliations. But Fanon remains a reliable guide. In some ways India's national form seems a colonial construct, a creation of the British, like Kenya. As late as the moment of Independence, the subcontinent contained, in addition to the territory under direct British rule, over 500 quasiautonomous princely states, some of which briefly tried to survive as independent nations of their own. We have made Italy, Cavour said, in placing that peninsula's crown on the head of the king of Sardinia; now we have to make the Italians. Or as Saleem's grandfather Aadam Aziz says to his wife on their honeymoon, " 'Forget about being a good Kashmiri girl. Start thinking about being a modern Indian woman' " (35). Yet even if India were nothing more than a geographical expression, geography is still, as Herder reminds us, one of the main constituents of national identity. And Rushdie himself suggests that if India was invented by the British it was nevertheless "a dream that everyone agreed to dream. And now I think there actually is a country called India"—and moreover one that's already 5000 years old.[22] For the British were not the first to attempt India's unification. Ashoka had done it before the birth of Christ, and the Mughal Emperor Akbar tried in the 16th century. Over the millennia religious movements had swept the whole subcontinent—Buddhism, the 8th century Hindu revivalism of Shankara, the syncretic *bhakti* movements that tried to fuse Hinduism and Islam in the 15th century. The Indian National Congress made a nonsectarian appeal, and it succeeded—"not wholly or in full measure," as Nehru admitted, "but very substantially"—because the community it imagined coincided, not only with the territory under British domination, but also with earlier movements to which it could look as a model.[23]

Yet in spite of its "secular and egalitarian pronouncements" Congress found itself, as both a resistance movement and a ruling party, appealing to what Akeel Bilgrami describes as "a monolithic and majoritarian Hinduism" that sought to impose the myth of "a pan-Indian Brahminical ideology" on India's heterogeneous past.[24] Fanon's analysis suggests that such a nativist politics grows from the attempt to find an identity anterior to the national form that colonialism leaves behind it. It is at best a reactive formation, limited by its failure to "take account of the . . . historical character" of human societies,[25] and it amounts as well to what Edward Said describes as an implicit acceptance of "the racial, religious, and political divisions" that imperialism imposes on its subject peoples.[26] For " 'Why should there be a good, right way of being a wog?' " as Zeeny Vakil asks, in rejecting "the confining myth of authenticity." " 'That's Hindu fundamentalism' " (SV, 52). Despite her Congress Party's increasingly sectarian identification, Mrs. Gandhi's authoritarian populism never hesitated to divide and rule itself, offering concessions to minority groups in exchange for bloc votes. This didn't cost her party much with the Hindu bourgeoisie that had moved—metaphorically, at least—into the houses the British left behind them. But it did with a newly prosperous and self-consciously Hindu middle class that has turned away from Congress and toward the Hindu nationalist Bharatiya Janata Party (BJP) in what, in the years since the publication of *Midnight's Children,* has become a far greater challenge to Nehru's legacy than that posed by the separatists of Kashmir or Assam. The fundamentalism of the BJP sees India as a single entity, with an essentially *Hindu* unity that long antedates the national state. For the country itself is unchanging and eternal, it is *Bharat Matya,* Mother India, the land of the *Mahabharata* and the *Ramayana*. The official secularism of the Indian constitution is but a foreign import, an attempt by British invaders to appease Muslim invaders. And so the nation must be redefined as an explicitly Hindu polity, and the pollution of the outsiders' touch expunged. It is no accident that the BJP's constituency is largely upper-caste.

Rushdie's conception of the "national culture" uses the necessary impurity of his own Angrezi to challenge not just the ideology of colonialism but that of such a "folkloristic straightjacket" as well. He depends instead on "an ethic of historically validated eclecticism," that rejects the myth of a pure and unadulterated *Bharat*.[27] His knowledge of what Fanon would call India's "historical character" tells him that the Aryan ancestors of the BJP were themselves invaders from the north, who imposed their rule and their Sanskrit tongue on the Dravidian South. Muslims have been in India for a thousand years, for longer than France has been France, and the glories of Rajput painting and architecture depend on Persian and Mughal models. The Bengali Renaissance of which the filmmaker Satyajit Ray was the last flower had its origins in an attempt, in the years before Macaulay, to demonstrate that the West was not antithetical to Hinduism. And the fact that such a book as *Midnight's Children* can exist at all?

For Rushdie puts Angrezi—puts English—at the very heart of modern India's national identity. As Saleem well knows, his mastery of English does indeed detach him from the affiliations of region or language or religion through which most of India's people have historically defined their identities. Yet in doing so that language paradoxically makes all India open to him.[28] He belongs nowhere—or anywhere, or everywhere in the imagined community of the independent nation-state. " 'Oh my shoes are Japanese,' " Gibreel sings in *The Satanic Verses,* translating the words of a Hindi film song into English. " 'These trousers English, if you please. On my head, red Russian hat; my heart's Indian for all that' " (SV, 5). No less Indian for all that because for Rushdie there is no *sine qua non* of Indianness. Saleem's biological parents are rich and poor, British and Hindu, but he grows up a Muslim. And an Indian—by choice, because the creation of Pakistan has given his family a choice, and they have consciously decided to think in terms of a national and not a communal identity. The very cosmopolitanism that might preclude Rushdie's solidarity with a mythical "people" is in itself a defense against the provincialism of sectarian politics. And so Saleem asserts his right to compare himself to Bombay's beloved Hindu god, "mammoth-trunked . . . garrulous" Ganesh (192). But his own great schnozz also recalls the great noses of Western literature, like Cyrano de Bergerac's or Tristram Shandy's, in a way that reveals the artificiality of any absolute distinction between India and the West. " 'We're all bad Indians' " (SV, 52), Zeeny says, for to believe that there's such a thing as a " 'good, right way' " of being Indian would force one to reject the very idea of the nation Rushdie has defined through the unfulfilled, but never abandoned, dream of the Midnight Children's Conference.

That India is as plural and impure as the Hindu pantheon itself, which finds room for Christ and Mohammed. It is a land of "non-stop self-regeneration," a collage of whatever clothes seem to fit—my metaphor is deliberately mixed—of hybrids like Urdu and the Sikhs and the Marxist Christians of Kerala. And the fundamentalist monoglot is the only one for whose beliefs its noble mansion does not have a room. The Angrezi of *Midnight's Children* is finally an attempt to imagine a sense of Indian national identity capacious enough to include someone like Saleem, or indeed like Rushdie himself. For neither British colonialism nor that "folkloristic straitjacket" has a place for such cultural conundrums, and his critique of the one is finally inseparable from his critique of the other.

Yet Rushdie's work is in the end far more than a celebration of Indian diversity. For his sense of the hubbub of voices within Saleem's mind can also stand as a model for the construction of both the postcolonial and the postmodern self: a self that depends on the impurity of his own "mixed language." As Saleem contains that multitude within him, so too must those who, whether abroad or in the land of their birth, have to live in two cultures at once. The postcolonial self is no more singular than India itself. It is never pure, never what *The Satanic Verses* terms "one one one" but is instead always "two or three or fifteen" (SV, 102), always plural, not a *chamcha* but instead a hybrid. Indeed Rushdie suggests that such a self should actively choose the hand that history has dealt it: should reject what in his postcolonial counterpart V. S. Naipaul is a wounded awareness of that lack of singularity for a ready acceptance of the fact that cultures are never inviolate; an acceptance that will allow one to learn the ways in which migrancy and mimicry can themselves become a creative force. "Perhaps we are all," he writes, "black and brown and white, leaking into one another . . . *like flavours when you cook*" (IH, 394).

But Rushdie also pushes that conception of the self beyond the postcolonial circumstances from which it grows to reject the very idea that it can ever be anywhere whole. "O, the conflicting selves jostling and joggling within these bags of skin," thinks the professional mimic Saladin at the end of *The Satanic Verses*, ". . . no wonder we invent remote-control channel-hopping devices. If we turned these instruments upon ourselves we'd discover more channels than a cable or satellite mogul ever dreamed of" (SV, 519). Lawrence called on the novel to abandon its belief in "the old stable ego of the character," and most modernist fiction has indeed dealt with the process of that ego's disintegration.[29] But Rushdie suggests that we shake off not just our customary belief in that stability but even the pain of the loss of that belief; the self becomes a pastiche, a collage of different styles, like the "national culture" that Zeeny Vakil describes, a set of masks improvised for different occasions. It is the point at which the postcolonial coalesces with the postmodern; a sense of the self as a series of impersonations—of the final inauthenticity of the self in itself—that corresponds to that in Philip Roth's *The Counterlife* (1986).

Yet the very fractures of the multiple self can be both a liberation and a source of strength. The Hindu faithful have traditionally believed that they lost caste in leaving India to travel over the black water. Because Rushdie's sense of the self has its roots in his imagination of an India that isn't bound by such notions of purity, his own Indianness has therefore become a portable identity, one that he could maintain through the years of English education and the emigration that culminated in the writing of *Midnight's Children*. And perhaps, one hopes, he has even been able to carry it with him into that strange half-life of safe houses and security guards in which he now lives.

III

Midnight's Children ends with a glimpse of apocalypse, in which Saleem finally explodes under "the awful pressure of the crowd" (445) inside him, cracking and crumbling into his constituent specks of "voiceless dust . . . two three, four hundred million five hundred six" (446), one for each individual citizen of the nation he has embodied. India falls to pieces, trampled in the dust by the people who comprise it. Within that house there are now a million mutinies, above all that led by Nehru's own daughter. Because of her the children of midnight will have no children themselves. And it is Saleem himself who will betray them to her, finally cooperating—against his will, under torture, yet cooperating just the same—with Mrs. Gandhi's identification of India with herself and herself alone. But Saleem also compares himself to her, pits his version of India against hers. Perhaps, he says, they are competing for "centrality," for they both see "the multitudinous realities of the land" as raw material on which to impose a form. Saleem describes his task as that of "sniffing-out-the-truth" (299) about a land in which the powers-that-be have remade that truth in their own image, and yet that competition forces him to use the same means. India as Indira, or India as Saleem? For he too wants to make the truth about India into what he instructs it to be.

Or rather into what Rushdie tells it to be. Before concluding I want briefly to explore my chief reservation about both *Midnight's Children* and his work as a whole. In a 1987 elegy for his brother Shiva, Naipaul argued that "There is a way currently in vogue of writing about degraded and corrupt countries . . . the way of fantasy and extravagance. It dodges all the issues. It is safe . . . empty, morally and intellectually; it makes writing . . . an aspect of the corruption of the countries out of which it emerges. I find . . . [an] insistence on rationality and the intellect more exhilarating."[30] Naipaul doesn't mention Rushdie, but it's hard to read these words without thinking of him as their target. And indeed one imagines a sense of rivalry between them, the English language's two most important writers of Indian descent. For Naipaul the nightmare of history is comprehensible, it can be explained through a rational analysis of historical processes; hence the classical restraint of his style. Anything else, any move into fantasy, any assignment of a metaphorical content to reality, is "empty." But though counter-arguments can be easily made, I want to take Naipaul's charge seriously. For both the fantasy and the rhetorical extravagance of *Midnight's Children* can numb its readers to anything but its own exhilaration. However entrancing—indeed, precisely because it is entrancing—Rushdie's style distances one from the horrors it describes, making his description of them not only bearable but even enjoyable. It keeps one from being disturbed by the things that happen to his characters, even by Saleem's treatment at the hands of the Widow.

Pushkin is said to have been surprised, in writing *Eugene Onegin,* to realize that his heroine Tatyana would turn one of her suitors down. But the contemporary novelist rarely endows his characters with that kind of freedom, and in reading, as Iris Murdoch writes, we feel instead their "ruthless subjection . . . to the will of their author."[31] Rushdie would be incapable of Pushkin's surprise. His characters' fates seem cartoonishly overdetermined, and not simply because they're handcuffed to history's crude ironies. The whole narrative of *Midnight's Children* remains so firmly under the thumb of his style that at times I find it hard to distinguish between the writer's fantasies on the one hand, and the Widow's on the other, between the book and the totalitarian world it purports to attack. The bombs in the 1965 Indo-Pak war fall in such a way as to wipe out Saleem's whole family; it's symbolically useful at that point for Rushdie's narrator to become an orphan.

Rushdie's style precludes the close involvement with individual characters on which the novel has traditionally depended, and that can indeed make his work seem an "aspect of the corruption of the [country] out of which it emerges." But in doing so it remains homologous to an age, to a politics, in which individuals as such do not greatly matter; a homology that isn't an echo so much as a parody of the Widow's lust for centrality. As we acknowledge the absurdity of Saleem's claim to be India, so should we recognize that of her own as well. Late in the novel Saleem finds a brief refuge from history in the magician's ghetto huddled in the shadow of the Jamma Masjid, Delhi's great Friday Mosque. And there he learns that for all their rope tricks and fire-eating, "the magicians were people whose hold on reality was absolute . . . they could bend it every which way in the service of their arts, but they never forgot what it was" (385). Those words can stand as Rushdie's own aesthetic principle: to bend Indian life this way or that, to make us believe in the illusions of telepathy or in metaphors that seem to come literally true—and yet always to remember what that reality is. The illusion becomes not an aspect of the country's corruption, but a comment on it. For in reading one no more forgets that reality than do either those Delhi magicians or their audience, which happily attends to the smoke and the mirrors, and so learns how easily one can be snared by fantasy, lured on by the promise of marvels. We even get to see how the trick's been done, and that does distinguish Saleem from the Widow, who would rather we didn't notice; he, at least, admits that his India is but one of all many millions of possible versions. And so we find that Rushdie has alienated us from the illusion even as he enthralls us, has made us think critically not only about Indian politics and identity, but also about the terrible seductive force of Saleem's—of his own—desire to encapsulate the whole of reality.

We are on this interpretation *meant* to be bothered by the ways in which the novel *doesn't* disturb us.[32] That is supremely true of the work of Rushdie's mentor, Günter Grass; in *The Tin Drum* both Oskar's grotesque moral distance from the events he describes and the reader's own response to that distance serve to indict the Nazi abuse of language. With Rushdie I'm not so sure; *Midnight's Children* seems too full of an unironized nostalgia for Saleem's

Bombay childhood to convince me that we're intended to read it with that kind of skepticism. And moreover Rushdie himself points to that failure to disturb as a weakness in his own work, telling an interviewer that his books have so far contained "very little stuff at all about the deep emotions . . . one of the things I have failed to do, at the center of my work, is write about strong feeling, cathartic emotion, obsession."[33] Even in *The Satanic Verses* it's only when Rushdie abandons fantasy, in the concluding scenes between Saladin and his dying father, that the novel manages to summon that "strong feeling"; and he considers that ending "the best thing I've ever written."[34]

The degree to which a novel like *Midnight's Children* maintains a tyrannical relation to its own characters does indeed mark a limitation in the great fiction of our age; we must learn to brush such works against the grain, to read them with the same kind of suspicion, the same attention to their implication in the corruptions of power, that we now direct toward the classic texts of 19th century realism. Too much of the most innovative postwar fiction has depended on "fantasy and extravagance" for me fully to share Naipaul's categorical condemnation. But neither can I wholly discount it, and in the end I remain troubled that a book about the nightmare of history cannot make me care about the individual characters to whom that history happens.

Yet that fantasy, that flamboyance, offers so much that I'm willing to accept such a fault as the price of the ticket: a way to deal with politics on a large scale, rather than in terms of individual ethical dilemmas; to present the ways in which history has transmuted us all into grotesquery; of dealing with events that the mind refuses to comprehend in terms of the rational explanations that realism presumes. And *Midnight's Children* could not do any of those things so vividly if it did not allow itself the freedom to find the metaphorical content of reality and render it a literal one. Any account of the Indian novel in English must recognize that Rushdie has given it a new start, a new and bolder life. No one has done so much to remake English into an Indian language; no one has so fully used that language to probe the nature of national identity, or to define a model for the postcolonial self. No writer in English has so energetically and joyously peopled the immigrants' London or the great city of Bombay; no one since Dickens has offered as engaging a gallery of self-dramatizing rogues and charlatans and madmen. And Rushdie's work moreover contains so powerful a sense of possibility as to render it a force for change. For Naipaul the nightmare of contemporary history is comprehensible, and yet his insistence on rationality can leave one with a sense of despair, locked into a nightmare from which there seems no escape. Rushdie's reliance on the fantastic may dodge some issues. It may also help keep the imagination alive in an otherwise intractable world.

Midnight's Children stands as an attempt to preserve the spirit of India's secular and democratic independence—a process that Saleem describes as the "chutnification of history." For as its final conceit the novel suggests that each of its chapters is a particular flavor of pickle, a jar in which Saleem has managed to preserve not just "fruit, vegetables, fish, vinegar, spices," but also "memories, dreams, ideas"; special recipes all ready to enter "mass-production [and] be unleashed upon the amnesiac nation" (443), helping it recall the majesty of the mansion that Nehru had left it. Sometimes, Saleem admits, he hasn't gotten the recipes quite right—there's an "overly harsh taste," for example, "from those jars containing memories of my father." And the process of pickling can lead, like the magicians' tricks, to some "inevitable distortions," for the flavors of history are altered and intensified by the spices and vinegars that preserve them—a metaphoric concentration of tamarind or lime, or indeed of India itself. Yet in the process, something quite unpalatable—an unripe mango, a massacre in Bangladesh—will be transformed, made bearable, even enjoyable, in a way that grants us a bit of sustenance out of which hope and action may grow. Saleem acknowledges that even so some pickles may remain "too strong for some palates, their smell may be overpowering, tears may rise to eyes." Yet he hopes that nevertheless each jar will contain "the authentic taste of truth." For they are all of them, "despite everything, acts of love" (444).

Notes

1. Page references to Rushdie's work will be included in the text. For *Midnight's Children* (New York: Knopf, 1981) this will simply be a page number in parentheses. For his other works, I use the abbreviations below, followed by a page number. These editions have been used:

S—*Shame*. New York: Knopf, 1983.
SV—*The Satanic Verses*. New York: Viking, 1989.

2. Timothy Brennan, *Salman Rushdie and the Third World: Myths of the Nation* (London: Macmillan, 1989), 142.
3. Ibid., 30.
4. Ibid., 27.
5. Tariq Ali, "*Midnight's Children*," *New Left Review*, November 1982, 94.
6. Frantz Fanon, *The Wretched of the Earth* (1961), trans. Constance Farrington (New York: Grove Press, 1968), 158.
7. Gauri Viswanathan, *Masks of Conquest: Literary Study and British Rule in India* (New York: Columbia University Press, 1989).
8. Rudyard Kipling, *Kim* (1901; reprint, Hardmonsworth: Penguin Books, 1987), 109. See also Richard Cronin, "The English Indian Novel: *Kim* and *Midnight's Children*," in *Imagining India* (New York: St. Martin's, 1989).
9. Raja Rao, Author's Foreword to *Kanthapura* (1937; reprint, New York: New Directions, 1967), vii.
10. Homi Bhabha, "Of Mimicry and Man" in *The Location of Culture* (London: Routledge, 1994), 86, 89. Emphasis in original.
11. Nirad C. Chaudhuri, *The Autobiography of an Unknown Indian* (1951; reprint, Bombay: Jaico, 1964), 492.
12. Anita Desai, "Indian Fiction Today," *Dedalus* 188, 4 (Fall 1989), 211.

13. Chaudhuri, 492.
14. G. V. Desani, *All About H. Hatterr* (1948; reprint, Harmondsworth: Penguin, 1972), passim.
15. Salman Rushdie, "The Empire Writes Back with a Vengeance," *The Times* (London), 3 July 1982, 8.
16. Desai, 212.
17. Bhabha, "Signs Taken for Wonders: Questions of Ambivalence and Authority under a Tree outside Delhi, May 1817," in *The Location of Culture,* 120.
18. Fanon, 209.
19. Chinua Achebe, "The Novelist as Teacher," in *Hopes and Impediments: Selected Essays* (New York: Anchor, 1989), 44–45.
20. Fanon, 211.
21. Ibid., 212.
22. Interview with Victoria Glendinning, "A Novelist in the Country of the Mind," *Sunday Times* (London) 25 October 1981, 38.
23. Quoted in M. J. Akbar, *India: The Siege Within* (Harmondsworth: Penguin, 1985), 10.
24. Akeel Bilgrami, "Cry, the Beloved Subcontinent," *New Republic,* 10 June 1981, 31–34.
25. Fanon, 216.
26. Edward Said, *Culture and Imperialism* (New York: Knopf, 1993), 227.
27. An important source for that conception—and, outside of Rushdie's own work, its most powerful articulation—can be found in the last chapter of Chaudhuri's *Autobiography,* "An Essay on the Course of Indian History."
28. See Cronin, 4–5.
29. From a letter to Edward Garnett, in *The Letters of D. H. Lawrence,* ed. Aldous Huxley (London: Heinemann, 1932), 198.
30. V. S. Naipaul, "My Brother's Tragic Sense," *Spectator,* 24 January 1987, 22.
31. Iris Murdoch, "The Sublime and the Beautiful Revisited," *Yale Review* Winter 1960, 265.
32. Brennan mounts such an argument in his chapter on *Midnight's Children*—"The National Longing for Form"—arguing that Rushdie treats his own novel "as if it were a paradigm of the state lie" (98). My own version of that argument is also indebted to Brechtian notions of epic theater.
33. Gerald Marzorati, "Rushdie in Hiding: An Interview," *New York Times Magazine,* 4 November 1990, 85.
34. Quoted in James Fenton, "Keeping Up with Salman Rushdie," *New York Review of Books,* 28 March 1991, 32.

Allegorizing the Emergency: Rushdie's *Midnight's Children* and Benjamin's Theory of Allegory

TODD M. KUCHTA

"The tradition of the oppressed teaches us that the 'state of emergency' in which we live is not the exception but the rule. We must attain to a conception of history that is in keeping with this insight."
—Walter Benjamin, "Theses on the Philosophy of History"

"The book exists to be a reaction to events as the author has reacted to them. It was written in the light of a very dark time."
—Salman Rushdie

While *Midnight's Children* is commonly read as an allegory of India's national history, critics fail to account for Rushdie's subversion of conventional allegorical structure through the "scraps, shreds, fragments" of memory that constitute narrator Saleem Sinai's resistance to "the banal chain of cause-and-effect."[1] Walter Benjamin's conception of allegory as a form of nonmimetic rupture provides a theory for reading the fragmentary structure of *Midnight's Children* as both a critique and a revision of the historical context framing the novel's composition. In 1975, Indira Gandhi declared a national state of emergency, attempting to squelch all opposition to her rule through censorship, suspension of civil liberties, mass imprisonment, and sterilization campaigns. Writing "in the light of a very dark time," both Rushdie and Saleem attempt to subvert Gandhi's authoritarian rule and her mythical status in the Indian political imaginary by allegorizing personal and national history within the context of the Emergency's repressive practices. The trajectory of recurrent though fragmentary allegorical objects in *Midnight's*

This essay was written specifically for this volume and is published for the first time by permission of the author.

Children, particularly the imagery of the finger and hand, connects the Emergency with various disparate moments in Indian history; in this way, Rushdie links and ultimately compares Gandhi's regime to the oppression of British imperial rule. Benjamin's theory of allegory allows us to trace this trajectory, for his ideas both inform the structure of *Midnight's Children* and offer a means of reading the novel as an attempt to "attain to a conception of history" that subverts "the 'state of emergency' in which we live."

I. Rushdie in Ruins

> "Allegories are, in the realm of thoughts, what ruins are in the realm of things."
> —Walter Benjamin, *The Origin of German Tragic Drama*

In a lecture delivered at the University of Aarhus in 1983, Salman Rushdie commented on the allegorical nature of *Midnight's Children*. "I didn't want to write a book which could be conventionally translated as allegory," Rushdie claimed, "because it seems to me that in India allegory is a kind of disease. . . . There is an assumption that every story is really another story which you haven't quite told, and what you have to do is translate the story that you have told into the story that you haven't told." Though Rushdie admitted his novel "clearly has allegorical elements," he nevertheless sought to "resist allegory," at least the kind for which readers must "translate the structure of the book into the secret meaning." Rushdie decided instead to use a "slightly different kind of thing, which is the *leitmotif*. The *leitmotif*, as described by Benjamin, involves the use of recurring things in the plot incidents or objects or phrases which in themselves have no meaning . . . but which form a kind of non-rational network of connections in the book."[2]

Rushdie's comments offer two significant insights into the structure of *Midnight's Children*. First, although the novel "clearly has allegorical elements," Rushdie attempted to resist the more conventional notion of allegory whereby a consistent network of one-to-one correspondences forces the reader to look for the "secret meaning"—an understanding of allegory that Rushdie claims is specifically Indian and that perhaps accounts for William Methwold's reference in *Midnight's Children* to "a very Indian lust for allegory" (*M*, 96). Second, while Rushdie goes on in his lecture to emphasize the often overlooked South Asian influences of *Midnight's Children*—the nonlinear, swooping shape of oral narrative; the parallels between narrator Saleem Sinai and the god Ganesh; the use and abuse of the family saga tradition; the architectural blueprint of the Hindu temple; and the problematic role of the hero in India—the novel's structure is nevertheless informed by the ideas of the early-twentieth-century German philosopher and critic Walter Benjamin.

Given Rushdie's desire to exchange traditional allegory for a more disruptive form of representation based in part on Benjamin's ideas, it seems problematic that, as Neil ten Kortenaar points out, the *Midnight's Children* is most commonly read "as a national allegory giving imaginative form to India and its history."[3] Of course, such a reading is encouraged by Rushdie's narrator, who, born at the exact moment of India's independence, claims that the nation "was not only my twin-in-birth but also joined to me (so to speak) at the hip, so that what happened to either of us, happened to us both" (*M*, 385). And indeed, as various readers have shown, the novel's allegorical elements work within a number of different registers, attesting to the structural complexity of allegory in *Midnight's Children*.[4] Fruitful though they may be in illuminating the prevalence of allegorical elements in *Midnight's Children*, however, such readings fail to acknowledge the unconventional nature of allegory in the novel by either ignoring its ruptured and fragmentary structure (as in the case of Kortenaar, Brennan, and Syed) or (as with Kane) treating that structure as a formal aberration that renders the novel's political and aesthetic values "irreconcilably divided."[5]

A different approach to the structure of *Midnight's Children* is suggested by Benjamin's conception of allegory.[6] For Benjamin, allegory is not "a mere mode of designation" that elaborates "a conventional relationship between an illustrative image and its abstract meaning"; rather, it is both a type of experience and "a form of expression, just as speech is expression, and, indeed, just as writing is" (Benjamin 1977, 162). Seeking to rehabilitate its debasement in romantic aesthetics, Benjamin distinguishes allegory from the symbol—the preferred figure of romanticism—by centering not on the relationship between part and whole but rather on "the decisive category of time." While "the measure of time for the experience of the symbol is the mystical instant," allegory involves "a corresponding dialectic" between the sign and its historical context (*O,* 165). Thus whereas the symbolic image shelters coherent meaning from the destructive passage of time, allegory recognizes the evolving relationship between signs and their meanings, viewing history as "a petrified, primordial landscape" whose emblems par excellence are the skull and the corpse (*O,* 166). But allegory's inevitable progression toward death is not without purpose: for the knowledge it brings, "the triumph of subjectivity and the onset of an arbitrary rule over things, is the origin of all allegorical contemplation" (*O,* 233).

As Azade Seyhan suggests, "Benjamin 'salvages' allegory from the 'inferior' position assigned to it in romantic usage and reinvents it as the informing trope of historical change."[7] Allegory thus responds to the decaying process of time in general, and to transitory historical moments in particular, with a melancholic desire to preserve the objects of the past by ripping them from their previous contexts and relocating them within the present. This violence toward an organic aesthetics results in "the destructive tendency of allegory, its emphasis on the fragmentary in the work of art."[8] With such an emphasis, "the false appearance of totality is extinguished" (*O*, 176), and the fragmentary images and objects that comprise an allegory become tantamount to ruins: for "in the ruin," as in the corpse, "history has physically merged into the setting" (*O*, 177–78). Thus, "if the object becomes allegorical under the gaze of melancholy, if melancholy causes life to flow out of it and it remains behind dead, but eternally secure, then it is exposed to the allegorist, it is unconditionally in his power" (*O*, 183–84). Allegory, in other words, promises to redeem subjectivity in the midst of dramatic historical change.

In the seventeenth century, baroque allegorists mobilized their "visions of the frenzy of destruction, in which all earthly things collapse into a heap of ruins," so that allegory could ultimately provide the means for "rediscover[ing] itself, not playfully in the earthly world of things, but seriously under the eyes of heaven" (*O*, 232). Only God offered redemption to the authors of the *Trauerspiel*. In the modern era, however, the fragmentary objects of allegorical contemplation uncover the potentially liberatory moments within the past that have been buried by tradition. Such an enterprise does not presume to discover the past itself, as a discrete entity of the Real. Rather, the subjective lens of memory serves as the primary tool for disinterring the ruins of the present from their sedimentation within the past. In his "Theses on the Philosophy of History," Benjamin, quoting Ranke, argues that "to articulate the past historically does not mean to recognize it 'the way it really was'. . . . It means to seize hold of a memory as it flashes up at a moment of danger."[9] Allegorical contemplation offers the basis for an epistemological and political awakening that is rooted in the present's memory of the past.

Benjamin's theory of allegory provides a means of reading *Midnight's Children* as a response to the historical conditions that frame its composition for both Rushdie and his narrator, Saleem Sinai. Indira Gandhi's State of Emergency, between 1975 and 1977, brought about India's most serious political crisis in almost 30 years of independence. Facing widespread discontent over the nation's economic instability, as well as mounting pressures from an increasingly united opposition, Gandhi revoked civil liberties, censored the media, enforced mass sterilizations, and imprisoned approximately 100,000 political enemies. In her address to the nation upon declaring the Emergency, Gandhi charged her opposition with "agitation, disruption, and incitement to industrial workers, police, and defence forces in an attempt to paralyze totally the Central Government."[10] She then implemented a "Twenty-Point Program" that bolstered the economy and produced a more efficient and industrious workforce. Thwarting any resistance, Gandhi strengthened her control over the nation, and by early 1976 ousted opposition rule at the state level and "postponed" scheduled national elections. Ruling largely with "the help of picked advisers, her so-called 'kitchen cabinet,'" "the normal processes of parliamentary debate . . . disintegrated," and India's parliament became a rubber stamp.[11] Perhaps unaware of mounting discontent, or believing she had fully silenced her opposition, Gandhi unexpectedly ended the Emergency in early 1977 and announced general elections. Voters elected Moraji Desai's Janata Party by a landslide, but disarray led Desai's government to crumble only three years later, and India once again placed itself under Indira Gandhi's leadership.[12]

"The book was conceived and begun during the Emergency," Rushdie claims of *Midnight's Children*, "and I was very angry about that. The stain of it is on the book."[13] His narrator Saleem is similarly haunted by Gandhi throughout the narrative and comes to believe that "the truest, deepest motive behind the declaration of the State of Emergency was the smashing, the pulverizing, the irreversible discombobulation of the children of midnight" (*M*, 427). As in Benjamin's conception of allegory, Saleem's own body becomes a decaying repository of history: "nine-fingered, horn-templed, monk's tonsured, stain-faced, bow-legged, cucumber-nosed, castrated, and now prematurely aged" (*M*, 447), Saleem is "literally disintegrating," "buffeted by too much history" (*M*, 37). But through allegory, Saleem seeks to subvert Gandhi's centralized authority as well as her severe restrictions on individual representation and expression during the Emergency. Allegory offers a means to reestablish individual and communal memory at a moment in India's history in which one of the greatest risks, according to Saleem, is the failure to remember.[14] Noting that "we are a nation of forgetters" (*M*, 37), Saleem devotes his narrative to reconstructing his own history "before memory cracks beyond hope of re-assembly" (*M*, 384). His project is especially significant during the Emergency, whose injustices were "rapidly being consigned to the oblivion of the past," so that many "had become so incapable of judgment, having forgotten everything to which they could compare anything that happened" (*M*, 444). Rushdie's nonfictional writing similarly emphasizes Indira Gandhi's ability to "persuade the world to forget the atrocities committed during her years of Emergency rule."[15] In *Midnight's Children*, Rushdie deploys Benjamin's notion of allegory—its ability to destabilize the apparently natural relationship between form and content, signifier and signified—as a historically situated response to the Emergency and to the communal amnesia that threatens to let Gandhi's actions fade from the nation's memory. Rushdie's project in *Midnight's Children* is to reconstruct that past through the fragmentary form of allegory.

II. Re: Imagining Home

"It may be that when the Indian writer who writes from outside India tries to reflect that world, he is obliged to deal in broken mirrors, some of whose fragments have been irretrievably lost."

—Salman Rushdie, "Imaginary Homelands"

> "That which is touched by the allegorical intention is torn from the context of life's interconnections: it is simultaneously shattered and conserved. Allegory . . . offers the image of transfixed unrest."
>
> —Walter Benjamin, "Central Park"

"It's my present that is foreign, and the past that is home," Rushdie writes in "Imaginary Homelands," perhaps his most famous statement on his position as an Indian-born novelist writing in England—what he elsewhere refers to as his "migrant sensibility" ("Imaginary," 9).[16] Rushdie claims that those who share his position, "exiles or emigrants or expatriates, are haunted by some sense of loss, some urge to reclaim, to look back, even at the risk of being mutated into pillars of salt. But if we do look back, we must also do so in the knowledge . . . that our physical alienation from India almost inevitably means that we will not be capable of reclaiming precisely the thing that was lost; that we will, in short, create fictions . . . imaginary homelands, Indias of the mind" ("Imaginary," 10). As his comments suggest, Rushdie's migrant sensibility shares with Benjamin's notion of melancholic allegorical contemplation a sense of loss and of displacement from an earlier time, an impossible desire to reconstruct the past. Like Benjamin, Rushdie recognizes the inherently skewed perspective of one forced "to deal in broken mirrors, some of whose fragments have been irretrievably lost," even as he claims that "the broken mirror may actually be as valuable as the one which was supposedly unflawed"("Imaginary," 11). Echoing Benjamin's suggestion that "allegories are, in the realm of thoughts, what ruins are in the realm of things" (*O,* 178), Rushdie claims that "the shards of memory" that constitute his attempts to reimagine his homeland "acquired greater status, greater resonance, because they were *remains.*" These remains owe their significance to the fact that "human beings do not perceive things whole; we are not gods but wounded creatures, cracked lenses, capable only of fractured perceptions. . . . Meaning is a shaky edifice we build out of scraps, dogmas, childhood injuries, newspaper articles, chance remarks, old films, small victories, people hated, people loved; perhaps it is because our sense of what is the case is constructed from such inadequate materials that we defend it . . . even to the death" ("Imaginary," 12).

Rushdie's claims about the work of memory and its recovery of the past through the present finds its fictional embodiment in *Midnight's Children.* Although he began writing the novel as a Proustian search for lost time, Rushdie became more interested while writing in "the way in which we remake the past to suit our present purposes, using memory as our tool."[17] *Midnight's Children* is thus not meant to be "some sort of inadequate reference book or encyclopedia" that produces a coherent account of the modern Indian nation; rather, Rushdie emphasizes the ambiguous and contingent nature of history by deploying Saleem's unreliable narration as "a useful analogy for the way in which we all, every day, attempt to 'read' the world."[18] But such an analogy should not suggest an abandonment of material concerns. Rushdie claims that "when your version differs from the official version" in moments of historical crisis like the Emergency, "then remembering becomes a political act."[19] Furthermore, Rushdie resists the notion that an interest in form and structure leads to a rarefied aestheticism, and he claims that "all description is itself a political act" ("Imaginary," 13).[20] Thus, like Benjamin, for whom modern allegory provides a resistance to orthodoxy and a return to subjectivity, thereby demanding a renewed historical mapping, Rushdie allegorizes Indian history through the perspective of the Emergency in an attempt to subvert Gandhi's mythological embodiment of the nation and to restore a memory of the past that can provide the foundation for political recognition and action. For Rushdie, as for Benjamin, allegory is the antidote to myth.[21]

III. Mythologizing the Emergency

"[T]he unity of India was never so strong and meaningful in all these years, before or since independence."
—Indira Gandhi, *My Truth*

"She told the world the horror stories about the Emergency were all fictions; and the world allowed her to get away with the lie."
—Salman Rushdie, "Dynasty"

In his essay "Dynasty," Rushdie claims that to understand the power of Indira Gandhi and the Nehru-Gandhi dynasty, "we must go beyond politics and history and enter the zone of myth."[22] Indeed, given the sharp divergence between the official and unofficial accounts of the Emergency, it should not be surprising that the Emergency has been transformed into the stuff of myth in India's national history.[23] An analysis of the Emergency reveals Gandhi's attempt to mythologize its events, helping her to maintain an almost divine aura in India and to convince its citizens, along with the citizens of the world, to forget her atrocities.

Years after the Emergency, Gandhi defended her decision to suspend democracy as a means of maintaining it, claiming that "democratic liberty does not include license to undermine democracy itself" (Gandhi, 170). According to Gandhi, the period before the Emergency was marked by severe political unrest. "Anti-Congress parties were not only obstructing development but also all normal functioning of the administration and economy. There were frequent calls to stop all work. Farmers were asked not to sell

their produce to the Government. Non-payment of taxes was preached....
They tried to persuade workers not to work but to agitate.... As if this were
not enough, they even attempted to undermine the loyalty of the police and
military.... The aim of the opposition parties was obviously to paralyze the
Government and indeed all national activity and thus walk to power over
the body of the nation" (Gandhi, *My Truth*, 171). But in a 1978 report to the
Commission on the Emergency, Supreme Court Chief Justice J. C. Shah
would categorically deny Gandhi's justifications for authoritarian rule in a
statement that is worth quoting at length:

> There is no evidence of any breakdown of law and order in any part of the
> country—nor of any apprehension in that behalf; the economic condition was
> well under control and had in no way deteriorated. There is not even a report
> of an apprehension of any serious breakdown of the law and order
> situation.... The public records of the times, secret, confidential or public,
> and publications in newspapers, speak with unanimity that there was no
> unusual event or even a tendency in that direction to justify the imposition of
> emergency.... But Madam Gandhi, in her anxiety to continue in power,
> brought about instead a situation which directly contributed to her continu-
> ance in power and also generated forces which sacrificed the interests of many
> to serve the ambitions of a few. Thousands were detained and a series of totally
> illegal and unwarranted actions followed involving untold human misery and
> suffering.[24]

Not surprisingly, Rushdie's own conclusions on the Emergency concur
with Shah's report. In "Dynasty," Rushdie compares Gandhi's Emergency
declaration with the opening of Pandora's box and claims that "many of the
evils besetting India today—notably the resurgence of religious extrem-
ism—can be traced back to those days of dictatorship and State violence.
The Emergency represented the triumph of cynicism in Indian public life,
and it would be difficult to say that that triumph has since been reversed"
("Dynasty," 52).

Perhaps as surprising as the continuing divergence over the origin, consequences, and overall significance of the Emergency was its general acceptance by the Indian population when it was imposed. As Inder Malhotra suggests, "[A]lmost literally no one raised his or her voice when Indira hit the
country with the hammer-blow of the Emergency proclamation. Indeed, the
apparently instant and complete acceptance of the Emergency was as stun-
ning as its sudden imposition."[25] The Emergency was accepted in this way
primarily because Gandhi had her political opponents swiftly imprisoned.
Gandhi declared the Emergency around midnight of June 26, 1975, and by
dawn, almost 700 opposition members were arrested under the Maintenance
of Internal Security Act.[26] "Acceptance" of the Emergency was also no doubt
encouraged by India's rapid economic improvement. Within a week of the
emergency, Gandhi unveiled the Twenty-Point Program of economic reform

whose main goal was to "bring down prices" and redistribute the nation's wealth. In 1975, a 6 percent rise in industrial production, sparked by the absence of strikes, led to a reversal of the previous year's 30 percent inflation rate. By 1976, agricultural output reached a record high, while significant increases in housing and surplus land were identified and reallocated to the poor. Gandhi's Emergency thus seemed the solution to India's recent political and economic instability. As Stanley Wolpert suggests, "[F]or twenty-one months India's trains ran on time! There were fewer strikes, less absentee 'illness,' less smuggling, hoarding, black marketeering, fewer complaints against government officials."[27] Even Saleem Sinai admits in *Midnight's Children* that "all sorts of things happen during an Emergency: trains run on time, black-money hoarders are frightened into paying taxes, even the weather is brought to heel, and bumper harvests are reaped" (*M,* 434).[28]

But Saleem also points out that "the Emergency had a black part as well as a white" (*M,* 427). As Stanley Wolpert suggests, "Fear motivated millions of Indians to greater efficiency. Police were free to do as they liked. . . . A chill climate of silent terror gripped many Indian homes, for no one knew who might be listening, recording, reporting 'treasonous' remarks."[29] Such fear was also sparked by the increasing power of Gandhi's son Sanjay, who "gathered around him a group of young thugs" and "reorganized the wing of the Congress Party known as the Youth Congress" (Gupte, 441). Although he implemented some rather innocuous demands in his own Five-Point Program—advocating adult literacy and tree planting—he was also the impetus behind enforced family planning and urban "beautification" processes that resulted in violent slum clearances. Between April and September of 1976, 3.7 million sterilizations were performed at Sanjay's behest, and in April he ordered the demolition of Muslim squatter settlements near the historic Turkman Gate in New Delhi, where six people were killed by police and tens of thousands lost their homes.[30]

In the long run, Sanjay's excesses contributed to his mother's expulsion from office.[31] Indira's mythic power would be significantly bolstered, however, by the Ministry of Information and Broadcasting, which set into motion an extensive propaganda campaign justifying the Emergency as a form of "Disciplined Democracy." Billboards proclaimed "hard work, clear vision, iron will, and strictest discipline," warning citizens that "the 'only magic' to eradicate Poverty is hard work" and reminding them to "work more, talk less."[32] Such propaganda not only used the nation's economic improvement to reinforce the disciplinary tone of the Emergency, it also exploited Gandhi's already mythic status in India. Gandhi herself had served as Minister of Information and Broadcasting between 1964 and 1966, and as Rushdie suggests in "Dynasty," she was always quite adept at crafting her political persona. "Her use of the cult of the mother—of Hindu mother-goddess symbols and allusions—and the idea of *shakti,* of the fact that the dynamic element of the Hindu pantheon is represented as female—was calculated and shrewd. . . .

And because it helped her mystique, she exploited the accident of her marriage to a quite different Gandhi, as well: the surname and its attendant confusions were not without uses" ("Dynasty," 50). The Emergency, in turn, would only bolster Gandhi's mythical image: posters of the prime minister sprung up throughout the nation, proclaiming "she stood between chaos and order," and Congress president Dev Kant Barooah famously declared that "India is Indira and Indira is India."[33]

But Indira's media censorship and dismantling of parliamentary procedure, designed to maintain her hold over the nation, would also be her downfall. Judith Brown claims that "by abandoning established mechanisms for receiving messages of the state of public opinion and for consulting with established local politicians, and by silencing public opposition and press debate, [Gandhi] isolated herself from the harsh realities of public dissent and fear, and probably from the truth about the acts of oppression and destruction of personal liberty and integrity done in the name of the government."[34] Finally given an opportunity to voice their opposition to Gandhi when she ended the Emergency and called for elections, Indians came to the polls in force. As Tariq Ali suggests, "Deprived by the emergency of virtually all forms of extra-parliamentary dissent such as strikes, street demonstrations or distribution of literature opposing the government, the Indian masses used the ballot-box to express their deep discontent. The result was a political earthquake. . . . The Empress had fallen."[35]

Despite her post-Emergency ouster, Indira's mythological status had its long-standing effects: in 1980 voters dismissed the ineffectual Janata Party government and brought Gandhi back to power. Pranay Gupte suggests that even more recently, "with chaos widening in the country, many Indians recall the Emergency days with a strange sort of yearning" (Gupte, 439). It is against such a sensibility—one that either looks with nostalgia on the Emergency or allows its events to fade from memory—that Rushdie deploys the allegorical structure of *Midnight's Children*. As Saleem suggests, the events of the Emergency remain hidden behind "the insidious clouds of amnesia" (*M*, 385), producing a "time which damaged reality so badly that nobody ever managed to put it together again" (*M*, 420). Saleem must struggle against this amnesia, for as he contends, the Emergency, like the hair on Indira Gandhi's head, "had a white part—public, visible, documented, a matter for historians—and a black part which, being secret macabre untold, must be a matter for us" (*M*, 421).

IV. Giving Indira the Finger

"Every image of the past that is not recognized by the present as one of its own concerns threatens to disappear irretrievably."

—Walter Benjamin, "Theses"

"Never knew a finger held so much blood."

—Saleem Sinai (*M*, 235)

I hope so far to have shown that, in contrast to allegorical readings that either overlook or view as aberrant the fragmentary structure of *Midnight's Children*, Walter Benjamin's theory of allegory offers an alternative framework for reading the novel's recursive though disjointed structure as an allegorical attempt by both Rushdie and Saleem to reconstruct the past in resistance to the authoritarian regime and attendant mythology of Indira Gandhi's Emergency rule. This is particularly the case with Saleem's admission that his story is based on "scraps of memory" (*M*, 426), as well as with his ultimate realization that he has been "consigned to the peripheries of history," with "the connections between my life and the nation's . . . broken for good and all" (*M*, 395). As J. Hillis Miller points out, allegory's capacity for speaking in other terms has always provided a way to "keep secret in the act of making public."[36] Yet Rushdie's "migrant sensibility" in general and the leitmotif structure of *Midnight's Children* in particular resonate with the specific characteristics that Benjamin associates with allegory: its seemingly amorphous structure and accumulation of fragmentary objects; its subversion of orthodoxy and emphasis on the subjective process of making meaning; its attempt to redeem the decaying progression of time by uprooting the past for its potentially liberatory moments. Benjamin thus allows us to recognize that Rushdie's novel does not constitute, as David Birch suggests, an allegory of indeterminacy wherein "history, the past, and memories are an absurdist allusion"; nor, as Kumkum Sangari argues, does Rushdie's "allegorical mode" simply establish Saleem "as both child and fate of independent India," attempting to "conjoin the two" in a "large-hearted assimilation."[37] Rather, Rushdie offers the fragmentary structure of allegory to demythologize the era of Gandhi's Emergency and to reconstruct a more critical version of its events.

In light of Benjamin's theory of allegory, I now wish to turn more closely to *Midnight's Children* itself, to follow the trajectory of one of its most significant allegorical images. As Rushdie suggests, *Midnight's Children* is constructed around "incidents or objects or phrases which in themselves have no meaning or no particular meaning but which form a kind of non-rational network of connections"; the significance of a particular element derives from "the sum total of the incidents in which it occurs," so it "accumulates meaning the more it is used."[38] *Midnight's Children* is itself a catalog of such recurrent objects: a sheet with a hole in the middle, a washing chest, a spittoon, and a number of prominent noses—all of which take on different meanings throughout the various contexts in which they occur. However, I would like to focus specifically on the recurrence of the hand and the finger. As we shall see, Saleem uses the image of the hand and finger to connect a number of disparate and seemingly disconnected moments within Indian national history that together offer a critical historical perspective on the Emergency and form an indictment of Indira Gandhi's rule.

The image of the finger first appears to Saleem when he is a baby in his crib—that is, within the context of India's partition and independence in 1947. "The fisherman's pointing finger: unforgettable focal point of the picture which hung on a sky-blue wall in Buckingham Villa.[39] . . . The young Raleigh—and who else?—sat, framed in teak, at the feet of an old, gnarled, net-minding sailor . . . whose right arm, fully extended, stretched out towards a watery horizon" (*M*, 122). The painting, which we later learn belonged to William Methwold (*M*, 128), operates, of course, within the context of the British colonization of India. This implication is strengthened when we remember that Saleem first refers to the picture in the opening pages of the novel—with the return of Saleem's grandfather Aadam Aziz from medical school in Germany and the subsequent argument between Aziz and Tai the ferryman. According to Saleem, Tai condemns Aziz for leaving India "before he's learned one damn thing" and for returning "a big doctor sahib with a big bag full of foreign machines . . . still as silly as an owl" (*M*, 19). Describing the ancient Tai evokes for Saleem a "memory of my blue bedroom wall," on which hung a picture of "the Boy Raleigh . . . gazing rapturously at an old fisherman" (*M*, 15). As such, the image of the pointing finger initially invokes tension over the European presence in India.[40]

Saleem imagines that the other figure in the picture, "another boy . . . sitting cross-legged in a frilly collar and button-down tunic," is himself. "In a picture hanging on a bedroom wall, I sat beside Walter Raleigh and followed a fisherman's pointing finger with my eyes; eyes straining beyond the horizon, beyond which lay—what?—my future, perhaps." For young Saleem, now himself a part of the picture, the fisherman's finger is "impossible to ignore" because it points "beyond the teak frame, across a brief expanse of sky-blue wall, driving my eyes toward another frame"—the one containing a congratulatory letter from Nehru and the newspaper photo announcing Saleem's birth (*M*, 122). But Saleem is not satisfied that the finger celebrates his status as India's first child. "Perhaps the fisherman's finger was not pointing at the letter in the frame; because if one followed it even further, it led one out through the window"; it becomes instead "an accusing finger . . . which obliged us to look at the city's dispossessed," thus undercutting Saleem's pride in his status as midnight's child by reminding him of the nation's continuing problems even as it seems to blame those problems on British imperialism. Saleem entertains one last option about the meaning of the finger. "Or maybe—and this idea makes me feel a little shivery despite the heat—it was a finger of warning, its purpose to draw attention to *itself*"; in other words, the fisherman's finger presents "a prophecy of another finger, a finger not dissimilar from itself, whose entry into my story would release the dreadful logic of Alpha and Omega. . . . [M]y God, what a notion!" (123). The finger finally prophecies the revelation of Saleem's mixed parentage.

Within this brief scene, then, the image of the fisherman's pointing finger participates in a complex network of signification that—shaped by Saleem's memory of India's independence from his perspective immediately after the Emergency—grants the finger little or no *inherent* meaning. The finger serves as an allegorical object whose meaning evolves within the dialectic of Saleem's present memory of the past. Initially a celebration of Saleem's status as midnight's child and thus of India's independence, it implicitly reminds Saleem of his homeland's colonization and its infusion by European domination and culture, and indicates India's present inability to sustain its poor. The finger thus undermines the notion of India's complete independence from imperialism and from the problems associated with imperial rule. Ultimately, however, Saleem suggests that the finger calls attention to itself—prophesying events that will reveal that he is not his parents' child. As a result, the finger becomes a signifier that blurs the boundaries between India and Europe, colonization and independence, self and family and nation.

The image of the finger does not significantly return until India's 10th year of independence and Saleem's burgeoning adolescent sexuality. Having recently been rejected by Evie Burns, Saleem attends his Cathedral School Social dance and meets an acquaintance of his sister's—Masha Miovic, the school's champion breast-stroker. Taunted by schoolmates Fat Perce and Glandy Keith, Saleem attempts to defend his masculinity before Masha. Saleem knees both his enemies in the groin and flees, as Masha calls after him, " 'Where are you running, little hero?' " Slipping inside the nearest classroom, Saleem is finally caught by Fat Perce and Glandy, who close the door behind them as Saleem struggles to escape. "They are pushing the door shut, but I'm pulling with the strength of my fear, I have it open a few inches, my hand curls around it, and now Fat Perce slams all his weight against the door and it shuts too fast for me to get my hand out of the way and it's shut. A thud. And outside, Masha Miovic arrives and looks down at the floor; and sees the top third of my middle finger lying there like a lump of well-chewed bubble gum" (*M,* 234–35). Once believing that the body is "indivisible, a one-piece suit, a sacred temple," Saleem claims that "the loss of my finger (which was conceivably foretold by the pointing digit of Raleigh's fisherman) . . . has undone all that" (*M,* 237). But the severed finger not only ruins the unity of Saleem's body and precipitates his exile from his family. Its figurative status as a severing of his manhood before Masha Miovic foreshadows the importance of the finger within the context of Saleem's sexual life.

Following the revelation of the finger—the revelation that he is not his parents' child—Saleem is shipped off to reside with his Uncle Hanif and Aunt Pia, a struggling screenplay writer and a histrionic movie actress. Saleem's stay with his uncle and aunt culminates in a sexual encounter between Saleem and Pia that is interrupted by the pain from his severed finger. Discovering that Pia has been discarded by her lover, Homi Catrack, Saleem attempts, not innocently, to console Pia, who lies sprawled across her bed, weeping. As Saleem, lying atop his aunt, offers her a hug, she begins to "thrash about beneath me in her despair and I thrash with her, remembering to keep my right hand clear of the action." Together their bodies "begin to acquire a kind of rhythm, unnameable unthinkable"; "as she writhes and twists" beneath Saleem, he brings down his right hand, having "forgotten my finger, and when it touches her breast, wound presses against skin. . . . 'Yaaaouuuu!' I scream with the pain; and my aunt, snapping out of the macabre spell of those few moments, pushes me off her and delivers a resounding wallop to my face" (*M*, 250).

Saleem's severed finger thus becomes associated with his stunted adolescent attempts to prove his manhood to Masha Miovic and to fulfill his sexual desire for his Aunt Pia—figurative castrations that, from Saleem's perspective after the Emergency, become inextricably tied to his actual castration at the hands of the Widow. But the severing of his finger is not merely indicative of Saleem's private sexual trauma; it also occurs within the more public context of India's 1957 national elections. Saleem claims that "on election day, 1957, the All-India Congress was badly shocked. Although it won the election, twelve million votes made the Communists the largest single opposition party." As Saleem points out,

> [O]ne member of the Midnight's Children Conference played a minor role in the elections. . . . Shiva was recruited by—well, perhaps I will not name the party; but only one part had really large sums to spend—and on polling day, he and his gang, who called themselves Cowboys, were to be seen standing outside a polling station in the north of the city, some holding long stout sticks, others juggling with stones, still others picking their teeth with knives, all of them encouraging the electorate to use its vote with wisdom and care. . . . [A]nd after polls closed, were seals broken on ballot boxes? Did ballot-stuffing occur? At any rate, when the votes were counted, it was discovered that Qasim the Red had narrowly failed to win the seat; and my rival's paymasters were well pleased. (*M*, 222)

From his post-Emergency perspective, Saleem's emphasis on his rival Shiva's role in coercing voters away from the Communist Party and toward Nehru's Congress suggests a potential moment within the past when the opposition might have broken Nehru's power and thus disrupted the dynasty that later would be established by his daughter Indira. The gesture is reminiscent of Benjamin's conviction that, as Terry Eagleton suggests, "dialectical thought, once released from the frozen correspondences of myth and historicism, must begin to weave its own 'magical' network of similarities across the face of history, seeking the dialectical image or shocking confrontation in which a present moment may re-read itself in the past and allow the past to interpret itself anew in the present."[41] Rather than reiterating clichés about the "Father of the Nation" claiming victory in "the world's largest democracy," Saleem's interest in the Communist defeat is part of an attempt to read the past through the perspective of the present. The event foreshadows his traumatic finger severing, thus implying a connection between his stunted sexual maturity and the impeded maturation of Indian politics. When read in relation to the earlier images of the fisherman's pointing finger, this more recent trajectory casts doubt on the democratic viability of India during Nehru's reign, and the nation's independence from forms of domination and repression tied to imperialism. This is not meant to suggest that Rushdie views Nehru as a protoimperialist but rather that Saleem sees the roots of Indira Gandhi's Emergency rule in Nehru's increasing power throughout the late fifties.

That Saleem implies a connection between the election of 1957 and Gandhi's Emergency is suggested not only by the suppression of Communist opposition during each period but also by the absence of the finger and hand imagery between these two sections in his narrative. When the imagery returns, it operates as one of the primary signifiers associated with Gandhi, whom Saleem renames the Widow. Much earlier in the novel (though contemporaneous with his act of writing), Saleem has a nightmare in which the Widow sits "on a high high chair" (*M*, 207) and hunts for children with "long and sharp and black" fingernails. "Now one by one the children mmff are stifled quiet the Widow's hand is lifting one by one the children green their blood is black there are no stars the Widow laughs. . . . And children torn in two in Widow hands which rolling rolling halves of children roll them into little balls. . . . And little balls fly into night" (*M*, 208). By renaming her the Widow, Saleem associates Gandhi with death even as he demythologizes her power simply by pointing out that "the Prime Minister of India was, in 1975, fifteen years a widow" (*M*, 421). As his brief biography of Gandhi reveals— for example, when he points out that "she was not related to 'Mahatma' M. K. Gandhi"—Saleem seeks to demythologize Indira's status in India's national and cultural Imaginary (*M*, 421). Saleem's demystification of Gandhi leads him to point out that the Widow not only was Prime Minister but "also aspired to be Devi, the Mother-goddess in her most terrible aspect" (*M*, 438).

Saleem's demythologizing of the Widow also involves appropriating the image of the hand, the historical correlation of which to Indira Gandhi is to be found in her Congress Party voter icon. Saleem turns the meaning of the signifier of Gandhi's party inside out, as it becomes a marker of Saleem's literal and figurative impotence. For it is the woman he refers to as the "Widow's Hand," a woman who "in newspaper articles . . . has been called 'a gorgeous girl with big rolling hips' " (*M*, 437), who performs his sterilization. And as Saleem points out, the operation is not simply a vasectomy: "because there was a chance, just a chance that such operations could be reversed . . . ectomies were performed, but irreversibly: testicles were removed from sacs, and wombs vanished forever" (*M*, 439). The imagery of the hand and the finger thus culminates with Saleem's sterilization: "the Widow drained me of past present future" (*M*, 402), a severing of his genitalia that parallels the earlier trauma of his severed finger. As a result, the imagery of the finger and the hand operates within a network of meaning that ties together the historical moments of Indian independence, the election of 1957, and the Emergency with Saleem's personal recollections of his celebrated but troubled youth, his burgeoning but stunted sexuality, and his castration at the hands of the Widow. The imagery of the hand and finger allows Saleem to discover a common thread between seemingly disconnected historical moments and thereby link the Widow's betrayal of India to earlier forms of imperial repression through the image of the fisherman's pointing finger and its relation to his own severed finger and his castration.

Toward the end of *Midnight's Children*, Saleem realizes that while he is "the sum total of everything that went before me, of all I have been seen done, of everything done-to-me," he has become at the same time an empty signifier in the hands of the Widow. "As the pouring-out of what-was-inside-me nears an end; as cracks widen within—I can hear and feel the rip tear crunch—I begin to grow thinner, translucent almost; there isn't much of me left, and soon there will be nothing at all" (*M*, 383). Saleem himself is left like an allegorical object, emptied of any inherent meaning, drained "of past present future" by the Widow (*M*, 402). His predicament is reminiscent of Benjamin's notion that, as Terry Eagleton reminds us, the allegorical object undergoes "a kind of haemorrhage of spirit: drained of all immanent meaning, it lies as a pure facticity under the manipulative hand of the allegorist, awaiting such meaning as he or she may imbue it with."[42] Yet as Eagleton points out, such barrenness also contains for Benjamin the seeds of allegorical redemption. By reimagining his past in relation to the allegorical image of the finger and the hand, Saleem is able to subvert Indira Gandhi's official version of the Emergency. As Azade Seyhan suggests, "Benjamin's concept of historical materialism operates by recalling and arresting moments of history that are then re-configured in new narratives in such a way as to release their liberating potential. This re-configuration distorts official or institutional histories that preserve and protect ruling class interests" (*M*, 234). Thus while Saleem has been drained of meaning by Gandhi, he has also appropriated her official use of the hand imagery and pointed it back at her as an indictment of her abuse of power during the Emergency. As such, Saleem has attempted to undermine both the mythology of the Emergency and the sense of communal amnesia surrounding it.

Following the trajectory in meaning of the hand and finger imagery reveals the extent to which Benjamin's theory of allegory both informs and provides a model for reading the fragmentary structure of *Midnight's Children*. Rushdie's use of allegory subverts the official history of the Emergency and its attendant mythology, indicting Gandhi's rule as a manifestation of the type of domination established by imperialism. Resisting conventional allegorical structure, Rushdie interrupts historical chronology by examining Indian history through the perspective of the Emergency and using recurrent allegorical objects such as the finger and hand to show the relationships between seemingly disconnected historical moments. Rushdie thus undermines the centralized authority and repressions on individual representation during the Emergency by reinstating a form of expression that, according to Benjamin, seeks "the triumph of subjectivity" (*O*, 233). The allegorical structure of *Midnight's Children* demands that we read Indian national history through the perspective of Indira Gandhi's Emergency regime and thereby attempt to "attain to a conception of history" that subverts "the 'state of emergency' in which we live."

Notes

1. Salman Rushdie, *Midnight's Children* (1981; reprint, London: Vintage, 1995), 428, 295; hereafter cited in the text as *MC*. As Timothy Brennan points out, "Rushdie deliberately prevents his readers from being caught up in a story with its own 'organic' life, that progresses uninterrupted, and that creates a completely imagined world" (*Salman Rushdie and the Third World: Myths of the Nation* [New York: St. Martin's, 1989], 85).
2. Salman Rushdie, "*Midnight's Children* and *Shame*," *Kunapipi* 7, no. 1 (1985): 3.
3. Neil ten Kortenaar, "*Midnight's Children* and the Allegory of History," *Ariel* 26, no. 2 (April 1995): 41.
4. For ten Kortenaar (see note 6), Rushdie's use of allegory makes literal the seemingly objective rhetoric of historical narratives of nationalism and thereby unmasks the ideology that underwrites them. Brennan suggests that allegory works in *Midnight's Children* through character: Padma's "plebeian aesthetics" and desire for linear narrative thus represent "the fatal immaturity of her class in the struggle for a meaningful democracy on a legitimately 'Indian' terrain" (104–5). For Mujeebuddin Syed, Rushdie deploys allegory at the level of plot: Ahmed Sinai's purchase of Methwold's estate reflects "the passing on of the colonial mantle to the Indian *petit bourgeoisie* which not only inherited political power from the colonial masters but also many of its peculiar colonial accoutrements after independence" ("Midnight's Children and Its Indian Con-Texts," *Journal of Commonwealth Literature* 29, no. 2 [1994]: 101). In a recent reading of *Midnight's Children*, Jean Kane argues that while the novel "allegorize[s] national history through the metaphor of the body politic," Rushdie "suppresses his protagonist's allegorical function while separating and opposing terms that the book insistently joins: that is, Saleem's 'personal' tragedy and India's political one." As a result, Kane claims "the fractures in the narrative's coalescent figural complexes and modes of production—between body and text, nation and subject, incorporation and division, imperial and postcolonial, male and female, past and future—contest the book's avowed political and formal values" ("The Migrant Intellectual and the Body of History: Salman Rushdie's *Midnight's Children*," *Contemporary Literature* 37, no. 1 [Spring 1996]: 115).

5. Kane, 97.

6. Benjamin's most coherent formulations on allegory are found in *The Origin of German Tragic Drama,* trans. John Osborne (London: Verso, 1977), particularly the section "Allegory and *Trauerspiel.*" Although this text focuses on the allegorical qualities of the seventeenth-century German baroque mourning play (*Trauerspiel*), Benjamin's interest in allegory resurfaces consistently—albeit in rather fragmentary form—throughout his later work: both his study of Baudelaire and his uncompleted *Arcades Project* chart the evolution of allegory into nineteenth-century literature and culture. For readings on Benjamin's theory of allegory, see Susan Buck-Morss, *The Dialectics of Seeing: Walter Benjamin and the Arcades Project* (Cambridge, Mass.: The MIT Press, 1989), 159–77; Bainard Cowan, "Walter Benjamin's Theory of Allegory," *New German Critique* 22 (Winter 1981): 109–22; Terry Eagleton, *Walter Benjamin, or Towards a Revolutionary Criticism* (London: New Left Books, 1981), 3–24; J. Hillis Miller, "The Two Allegories," in *Allegory, Myth, and Symbol,* ed. Morton W. Bloomfield (Cambridge, Mass.: Harvard University Press, 1981), 355–70; Charles Rosen, "The Ruins of Walter Benjamin," in *On Walter Benjamin,* ed. Gary Smith (Cambridge, Mass.: The MIT Press, 1988), 129–75; and Azade Seyhan, "Allegories of History: The Politics of Representation in Walter Benjamin," in *Image and Ideology in Modern/PostModern Discourse,* ed. David B. Downing and Susan Bazargan (Albany, N.Y.: SUNY Press, 1991), 231–48. A number of commentators, including Cowan and Paul Smith ("The Will to Allegory in Postmodernism," *Dalhousie Review* 62, no. 1 [Spring 1982]: 105–22), have commented on and encouraged the applicability of Benjamin's theory of allegory to twentieth-century texts.

7. Seyhan, 237.

8. Walter Benjamin, "Central Park," trans. Lloyd Spencer (with Mark Harrington), *New German Critique* 34 (Winter 1985): 55.

9. Walter Benjamin, "Theses on the Philosophy of History," in *Illuminations,* trans. Harry Zohn (New York: Schocken, 1968), 255.

10. Qtd. in Indira Gandhi, *My Truth* (New York: Grove Press, 1982), 161; hereafter cited in the text.

11. Judith M. Brown, *Modern India: The Origins of an Asian Democracy* (Oxford, England: Oxford University Press, 1994), 377.

12. I hope not to offer an Orientalist reading of the events surrounding the Emergency or of Indira Gandhi's reelection in which Indians are cast as the ignorant dupes or willing servants of an authoritarian despot. As M. Keith Booker has reminded me, Gandhi is still greatly admired by many in India and the Third World as a modernizer and female head of state and is treated less condescendingly by Soviet scholars than by Americans. Nevertheless, the Emergency represents for many—including Rushdie—among the most significant historical dilemmas of India's national history. It is such an understanding of the Emergency that I am attempting to articulate.

13. Salman Rushdie, interview by John Haffenden, in *Novelists in Interview* (London: Methuen, 1985), 240.

14. David Price suggests that for Rushdie, Gandhi's Emergency rule exemplifies Nietzsche's concept of monumental history (as defined in the essay "On the Uses and Disadvantages of History for Life"). Nietzsche claims that when the monumental mode predominates, "whole segments of [the past] are forgotten, despised, and flow away in an uninterrupted colourless flood" (qtd. in Price, "Salman Rushdie's 'Use and Abuse of History' in *Midnight's Children,*" *Ariel* 25, no. 2 [April 1994]: 97).

15. Rushdie, "The Assassination of Indira Gandhi," in *Imaginary Homelands: Essays and Criticism, 1981–1991* (London: Granta, 1991), 45.

16. Rushdie, "Imaginary Homelands," in *Imaginary Homelands,* 10–11; hereafter cited in the text as "Imaginary." See also "The Location of Brazil" in *Imaginary Homelands.* For readings on the relation between Rushdie's "migrant sensibility" and his fiction, see Anuradha Dingwaney (Needham), "Author(iz)ing *Midnight's Children* and *Shame:* Salman Rushdie's Con-

structions of Authority," in *Reworlding: The Literature of the Indian Diaspora,* ed. Emmanuel S. Nelson (New York: Greenwood, 1992), 157–68, and "The Politics of Post-Colonial Identity in Salman Rushdie," *The Massachusetts Review* 29, no. 4 (Winter 1988–1989): 609–24.

17. Rushdie, "Errata," in *Imaginary Homelands,* 24.
18. Ibid., 25.
19. Interview, 251.
20. See also Una Chaudhuri's interview, in which Rushdie discusses "an essay or letter of Brecht's—maybe it's a letter he wrote to Walter Benjamin—where he says the trouble is that people in literature discuss form as if it was only an aesthetic problem, whereas, he says, it's a political problem, it's a moral problem, it's all sorts of things—certainly not just simply a matter of aesthetics" ("Imaginative Maps: Excerpts from a Conversation with Salman Rushdie," http://www.crl.com/ỹsubir/rushdie/uc_maps.html, 2).
21. See Benjamin 1985, 46, and Winfried Menninghaus, "Walter Benjamin's Theory of Myth," trans. Gary Smith, in *On Walter Benjamin,* 292–325.
22. Rushdie, "Dynasty," in *Imaginary Homelands,* 48; hereafter cited in the text.
23. I am using the term *myth* in its Barthesian sense, that is, an attempt to render natural that which is culturally constructed. According to Roland Barthes, "[M]ythical speech is made of a material which has *already* been worked on so as to make it suitable for communication: it is because all the materials of myth (whether pictorial or written) presuppose a signifying consciousness, that one can reason about them while discounting their substance" (*Mythologies,* trans. Annette Lavers [New York: Hill and Wang, 1972]), 110.
24. Quoted in Pranay Gupte, *Mother India: A Political Biography of Indira Gandhi* (New York: Scribner's, 1992), 440; hereafter cited in the text.
25. Inder Malhotra, *Indira Gandhi* (London: Hodder and Stoughton, 1989), 173.
26. Although the Emergency put unlimited power and authoritarian rule in the hands of Indira and her close circle of advisers, most notably her son Sanjay, the right to declare the Emergency was itself legal, provided by article 352(I) of the Indian constitution. "Although Congress . . . had bitterly opposed government's ability to rule with emergency powers," Judith Brown claims that "as the party of government intent on wielding a new state, [the Congress Party] incorporated into the constitution very significant provisions for just such rule after 1947." Gandhi also made use of the Defence of India Act, which demanded the detention of "anyone thought likely to prejudice the defence of India," as well as the President's Rule, allowing the president to suspend state government and enforce union control (Brown, 357). Of course, Gandhi also stretched the limits of the constitution by banning 26 political organizations and forcing two historic amendments into the constitution—one refusing any legal challenges to the Emergency, the other exonerating her from any past or future legal charges (Gupte, 439).
27. Stanley Wolpert, *India* (Berkeley: University of California Press, 1991), 214.
28. As the juxtaposition of these two passages reveals, *Midnight's Children* often appropriates and subverts the language of conventional histories like Stanley Wolpert's *India* and *A New History of India.* On Rushdie's use of Wolpert, see Kortenaar, 42, 44–46, 48; and David Lipscomb, "Caught in a Strange Middle Ground: Contesting Rushdie's History in Salman Rushdie's *Midnight's Children,*" *Diaspora* 1, no. 2 (1991): 163–89.
29. Wolpert 1991, 214.
30. Malhotra, 179–80.
31. Paul R. Brass, *The Politics of India Since Independence* (Cambridge, England: Cambridge University Press, 1990), 42.
32. Stanley Wolpert, *A New History of India,* 4th ed. (New York: Oxford University Press, 1993), 400.
33. Wolpert 1993, 399.
34. Brown, 377.
35. Tariq Ali, *An Indian Dynasty: The Story of the Nehru-Gandhi Family* (New York: G. P. Putnam's Sons, 1985), 194.

36. Miller, 357. Miller points out that the word *allegory* means "to speak figuratively, or to speak in other terms, or to speak of other things in public, from the Greek *allegorein, allos,* other, plus *agoreuein,* to speak (in public), from *agora,* an assembly, but also the marketplace or customary place of assembly.... The word *allegory* always implies not only the use of figures, but a making public, available to profane ears, of something which would otherwise remain secret" (356).

37. David Birch, "Postmodernist Chutneys," *Textual Practice* 5, no. 1 (Spring 1991): 2; Kumkum Sangari, "The Politics of the Possible," *Cultural Critique* 7 (Fall 1987): 179.

38. "*Midnight's Children* and *Shame,*" 3.

39. Given Rushdie's frequent use of ellipses in the text of *Midnight's Children,* I shall hereafter bracket my own for clarity.

40. For a more developed reading of the painting than I can provide here, see Neil ten Kortenaar, "Postcolonial Ekphrasis: Salman Rushdie Gives the Finger Back to the Empire," *Contemporary Literature* 38 (Summer 1997): 232–59. Though Kortenaar's subtitle is mirrored by my own title for this section, I first drafted this essay before Kortenaar's was published. I thank M. Keith Booker for bringing Kortenaar's essay to my attention.

41. Eagleton, 41.

42. Ibid., 6.

Rewriting History and Identity: The Reinvention of Myth, Epic, and Allegory in Salman Rushdie's *Midnight's Children*

MICHAEL REDER

PERSONALIZING HISTORY

In the first paragraph of Salman Rushdie's *Midnight's Children* (1981), Saleem Sinai conflates his life with that of his country, claiming: "I had been mysteriously handcuffed to history, my destinies indissolubly chained to those of my country."[1] But what version of history does Saleem speak of? There are many histories of India, and Rushdie, through Saleem, engages in writing a version of his own. Saleem feels compelled to tell his story because he seems to be, both literally and metaphorically, falling apart. Although he claims that his death is inevitable, he fears most a loss of meaning: "I must work fast, faster than Scheherazade, if I am to end up meaning—yes, meaning—something. I admit it: above all things, I fear absurdity" (11).

Saleem thus tells his own story to form his identity and give his life meaning. In doing so, Saleem appropriates history, shaping it to fit his version of the world. This self-narration is empowering, particularly for a person who could easily be viewed as the victim of history: not only as an individual "to whom things have been done" (232) but also as a representative of a culture whose history has been supplanted by a dominant, European history that has controlled the continent. Simon During reminds us that "The post-colonial desire is the desire of decolonized communities of an identity."[2] Related to Saleem's individual crisis is India's own crisis: Saleem tells his tale just after Indira Gandhi has declared the Emergency. India itself, and the generation of Indians who grew up in the new nation called India, are experiencing their own crisis of identity. By attempting to answer the questions "Who am I? Who were we?" (422), Saleem places himself at the center of a history that he

---

This essay was written specifically for this volume and is published for the first time by permission of the author.

himself creates, carving out an individual identity in a manner that has national implications. As we shall see, the answers to these questions are less important than the manner in which Saleem—and Rushdie—set about answering them.

In the process of narrating his story, Saleem creates a radically individual type of historical discourse that challenges the powerful but potentially oppressive notions of national mythology, a version of official history that often overshadows the lives of the individuals who populate a nation. Rushdie's novel explodes traditional notions of myth and epic, offering us a type of historical discourse that focuses on individual, personalized mythology. At the same time, Saleem's story also undermines the conventional use of allegory, in which individual identity is often subsumed under larger, seemingly more significant meanings and events. Saleem creates personal meaning from history, assigning historical events significance in relation to himself as an individual.

In the process of personalizing history, Saleem fragments official history.[3] Rushdie's history is not continuous or monolithic; it is fragmented, individual, personalized. Rushdie confirms that Saleem "wants to shape his material [so] that the reader will be forced to concede his central role. He is cutting up history to suit himself."[4] Rushdie admits that *Midnight's Children* is constructed in a "fragmentary way": "It tries to recognize the way in which memory operates: it exalts certain things which may be unimportant in themselves and become very important because they have lodged in your mind."[5] When Rushdie speaks of "memory," he is speaking not of cultural memory or national consciousness but of individual memory. But history seen through a personal lens becomes distorted. As Rushdie notes, "What seem to be irrelevant things become very big. What seem to be very big things are treated very slightly."[6] In other words, the history in *Midnight's Children* is a history filtered through the eyes of an individual: it is not the dominant, official "History" but a history that is personalized and therefore given life, significance, and meaning. In the process of creating this new mode of historical discourse, Rushdie replaces an absolute notion of identity—as something easily defined but therefore as limited as it is limiting—with a humanistically centered, multiply defined individual identity, one that must literally write itself into existence. Rushdie exposes the myth that is modern India but at the same time offers a new methodology for myth making: not a cultural or epic myth meant to represent an entire people but an individual myth that is multiply signifiable.

Midnight's Children challenges the notion that any type of historical discourse can make claims of accurately representing past events. Keith Booker contends that the "self-conscious fictionality of the narrative is directly linked to the artificiality of our constructions of history."[7] Booker notes that by "tying his text so closely to history, Rushdie suggests that the authority of all of our representations of the past may be somewhat questionable" (Booker,

983). Rushdie finds this authority more than questionable and criticizes the idea of the possibility of an "objective" view of the world. In his essay " 'Errata': Or, Unreliable Narration in *Midnight's Children*" (1983), Rushdie writes:

> History is always ambiguous. Facts are hard to establish, and capable of being given many meanings. Reality is built on our prejudices, misconceptions and ignorance as well as on our perceptiveness and knowledge. The reading of Saleem's unreliable narration might be, I believed, a useful analogy for the way in which we all, every day, attempt to "read" the world. (*Imaginary*, 25)

Rushdie does not attack individual authority as much as he attacks the notion of the existence of objective "facts." History is ambiguous because reality is ambiguous. If Rushdie believes that our everyday "reality" is built not upon fact but upon opinion, then by extension, the act of creating history must be equally unreliable.

YOURSTORY, MYSTORY, HISTORY

The individual is the site of the clash between competing histories.[8] India's history is reflected—and in many ways magnified—in Saleem and his own fractured history. Saleem fights what David Spurr terms "Negative History": "The discourse of negation denies history as well as place, constituting the past as absence, but also designating that absence as a negative presence: a people without history is one which exists only in a negative sense; like the bare earth, they can be transformed by history, but they cannot make their own."[9] Yet as Saleem's story demonstrates, individuals can fall victim to a discourse—such as a national myth—in which they themselves are denied a role. Saleem's narration represents a struggle with all official histories that attempt to totalize the individual. In his essay "Discourse in the Novel," M. M. Bakhtin asserts that "The importance of struggling with another's discourse, its influence in the history of an individual's coming to ideological consciousness, is enormous. One's own discourse and one's own voice, although born of another or dynamically stimulated by another, will sooner or later begin to liberate themselves from the authority of the other's discourse."[10] Saleem must write his own history, relating it to the history that has been imposed upon him by the fate of his birth.[11] Through Saleem's struggle the reader witnesses the struggle for individual narration.

Part of Saleem's project, therefore, is similar to that of his grandfather Aadam Aziz, who feels, on returning home with a European medical education, "caught in a strange middle ground between belief and disbelief" and seeks "to re-unite himself with an earlier self" (13). Aadam Aziz needs to come to terms with his past self to understand his present self: he needs to reclaim the validity of his past, fusing it with his present self.[12] The same can be said of Saleem and his individual history: he must literally write—or tell—himself into existence, bridging the gap between the past and the present. The project of mediating between the past and the present is not uniquely postcolonial; all psychologically healthy humans must bridge this gap. However, when an individual's historical past is disrupted—by personal or political events—then negotiating between the past and the present is more difficult. Rushdie recognizes the universal need to bridge this gap, describing the past as "a country from which we are all exiled."[13] And since the past is accessible only through an individual's version of events—stories, one might say—what better way to reconcile the past and the present than by narrating a tale? Rushdie himself has stated, more than once, that he wrote *Midnight's Children* because "I wanted to restore that past to myself."[14] Saleem's narration of his own story represents a similar historical project, a quest for a cohesive identity, the coming together of past and present. To exist in the present, Saleem must make sense of his past.

Rushdie offers the notion of a radically individual history as an alternative historiography for the recapturing of Indian history. By allowing Saleem to narrate his own individual history, Rushdie avoids creating a version of history that homogenizes as much as it defines. Rather than playing the "Western game of History" and attempting to write—or rewrite—a history of the subcontinent, Rushdie has decided to challenge Western history on alternative grounds.[15] Saleem is able to place himself within the historical process without falling prey to it; he remains individual and dynamic. History itself, Rushdie's work proclaims, is always becoming; it is always being lived and always being evaluated and written.[16] Relating the process of the postcolonial recovery of history and identity, Helen Tiffin states that "Decolonization is process, not arrival; it invokes an ongoing dialectic between hegemonic centrist systems and peripheral subversion of them."[17] Saleem—and his story—are constantly in the state of redefinition. Saleem as historian produces a personal and alternative history—one that liberates him not only as an individual but also as a representative victim of colonization.

Saleem's rather odd, self-conscious narration—with its obvious distortions and its constant references to Saleem's own disintegration, cracks, and imminent death—represents Rushdie's attempt to define a radically different mode of historical discourse. When discussing the need for a new type of historical discourse, Dipesh Chakrabarty declares, "I ask for a history that deliberately makes visible, within the very structure of its narrative forms, its own repressive strategies and practices."[18] Saleem as narrator is well aware of his strategy of representation, and Rushdie himself seems aware of Saleem's shortcomings and distortions.[19] In much the same way Chakrabarty calls for "a history that will attempt the impossible: to look toward its own death by tracing that which resists and escapes the best human effort at translation across cultural and other semiotic systems, so that the world may once again be imagined as radically heterogeneous."[20] Rushdie—via Saleem—is creating a radically individual narrative that is meant to supplant a dominant, hegemonic conception of history.

Midnight's Children and Myth/Epic/Allegory

Rushdie does, however, connect this notion of individual history with the creation of a type of mythology. Saleem's mythology is personal and, unlike classical myth, does not purport to represent a system of hereditary stories that are believed to be true or that explain the rationales for social customs or cultural norms. Saleem's myth is placed in relation to and draws from a national and cultural mythology, but ultimately Saleem's myth is about explaining *Saleem,* not the culture in which he lives or his nation's history. As Saleem points out, "There are as many versions of India as Indians" (261). His narrative represents his own, personal set of accumulated stories, which includes that of his erstwhile family. It is beyond the power of Rushdie—or even Saleem—to write a new national mythology, but both are free to suggest a new mode with which Indians may come to terms with their own personal and cultural pasts. This mode is the creation of a personal mythology that resonates in relation to, but independent of, the national culture from which it emerges.

Rushdie himself admits: "I'm also very fond of myth, but it isn't possible to sit down and say that I will now write a myth. Myth is a cultural accumulation—a collective experience, not an individual achievement—and you can learn from and use its shapes, since they provide a strength in the work."[21] Rushdie seems to be saying that the new myth of India is no myth: it is simply the story of the individual. Indira Karamcheti, however, contends that Saleem chronicles his nation's identity, "inventing its national mythology, that is its causes and significance."[22] Notions of "causes and significance" are radically subjective, concepts that must be filtered through the individual. Karamcheti claims that "Saleem creates literary identity out of time, which is his embroilment in history, and out of origins, which embroil him in causes and mythologies."[23] Clearly, even if Saleem and Rushdie create a mythology that other people want to claim as their own, Saleem creates a personal mythology that implicates and has implications for India as a whole.

Saleem claims that India is a "new myth—a collective fiction in which anything was possible, a fable rivalled only by the two other mighty fantasies: money and God" (111). Rushdie chooses his words carefully, because the myths of God and money—the two main driving forces behind colonial expansion—are the basis for the foundation of "European civilization" and its domination of the once nonindustrialized heathens. In other words, the whole concept of a "new" India—when Indian civilization has been around for thousands of years—is itself a story, a fiction, a myth. As Saleem describes the approach of independence, he sarcastically declares that there is "a new myth to celebrate, because a nation which had never previously existed was about to win its freedom, catapulting us into a world, which, although it had five thousand years of history, although it had invented chess and traded with Middle Kingdom Egypt, was nevertheless quite imaginary" (111). As odd or dreamlike as it seems, August 1947 is almost universally recognized as "the birth" of India. Saleem—and Rushdie—must share ambivalent feelings surrounding the notion of India's "independence"—as if the culture had never existed independently before that fateful day in 1947. India, Rushdie proclaims, is "a kind of collective fantasy."[24] Saleem's narration makes it clear that history is "unreliable" because it is comprised of individual(s') stories. In *Midnight's Children*, history itself is revealed to be little more than myth, a collective fiction in which people choose to participate.

Epic/Anti-Epic

Narratives centered on an individual—such as the epic hero—often compose a national mythology. Classical epics, such as Homer's *Iliad* and *Odyssey*, Virgil's *Aeneid*, or the Hindu *Mahabharata* and *Ramayana*, were usually composed both to celebrate and solidify the founding of a nation or culture. Epics are highly conventional and, in general, share similar features and conventions.[25] The epic is static: its characters are well defined and fixed. The general features of an epic include a hero of national or cosmic importance, a setting of wide or ample scale, action that involves superhuman deeds in battle, gods or other supernatural creatures who take an interest or active role in the adventure, and finally, an elevated or ceremonial style of writing. At first glance, *Midnight's Children* seems to resemble an epic: it is (ostensibly) about the birth of a nation, and its form of transmission represents an oral tale that is written down (Saleem's telling his story to Padma as he writes). However, the novel dispels the notion of its being an epic within its very first pages: "the hero," Saleem Sinai, presents himself as a passive victim; the setting, although expansive in that it addresses both India and Pakistan, is basically the office of a pickle factory in Bombay; the action consists of Saleem's writing and reading his story, a story that, although it addresses battles, contains few traditionally heroic deeds; Padma, a pickle-factory employee, is the only person—natural or supernatural—to show any interest in the story's action; and finally, the style Saleem adopts is personal and conversational, filled with self-conscious musings and casual remarks. Saleem's story also breaks the three basic epic conventions: there is no statement of argument or invocation of a muse, and Saleem goes so far as to retract his first statement, arguing with himself; the story begins not *in medias res* but *in medias ruinas* ("de-cay"), at a specific time in history, with Saleem's birth; and Saleem provides the listener/reader with no catalog of characters, who, far from being introduced in detail, are often referred or alluded to before their identity is made clear. The epic form is not the proper form for Saleem's journey of self-definition. *Midnight's Children* plays with the form of the traditional epic and the limited possibilities and views that it presents, expanding it to suit Rushdie's own purposes.

In fact, as Rushdie himself has discussed, Saleem's story is an "anti-epic" in the tradition of Rabelais, Gogol, or Boccaccio.[26] For Rushdie (and Saleem) the individual, and therefore history, are dynamic. Only as the silent, dog-like "buddha" does Saleem become static. As the buddha-dog, Saleem is asked about his family, feeling, and memories, and replies: "Don't try and fill my head with all that history. I am who I am, that's all there is" (340; see also 346). This simple, Popeye-esque declaration of identity reveals what Rushdie finds wrong with the epic hero, who is static and therefore dead.[27] Saleem is continually redefining himself, which is the antithesis of an epic hero, who "is always equal to himself; he is definable, and that definition belongs to all."[28] *Midnight's Children* cannot be an epic in the traditional sense because Saleem is not an epic hero, the type of character who has already reached perfection and lives an exemplary life. Saleem, whose whole narration represents the evaluation, reevaluation, and definition of his life, is in the process of becoming.

In the diverse and fragmented world of India—in the postcolonial, postmodern world in general—the epic hero is no longer universally applicable and has no place in the individual formation of identity. *Midnight's Children* above all emphasizes the importance of the individual, and the individual's relationship to history. Saleem's story represents the process of self-, not epic, definition. Rushdie presents an alternative to the epic hero: the anti-epic hero, whose process of self-definition—his self-narration—is accessible and applicable to all. Rushdie insists that the individual, too often subsumed by colonizers, the idea of the nation-state, or national mythology, must be understood as part of history. Rushdie implies the availability of this mode of (self-)definition throughout Saleem's narrative; to quote Saleem again: "There are as many versions of India as Indians" (261). *Midnight's Children* and Saleem explode the notion of epic, offering the reader a personalized view of the individual and his or her relationship to history.

READING *MIDNIGHT'S CHILDREN* AS ANTI-ALLEGORY

Simply reading *Midnight's Children* as an anti-epic fails to discern the many traditions—not only epic—that Rushdie addresses in his novel. I believe that

Saleem's story is most productively read as an *"anti-*allegory." I use the term "anti-allegory" to imply a style of reading that is invited by a text, a method of *reading against* suggested or typically allegorical figures and connections.[29] In other words, Saleem's story as a whole is meant to be read not only in the anti-epic tradition of European literature but also as a parody of an allegory that reveals the potentially repressive use of allegorical representations and readings. Reading *Midnight's Children* as an anti-allegory, then, gives the reader greater insight into the critique of history and traditional historical discourse that Rushdie presents.

Ron Shepherd reasons that the traditionally Hindu penchant for using allegory (to which Rushdie refers in *Midnight's Children*) is a method of seeing reality through the veil of *maya*. Rushdie, Shepherd believes, replaces the traditional Hindu veil with a veil of his own construction: "To create this new order of reality he uses a device which can be seen at every point in the novel: that is, he insists on mistaking metaphor for reality, metaphoric meaning for actual meaning." One example of this is Saleem's connection to his country: "Saleem doesn't just claim a close connection as a figure of speech, but turns this figure of speech into an actual literal connection."[30] Shepherd fails to see that, contrary to creating a new veil, Rushdie reveals the problems of trying to use allegory to access "reality." The allegory in *Midnight's Children* presents a critique of itself, revealing that there exists no one true reality for it to access.

Other critics have also misread Rushdie's complex use of allegory. Although Ashutosh Banerjee notes that "*Midnight's Children* achieves a singular synthesis between the recent Anglo-American genre of 'Non-fiction Novel' and the far older one of political allegory," he fails to understand fully the implications of the allegorical connections that Saleem makes. Of the Saleem-India connection, Banerjee states that it "taxes the author's abilities sorely to sustain Saleem Sinai's credibility as a human being while at the same time capturing within his person all of the euphoria, the tensions and the trauma of Independence."[31] Like many other critics, Banerjee imposes the notion that Saleem needs to be representative of all Indians and all of India. He fails to read Saleem as an individual, and in Saleem's story he fails to see Rushdie's implicit critique of allegory. Banerjee does not see the comic and ironic elements in Saleem's story, how Rushdie uses allegory in such a heavy-handed manner to draw attention to its shortcomings. Banerjee complains that the convergence of personal and national events "is often artificially imposed on the narrative." As an example he cites Saleem's "[o]ne last fact" that connects the death of his grandfather with Prime Minister Nehru's falling ill and complains that "This connection seems rather gratuitous."[32] Banerjee fails to see that Rushdie wants to make the connection seem "gratuitous"—that is *precisely* the point that Rushdie wishes to make. Such a scene shows Saleem's conscious imposition of his history on the nation's narration (and that Rushdie does not go to great lengths to hide Saleem's tendency to do this). The "gratuitous" connection to which Banerjee refers reveals *Saleem's* obsession with connections—not Rushdie's.[33]

Allegory is a mode popular in traditionally colonial texts. Writers such as Forster, Scott, Kipling, Conrad, and Cary—to name just a few—all employed allegory in their stories about Africa and India. Stephen Slemon observes that "if allegory literally means 'other speaking,' it has historically meant a way of speaking *for* the subjugated Others of the European colonial enterprise—a way of subordinating the colonised, that is, through the politics of representation."[34] Slemon goes on to examine how postcolonial texts use allegory not as a conservative mode to express existing values and structures but as a "site for the struggle between colonialist discourse and post-colonial counter-discourse." Slemon recognizes that allegory has often been used as a tool of the colonizer, and "in a dialectical sense, [it] becomes an especially charged site for the discursive manifestations for what is at heart a *cultural* form of struggle."[35] However, precisely by setting up opposing binary values—in which one term in the relationship is constantly subjugated to the other—allegory provides the locus for meaning within colonial discourse.

Abdul JanMohamed has shown how the binary pairs used in allegory can be repressive. He uses the term "Manichean allegory" to refer to the simple binary oppositions (good/bad, white/black) used in the colonial context to simplify and devalue the colonized.[36] Frantz Fanon believes that the problem with the juxtaposition of terms such as black/white, insider/outsider is that the two terms are opposed to one another, not in the service of a higher unity. In other words, one term in the pair is superfluous, so no "Hegelian" recognition—and consequently no reconciliation—is possible. Therefore such a binary division is nondialectical.[37] The split from which colonialist allegory creates its meaning is irreconcilable and is dependent upon the subjugation of the lesser of the terms. Slemon argues that "Allegory becomes a site upon which post-colonial cultures seek to contest and subvert colonialist appropriation through the production of a literary, and specifically anti-imperialist, figurative opposition or textual *counter-discourse*." Slemon fails to see that the relationship he sets up between allegorical discourse and counterdiscourse is dialectical in nature. If, as Slemon claims, allegory is "colonialism's most visible figurative technology," then why would it be necessary to "engage head-on" with this form of representation?[38] Would it not be all the more powerful for a postcolonial text to undermine this repressive form, revealing allegory, in all of its seeming power, to be a sham, non-sense? Even if allegory can be turned and used effectively as a tool to undermine oppressive imperial and cultural values, why valorize the allegorical mode of expression by willingly engaging it? In *Midnight's Children* Rushdie seeks to diffuse the seemingly monolithic power of allegory, focusing instead on a multiplicity of views better read in terms of anti-allegory.[39] In other words, to diffuse the oppressive power of allegory, the postcolonial text must bring into question the cohesiveness of any implied allegorical reading. Hence, Rushdie is able to show allegory as it truly is: a literary device that can be used not only in the service of revealing truths but also in the service of revealing absurdities and inconsistencies. Keith Booker asserts that the "theme of two contradictory realities occupying the same space is a favorite one in Rushdie's fiction." And if two opposed identities, "two incompatible and contradictory alternative realities, can occupy the same space, then clearly the very notions of 'identity' and 'reality' are called into question" (Booker, 990).

There are many reasons why Rushdie in *Midnight's Children* might want to pick apart the validity of allegorical representation. First, and most basic, is the traditionally repressive role that allegory has played in colonialist literature. As David Spurr states in *The Rhetoric of Empire:*

> In colonial discourse every individual weakness has its political counterpart—uncivilized society, according to this logic, being little more than the uncivilized mind and body writ large. Hence a certain parallelism in the themes of debasement employed by the discourse: the qualities assigned to the individual savage—dishonesty, suspicion, superstition, lack of self-discipline—are reflected more generally in societies characterized by corruption, xenophobia, tribalism, and the inability to govern themselves.[40]

By using allegorical representation, colonialist literature creates binary oppositions that lower the colonized subjects as they elevate the colonizers. Although Slemon identifies the process in which postcolonial writing engages allegory head-on, he fails to see that the willingness to engage a colonial text on its own allegorical grounds valorizes this potentially repressive mode of representation. Rushdie is not simply attempting to negate the view of the colonizers—a view that contains, certainly, some truth—he wishes, rather, to decenter it. Rushdie wants to open up the notion of one "Truth," showing the many versions of possible *truths*.[41] Rather than appropriate allegory and use it as a weapon to fight colonial representation, Rushdie explodes the allegorical relationship, leaving a text that cannot be read through a single, layered interpretation but demands to be read in a multiplicity of manners. Saleem not only contradicts himself, misstates dates, and lies but also constantly claims that he *is* India (and is therefore representative, not unique but one among many) while at the same time he insists on the importance of his life in India's history.

While discussing the various "modes" of Rushdie's narratives, Kumkum Sangari singles out both the parodic and the allegorical. Rushdie's conflation of an "oral" narrator with a modernist narrator ("If Ganesh breeds with Tristram Shandy to hatch Saleem . . .") leads to parody.[42] Sangari shows how Saleem asserts his humility but continually attempts to establish himself as more important than the story, as the agent of history. Sangari suggests that Saleem's double action parodies both the historical aggrandizement of the (impotent) individual—the paradigmatic protagonist of nineteenth century realist fiction—and the vaunted epicality of his own narrative. The often indulgent autoreferentiality of the postmodern idiom is opened up for inspection and irony, especially as the narrative's own substantive alignment is with the specificity of colonial and contemporary experience on the Indian subcontinent.[43]

Sangari points out that "While the parodic mode works at the expense of both epistemologies, the allegorical mode (albeit problematized and contested), which sets up the narrator as both child and fate of independent India, attempts to conjoin the two." Saleem, then, is at once "the voice of the individual and of a collectivity, spectator and participant, unique and representative."[44] By showing the inadequacies of allegory, Rushdie shows that reality cannot be read allegorically, it must be created individually.

In playing with the traditionally colonialistic and repressive trope of allegory, Rushdie also addresses a potentially repressive notion in current Western literary theory. In his important but deeply flawed essay "Third-World Literature and the Era of Multinational Capitalism," Fredric Jameson declares:

All third-world texts are necessarily, I want to argue, allegorical, and in a very specific way: they are to be read as what I will call *national allegories,* even when, or perhaps I should say, particularly when their forms develop out of predominantly western machineries of representation, such as the novel.... Third-world texts, even those which are seemingly private and invested with a properly libidinal dynamic—necessarily project a political dimension in the form of national allegory: *the story of the private individual destiny is always an allegory of the embattled situation of the public third-world culture and society.*[45]

Jameson's self-described "sweeping hypothesis" seeks to define "Third World" novelists in opposition to their "First World" counterparts, suggesting, it seems, that when non-Western writers attempt to employ the Western novelistic form, they end up writing national allegories. Once a weapon of colonialist writers, allegory has been appropriated by seemingly colonialist critics.[46] In *Midnight's Children* Rushdie "turns" the allegorical trope, so obviously connecting Saleem to his nation's history that allegory is parodied. Through Saleem's constant and absurd assertions regarding his individual fate and the fate of India, Rushdie offers a critique of the traditional use of allegory.

The critique of allegory contained in *Midnight's Children* extends beyond its repressive use by Western writers and critics. Rushdie has identified the problematic use of allegory within Indian literary criticism. In various interviews Rushdie has expressed negative sentiments about the limits of allegorical interpretation:

In India allegory is a kind of disease. Indian philosophy has this idea of Maya, of reality as a veil, in which what we in fact can think of as being real is an illusion born out of our limited perception, and if you can move this veil aside then somewhere behind it there is reality. And you move this veil aside through a process called religion. Because there is this idea of the veil, almost all great classical Indian literature has been allegorical in its form, and so—we're talking about the limitations of Indian criticism—one of the problems is that there's an expectation of allegory which is so great that almost everything you do is always translated allegorically. I don't think anything I've done can be translated in that simple way.[47]

Rushdie believes that Indian literary criticism overemphasizes allegory "as though every text is not what it seems but only a veil behind which is the real text." As Rushdie complains, "I quite dislike the notion that what you are reading is really something else."[48] Ron Shepherd believes that although *Midnight's Children* is "a replica of India and Indian consciousness," it is modified, personalized, disguised, and parodied.[49] Writing against both the West's repressive allegorical representation of the Orient and a potentially limited manner of Indian reading and writing, Rushdie undermines the use of allegory as both a discursive practice and a mode of critical interpretation.

The action within *Midnight's Children* supports its critique of the multiple uses and abuses of allegory. The text directly addresses the West's notion of the Indian penchant for allegory. In *Midnight's Children,* the only character who speaks directly of this "Indian lust for allegory" is the oh-so-British William Methwold. Within *Midnight's Children* itself, allegory is shown to be a tool of the colonizer: Methwold states that "beneath this stiff English exterior lurks a mind with a very Indian lust for allegory" (96). In Methwold's hand allegory is repressive and hierarchical, and Saleem speaks of this "Englishman's lust for an Indian allegory and the seduction of an accordionist's wife" (108). Methwold's seduction of Vanita—read allegorically as the seduction of the Indians by the British—is the event that precipitates Saleem's birth. Saleem is in many ways a "victim" of allegory; because Methwold's seduction leads to Saleem's birth, Saleem is both dependent on allegory for his existence—a product of allegory—but, abandoned by his father, spurned by allegory nonetheless. Methwold's penchant for the allegorical has its limits: he may father an Indian child (as the British fathered a country), but that does not mean he needs to take any responsibility for it. Methwold's "parting" act of irony in this small allegory is that his center-parting hair—which he reveals as fake at the moment of independence—was his one feature that Vanita could not resist. Thus Vanita is seduced by something false, and Methwold, hairpiece and all, departs, leaving his offspring, Saleem (113).

Saleem's Story as Self and All

From the beginning of *Midnight's Children* Rushdie seems to be challenging this allegorical mode, subtly undercutting the obvious signs that Saleem's life should be read as a historical or national allegory. Rushdie addresses the notion of historical allegory by claiming that Saleem is "handcuffed to history" (11): not merely attached to history—not held or embraced, walking beside in partnership with, but handcuffed—dragged along, like an unwilling criminal. This statement can be read as Rushdie's metacommentary on his own narrative process: Saleem has been "handcuffed" to the history of his country by Rushdie himself. As regarding his birth, Saleem has no say in the matter: he is just taken along for history's ride. In much the same way, Saleem's own allegorical obsessions are imposed on him from the moment of his birth. The idea that his birth is special—occurring at the moment of independence and therefore representative of the new Indian, and therefore the new India—is itself an idea that is allegorical in nature. Prime Minister Jawaharlal Nehru's letter also suggests this allegorical connection: "You are the newest bearer of that ancient face of India which is also eternally young. We shall be watching over your life with the closest attention; it will be, in a sense, the mirror of our own" (122). Saleem takes this letter too literally and becomes obsessed with finding purpose in his life. As a child Saleem fears that his "much-trumpeted existence might turn out to be utterly useless, void, and without the shred of purpose" (152). He notes that "It was a very early age ['nearlyeight'] at which to be perplexed by meaning" (152). As a teen, Saleem suggests that the Midnight's Children Club address "the notions which plagued me all this time: the notions of purpose, and meaning. 'We must think,' I said, 'what we are for'" (222). Later, Saleem notes "the question of purpose which had plagued me all my life" (410). Saleem has once again become a victim of allegory—the allegorical connection made, because of the time of his birth, by the PM's letter. Later, Saleem recognizes this Indian need to allegorize, although he fails to identify this desire in himself. Referring to Indians, Saleem claims that "As a people, we are obsessed with correspondences. Similarities between this and that, between apparently unconnected things, make us clap our hands delightedly when we find them out. It is a sort of national longing for form—or perhaps simply an expression of our deep belief that forms lie hidden within reality; that meaning reveals itself only in flashes" (291). Rushdie paints a portrait of Saleem as a person who is obsessed with connections, a person who imposes his life and the life of his family onto history. Through Saleem's allegorization of his own history, Rushdie parodies allegory, showing its dangers.

It is important to make the distinction between Saleem as narrator and Rushdie as author, something many of the critics who "blame" Rushdie for

Saleem's actions or statements have failed to do. Keith Booker notes this problem, confirming that "Certainly it would be an egregiously naive interpretive error to mistake statements made by any of Rushdie's rhetorically complex narrators for the opinions of Rushdie himself, though one might have a difficult time explaining that fact to certain Islamic fundamentalist elements" (Booker, 978). Rushdie states in an interview that one difficulty with first-person narration is "a problem with having a figure who swamps the book like that, which is that it is very difficult to give the reader the impression that the narrator's point of view sometimes diverges from the writer's. And it *is* a problem with *Midnight's Children* because I think the older he gets particularly, there are more and more occasions when I'm not in sympathy with him."[50]

Rushdie shows Saleem's obsession, both by making the connections Saleem makes between historical events and his personal life more and more tenuous and by using the other characters to comment on Saleem's sense of self-importance.[51] When Saleem appears on his Aunt Sonia's doorstep as an adult, she greets him: " 'Saleem, is it? Yes, I remember you. Nasty little brat you were. And why? Some stupid letter the P.M.'s fifteenth assistant undersecretary must have sent you' " (378). Saleem creates his story to fit his view of reality and his life: "[T]he Midnight Children's Conference fulfilled the prophecy of the Prime Minister and became, in truth, a mirror of the nation" (248). But as Aunt Sonia points out, the PM's letter was probably written by some assistant—hardly a prophecy. This not only demonstrates the power of words—the words that led to Saleem's obsession with his "purpose"—but shows how the individual can distort experience. Ironically, perhaps to Saleem's credit, even at the age of almost 30, he still seems to believe the PM's words: the story he creates now, even as an adult, reflects his obsession with purpose, meaning, and his own life's parallel to the "life" of his country: his own obsession with allegory.

Saleem is aware of himself as a storyteller, as the creator of the narrative into which the reader is drawn. Rushdie purposely draws attention to Saleem's methods of creating Saleem's story. The most obvious of these methods are Saleem's allegorical connections, which serve to amplify Saleem's "claim to a place at the centre of things." Saleem constantly obsesses on his relationship to India. Regarding the Prime Minister's statement that "Your life, which will be, in a sense, the mirror of our own," Saleem asks: "*In what sense?* How, in what terms, may the career of a single individual be said to impinge on the fate of a nation?" (232; emphasis in original). Saleem replies: "I was linked to history both literally and metaphorically, both actively and passively" (232). In other words, Saleem reveals his historical linkage to be what it literally is: a literary device. At various points in the novel Salem goes so far as to point out and label ("passive-literal," "active-metaphorical," etc.) the modes of connection that he is currently establishing (see 232–33, 248,

278). Through his metacommentary, Rushdie reveals Saleem in all of his glory, as the teller of the tale.

Truth in History and Narration

Saleem states that "Sometimes legends make reality, and become more useful than the facts" (47). Rushdie intimates that "legends"—in other words "stories"—are reality. This is certainly true if, as Rushdie seems to imply, historical "facts" are hard to come by and are often composed of stories to begin with. Nancy Batty believes that "Rushdie's implication—that if history is composed of fictions, then fiction can be composed of history—is perhaps the most potent message of *Midnight's Children*."[52] Rushdie believes that history is not scientific or objective; history is the same as "fiction." In *Midnight's Children* even something as seemingly absolute (not to mention scientific) as the passing of time can be brought into question. As one character asks in reaction to the suggestion that Pakistani clocks run a half an hour ahead of clocks in India: "If they can change the time just like that, what's real any more? I ask you? What's true?" (79).[53] The whole notion of truth and reality is relative and dialogic—not absolute and monologic, to use Bakhtin's term. It is the job of the artist—of the writer of "fiction"—to bring these "truths" to light. Saleem notes that "Picture Singh and the magicians were people whose hold on reality was absolute; they gripped it so powerfully that they could bend it every which way in the service of their arts, but they never forgot what it was" (385). In other words, the artist, the magician, the storyteller—those who base their art on the manipulation of "reality"—best understand what reality is about. Although Saleem later claims that he could "never fully enter the world-according-to-Picture-Singh; that, in fact, my dream of saving the country was a thing of mirrors and smoke; insubstantial, the maunderings of a fool" (399), this itself may be a smoke screen. After all, if Picture-Singh and the magicians did not believe in magic, they must have believed in sleight of hand and tricks, that is, smoke and mirrors. Even if Saleem's "hold on reality" is not absolute (no one's is—that is the message), he may still have a firm grip on his own magical reality: the art of telling a story.

Saleem's artistic truths are personal, and they are far from "perfect." After admitting to lying, Saleem reasons: "That's why I fibbed, anyway; for the first time, I fell victim to the temptation of every autobiographer, to the illusion that since the past exists only in one's memories and the words which strive vainly to encapsulate them, it is possible to create events simply by saying they occurred" (427). To some extent, at least for the storyteller, it *is* possible "to create" events simply by stating that they occurred. Critics such as

John Stephens have misread Saleem's declarations, hearing and criticizing Saleem's words without paying attention to his actions. In his article, Stephens misquotes the passage above—leaving off "the illusion that"—and makes the illogical assertion that "In other words, there is no relationship between signifier and signified, and floating signifiers may be used to deconstruct the present in order to recreate the past in order to explain the present." Stephens concludes that Rushdie's message is "History is meaningless."[54] Stephens's misuse of poststructuralist thought leads him to read meaninglessness into a novel that is constantly *creating* meaning. In failing to understand Rushdie's message, Stephens arrives at an erroneous conclusion. Stephens does not see how the gap between signifier and signified may be exploited to *create* meaning. *Midnight's Children* is out to show that history does have meaning; in fact, history has *many* meanings. For Rushdie, history is individual, and history's meaning is determined by the present. The message is, to a great extent, that history is not logical, it is not scientific or even objective—but it still can have meaning.

SALEEM AS STORYTELLER

Saleem suggests that "in autobiography, as in all literature, what actually happened is less important than what the author can manage to persuade his audience to believe" (263). In other words, truth is contained in the creative act. Saleem tells us "[m]emory's truth, because memory has its own special kind" (207). After all, beyond the cold, vacant "truth" preserved by the pure logic in philosophy and mathematics, truth is no more than memory. Memory mimics the artistic process, which itself "selects, eliminates, alters, exaggerates, minimizes." Saleem asks: "What is truth?" He continues: "What is sanity? Did Jesus rise up from the grave? Do Hindus not accept . . . that the world is a kind of dream; that Brahma dreamed, is dreaming the universe; that we only see dimly through that dream-web, which is Maya. Maya . . . may be defined as all that is illusory; as trickery, artifice, deceit" (207; my ellipsis). But art does not have to involve trickery. What might be viewed as Saleem's most fantastic and unbelievable claim, his ability to "look into the hearts and minds of men" (196), when viewed as an artistic conceit makes perfect sense.[55] In his act of telling this story Saleem manages to prove his most outrageous claim: that he has telepathic powers. His ability to enter the hearts and minds of others is as "genuine" as the story itself; the *act* of telling the story gives him the powers he claims. Saleem as telepath and Saleem as storyteller are one and the same.

Saleem's self-proclaimed ability to read minds—a claim that at first resembles a magical act—describes his artistic ability to create. As novelist, Rushdie looks into the hearts and minds of humans, and as storyteller, Saleem is endowed with similar powers. Saleem invites his readers to understand his life and, by implication, to understand the world: "I have been a swallower of lives; and to know me, just one of me, you'll have to swallow the lot as well" (11). This statement can be read in many ways: to understand his own life, Saleem must put it in context; or, one life contains all lives, and therefore each life is a world—an idea akin to Leibniz's Monadology. Saleem does not claim to represent an entire people or world, he claims to be one among many. As storyteller Saleem does in fact "swallow lives," and as readers of Rushdie we are asked to do the same. Saleem is well aware that his story is only one among many. By suggesting that Saleem's project of self-narration contains the stories of many people, Rushdie asserts that his project, *Midnight's Children* per se, is just a beginning. Saleem's story represents one person's discourse, and its assertion of the importance of individual narration is the base of that "national myth" of which Rushdie speaks.

CREATING MEANING, CREATING REALITY, CREATING HISTORY

Saleem's tale in *Midnight's Children* is his attempt to come to terms with his past, thereby bridging the gap between his experience and his future. Saleem states that "consciousness, the awareness of oneself as a homogeneous entity in time, a blend of past and present, is the glue of personality, holding together our then and now" (341). Rushdie asserts that history needs to be given meaning, or, more precisely, history is the *process of discerning meaning*. Saleem declares: "Reality is a question of perspective; the further you get from the past, the more concrete and plausible it seems—but as you approach the present, it inevitably seems more and more incredible" (164). He gives the example of a movie screen: as one moves closer, "tiny details assume grotesque proportions; the illusion dissolves—or rather, it becomes clear that the illusion itself *is* reality" (164).[56] In Rushdie's world, reality is subjective; it must be narrated, given form. In shaping his story, Saleem discerns the meanings in his experiences. "Everything has a shape if you look for it," Saleem insists. "There is no escape from form" (221). If there is no absolute reality, then what is "real," like form, must be discerned by the historian or the artist. The reality or form lies dormant—within history or a work of art—and the job of the individual historian or artist is to make manifest one particular history or reality. Rushdie shows that there is no one single "correct" form that is waiting to be brought out but a multitude of forms that are accessible to all. Different artists, historians, and individuals bring out different forms. Hence *Midnight's Children* emphasizes the importance of the individual not only in making but in interpreting—and therefore creating—history.

Saleem's self-proclaimed helplessness is a combination of his modesty, his exhaustion, and his feeling of impotence. This feeling of impotence is common in most people, especially in the shadow of national and international events. In this way Saleem represents the political everyman—impotent in the face of history yet witness to it all. His power lies in his ability to tell, retell, mold, and shape history into the story he narrates. We see Saleem as a child participating in the reshaping of history when he alters the headlines in the newspaper (252–53). People constantly reclaim and reinterpret their history and pasts, on both an individual and a national level. This reclamation and reinterpretation is the essence of the dynamic historical process in which Saleem is embroiled. Rushdie's major assertion is that we are all the children of history, and that history is not an objective science. Saleem not only writes his own history, he creates a new myth of and for India: that of the celebration of the individual.

The act of narration, therefore, is the act of creating history. Rushdie recognizes the inherent historical and political ramifications of all art. In his essay "Outside the Whale" (1984), Rushdie believes "that works of art, even works of entertainment, do not come into being in a social and political vacuum; and that the way they operate in society cannot be separated from politics, from history" (*Imaginary,* 92). In *Midnight's Children,* Saleem parallels his own life with that of India, writing his history and forming his identity. Through his story Saleem creates his India. I am not implying that without Saleem there would be no India, only that we would not have the India that Rushdie gives us, this particular view of history and of midnight's children.

Rushdie's main metaphor for Saleem's creation of historical form is that of "pickling." Saleem, we must not forget, is the "pickler-in-chief" at a Bombay chutney factory. History, like making chutney, involves both preserving and combining a finite number of ingredients from an almost infinite number of choices. It also involves the altering of form, changing yet preserving. Saleem states of pickling: "The art is to change the flavour in degree, but not in kind, and above all (in my thirty jars and a jar) to give it shape and form— that is to say, meaning. (I have mentioned my fear of absurdity)" (444). Pickling, like history, is subjective because the process involves individual opinions or "taste." Saleem conflates his writing with the pickling process, investing the latter with a symbolic meaning that, like his writing, explodes notions of scale: if a single spoon and jar can contain the genetic materials for a whole country, a whole person can contain "the world," and a single book can contain all of a country's history.

Saleem is not after perfect comprehensiveness; he desires expansiveness. The dangers of attempting a comprehensiveness are shown through the characters of the painter, who "tried to get the whole of life into his art," and the peep-show man, Lifafa Das. The painter kills himself, declaring, " 'I wanted to be a miniaturist and I've got elephantiasis instead!' " (48–49). Das, while advertising his show, cries: " 'See the whole world, come see everything!' " (75). Das's "hyperbolic formula began, after a time, to prey upon his [Das's] mind" (75). Saleem recognizes what he terms "an Indian disease, this urge to encapsulate the whole of reality." He asks: "Worse: am I infected, too?" (75). Saleem may be infected, but he is well aware of his limitations as an artist. When Saleem reaches his final chapter, he states: "I reach the end of my long-winded autobiography; in words and pickles, I have immortalized my memories, although distortions are inevitable in both methods. We must live, I'm afraid, with the shadows of imperfection" (442). What is required of the writer to tell the story of himself or herself? Great talent? A claim to be representative of all? None of these, merely a certain "nose" or sensitivity. The characteristics required for pickling are much the same as those of the artist. Saleem asks: "What is required for chutnification? . . . [A]bove all a nose capable of discerning the hidden languages of what-must-be-pickled, its humours and messages and emotions" (443). Similar to his "mundane" work in a factory making condiments, Saleem's artistic self-narration is also temporally bound:

> [I]n the pickles' version of history, Saleem appears to have known too little; at other times, too much . . . yes, I should revise and revise, improve and improve; but there is neither the time nor the energy. I am obliged to offer no more than this stubborn sentence: It happened that way because that's how it happened. (443; ellipses in original)

Saleem once again asserts the individuality of his version of the past. Telling (and creating) one's history is like preserving: "To pickle is to give immortality" (444). Much like Rushdie's writing (and Saleem's story), particular chutneys are a matter of taste that may not be to everyone's liking. To the end, Saleem asserts the importance of subjectivity. Interestingly, however, Saleem describes his narrative pickling as "acts of love," implying that his story is not as solipsistic and self-interested as it may first appear.

The ending of *Midnight's Children* has been a source of great disagreement, and critics interpret it alternately as full of despair and pessimism or reservedly hopeful. While discussing the ending of *Midnight's Children,* Rushdie reports: "What I tried to do was to set up a tension in the text, a paradoxical opposition between the form and content of the narrative."[57] Rushdie believes that although the story of Saleem does lead Saleem to despair, the story is told in a manner to show, in Rushdie's words, "the Indian talent for non-stop self-regeneration." Rushdie continues: "This is why the narrative constantly throws up new stories, why it 'teems.' The form—multitudinous, hinting at the infinite possibilities of the country—is the optimistic counterweight to Saleem's personal tragedy."[58] Saleem's own cynical protestations of inaction and weakness are balanced by his incredible power to tell his story. Saleem remains active by telling his tale, forging his own identity through his own words. He places this identity within a historical context, relating it not in relation to his family but in relation to the history of India. In this manner, Saleem's project of self-narration not only accomplishes its explicit goal of "meaning something," it also has further-reaching impact. In the process of telling his own personal and family history, Saleem "recaptures" the history of India. Through Saleem, Rushdie offers his commentary not only on the nature of narration and history but also on the importance of forming an individual identity that is defined in relation to one's historical past. Rushdie uses Saleem's tale to critique the abuses of allegorical representation and interpretation in both colonial writers and in Indian literature and criticism.

Rushdie himself may be understating Saleem's achievement; Rushdie may fail to see that in the act of narration Saleem creates and re-creates himself. In fact, through his writing Saleem, the pickler-in-chief, makes himself immortal (444). The final paragraph of *Midnight's Children* begins not with negation but with *affirmation:*

> Yes, they will trample me underfoot, the numbers marching one two three, four hundred million five hundred six, reducing me to specks of voiceless dust, just as, all in good time, they will trample my son, and his son who will not be his, and his who will not be his, until, the thousand and first generation, until a thousand and one midnights have bestowed their terrible gifts and a thousand and one children have died, because it is the privilege and the curse of midnight's children to be both masters and victims of their times, to forsake privacy and be sucked into the annihilating whirlpool of the multitudes, and to be unable to live or die in peace. (446)

The "Yes" recalls Molly Bloom's "Yes" in James Joyce's *Ulysses* and implies a letting go and acceptance: "yes I said yes I will Yes."[59] In spite of the images of trampling and "annihilating whirlpools," and Saleem's claim that midnight's children will be "unable to live or die in peace," the ending is far from pessimistic. These images imply an engagement with reality, and the conclusion represents, to a great extent, a spiritual union of the individual with the world. For Rushdie this union is a union with history, with the world—in all of its gritty reality. Rushdie offers us a mystical acceptance of the somewhat harsh realities of today's world, because he believes that we must actively participate in history, not try to escape from it. Hence, although employing postmodernist narrative techniques, Rushdie's writing does not imply the moral cynicism often attributed to postmodernism. Instead, his message emphasizes the need to play an active role in shaping one's destiny, to engage with—not withdraw from—the historical and cultural forces that shape our time.

By placing Saleem at the center of his own universe, Rushdie offers us a radically humanist view of history, narration, and identity. The answer to Saleem's questions "Who am I? Who were we?" (422) is actually quite simple: we are the stories we tell about ourselves. To understand Saleem, we have to swallow the world, but Saleem's world, in spite of its tragedies and sorrows, remains full of humor and resilience.

Notes

1. Salman Rushdie, *Midnight's Children* (New York: Knopf, 1981), 11; hereafter cited in the text.
2. Simon During, "Postmodernism or Post-colonialism Today," *Textual Practice* 1, no. 1 (1987): 43.
3. Rustom Bharucha claims that Rushdie does not write about history: "He *weaves* it into his fiction" (229; emphasis in original). Bharucha believes that Rushdie is least effective when he summarizes facts. See Rustom Bharucha, "Rushdie's Whale," *Massachusetts Review* 27 (1986): 221–37. Interestingly, David Lipscomb has recently identified these passages that summarize history as being taken from an introductory textbook on Indian history. Rushdie takes many historical descriptions from Stanley Wolpert, *A New History of India* (New York: Oxford University Press, 1977), 166. Lipscomb believes that Rushdie uses Wolpert, who is a professor at UCLA, as the generic "historical voice," the validity of which Rushdie wants to call into question. For an intriguing reading of Rushdie's use of Wolpert's passages see David Lipscomb, "Caught in a Strange Middle Ground: Contesting History in Salman Rushdie's *Midnight's Children*," *Diaspora* 1, no. 2 (1991): 163–88.

Bharucha also notes Rushdie's use of "performance" to incorporate history into fiction: the pepper-pot "revolution" that Saleem helps orchestrate on his dining table, or Saleem's encounter with the language demonstrators. Saleem's words touch off the language riots, perpetuating and creating history through language (230). Bharucha suggests that the most obvious method that Rushdie uses to rewrite Indian history is analogical: "It is a freewheeling narrative device that links a moment from Saleem's biography to an historical event either through inference or a verbal echo" (230–31).

4. Salman Rushdie, " 'Errata': Or, Unreliable Narration in *Midnight's Children*" (1983), in *Imaginary Homelands: Essays and Criticism 1981–1991* (New York: Viking, 1991), 24; *Imaginary Homelands* is hereafter cited in the text as *Imaginary*.
5. Salman Rushdie, interview with Jean-Pierre Durix, *Kunapipi* 4, no. 2 (1982): 22. Fawzia Afzal-Khan asserts that for Rushdie "neither myth nor realism (with their stress on 'wholeness') seems to be an appropriate fictive strategy for depicting a world that he sees as fragmented in the aftermath of colonialism." See Fawzia Afzal-Khan, *Cultural Imperialism and the Indo-English Novel: Genre and Ideology in R. K. Narayan, Anita Desai, Kamala Markandaya, and Salman Rushdie* (University Park: Pennsylvania State University Press, 1993), 177.
6. Interview 1982, 22.
7. M. Keith Booker, "Beauty and the Beast: Dualism as Despotism in the Fiction of Salman Rushdie," *ELH* 57, no. 4 (1990): 984; hereafter cited in the text.
8. The body of the colonized person is often read—literally and allegorically—in light of the clash between colonizer and colonized; although this often leads to fruitful readings, several critics have already read Saleem in such a way, most recently Jean M. Kane in "The Migrant Intellectual and the Body of History: Salman Rushdie's *Midnight's Children*," *Contemporary Literature* 37, no. 1 (1996): 94–118.
9. David Spurr, *The Rhetoric of Empire: Colonial Discourse in Journalism, Travel Writing, and Imperial Administration* (Durham, N.C.: Duke University Press, 1993), 98.
10. Mikhail M. Bakhtin, "Discourse in the Novel," in *The Dialogic Imagination: Four Essays,* ed. Michael Holquist, trans. Caryl Emerson and Michael Holquist (Austin: University of Texas Press, 1981), 348.
11. Aruna Srivastava sees in Saleem the impotence of the "Nietzschean" historical person, an impotence that "results from the desire of those in power to control history." See Srivastava's " 'The Empire Writes Back': Language and History in *Shame* and *Midnight's Children*," *Ariel* 20, no. 4 (1989): 63. Srivastava asks: "Is Saleem indeed 'fathered' by this chronological, British-born(e) manipulation of history?" "If he is," she answers, "he must live with his feeling

of impotence, which is also reflected physically, in the face of an oppressive sense of destiny or fate that this mode entails."

12. The danger of attempting to fuse together these clashing belief systems is shown in Aadam Aziz's "attempt to fuse the skills of Western and hakimi medicine, an attempt which would gradually wear him down." As Aadam "aged and the world became less real he began to doubt his own beliefs" (67).

13. Salman Rushdie, interview with Chandrabhanu Pattanayak, *The Literary Criterion* 18, no. 3 (1983): 19.

14. Interview 1983, 21.

15. For a concise discussion of the tradition of privileging "history" over "literature" (and its relationship to Derrida's critique of the metaphysics of presence), see Michael Ryan, *Marxism and Deconstruction: A Critical Articulation* (Baltimore, Md.: Johns Hopkins University Press, 1982), 21. For a general discussion of the relationship between literature and history, see Tony Bennett, *Outside Literature* (London: Routledge, 1990), 41–77.

16. Bakhtin believed that the novel was the perfect form through which to advance a multiplicity of competing views that challenge a monologic view of the world. Gary Saul Morson develops Bakhtin's ideas in a manner particularly applicable to Saleem's story: "The defining characteristic of the novel . . . may be stated in terms of its relationship to time, to the historical process. The novel is ever novel. Unlike every other genre, it conceives of itself as of the present moment, and is aware of its position within the historical flux." Morson continues: "The novelistic perception of the world is deeply relativistic; it sees all assertions of timeless norms as temporally bound. . . . [T]he novel is the genre of Becoming." Gary Saul Morson, "The Heresiarch of *Meta*," *PTL: A Journal for Descriptive Poetics and Theory of Literature* 3 (1978), 418–19.

17. Helen Tiffin, "Post-Colonial Literatures and Counter-Discourse," *Kunapipi* 9, no. 3 (1987): 17.

18. Dipesh Chakrabarty, "Postcoloniality and the Artifice of History: Who Speaks for 'Indian' Pasts?" *Representations* 37 (1992): 23.

19. See " 'Errata,' " in *Imaginary*, 22–25.

20. Chakrabarty, 23. Compare Chakrabarty's description of this historical discourse to the final paragraph of *Midnight's Children*.

21. Quoted in John Haffenden, ed., *Novelists in Interview* (London: Methuen, 1985), 247. Rushdie states in this interview, which took place in 1983: "The greatest compliment I received for *Midnight's Children* was when students in Bombay, and not only in Bombay, said that they knew everything in the book and that I had just written it down" (247–48). Rushdie continues, demurely: "Naturally, I had not made a conscious attempt to articulate the shared experience of my generation, but the students were saying that the book had some mythic content" (248).

22. Indira Karamcheti, "Salman Rushdie's *Midnight's Children* and an Alternate Genesis," *Pacific Coast Philology* 21, nos. 1–2 (1986): 81–82.

23. Ibid., 82.

24. See Rushdie, "A Fantasy Called India," *India Today International* (18 August 1997): 36. Rushdie continues: "I suppose what he [Saleem]—or I, through him—was saying was that there never had been a political entity called India in 1947. The thing that became independent had never previously existed, except that there had been an area, a zone called India. So it struck me that what was coming into being, this idea of a nation-state, was an invention. It was an invention of the nationalist movement. And a very successful invention. One could argue that nation-states are that kind of collective fantasies." Rushdie may be the first person to clearly articulate the role the collective imagination plays in nationalism. Josna Rege notes that the publication of *Midnight's Children* in 1981 preceded the contemporary critique of nationalism as advanced by scholars such as Benedict Anderson. See Rege, "Victim into Pro-

tagonist? *Midnight's Children* and the Post-Rushdie National Narratives of the Eighties," *Studies in the Novel* 29, no. 3 (Fall 1997): 244.

25. I have gleaned the following information about epics from three specific reference works: M. H. Abrams, *A Glossary of Literary Terms*, 6th ed. (Fort Worth, Tx.: Harcourt, 1993); Margaret Drabble, ed., *The Oxford Companion to English Literature*, 5th ed. (Oxford, England: Oxford University Press, 1985); and Alex Preminger, ed., *Princeton Encyclopedia of Poetry and Poetics*, enlarged ed. (Princeton, N.J.: Princeton University Press, 1974).

26. Interview 1982, 20.

27. Of course, "I am what I am" also alludes to the God of the Old Testament, who is static because he is basically absent from the action that takes place. Gary Saul Morson notes that the novelistic hero's "existence must be a continual process of re-definition and re-evaluation" (419). Morson states that "For the novelist, personality is always in the making. . . . [N]othing could be further from the novel than the epic, whose hero is, like the world he inhabits, completely finished." The novel, not the epic, is the perfect form for interrogating history: "The epic knows, the novel asks how we know." See Morson, 419, 420.

28. Morson, 419. Of course, Saleem cannot simply be who he is, because he is not, to use Morson's phrase, "equal to himself": his parentage and his identity, like those of modern India, is continually under redefinition.

29. For a lengthy examination of allegory and its multiple uses, see Carolynn Van Dyke, *The Fiction of Truth: Structures of Meaning in Narrative and Dramatic Allegory* (Ithaca, N.Y.: Cornell University Press, 1985). See also Stephen Greenblatt, ed., *Allegory and Representation* (Baltimore, Md.: Johns Hopkins University Press, 1981).

30. Ron Shepard, "*Midnight's Children:* The Parody of an Indian Novel," *SPAN* 21 (1985): 186.

31. Ashutosh Banerjee, "Narrative Technique in *Midnight's Children*," *Commonwealth Review* 1, no. 2 (1990): 24.

32. Ibid., 26–27.

33. For an interesting discussion of Rushdie's "literalization of metaphor" and how this relates to allegory and magic realism, see Neil ten Kortenaar's "*Midnight's Children* and the Allegory of History," *Ariel* 26, no. 2 (April 1995): 41–62.

34. Stephen Slemon, "Monuments of Empire: Allegory/Counter-Discourse/Post-Colonial Writing," *Kunapipi* 9, no. 3 (1987): 8.

35. Ibid., 11.

36. See Abdul JanMohamed, "The Economy of Manichean Allegory: The Function of Racial Difference in Colonialist Literature," *Critical Inquiry* 12, no. 1 (1985): 59–87, and JanMohamed, *Manichean Aesthetics: The Politics of Literature in Colonial Africa* (Amherst: University of Massachusetts Press, 1983).

37. See Homi K. Bhabha, foreword to Frantz Fanon, *Black Skin, White Masks* (London: Pluto, 1986), reprinted as Bhabha, "Remembering Fanon: Self, Psyche and the Colonial Condition," in *Colonial Discourse and Post-Colonial Theory: A Reader,* ed. Patrick Williams and Laura Chrisman (New York: Columbia University Press, 1994), 112–23.

38. Slemon, 11. Ultimately, Slemon asserts that postcolonial writing cannot be "read as literature" only but must be read also as a form of cultural critique and criticism, "a mode of disidentifying whole societies from the sovereign codes of cultural organisation, and an inherently dialectical intervention in the hegemonic production of cultural meaning" (14). Slemon's insistence on a dialectical relationship—traditionally Hegelian and therefore traditionally Western—limits the modes in which postcolonial writing can undermine the dominant discourse. Slemon refuses to see that binary oppositions by nature cannot be reconciled (and brought to a higher level) because the terms are mutually dependent on each other for their definition.

39. Keith Booker, in "Beauty and the Beast," observes that Rushdie, and what he terms Rushdie's "deconstruction" of polar oppositions, has precursors in modern discourse, all of

whom want to challenge the potentially oppressive powers of "monological" authorities. Booker cites Nietzsche's transvaluation of values, Derrida's deconstruction, and Bakhtin's dialogics (991). Booker connects Rushdie's challenge to dualistic thinking not only to modern philosophy (running from Nietzsche to Derrida) but to earlier authors like Swift, Rabelais, and Sterne (and their more contemporary counterparts: Grass, Joyce, and Pynchon) because of their common carnivalesque tradition. "Central to the work of all of these writers (and to Menippean satire in general) is a questioning of traditional authority, and particularly of traditional forms of logic, forms that depend greatly on dualistic oppositions (especially the Aristotelian principle of non-contradiction) for their structure" (992).

40. Spurr, 76.

41. Kelly Hewson notes that "Saleem, we can see, will not lay claim to absolute knowledge of, or offer total explanations for, anything. His art has a deliberate air of uncertainty and unreliability about it." Kelly Hewson, "Opening Up the Universe a Little More: Salman Rushdie and the Migrant as Story-Teller," *SPAN* 29 (1989): 89.

42. See Kumkum Sangari, "The Politics of Possible," *Cultural Critique* (Fall 1987): 179.

43. Ibid., 179. Sangari believes that by overtly displaying this technique, the narrative displays to the Indian middle class the "doubleness of its own parentage," showing the hybridity of its own culture—that many things have "leaked" into each other.

44. Ibid. Sangari reasons: "Through the diversity of its narrative techniques and the diversity it seeks to record, *Midnight's Children* effects something that verges on an indigenized 'tropicalization' of the subcontinent" (180). She acknowledges the transformative capacity of indigenous narratives but asks if *Midnight's Children* itself is transformative: can it "effect a different mode of understanding, . . . offer to remake the reader?" (180).

"However," Sangari writes, "in the ability and attempt to play both with different conceptions of the subject and with different ways of seeing, a play licensed by this historical moment as well as by the intersection between the non-Western and the postmodern, his narratives open the way toward more incisive descriptions of interpretative cultural formation" (180). In other words, Rushdie's approach—his exploitation of the postmodern "gap" in meaning and the cultural gap between West and non-West—leaves India open to a potentially damaging critique.

45. Fredric Jameson, "Third World Literature in the Era of Multinational Capitalism," *Social Text* 5, no. 3 (1986): 69; emphasis in original.

46. For a more extensive discussion of Jameson's essay, see Aijaz Ahmad, "Jameson's Rhetoric of Otherness and the 'National Allegory,' " in *In Theory: Classes, Nations, Literatures* (London: Verso, 1992), 95–122. For a concise discussion of Jameson's essay and Aijaz Ahmad's criticisms of Jameson, see Slemon, 8–10.

47. Salman Rushdie, interview with David Brooks, *Helix* 19/20 (1984): 61. When Brooks asks Rushdie if he finds himself actually fighting the possibility of writing allegorically, Rushdie replies: "Yes, except, if it's an Indian disease, it also affects me, so it does get into the books every so often. But I keep trying to sidetrack it" (61).

48. Quoted in Haffenden, 243.

49. Shepard, 190. Shepherd notes that in addition to allegory, two other concepts "central to Indian Hindu thought" are at work in *Midnight's Children:* themes of birth/creation and of death/destruction (188–90). It is important not to confuse allegory or allegorical symbolism with what Rushdie identifies as leitmotif—the recurrence of certain objects, words, or phrases that connect what might be otherwise unconnected events. Rushdie uses the spittoon, center-parting hair, "whatsitsname," and the like as leitmotifs, as symbolic touchstones that provide connections and give shape to the mass of material that *Midnight's Children* presents. In a lecture and interview at the University of Aarhus, Rushdie stated: "The book is really constructed around that kind of *leitmotif,* and not on the conventional Indian allegorical symbolic model." See *"Midnight's Children* and *Shame,"* 4.

50. Quoted in Rani Dharker, "An Interview with Salman Rushdie," *New Quest* 42 (1983): 352. Later Rushdie reasons that "because the book is narrated in his [Saleem's] voice it

is the authority in the book. And it's very difficult for the reader to see through that authority to another point of view about *him*" (352).

51. For example, see Mary Pereira's role in Indian history (103) or Saleem's purported explanation for the Emergency (412).

52. Nancy E. Batty, "The Art of Suspense: Rushdie's 1001 (Mid-) Nights," *Ariel* 18, no. 3 (1987): 64. Batty believes that "Only future critical exegesis which takes into account the dialectic between the historical and literary dimensions of *Midnight's Children* can hope to measure the efficacy and effects of Rushdie's project" (64). Although I agree with her focus, I believe that the relationship between the historical and the literary dimensions of the novel is not necessarily dialectical: that literature and history are sometimes one and the same thing seems to be Rushdie's assertion.

53. Kelly Hewson correctly asserts that in Rushdie's novel, then, there are few absolute truths but "many kinds of truths and many levels of reality" (89).

54. John Stephens, " 'To tell the truth, I lied . . .': Retrospectivity and Deconstruction as (Contributing) Strategies for Reading Salman Rushdie's *Midnight's Children,*" *SPAN* 21 (1985): 206.

55. Saleem's telepathic ability to look into the hearts and minds of humans can be understood as Walt Whitman's idea of artistic self-projection. Whitman proclaims in the first lines of "Song of Myself": "I celebrate myself and sing myself, / And what I assume you shall assume, / For every atom belonging to me as good belongs to you" (1.1–3). For Whitman, celebrating himself meant celebrating and experiencing the world in all its diversity. Whitman's poetry shows his ability as an artist to project himself out into the world and empathize with—and hence become one with—his subject. Saleem declares: "To understand just one life, you have to swallow the world" (108).

56. In his essay "Imaginary Homelands" (1982), Rushdie comments: "The movement towards the cinema screen is a metaphor for the narrative's movement through time towards the present, and the book itself, as it nears contemporary events, quite deliberately loses deep perspective, becomes more 'partial.' . . . I felt that it would be dishonest to pretend, when writing about the day before yesterday, that it was possible to see the whole picture" See *Imaginary,* 13.

57. Ibid., 16.

58. Ibid.

59. James Joyce, *Ulysses: The Corrected Text*, ed. Hans Walter Gabler with Wolfhard Steppe and Claus Melchior (New York: Vintage, 1984), 644. I am grateful to Stephen Clingman for first pointing out the connections between Saleem's and Molly's "Yes." Thanks also to Chaman Sahni, Andrea Rossi, Keith Booker, and others who took the time to read and comment upon various drafts of this article.

Victim into Protagonist?
Midnight's Children and the Post-Rushdie National Narratives of the Eighties

Josna E. Rege

Midnight's Children as a Breakthrough

The 1981 publication of Salman Rushdie's *Midnight's Children* was a watershed in the post-independence development of the Indian English novel, so much so that the term "post-Rushdie" has come to refer to the decade or so afterwards in which a wave of novels appeared by established as well as by young writers that were clearly influenced by *Midnight's Children*.[1] Unashamedly self-centered, Rushdie's novel celebrates the creative tensions between personal and national identity, playing up and playing with both their polarity and their unity, recognizing, like its protagonist Saleem Sinai, that if the individual is "handcuffed to history" whether he likes it or not, he can make a virtue out of that necessity. Sparks fly between the private and public realms, making artistic fireworks where there had previously been deadening dichotomies. *Midnight's Children* neither denies nor seeks to transcend polarities, but embraces them as artistic method, rejecting nothing, celebrating the resulting chaotic multiplicity, even if it crushes the protagonist himself into a billion pieces. *MC* brings heresies into the open and transforms them into prophecies. What had been the Indian English novel's problems now suddenly became its trademarks.

The number of new Indian English novelists published throughout the 1980s testifies to *MC*'s tremendous influence, not merely on superficial would-be imitators (of which there were several), or on the metropolitan demand for Indian fiction (which was considerable), but also on the fundamental conception of the national narrative. My central claim in this essay is that *Midnight's Children* enacted a discursive reconfiguration of the relationship between Self and Nation. I seek to demonstrate how it did so, and also why and how it opened up new spaces for a new crop of writers in English.

Reprinted from *Studies in the Novel* 29, no. 3 (Fall 1997): 342–75.

Midnight's Children declared that there were as many equally valid versions of Indian identity as there were Indians. This concept proved to be very liberating for many Indian English writers, allowing them to break the polarized stalemate between Self and Nation that had caught the Indian English novel in a kind of ideological and artistic holding pattern for two decades. The eighties and nineties have been distinguished by an Indian English literary explosion as writers have found themselves free to speak in a multiplicity of voices and write in a multiplicity of modes.

When *Midnight's Children* was published in 1981, winning that year's prestigious Booker Prize (and subsequently, the prize for the best of 25 years of Bookers), it was hailed both in and out of India as a literary masterpiece, and almost immediately became a kind of benchmark against which both writers and readers began to assess new novels. But it has become virtually impossible to look back at *MC* from the late nineties without seeing the novel through the filter of the events of the past 15 years. It is hard to remember, or even to acknowledge, the enthusiasm with which its publication was greeted in India—not because of its politics (there were always quarrels with that), or because of the accuracy of its representation of Indian history (it did not even pretend to that), but because of its exuberance of language and style, its combination of hilarious comedy and scathing political satire, its triumphant over-confidence, and, not least, its very success. When Rushdie toured the country in 1983 in a "triumphal homecoming," hundreds of people flocked to see him.[2] At the British Council in Delhi, fully 700 people arrived at a reading where no more than 300 had been expected and the organizers had to set up loudspeakers on the lawns outside.[3] According to a 1988 article in the Indian weekly, *Sunday,* "copies of pirated editions (of *MC*) flooded the pavements before the paperback edition reached India."[4] In 1984, Shyamala Narayan wrote: "Publishers claim that the novel has sold 4,000 copies in hardcover, and 45,000 in paperback (in addition to the pirated editions); these sales figures are unprecedented for an Indian-English novelist."[5] *MC*'s commercial success certainly helped to pave the way for future Indian English writers as publishers in India became more attentive to the domestic market for fiction in English, and publishers in Britain and the United States became more receptive to new writers from India.[6]

In the late nineties, critics both inside and out of India are much more cautious, much less likely to embrace Rushdie or claim him for India; he tends to be discussed as a diasporic writer, and his influence on the Indian literary scene is often criticized as having negatively influenced a group of already elite, alienated, or expatriate Indian English writers, and intensified the neglect of Indian language writers.[7] Of course, chief among the events that have so radically changed our perceptions of *MC* and its author since 1981 has been the 1989 Irani *fatwa* on Rushdie's *The Satanic Verses.* Its intellectual and political fallout has been disastrous, both for the literary reputation and literal survival of Rushdie himself and for the dialogue between

North and South, always strained, now more polarized than ever (ironic, this, for a writer whose stated aim was to open up space on the very horns of a dilemma). And at least as important as the *fatwa* to our changed view of *Midnight's Children* has been the deepening crisis of the Nation-state and the worldwide rise of myriad Indian and other sub-nationalisms throughout the eighties and nineties. To take a few landmark events in one rather prominent Indian family as an example: when *MC* was written, Indira Gandhi, demonized in the novel as the Widow, was still very much alive; she was assassinated by her Sikh bodyguards in 1984. Her son Sanjay, whom she was grooming as her successor and who figured as the "labia-lipped" goon squad leader in *MC,* was still alive; but he was killed in a plane crash in 1980, after the novel had been completed. Her son the airline pilot, Rajiv, who was never meant for the limelight, and who received barely a mention in *MC,* succeeded her as Prime Minister and was himself assassinated by the Tamil Tigers in 1991. Historical events have indeed proven stranger than works of fiction, even one with Salman Rushdie's own fantastic mix of ingredients, and the megalomaniacal claim of protagonist Saleem Sinai, that the elimination of his family from the face of the earth was the hidden purpose of the entire Indo-Pakistani war of 1965, no longer seems so very far-fetched.

It may also be useful to remember that the publication of *MC* preceded the contemporary critique of nationalism and the social and political fragmentation of the large universalizing nation-state. It preceded the worldwide explosion of ethnic and religious nationalisms, from the Punjab to Bosnia. It also preceded the end of the Cold War, and the rise of the New World Order and the global economy of the nineties. And as for scholars of nationalism and postcoloniality, in 1981 Partha Chatterjee, Eric Hobsbawm, Benedict Anderson, and Ernest Gellner had not yet published their works on nationalism, colonialism, and the nation-state. Fredric Jameson and Aijaz Ahmed had not yet begun their now-famous debate about whether the Third World novel is necessarily a national allegory. Still years away from its now-widespread "dissemiNation" was Homi Bhabha's Nation and Narration, and scholars were not yet speaking of nations as acts of the collective imagination and "India" in quotation marks. Rushdie's beloved Bombay was still a tolerant, cosmopolitan city years away from the Muslim pogroms and bombings of 1993, from the nativist Shiv Sena government of 1994, and from changing its name to Mumbai in 1995. Rushdie as a Bombay Muslim, albeit a thoroughly secular one, could in 1981 identify affectionately with the elephant-headed God Ganesh, the scribe of the epic Mahabharata,[8] while less than 15 years later in *The Moor's Last Sigh,* that chubby, endearing deity, the epitome of auspiciousness, the one who brings all newly-begun enterprises to a happy conclusion, becomes a "menacing grotesque" representing the corrupt and cynically manipulative forces of the religious right. In 1981, the world was certainly a fresher place in which to entertain notions of self and nation, although perhaps also a more confined one. But, like the garrulous protagonist of Rushdie's novel, I digress.

In the contemporary context, Rushdie's works have come to be seen as the foundational texts for a new kind of postcolonial novel, one in which a migrant, diasporic, cosmopolitan consciousness dominates, and also as the foundational texts for a new kind of postcolonialism being established in the metropolitan academy. Therefore few critics of whatever theoretical bent or political stripe, especially those in the US-UK, have placed *MC* in its Indian literary context, and investigated the nature of and reasons for its considerable influence on the Indian novel in English and the legacy it has passed on to a generation of new writers. This is what I want to begin to do in this essay.

There has been a flood of critical writing, some of it very good indeed, accounting for different aspects of *MC*'s success and literary influence. Critics have written of Rushdie's multiple literary influences, his postmodernism, his narrative art, and his deconstructive use of history.[9] Critics in India have noted, first and foremost, that nothing succeeds like success, and that the novel's commercial success outside India created a metropolitan demand for Indian writing in English and a corresponding new confidence and productivity on the part of writers in English within India. For example, *Sunday* characterized *MC* as "a confident novel," one which "offered no explanations, proffered no apologies, sought no compromise."[10] This confidence was seen as a "refreshing departure from the past," when Indian writers were "far too apologetic about writing in English." Professor Vrinda Nabar of Bombay University recalled the sixties, when "there was a strong feeling against English and writers were criticized for using it." Indian critics who might have tended to dismiss the expatriate Rushdie as a cocky, elite, alienated outsider, found themselves prepared to be charmed by him (albeit sometimes grudgingly), at least until the controversy over *The Satanic Verses* erupted. But much of this criticism is descriptive or impressionistic, without closely examining the underlying conditions that contributed to the success. Many Indians were annoyed by the kind of reception with which *MC* was hailed, exemplified by the *New York Times* reviewer's phrase, "a continent finding its voice"—as if India's millions had been silent through the millennia until Rushdie came along to speak for them. And more relevant to my purpose, Indians have been critical of the weight, following *MC,* given to the narrative of nation— as if there were no other way for people to tell their story—thereby silencing or sidelining other voices using other terms.

In asserting the literary influence of *MC,* I do not assign it a uniquely privileged status or make an exaggerated claim for its centrality. Clearly I believe it had an important influence on Indian English fiction in the eighties. I employ it as a literary marker of the post-Emergency crisis in the Indian national idea, both expressing and embodying the crisis, both celebrating and mourning the idea. I discuss the formal and conceptual breakthroughs that

Rushdie's novel achieved, how it set the tone for the eighties, how it broke out of a certain stagnation of both form and content that had characterized the Indian English novel of the previous two decades. I explore how both *Midnight's Children* and the increasing fragmentation of the times, primarily brought on by the crisis of the dominant model of nationalism, influenced other Indian English writers and enabled them to enter imaginatively into new relationships with the nation. I also suggest the limits and limitations of that influence.

One of the secondary relationships I want to chart in this essay is the relationship between the kind of discursive configuration Rushdie sets up in *MC* and the problematic relationship of Indian writing in English since Independence. Timothy Brennan has characterized Rushdie's novels as "metafictions . . . novels about Third-World novels," and *MC* as a critique of the rise of the neocolonial elite that Rushdie links to "the production of Third-World fiction itself." Here Brennan is referring to what he sees as *MC*'s obsessive delineation, through the person and position of Saleem, of the degree to which the privileges of Third-World writers distance them from the realities of their subjects, and render them complicit with their subaltern compatriots' continued neocolonial suppression.[11] While I agree that a sense of distance and neocolonial complicity is certainly there, I also see a sense of rejection and hurt, accompanied by a concomitant desire to claim and be reclaimed by India. I would argue that *MC* is not so much about the neocolonial positioning of the Third-World novel(ist), but perhaps more accurately about the predicament of the neocolonial Indian nation-state and its inheritors, which is itself mirrored by the ambivalent position of the Indian English novel.

In a recent talk at Amherst College on post-Independence Indian writing, Rushdie referred to Indian English writing as "Empire's bastard child,"[12] which is exactly what Saleem Sinai was in *MC;* so at one level his protagonist can be seen as Indian writing in English, claiming centrality for itself. Rushdie himself is doing the same today when he asserts—characteristically over-aggressively—that the best prose writing in India since independence has been in English, which has by now become an Indian language. And furthermore, against all evidence and internal assertions to the contrary, he argues in his usual hyperbolic fashion that Indian English writing has not just a place for itself among other Indian literatures, but a pre-eminent place. I suspect that Rushdie's position here is something that needs to be understood in the light of his own feelings of rejection by and displacement from India. He needs to lay claim to India—and further, to centrality within it—in order to feel a sense of engagement, just as Saleem needed to feel an egotistical sense of mission in order to allow himself a new kind of engagement with India. Rushdie's act of claiming must also be seen in another light: he returned to India in the late seventies at thirty-something, in the aftermath of Indira Gandhi's Emergency, a time when large numbers of expatriate and emigrant Indians (many acting against their instinct not to wash dirty linen in public) had expressed their outrage at Gandhi and the Congress Party's betrayal of all the secular social-democratic ideals on which they, as the early post-independence generation, had been raised. In *MC,* Rushdie reaffirms and seeks to reclaim those ideals, even as he recognizes that their time may be past, and that he and his generation may be out of touch and out of time.[13]

MIDNIGHT'S CHILDREN'S CONCEPTUAL CONJURING

In *Midnight's Children,* Rushdie's reconfiguration of the relationship between the Self and the Nation opened up space that proved to be very enabling for new Indian English writers in the eighties. The novel's publication was a watershed for the Indian novel in English, coming at a time when the dominant Congress model of nationalism was cracking up—a time of fragmentation but therefore also a time of possibility. Many critics have commented upon *MC*'s influence on the Indian English novel, and several studies have analyzed the use of history and memory in the novel, its identification of Self and Nation, and its struggle to overcome duality. Few, however, have discussed how such elements of the novel combined to influence Indian writing in English.

In an early interview, Rushdie characterized *MC* as more a political novel than a historical novel, and most of all, as a novel about the nature of memory, "about one person's passage through history," in which the individual's version of the truth was presented as at once coherent and suspect. This personal view of history, Rushdie explained, allowed him to discuss and explore the nature of "the relationship between the individual and history, between private lives and public affairs."[14]

In his most recent novel, *The Moor's Last Sigh,* Rushdie's protagonist-narrator discusses his mother Aurora's artistic withdrawal in the decade after independence:

> It was easy for an artist to lose her identity at a time when so many thinkers believed that the poignancy and passion of the country's immense life could only be represented by a kind of selfless, dedicated—even patriotic—mimesis.
> Public opinion—not for the last time—swung against Aurora ... Scoundrelly patriots called her a traitress, the godly called her godless, self-styled spokesmen for the poor berated her for being rich ... those artists truly in thrall to the West ... abused her for "parochialism," while ... other artists ... reviled her just as loudly for losing touch with her roots. ...
> Aurora retreated somewhat from public life ... turned once and for all ... inwards, to the reality of dreams ... (and, in her bitterness and isolation), announced that neither Marathi nor Gujarati would be spoken within her wall; the language of her kingdom was English and nothing but.[15]

He could as accurately be speaking of the post-Independence Indian novel in English.

In the dynamic nationalist period of an independence struggle, individuals actively give themselves over to the struggle, willingly subordinating their personal desires to the urgency of the political moment, shaping themselves in the image of the nation. Quite naturally, the novels written during the period of the nationalist movement for independence, aptly called the Gandhian period of Indian literature, tended to identify themselves and their protagonists idealistically with the struggle. In order to unite the country in a shared vision, they portrayed the aspirations of the rural masses and the poor, and showed middle-class or educated characters either throwing in their lot with these masses or betraying them as enemies of the people. This period lasted into the first decade after Independence, and then, from the early sixties, tended to give way to a period in which writers expressed disillusionment with the corruption and failures of the government and its bureaucracy and often turned away from the public sphere altogether, in angry, bleak existentialist novels that charted alienation, interiority, and madness.

In the early post-independence period, the new-forged nation-state presses particularly heavily on the individual, molding the personal to the national, reproducing, maintaining and consolidating the national ideology at every level of society. In this ideological straitjacket, the Indian English novel which is, after all, the genre of the individual, stagnated and grew schizoid as the overriding story of nation increasingly gave the lie to individual realities. Nationalist speech-making often gave way to deafening literary silences. Faced with a centrally imposed nationalism that purported to speak for the individual, many writers of the sixties and seventies turned away from the larger social realm, forced into alienation. Their protagonists were often destroyed by the tensions between their personal realities and the nationalist ideal, their novels deadened by the creative deadlock that ensued.

In this period of postcolonial consolidation of the nation-state, the Indian English novel, once caught up in the dynamism of the nationalist movement, settled into a rather tired social realism that no longer throbbed with urgency or captured the creative imagination. It seemed as if the drive toward freedom that had engaged the Gandhian novels now gave way either to mechanically formulaic, politically correct nation-building or, on the other hand, to rejections of the public sphere. The national idea, which had once been an inclusive vision of "unity in diversity," shrank into a more rigid, centralizing monolithic concept as the Congress Party sought to secure centralized state power.[16] In terms of the relationship between the individual and the state, it seemed that either one was a patriot, wholly identified with the nation and its symbols, or else a traitor; there was little middle ground. This was especially so for the Indian English novel, whose loyalties were already suspect in its use of the former colonizer's language. As a result, the Indian English novel—or Indo-Anglian novel, as it was more commonly called at that time—began to stagnate, robbed of "authenticity," unable to find an acceptable voice, form, or subject matter that was at once uniquely its own and indisputably Indian.

In the aftermath of political independence, as the new nation-state sought to consolidate its power, the expansive, multiple languages of the freedom movement shrank and hardened into a more limited, coercive discourse, in a kind of "collective failure of the imagination," as Rushdie might have characterized it. This meant that different worldviews no longer creatively interpenetrated, throwing up innumerable new possibilities, and that the arena of action narrowed into sharply opposed polarities in a postcolonial throwback to Orientalist categories of thought which privileged rationalism, action, and literalism, and invested them with state powers and legitimacy.[17] Thus the protagonists of the early post-independence novel were routinely faced with and forced to embody drastic, impossible choices: self or nation, loyalty or betrayal, modernity or tradition—choices which, because they did not reflect the richness of lived reality, often proved self-destructive to the characters. Such choices were conceptually limiting and artistically stultifying.

In general, then, the Indian English literary scene in the late seventies and early eighties was in the doldrums. In the official Sahitya Akademi publication, Indian Literature, the annual review of 1980 summed up the contemporary Indian English literary scene as "mediocre and . . . meretricious."[18] The novel in English seemed to be stagnating, in terms of both content and form, neither engaged in social movements nor literary experimentation. By 1980, nation and novel had reached a state of impasse: both the unitary model of the modern nation-state and the narrative of the modern Indian English novel needed radical rethinking. The publication of *Midnight's Children* broke both deadlocks simultaneously: at once eulogy and elegy for the unitary model of nation-state that had failed to deliver the promises of the Indian freedom movement, and a new literary and conceptual model that opened new worlds of possibility for re-imagining and representing enabling relationships between individual and nation.

Without denying historical necessity, *MC* reconceptualized the dichotomy between personal and national identity in a way that made a new kind of social engagement possible. Rather than merely forcing the self into the image of the nation, Rushdie comically and mock-heroically insists on creating Nation in the imaginative image of Self. He takes on History, too, in the same way. The individual must either acquiesce to History's grand narratives or be destroyed—swept aside, or crushed underfoot. Rushdie's protagonist Saleem Sinai must also eventually succumb to the relentless march of History, but not before he tells his own story on his own terms.

Midnight's Children opened up space—conceptual and narrative—for play. Nevertheless, Rushdie's project is not merely post-modern free play, or flirting dangerously with a fashionable crisis of meaning, as Kumkum Sangari has argued in her influential essay, "The Politics of the Possible."[19] Rushdie certainly does not seek to avert his—or our—eyes from the threatening loss-of-meaning implicit in the crisis of nation, but neither does he seek to trivialize it. Sangari suggests that through "double-coded" works like *MC*, "the crisis of meaning in the West" is imported into the "non-West." I recognize Sangari's concern that Rushdie's novel and others like it are all too easily appropriated into the academic discourse of poststructuralism as "texts of a near-canonical Euro-American postmodernism." However, the crisis that Sangari fears was already built into the epistemological categories of nation and history within which Rushdie was working, and these categories were already deconstructing themselves through their own inner conflicts. The crisis of the nation-state is inherent in the underlying formulations of the modern secular Nehruvian nation-state, and is one that *MC* prophesies, but surely cannot determine.

Identifying with Meaning itself, Saleem stands to lose everything by its loss, and thus making sense of the crisis takes on the proportions of a life-and-death struggle. "I must work fast," he pants as he introduces himself and underscores the urgency of his literary endeavor on the very first page of the novel, "if I am to end up meaning—yes, meaning—something. I admit it: above all things, I fear absurdity" (p. 9). While he is all too aware of his impotence and impending demise, his prophetic awareness does not lead him into fatalism or disillusionment. Instead, it spurs him on, not to struggle for his personal survival, but to reach toward the meanings-within-the-loss-of-meaning of the national idea that he embodies.

Interpenetration of Self and Nation

Born on the stroke of midnight, August 14–15, 1947, baby Saleem Sinai receives a letter of congratulations from Prime Minister Nehru himself, worded with all the promises and truth-claims of the newly independent nation. Confidently identifying Saleem's life with the life of India itself, the letter links the unlimited potential of the newborn infant both with that of the nascent state, with all its future glory lying before it, and with the India of timeless antiquity, tales of whose past glories inspired and unified the nationalist movement: "You are the newest bearer of that ancient face of India which is also eternally young. We shall be watching over your life with the closest attention; it will be, in a sense, the mirror of our own" (p. 122).

"In what sense?" asks narrator-protagonist Saleem thirty-two years later as, battered by history, castrated by a Prime Minister, thoroughly disillusioned and "fullofcracks," he struggles desperately to preserve his version of India's history and his own before he completely falls to pieces. In what sense can it be said that his life and the lives of all the *Midnight's Children*—those 1001 babies born within an hour of the moment of independence—has mirrored that of the nation (which, it must be remembered, held out the promise of self-determination to the greatest and the least of its people)? And writer-storyteller Saleem answers his own rhetorical question, mock-heroically, pseudo-scientifically, in rhetorical terms, in "adverbs and hyphens":

> I was linked to history both literally and metaphorically, both actively and passively, in what our (admirably modern) scientists might term "modes of connection" composed of "dualistically combined configurations" of the two pairs of opposed adverbs given above. This is why hyphens are necessary: actively-literally, passively-metaphorically, actively-metaphorically and passively-literally, I was inextricably intertwined with my world. (p. 238)

The device of the "modes of connection" enables writer/narrator Saleem/Salman to grant his postcolonial protagonist multiple methods of engagement with the larger social realm and gives his characters room to move in ways which would be impossible within a unitary, social-realist structure, saving him, disillusioned as he becomes, from alienation and despair ("I was inextricably intertwined . . ."). Unlike a realistic novel form which privileges action and the actual, *MC* recognizes the passive and metaphorical modes as well, expanding the stage of action (at least) fourfold, and giving both formal and metaphysical realization to the fervent prayer quoted in Rushdie's essay, "Imaginary Homelands": "For God's sake, open the universe a little bit more."[20]

In *Midnight's Children,* women are seen to be the powerful practitioners of yet another mode of connection, the passive-aggressive. In spite of their seeming lack of control in the public sphere, they loom large in Saleem's family life, feeding all their repressed sorrow, guilt, jealousy, and bitterness into him like mother's milk, as did his Aunt Alia, who "fed us the birianis of dissension and the nargisi koftas of discord," and whose kormas, "spiced with forebodings as well as cardamoms," wrought a terrible vengeance upon his mother. Saleem's postcolonial status gives him an intimate connection with the passive modes of interaction with the world. Women's status within a patriarchal structure and the weapons of the weak that they wield mirror the weapons that the postcolonial subject can wield in the uneven struggle for self-determination. As the women do in the private sphere, so does Saleem in the universe of his narrative, namely, elevate the passive mode into equal significance with the active, and the metaphorical into equal prominence with the literal.[21] The Manichean dynamics of the neocolonial Indian nation-state maintain its sovereign subjects in a female/passive relationship to the Center even as the nationalist rhetoric exhorts them to work and action.

R. S. Pathak describes "the interplay of personal and national histories" as "the most significant feature of *Midnight's Children*," the inextricable intertwining of "the public and the private strands" as giving the novel its coherence, and "the interaction of historical and individual forces" as having "made the narrator what he is." Given that Indian history has been mutilated by the British, Pathak sees Rushdie's re-creation and reappropriation of Indian history and his charting of the "interlocking and interdependent relationships of history and the individual" as restoring a "much-needed sense of dignity" to the individual.[22] Pathak also points to Rushdie's savage satire and entertaining comedy as a winning combination, as does Thakur Guruprasad, who echoes similar sentiments in ascribing Rushdie's disarming charm to his having "conjured up a . . . new genre" that combines "fairy tale with savage political indictment" through "a fictional family story intertwined with dismal political history in a comic strain."[23]

In an early review of *Midnight's Children,* Anita Desai hesitates to call the novel "historical" because of Rushdie's insistence upon the interpenetration of the individual and the national, his belief that "while individual history does not make sense unless seen against its national background, neither does national history make sense unless seen in the form of individual lives and histories."[24] *MC* does not deny the nation's power over individual lives, neither does it subordinate individual to nation, but it acknowledges and makes creative capital of both their polarity and their unity. In the same review, Desai (in whose novels of the interior the protagonists are often helpless victims of History) speaks of the novel's purpose as "wholly serious" and its subject as tragic, "the tragedy of individual lives harried and wrecked by history, and of history harried and wrecked by individuals." However, part of the novel's appeal lies in its refusal to accept the relentless march of History as inevitably tragic. Rather than the individual being altogether obliterated by the Nation-state or matters of state being subordinated to the individual, it is the interesting space-in-between that is explored, and thereby what is patently the stuff of tragedy made comic. Rushdie doesn't deny the dichotomy between the private and the public; rather, he demonstrates how the two partake of each other in curious and often unexpected ways and how the possibilities of a situation may differ depending upon how it is perceived: baby Saleem was handcuffed to history, forcefed by events (passive-metaphorical), yet as the narrator, he can turn this around. History is both violent menace and nourishment for baby-to-be Saleem: "He, too, has to swallow all his past, all that made him—or, put another way, it feeds him" (pp. 107–08). Rushdie's triumphant technique in *MC* is simply yet supremely the discursive room-to-move gained by putting it another way.

Rushdie's playful handling of previously implacable categories opens up possibilities within language where there would seem to have been none, thus delivering a measure of discursive room-to-move. Says protagonist Saleem Sinai, "Setting my face against all indications to the contrary, I shall now amplify . . . my claim to a place at the centre of things." This is exactly what Rushdie's modes of connection enable him to achieve in *Midnight's Children.* Saleem and his age group have no agency in the active and the literal modes where he is perennially the victim, the one-to-whom-things-are-done; it is only in the metaphorical and, interestingly, in the passive realms of reality that he and his compatriots are controlling Subjects. " 'Passive-metaphorical,' 'passive-literal', 'active-metaphorical': the Midnight's Children's Conference was all three; but it never became what I most wanted it to be; we never operated in the first, most significant of the 'modes of connection.' The 'active-literal' passed us by" (pp. 238–39). Powerlessness and lack-of-choice continually characterize Saleem's predicament, yet he doggedly persists in positioning himself, the bestower of meaning and form, at the center of his story—as indeed he is, in the role of author-narrator. Even though Saleem is supremely the person to whom things have been done, it is Rushdie's magic that, "against all indications to the contrary," transforms victim to protagonist.

Action and Engagement

What does Rushdie achieve by the creation of his larger-than-life, tragi-comic hero and how might this fiat be said to have enabled a new kind of social engagement for a new generation of writers? Perhaps the success or failure of this engagement may be judged by the degree to which his protagonist Saleem is able to engage with the public sphere; if so, we may chart his progress through the novel. Or perhaps the success or failure of a character, who starts life with the optimistic faith that his country's achievements will be his own, tests the truth claims of a nation which has promised to deliver self-determination to the greatest and least of its citizens.

In a 1983 interview, Rushdie explained that his "comic inversion" of the relationship between the individual and history enabled him to discuss the problematics of that relationship in modern India. His protagonist Saleem begins his life with supreme confidence in his centrality and agency, but his unbounded optimism is besieged and eventually destroyed by disillusionment. Rushdie charts the disillusioning "series of retreats" that lead Saleem and the reader from his youthful omnipotence at the moment of Independence to his premature impotence and decrepitude at the age of thirty-two.

> Saleem believes that there is a relationship (between the individual and the nation), Saleem has a thesis, as it were, and the book tests the thesis. It turns out to be a destruction-test, because by the end of the book, it is clear that the thesis doesn't hold up: he's not in charge. And he can't stand it—at the moment at which he begins to be faced with the facts of life, he performs a series of retreats, whether into a kind of catatonic state, or into quiescence or acceptance, or finally, into the pickle factory.[25]

Midnight's Children is an ironic, quirky, but deadly serious critique of quiescence, of withdrawal, of forgetting. Being pulled forcibly from his roots by his parents' relocation to Pakistan begins the process of disconnection for Saleem. Across the political border he can neither receive nor broadcast signals to the *Midnight's Children*, and thereby becomes isolated within his own head. He succumbs first to a fatalism that allows him to accept all that is done to him. When he is struck by a flying spittoon in the Indo-Pakistan war of 1965, he loses his memory altogether, and with it, six years of his life. The narrative picks up in the midst of West Pakistan's foray into what was soon to become Bangladesh to quell the Eastern rebellion. Saleem is no longer the youthful "I" but is presented at a third-person remove as "the Buddha"—referring both to an old man, prematurely aged by history, and one who—like the prince who found enlightenment under the Bo tree—has withdrawn in spirit from the world of pain and sorrow. Here Rushdie makes a stereotypical (mis)representation of Buddhism as escapism and quiescence. He depicts the Buddha's "not-living-in-the-world as well as living in it" as an act of weakness and submission; as indeed it is for his buddha, the former Saleem, who has become a man-dog, silently and obediently carrying out the function of a canine tracker for a Pakistani military intelligence unit, tracking down rebels—"undesirable elements"—and destroying them. Saleem's state of amnesia prevents him from taking responsibility for his betrayals of his own countrymen. "Emptied of history, the buddha learned the arts of submission, and did only what was required of him" (p. 350).

Withdrawal, however, is achieved at a price. The man-dog leads his unit into the Sundarbans, steamy jungles of the subconscious, where his own mind leads him tortuously and inexorably through fevered, shifting nightmare landscapes towards a recognition of his own true identity and the responsibility which he must take for his actions. As he runs from the conflicts of the physical battlegrounds, he is drawn into the depths of his insanity, an experience which may lead him towards a recognition of the truth of his situation, but is fraught with its own dangers—madness and the risk of never being able to return.

Even when the poison from a forest snake awakens him to himself and to the realities—and the dangers—of his predicament, he still cannot remember his name. It takes Parvati-the-witch to name him and recall him fully to himself. (Parvati, after Shiva, Saleem's arch-rival, his other half, who was also born on the stroke of midnight, is the child born next-closest to midnight, the Third who embodies a point of meeting for the polarized pair. Parvati is also the name of the Hindu goddess, consort of the god Shiva.)

It is Parvati's magic that conveys him safely back into India, but again, survival exacts a price. To survive, Saleem is made invisible, and carried into Delhi crouched inside a basket. But, ironically, the invisibility that saves him also carries the risk of robbing him of his very essence. What saves Saleem from the enervation that accompanies invisibility is anger, a righteous anger on behalf of India's oppressed people that brings with it an exalted sense of mission: a mission no less than that of saving the country. However, like the self-appointed leaders of the Indian nationalist movement, he is to betray the people he claims to represent, and he fails to overcome the isolation that followed his rejection of Shiva, his nemesis and polar opposite, and his loss-of-connection with the Midnight's Children. Far from saving the country, he is sucked down into the vortex of its crisis. In the attempt to restore his own fortunes by contacting his despicably toadying uncle Mustapha, who is a high official in the Indira Congress bureaucracy, he abandons Parvati and his adopted family in the communist magicians' ghetto. He returns, but what might have been is derailed by the squashy bellied, labia-lipped Youth Congress leader and his goons as the slum is razed. He falls victim, like so many others, to "the Widow's" 1975 State of Emergency, in which he is tortured and made to reveal the names and addresses of all the surviving children of midnight, the hopes and possibilities contained within that moment of history. They are then given a fiendishly efficient operation—a "sperectomy"—which not only ensures their irreversible sterilization but also removes all hope.

For Saleem, it is a time of endings. For his son, however, and for the legion of bastard children whom Shiva has implanted in wealthy women across the nation, it is the beginning of a new chapter in India's history. Saleem's success in writing down his story—which is, in so many senses, the story of his generation—may or may not ensure that it is passed on and remembered. Against the evidence even of the narrative itself, the powers of Saleem's son and, by extension, of the new generation, project the hope that the times have bestowed upon them what it takes to survive and move forward collectively even to create new myths.[26]

Rushdie's narrative, which so fiercely advocates political engagement and social responsibility and so firmly condemns quiescence as betrayal, characteristically shows his naive protagonist's progressive withdrawal and eventual destruction to be both beyond his control and of his own making. Saleem's family, and his own sense of connection with the pulse of India, was destroyed by internal divisiveness as well as the will-to-power. In his bitter disillusionment and loss of his sense of centrality, he withdraws into himself, destroying himself and betraying his fellow-Indians. Rushdie explains social and political withdrawal of writers of his generation in terms of a profound disillusionment with the myths of the secular-socialist nation, myths which failed to deliver either material or spiritual results to a generation of believers. Yet at the same time, paradoxically, he reaffirms those very myths, even as he pronounces their obsolescence; both author and protagonist are bedevilled by duality and ambivalence.

Duality and Ambivalence

As Homi Bhabha points out in his introduction to *Nation and Narration,* nationalism is by definition ambivalent, and the ambivalence of the nation is mirrored in the very form of the national narrative. It is significant, too, that Bhabha uses Tom Nairn's term, "the modern Janus," for the nation, since the Indian English novel was, sometimes with dubious distinction, dubbed "Janus-faced" by Indian critics in the seventies. In this early post-independence context, the term was used in its sense of "two-faced," to cast aspersions on the pedigree of the Indian English—or "Indo-Anglian"—novel as insufficiently Indian, of dubious loyalty because of its dual parentage. This view, preceding the contemporary critique of nationalism, failed to consider the ambivalence inherent in nationalism and the nationalist discourse itself, which also has a dual parentage regardless of which modern Indian language it speaks through. Another sense of Janus-faced, however, is "sensitive to dualities and polarities," and this is the spirit in which Rushdie writes, sensitive to the dualities inherent in post-coloniality, accepting—even flaunting—them rather than attempting to deny or conceal them, and elevating condition into method in his metanarrative.[27] Bhabha's use of the Janus metaphor aptly characterizes *MC*'s narrative approach, that of turning "the two-faced god into a figure of prodigious doubling," so that the condition of ambivalence is transformed into a dynamic process.[28]

Rushdie's successful inversion in *Midnight's Children,* his formula for overcoming post-independence alienation, whether in the postcolonial subject, Indian English, or the Indian English novel itself, might have been summed up in his latest novel, *The Moor's Last Sigh,* in the advice given to the freakish Moor by the boy-guru Lord Khusro: "Embrace your fate . . . Rejoice in what gives you grief. That which you would flee, turn and run towards it with all your heart. Only by becoming your misfortune will you transcend it." The Moor declares, "By embracing the inescapable, I lost my fear of it."[29] Rather than withdrawing in alienation if he is unable to identify fully with the nation, the individual may embrace his ambivalence, flaunting it publicly, rather than hiding in embarrassment, turning a liability into an asset, a birthmark into a trademark. Or in the words of the Anglo-Indian artist Vasco Miranda, himself doomed like Saleem: "A man's weakness is his strength, and versy visa" . . . "Would Achilles have been a great warrior without his heel?"[30]

M. Keith Booker has rightly identified one of the central themes and strategies of Rushdie's fiction as "embracing contradiction," both constructing and deconstructing dual oppositions "by demonstrating that the apparent polar opposites are in fact interchangeable and mutually interdependent."[31] I think that Rushdie's approach to duality in *MC* functions as theme, as form, and as a method that enables a shift in postcolonial nationalist discourse by exposing and enacting the radical ambivalence of the Indian nation. However, as Booker also notes, Rushdie constructs and inhabits his opposing dualities only to expose their limitations; duality as method enables him to expose dualism as prison. I see Rushdie's reproduction, reconfiguration, and critique of nationalist dualities as creating new possibilities for postcolonial narrative discourse in the eighties, but also as raising doubts about the outcome of the swirling embrace of polar opposites: will it be perpetual motion, fusion, or fission? Rushdie portrays Saleem as a victim of the paradoxes of Indian nationalism, among them the splits between pragmatism and idealism, the elite and the masses, centralization and federalism, rationalism and spirituality. As Krishna, in the Bhagavad-Gita, exhorted the doubt-torn Arjuna to rise above the pairs of opposites so that he might see clearly and act, so Rushdie's hero longs for a Third Principle that can overcome the dualities within and around him and break through to another level of truth. At meetings of the Midnight Children's Conference (or M.C.C.), through which the children meet telepathically, the idealistic young Saleem as convenor and central switchboard operator implores the squabbling Midnight's Children to overcome their differences. Their miraculous powers, so full of possibility, are powerless to prevent the apparently inevitable conflicts that break out among them:

> "We," I cried passionately, "must be a third principle, we must be the force which drives between the horns of the dilemma; for only by being other, by being new, can we fulfill the promise of our birth" (p. 255).

But Saleem himself—like the Indian nation and the Indian English novel—has internalized the very dualities that he seeks to unite. He is as yet unaware of his own mixed parentage, ironic evidence of the dual heritage of the Indian nation-state. And as he finds out, his own continued privilege is predicated upon the disinheritance of Shiva, his alter-ego and arch-rival. Even though Saleem desperately seeks to avoid Shiva, it would seem that the enmity between the two of them is inevitable: "Shiva and Saleem, victor and victim; understand our rivalry and you will gain an understanding of the age in which you live" (p. 432). And the enmity of Shiva and Saleem ("knees-and-nose, a nose and knees"), polar opposites, split selves, drives the novel to its tragic climax and its ambiguous conclusion.

When Saleem excludes Shiva from the *lok sabha* (lit. people's assembly or parliament) of his mind because he is afraid that Shiva will "insist on claiming his birthright" (p. 282), he closes off the option of regaining the harmony that the children had shared in the early days of the Midnight Children's Conference. It is this active rejection on his part, as much the passive-literal act of being taken across the border to Pakistan, that is responsible for his loss of connection with the Midnight's Children. Instead of accepting Shiva as an equal member of the group, even as equal to himself, Saleem perceives him as a threat (which, indeed, he is) and relegates him to the realm of an eternal

Other. The possibility of a Third Principle is forever closed off for Saleem, as the polarization of knees-and-nose takes hold:

> he became, for me, first a stabbing twinge of guilt, then an obsession; and finally, as the memory of his actuality grew dull, he became a sort of principle; he came to represent, in my mind, all the vengefulness and violence and simultaneous-love-and-hate-of-things in the world. (pp. 298–99)

Still, Parvati-the-Witch, who always believed in Saleem, remains open to the possibility of reconciliation. Even as Saleem dreads the return of Shiva, the principle of destruction, Parvati is able to see him as a principle of Creation as well; after all, he is the father of her child—Saleem's son-who-is-not-his-son—and the father of thousands more throughout the land. Parvati the witch, perhaps the mediator/medium who can transform a vicious circle into a triangle, welcomes the return of the repressed: "Maybe he will come when he has time; and then we will be three!" (p. 389).

Salman Rushdie is able to break the stranglehold of Manichean dualities in the realm of language, even though neither Saleem Sinai nor his creator is able to find a way to transcend duality in his own life. And he accomplishes this simply, just as he opened up more breathing space for the Self in his deadlock with the Nation. Can anything capture the essence of duality more simply and ineluctably than the children's game of Snakes and Ladders?

> implicit in the game is the unchanging twoness of things, the duality of up against down, good against evil; the solid rationality of ladders balances the occult sinuosities of the serpent; in the opposition of staircase and cobra we can see, metaphorically, all conceivable oppositions, Alpha against Omega, father against mother; here is the war of Mary and Musa, and the polarities of knees and nose . . . but I found, very early in my life, that the game lacked one crucial dimension, that of ambiguity—because, as events were to show, it is also possible to slither down a ladder and climb to triumph on the venom of a snake. (p. 141)

Beyond realizing the ability of each opposed half to turn into its opposite, Saleem begins to recognize that, rather than becoming paralyzed and alienated by seemingly irreconcilable dualities, an individual can aspire to partake of both (either/or becoming and . . . and). He invokes the spiritual image of the *paramahamsa,* "symbol of the ability to live in two worlds, the physical and the spiritual" (p. 223). The *paramahamsa* symbolizes divinity and spiritual freedom, the creative ability to live in the world and rise above its dualities, at once engaged and detached.[32] Rushdie also employs as an antidote to Manichean dualism the traditional Indian conception of the multiple levels of correspondence between microcosm and macrocosm: "As a people, we are obsessed with correspondences . . . It is a sort of national longing for form—or perhaps simply an expression of our deep belief that forms lie hidden within reality; that meaning reveals itself only in flashes" (p. 300). But the older Saleem, despite everything, remains earthbound like his grandfather before him, who was struck on the nose with a frozen clod of earth when, "foreign-returned," he attempted to pray. The cause? "Altered vision"—he "saw things differently" (p. 11). From the moment he returned to his native Kashmir from medical study in Germany and found himself unable to pray, Saleem's grandfather Aadam Aziz finds himself knocked into a place in which he is able neither to believe nor disbelieve in God. Throughout the novel, however, when real life continually breaks the bounds of reason, Saleem tells the reader, "believedon'tbelieve. But it happened anyway."

While Saleem is able to communicate with the midnight's children, he is able to inhabit two worlds; but when the powers and possibilities of the M.C.C. are cut off, his connections with both are severed. In his disillusionment, he bids farewell to his hopes: "If there is a third principle, its name is childhood. But it dies; or rather, it is murdered" (p. 256). Fear and cynicism murder it; it is blocked in the closing-off of possibilities, the hardening of the mind and heart, the loss of the ability or desire to put things another way.

Finally, *MC* accepts the dual legacy of midnight, a legacy split at the very root. Saleem does not come without Shiva, Shiva would not be Shiva if it had not been for Saleem. There is an acceptance of ambivalence, of the degree to which polarized opposites partake of each other, so much so that one cannot exist without the other, one feeds the other. Even as Saleem-the-narrator finally succumbs to the cracks and is trampled into dust, Rushdie-the-author triumphs. He has succeeded in creating a space between the horns of the dilemma, not by transcending them or denying them, but by reconfiguring them. For his generation are privileged and cursed "to be both masters and victims of their times."

Rushdie, as well as Saleem his creation, is a child of midnight, formed and raised by the secular ideals of the Nehru Congress in the days when Independent India itself was young. As a student of history and a left-leaning social democrat, he has recognized intellectually the limitations and ambivalence of the Indian inheritors of the colonial state, and *Midnight's Children* subjects them to a serious critique. As an antidote to the paralyzing polarities of endlessly contending dualities, Rushdie poses the notion of multiplicity—many Indias, many versions of truth, and infinite capacities for regeneration. Nevertheless, ambivalence remains, because of his continued emotional investment in a unitary idea of India, the India of his lost innocence, and his own inability, despite everything, to conceive constructive possibilities in its demise.[33]

FRAGMENTATION AND THE WHOLE

Kathleen Flanagan, writing on the fragmented self in *MC,* recognizes divided selves in Rushdie's works as "the products of crises of faith in political and religious institutions" and stresses the importance for Rushdie of the individual's responsibility to society. She makes the important point that Saleem's act of writing down his story combines for him both "public good and private need" as it connects self to society by making the individual a "speaking subject" who recognizes his private acts as having public consequences. She further points out that Rushdie draws attention to the disjunction between the individual and the official views of history through what she calls the child Saleem's "ridiculous" and socially destructive self-centeredness. Taking from Lukács a developmental view of Saleem's consciousness, she argues that he must progress from seeing "himself as the center of the state to seeing himself as a responsible part of the state." Although he desires to place himself at the controlling center of an "ordered reality," he is forced to recognize the power of "the fragmented forces of society" and the "preeminence of the social and the historical over the private." In Flanagan's Lukácsian argument, Rushdie's child-narrator starts with the problem of seeing history in isolated parts, and only as they relate to him as the center of his childish universe. His problem is that he should be seeing these parts "as aspects of the historical process and integrat(ing) them in a totality" if his knowledge is ever to be brought into line with reality, and that he must come to terms with the self as "decentered, yet responsible" vis-a-vis the state.[34]

It is here, in the insistence that Saleem's "absurd" self-centeredness must be decentered in order for him to mature into a truly responsible member of society, that I part company with both the teleology and the spirit of the argument. For while Saleem's childish megalomania is of course absurd, it is also quite clearly privileged in the novel. At the same time as Rushdie parodies and undermines the over-centralized nation-state that seeks to control and speak for all its "children," he also romanticizes the Congress Party ideal of "unity in diversity" in which the center provides a forum through which all the children can speak to one another. While the progression of the novel may certainly be seen as a movement from an immature megalomania to a more realistic, down-sized sense of self, it is also a movement from idealism to disillusionment; from dynamic growth to castration and impotence, premature aging, and death; from a deep sense of connectedness with the pulse of India to alienation, betrayal, and insignificance. Saleem's irrepressible megalomania was precisely what post-Rushdie novelists found so attractive and inspiring. The lesson they drew was not that he needed to be cut down to size, so that he might learn to become a humble, socially responsible pickle-factory worker. They saw instead that, in spite of the fact that his story was just one story among millions, it was his own story, and therefore truer for him than any other. It was possible for an insignificant fragment to speak in his own voice from the center of his universe and tell that story. Ironically, however, even as Rushdie's novel may have inspired a myriad of speaking subjects, his elite narrator Saleem recognized that it was only at the expense of his own sense of wholeness that the subaltern voices of the other

Midnight's Children could begin to be heard. For Rushdie, as for Saleem, fragmentation presents both the terrifying prospects of chaos and the productive possibilities unleashed by the breakdown of the controlling center. But as a true child of his time he is unable, in spite of everything, to fully accept that breakdown.

An interviewer once reported that Salman Rushdie kept on his writing desk a little sculpture of an unpartitioned India. Even as he wrote of the realities of a divided subcontinent, he couldn't help but persist in holding on to India's geopolitical wholeness as both an idea and an ideal. His protagonist Saleem shares some of his creator's nostalgic idealism. Once a kind of radio who was able to tune in to voices from all over India, and more importantly, the instrument through which they were enabled to tune in to each other, Saleem has been drained of his powers, has aged prematurely, and is cracking apart. He hastens to record his memories before it is too late. And he seals his last chapter of pickled memories not a moment too soon, for now he is breaking into a myriad of fragments and his particles are being scattered and trampled into the Indian dust. And for Saleem, the vicissitudes of whose life area mirror of his country's, whose battered, misshapen body is a grotesque caricature of the national map, fragmentation is something to be resisted to the end, even as he accepts its inevitability and indeed its desirability.

In 1957 Saleem was confidently in control—the prime minister, so to speak, of the "*lok sabha* of my brain," as he called the diverse, clamorous gathering of 581 ten-year-olds who convened inside his head. His idealistic quest for meaning and purpose drove him to declaim earnestly and endlessly to his agemates ("we must think . . . what we are for"), while his birth at the very stroke of midnight gave him greater powers than any other—excepting only one, his polar twin, his arch-rival, Shiva the cynical, Shiva the streetwise gang leader who mocked him and his ideals as a "pampered rich boy," Shiva whom he strove to shut out of his head, to his own cost. ". . . I was not immune to the lure of leadership," he acknowledges with rueful hindsight (p. 227). But then, while few of the children had his privilege, few had his larger sense of purpose or his powers. It was undeniable that the powers themselves had been granted hierarchically, and it was equally undeniable that, without Saleem, the children would have been unaware of the larger national arena, and unable to communicate with each other. Was the M.C.C. an institution of tremendous promise, or was it rather the vehicle of the children's eventual undoing?[35] Was Saleem, as its founder, their saviour or their betrayer? Was the break-up of the M.C.C., of Saleem, of India itself, the end of possibility, a tragedy to be averted at all costs, or was it, on the contrary, an opportunity to be welcomed? Like many others in *Midnight's Children,* the answer to all these questions is—well—both. And yet, from Saleem/Salman's personal perspective, it comes down quite clearly on one side.

As Saleem's bedeviled body begins to disintegrate, he naturally resists. Who in his position would not have striven to remain intact, healthy, whole?

O eternal opposition of inside and outside! Because a human being, inside himself, is anything but a whole, anything but homogeneous; all kinds of everywhichthing are jumbled up inside him, and he is one person one minute and another the next. The body, on the other hand, is as homogeneous as anything. Indivisible, a one-piece suit, a sacred temple, if you will. It is important to preserve this wholeness . . . Uncork the body, and God knows . . . The consequences for the sphere of public action . . . are . . . no less profound. (pp. 236–37)

The individual body, once intact and indivisible but now falling apart, allows a life to the myriad voices that it contained, controlled, suppressed, denied. It also allows the fragments to take on a life of their own.[36] It accepts the inevitability of the fragments breaking through but persists in holding on to an idea of the whole. Saleem's cracking up allows the voices to escape and be heard, and yet without Saleem they would not have been able to hear each other in the first place. "Midnight's other children . . . are pressing extremely hard. Soon the cracks will be wide enough for them to escape" (p. 179). From the first page of the novel, the cracks signal the beginning of the end for Saleem as a unitary individual. He already more than half acknowledges the absurdity of his enterprise, yet persists stubbornly, ultimately succeeding in "pickling" all thirteen chapters of his story before the forces of disintegration prevail.

During the Quit India movement of 1942, Aadam Aziz, the patriarch, is infected with the optimism disease, the blind nationalism which prevents him from seeing the incipient divisions within nation and family, from failing to anticipate Partition and from responding to his wife's deep dissatisfaction. Later, the narrator/protagonist Saleem Sinai suggests that "the urge to encapsulate the whole of reality" is another Indian disease. Lifafa Das tries to put the whole world ("Dunya Dekho") in his peepshow. Nadir Khan's painter friend had drawn ever larger paintings, trying to "get the whole of life into his art." In the end he had committed suicide, saying, "I wanted to be a miniaturist and I've got elephantiasis instead." Saleem Sinai worries, "Am I infected too?"[37]

Richard Cronin's essay, "The Indian English Novel: *Kim* and *Midnight's Children*," asserts that Saleem's urge to encapsulate the whole of reality is "a disease to which only those like Rushdie who write about India in English are vulnerable," and that "it is only because he (the young Saleem) is an outsider that India seems one to him" and "he can aspire to encapsulate the whole of it."[38] Cronin calls Kipling and Rushdie, in the same breath, impudent "trespassers" in India. Further, he claims that, for Indians who write in a regional language, a regional identity "unavoidably" takes precedence over an Indian identity. Cronin's essay is full of categorical statements. First, if the young Saleem had a unitary conception of the nation, so did many of the educated Indians of his generation in the post-Independence Nehruvian era. Second,

Rushdie's conception of the nation, while still holding emotional allegiance to the Nehruvian model, at the same time questions it deeply. Third, if Saleem is an "outsider" because he is from a wealthy family and does not speak Marathi or Gujarati in cosmopolitan Bombay, then legions of the Indian urban middle classes are outsiders as well. (In Maharashtra, the xenophobic Shiv Sena organization built its power base by organizing against South Indian "outsiders" in Bombay and it now seeks to expel the city's Muslims as well.) Fourth, the meaning of "reality" for Rushdie here is clearly not restricted to the unitary Indian nation—in fact, it is the very multiplicity of India, and beyond India, the multifaceted nature of reality itself, that he is attempting to convey.

Midnight's Children mocks its own melodrama but makes literary fireworks out of events which persistently refuse "to remain life-sized." Like India, Saleem Sinai finds himself cracking up into tiny pieces, like the pieces of his grandmother that his grandfather fell in love with and the pieces of his father that his mother tried to love; but, like Partition, it seems, his eventual fragmentation is inevitable, just as his grandfather never succeeds in seeing his wife whole and his mother is never able to love her husband wholly. The urge of the work is to resist (however vainly) fragmentation and compartmentalization, providing a strong contrary current of inclusiveness (like the epic *Mahabharata,* of which it is said that what is not in it, is not). Thus the text thrives on and is driven by a contrary dynamic, a dialectic that simultaneously undermines and valorizes its totalizing urges, recognizing their obsolescence while refusing to let go of their emotional power. In this dynamic polarization lies the explosive success of the novel—and perhaps, also, Saleem's ultimate fate. In the end, which is the madness and which the disease, the desire to embrace reality and to swallow the world whole, or the tendency to fragment, to compartmentalize oneself and the world into internally homogeneous, manageable, bite-sized pieces? Or is it both?

In this current crisis of the once-dominant Congress model of nationalism, polarized political forces intensify their struggle in a swirling deathgrip, and it would seem that there is nothing beyond the dualities of endlessly contending extremes. And yet in the fragmentation of the national ideal of unity-in-diversity, of the Midnight Children's Conference, deep fissures in the once-impermeable national membrane allow new ideas entry; flames curl up through the cracks and set the nation ablaze, destroying but also illuminating, firing the national imagination. With his final words, the disintegrating Saleem prophesies his fate and articulates the postcolonial condition of his generation:

> Yes, they will trample me underfoot, . . . reducing me to specks of voiceless dust . . . because it is the privilege and the curse of the *Midnight's Children* to be both masters and victims of their times, to forsake privacy and be sucked into

the annihilating whirlpool of the multitudes, and to be unable to live or die in peace. (p. 463)

Even though Saleem is cracking into as many pieces as there are Indians, as there are stories to tell, he has successfully told his story—imperfect, unreliable, distorted, needing endless revising to be sure—but nonetheless triumphantly his own.

When Saleem Sinai tells his readers that they will have to swallow him and his story whole, "whole" does not imply unitary, seamless. Whole means multiple, fault-ridden, contradictory, "fullofcracks." Is he doomed? Yes, inevitably. But wholly defined by Nation and colonial History? Never! Stubbornly and against all the odds, Victim transforms himself into Protagonist, simply through the telling of his own story.

POST–*MIDNIGHT'S CHILDREN*: NATIONAL NARRATIVES OF THE EIGHTIES

When *Midnight's Children* was first published, Rushdie's refusal to censor or sanitize his story, his unembarrassed washing of dirty linen in public, was refreshing to the world of Indian English writing, which had trodden so carefully for so long, walking a tightrope between "Indian" authenticity and "English" correctness.[39] Unafraid either of public censure or government censors, Rushdie sought to embrace the sights, sounds, and smells of the India of his dreams and memories in all their multiplicity, and was determined to leave nothing out. Had he been living in middle-class Indian society, he might have been more circumspect. But then, surely, the novel would have lost much of its dynamism.

In an early review, written before *MC*'s success in India, Anita Desai expressed the belief that Rushdie's message would fall on deaf ears in the unself-critical intellectual climate of post-independence India. She wrote, somewhat bitterly, ". . . it is tragic to think how unlikely that it will be published, distributed or read in a land that prefers to avert its eyes from the intolerable reality and gaze upon maya, the shimmer of illusion." In fact, as noted earlier, the Indian sales of the novel were unprecedentedly high, heralding a new spirit of freedom and a willingness to experiment with subject, language, and narrative strategy. Desai, whose five novels of the sixties and seventies were pre-eminently novels of interiority, told me in a 1992 interview that *MC* gave her the courage and artistic room to move into the public sphere in her own fiction.[40] Rushdie's playfulness actually created discursive space for her where there was none before.

Indian English writers of the eighties found that Rushdie's paradigm allowed them a new freedom of both form and content. His narrative sleight-of-hand juggled multiple modes of engagement between the individual and the national narrative, teased apart the cracks within and between the master discourses, and conjured up space for (relatively) free play—or at least the illusion of it—in a terrain where there had previously been a polarized paralysis. New writers found his acknowledgement of multiplicity and his hybridity of language particularly liberating. It enabled them to tell their personal stories in their own voices as national epics. Just as the crisis of the unitary nation-state appeared to open up space for the clamor of a thousand contending claims, so it seemed that the crisis of the once-dominant nationalism opened up space for new discursive models.

Over the course of the eighties, a wave of Indian English novels followed *MC,* clearly influenced by it in language, style, and structure. Some prominent new novelists of the 1980s whose work is indebted to Rushdie include Namita Gokhale (*Paro, Dreams of Passion*), Amitav Ghosh (*The Circle of Reason* and *The Shadow Lines*), Upamanyu Chatterjee (*English, August* and *The Last Burden*), I. Allan Sealy (*The Trotter-Nama* and *Hero*), Boman Desai (*The Memory of Elephants*), Shashi Tharoor (*The Great Indian Novel* and *Show Business*), and Nina Sibal (*Yatra*).[41] Of course these novels did not represent the only tendency within Indian English writing during the period, but this was certainly the dominant one, and it brought a new vitality to what had become rather a stagnant tradition with little experimentation and few new names. Rushdie-influenced works by new novelists have variously been seen to include one or more of the following features: 1) a multigenerational, mock-epic family saga, complete with family trees, maps, and a long list of dramatis personae, that tells the story of the protagonist's family as a national history; 2) a rejection of the traditional, social realist novel: larger-than-life allegorical characters and events in the tradition of magical realism; 3) both a fluency in standard English and a confidence with the language that allows the confident use of various kinds of Indian English; 4) a sprawling, rambling style, full of digressions and humor; 5) the use of myth, oral tradition, and different versions and ideas of history; 6) a playful irreverence for the sacred cows of nationalism and religion. Aside from these similarities, however, there is a broad range of tendencies among these post-Rushdie novels, even if one were to focus solely on their conception of the relationship of the individual to the nation and to History.

Less commonly noted is the opportunity these novels give to members of marginalized groups or national minorities to place themselves centerstage in the drama of national history, rather than feeling the pressure to subsume themselves in the mainstream, official version. For example, Parsis and Anglo-Indians are two groups whose "Indianness" is often called into question, but Parsis like Boman Desai (*The Memory of Elephants,* 1988) and Anglo-Indians like I. Allan Sealy (*The Trotter-Nama,* 1988), range back over the centuries in their novels to celebrate the long and colorful histories of their respective communities in India.[42] In his comic, digressive, mock-heroic mode, I. Allan Sealy's protagonist is able to present the checkered past of his "glorious" Anglo-Indian ancestors and to poignantly acknowledge their marginalization in post-independence India. Boman Desai draws on *MC*'s notion that there are competing histories that are equally valid—for the individual, at least—and that the individual has moral authority and willpower, if not political power. In *The Memory of Elephants,* Desai's protagonist gains access to the collective unconscious of his contentious family in particular and the Parsis in general, but although he is able to tune in to them, he has no control over the events he sees. However, just before he is forced to relinquish his dangerous powers, he is able, just for a moment and by a tremendous effort of will, to bring all his ancestors together and hold a united family tableau in his mind.

Besides giving new novelists the courage to tell their own stories as Indian stories, *Midnight's Children* also gave them permission to be ironic and ambivalent about their relationship to the nation-state. Upamanyu Chatterjee, in his first novel, *English, August: An Indian Story* (1988), is able to portray a disaffected protagonist within the Indian Civil Service who suffers deep and prolonged alienation and indecision in his provincial posting. And Shashi Tharoor, in *The Great Indian Novel* (1989), is able simultaneously to allegorize the story of modern India in terms of the epic *Mahabharata* and to question the very notion of using the authority of tradition to offer certitudes in the seeming chaos of the present. Despite its conceptual freshness and vitality, *Midnight's Children* remains very much emotionally committed to the narrative of nation. In the end, it can only reconfigure the ideological categories, not step out of them altogether. If they were to remain within the self-as-nation framework, it might be that the new trajectories set in motion by Rushdie's reconceptualization of Self and Nation would eventually mire themselves in the same dualities as the novels of the earlier sixties and seventies, the possibility of alternative realities remaining just that, a possibility—a spectacular, but ultimately illusory, authorial conjuring trick. Is the discursive space in which they function merely in the realm of virtual reality, or do they posit alternate realities that in fact create new possibilities for public discourse?

In the eighties the new narratives of nation burst forth in a dazzling display of artistic pyrotechnics with a new confidence in self, language, and form. Their energy was based on a celebration of the simultaneous identity and duality of self and nation, a recognition of the creative potential of ambivalence. But ultimately life must be lived, and it cannot be lived for long on the fence—on the hyphen, as it were.[43] The energy that breaks forth from the crisis of the nation must eventually be redirected. As Rushdie/Saleem himself acknowledges, "new myths must be made." When allegiance to an idea is lost in disillusionment, new allegiances must be affirmed (or old ones reaffirmed) and new commitments made, in order for life to go on. In the meantime, of course, life goes on anyway, and the interregnum is characterized by "a great diversity of morbid symptoms."[44]

Just as the narrative of nation may marginalize other kinds of narratives, marginalized groups attempting to lay claim to the nation may themselves be written out of their own texts by the very terms in which the nationalist discourse is framed. Rajeswari Sunder Rajan observes in an essay on Nina Sibal's *Yatra* that women writers who have attempted to employ the narrative of nation find themselves condemned to rehearse a story that excludes them.[45] And recent feminist research on the colonial construction of Indian nationalism has demonstrated the extent to which "traditional" conceptions of Indian womanhood have been bound up with the nationalist project. Women's experiences in the postcolonial period have shown, again and again, that their interests are incompatible with the interests of the nation-state. Protagonists of post-independence literary texts—particularly, but not exclusively, female protagonists—have become deadlocked when they have attempted to live out the conflicting demands of the nationalist synthesis. In general, minorities and women writers, who have found that the exclusive discourse of nation cannot be made to tell their story, have been less likely to employ the narrative of nation. Women writers, such as Shashi Deshpande and Jai Nimbkar, who have come to prominence recently in the late eighties and nineties, have been working relatively unnoticed for decades. Deshpande and Nimbkar, along with the younger Githa Hariharan and Anjana Appachana, are neither shoring up a disintegrating discourse of nation nor making dramatic departures from women's traditional conflicts and concerns, but are exploring the possibilities of coming to terms with the past in new ways.

Some of the new Indian English writers of the eighties used the nation as a framework to define themselves against, either as a peg on which to hang their identities or a boundary that demarcates their own liminal positioning. Thus they tended to gravitate towards two extremes, either a romantic clinging to the ideal of Nation, or its opposite, a fashionably disillusioned individuality answerable to no one: either an obsession with the need to belong to a Nation-State, or a defiant declaration of one's alienation. In a thoughtful review of Salman Rushdie's *East, West* in the *Indian Review of Books,* Sanjay Iyer argues that the Rushdie-inspired narratives of nation have been privileged to the extent of obscuring other Indian novels that work out of different paradigms:

> In privileging the experiences of nation and post-colonialism, Rushdie, as a literary giant, has powerfully set the terms for inclusion in this countercanon [of Third World Literature]. The result is apparent to us every day, in the spate of novels that do take the personal as national . . . The price of this has been the marginalization of countless works that are not obsessed with national experience.[46]

I would agree that the continued conflation of Self and Nation eventually ceases to be productive during a period when the Indian nation-state has quite clearly shown itself to be in a prolonged political and epistemological crisis. It is important to recognize that Rushdie's model in *MC* is not the only one operating in the contemporary Indian English novel, and perhaps no longer even the dominant one.

The first wave of exhilaration that produced a score of epic national/personal narratives directly inspired by *Midnight's Children* may well have run its course. For as long as post-Rushdie narratives remain ideologically bound to Nation, they will be forced to follow the contours of its crisis and recuperation in the eighties and nineties. If they are not to trickle out into what Saleem Sinai dreaded most, meaninglessness and flippant indeterminacy, they will have to move beyond ambivalence, and so perhaps beyond nation itself. However, from the vantage point of the late nineties, indications are that these fears are not being borne out. Rather than taking Indian English writing down a slippery slope into global capitalism, with its post-modern free play and radical indeterminacy, the post-Rushdie novel would seem to be moving beyond ambivalence to new commitments. For instance, in Mukul Kesavan's first novel, *Looking Through Glass* (1995), the protagonist starts out as a disengaged young photographer who looks at history and politics only through the lens of his camera, but moves progressively closer to his subjects until his point of view merges altogether with theirs. Sudden and involuntary time-travel magically plunges him into the politically turbulent period of the Quit India Movement of 1942 and forces him to live a Muslim Indian version of history from the inside. This was a period when Muslim points of view began to be erased first from Congress Party politics and later from official Indian histories, and Kesavan dramatizes this erasure by allegorizing it, Rushdie-style: overnight, hundreds of Muslims literally disappear. *Looking Through Glass* carries many of the hallmarks of the post-Rushdie novel: its portrayal of the vexed but intimate relationship of the personal and the political, the ambivalence of its protagonist, its challenging of official histories and parallel presentation of alternative versions, the magic realism of its time travel, the making concrete of its metaphors, and its valorization of political engagement.[47] In the tradition of *Midnight's Children,* it does not allow itself to be mired in disabling ambivalence. But we have seen that *MC* simultaneously challenges and reinforces the dominant model of Indian nationalism, and is ultimately unable and unwilling to step out of the framework of the nation. *Looking Through Glass* is equally caught up with national history, challenging the official nationalist version both by applying a corrective lens and by progressively removing the lens between history and life; it does not reject the national altogether, but replaces nationalist politics with a more local allegiance to people and to places.

Midnight's Children ends with the recognition that Saleem is at the end of a line. Nehru's promise has been drained of all possibility for him personally and perhaps even India itself has come to the end of that particular road in its history. Saleem recognizes that the country will have to fashion new ideals to inspire its people and move forward, but that will have to be the task of a new generation: "New myths are needed," he acknowledges, "but that's none of my business."[48] Another post-Rushdie first novel, Amitav Ghosh's 1986 *The Circle of Reason,* ends with its orphan protagonist's return to India. The discourse of secular rationalism that reared him has finally been discredited and consigned to the flames. He has been forced to live a life on the run from his own native land, and now he is free to return and make a new beginning. But it is clear that he will not be able to make it anew; he will have to work with the fragments he has. As one character says, "Nothing's whole any more. If we wait for everything to be right again, we'll wait for ever while the world falls apart. The only hope is to make do with what we've got."[49]

CODA, 1999

Ever since the advent of the novel in mid-nineteenth century colonial India, Indian writers have been reappropriating official versions of history to serve their own purposes. The Indian novel has had a role in the anti-colonial struggle as well as a role in forging an Indian national identity and an independent nation, its narrative vision shaping the ideal, and its language and discourse bodying forth the forms of the nation.[50] In the postcolonial period, with the crisis of the neo-colonial nation-state, the Indian novelist has both old tasks and new: first, in order to find, in Chinua Achebe's words, "where the rain began to beat us," to challenge official versions of history and nation and to recover the dignity and subjecthood of its people in their many and various voices; second, to envision and articulate new forms, new allegiances, that can carry them forward, giving meaning and coherence to fragmented, contending realities and forms of knowledge. In so doing, the novel necessarily becomes self-conscious, and the Indian English novel all the more so, because of its own complicity in the process of nation-building. I have argued that Salman Rushdie's *Midnight's Children* played a role in this process at a critical juncture in the postcolonial period, and that the novels that have succeeded it in the post-Rushdie period continue the tasks of vision and revision, telling their own stories in their multiple voices and imagining new languages and forms that can help give meaning and agency to individuals and communities during a time of crisis and change.

In March 1998, a new prime minister took office in Delhi for the fourth time in less than two years, heading a fragile coalition of minority parties. Coalition politics is clearly here to stay now that the long-dominant Congress Party has lost its popular mandate. The party that led India to independence in 1947 and held power at the center for 44 of the next 50 years was headed by three successive generations of the Nehru family in an often fantastic dynastic saga rivalled and mirrored by Saleem Sinai's own in *Midnight's Children.* It is clear that a unitary, centralized model of nation no longer holds.

But frightening as the seeming instability may be, the present situation might also offer some hope for formerly disenfranchised fragments of the nation to realize a more decentralized vision, for the Midnight's Children—and their children—to continue talking to each other without any one privileged voice controlling them.

In these embattled, polarized times, it is perhaps all the more crucial to keep open the space for ambivalence, uncertainties, and multiple truths, rather than rushing to premature closure on questions of identity, whether personal or public. In spite of the resulting fear of instability and chaos, history has demonstrated the danger of imposing false unity upon either the nation or the novel form. Ultimately, *MC* is unable to reconcile the timebound, linear model of history with the timeless, cyclical mode of myth. It is similarly unable to reconcile the unitary narratives of History and Nation with the multiple viewpoints of its individual and subaltern stories. And it fails to transcend the duality or reverse the fragmentation that defines its protagonist's life and eventually leads to his demise. But surely this failure is the novel's very point: its success lies in its willingness to point out the fatal flaws of the nation-state and to acknowledge its internal divisions and disjunctures, even at the risk of the protagonist's very life.

From the health and diversity of Indian writing in English in the eighties and nineties I would conclude that *MC* has had a salutary effect, but there are no easy conclusions to draw about the writers who have followed. Both nationalism and its critique continue to thrive in their work, which, like *MC* itself, simultaneously acknowledges and thematizes the limitations of the national narrative. And the latest crop of young writers—many of them women—have refreshingly begun to dispense with the language and forms of Nation altogether. Of course no single novel can be said to give a people agency, but the very multiplicity of modes and voices in the Indian novel of the nineties, even as the Indian nation-state flounders, is a testament to the hyperbolic claim of *Midnight's Children,* despite all evidence to the contrary, to have turned Victim into Protagonist.

Sitting down to write this essay, it seems an age since Saleem Sinai's opening lines sprang forth fresh on the page—almost when the world was still young. If *MC* were to be published today, sixteen years later, it might not receive the same positive welcome in the current social and political climate. If it had been published in India by an Indian publisher, it might not have won the Booker Prize. And without the acclaim outside India, it might not have been read with such eagerness inside India and been able to say things, and in a new way for the Indian English novel, that would otherwise not have been so well received. No doubt its post-Emergency timing was a factor in its success, and so was the novelist's gender, location, and positioning. But the novel's impact on Indian English writing of the eighties and nineties is undeniable. Re-reading *Midnight's Children,* I do not find it dated, neither do I read it merely as elegy/eulogy to a failed experiment; it remains a celebration of India, a paean to both unity and multiplicity, and both inspiration and challenge to a new generation to supercede it in style.

Notes

1. Salman Rushdie, *Midnight's Children* (London: Picador, 1982). Further references to this work will be abbreviated *MC* and all citations are from this edition.
2. Quoted from Shyamala Narayan, in the 1983 Bibliography, *Journal of Commonwealth Literature* 19.2 (1984): 79–82. Rushdie had lived in England since 1962, when his father sent him to Rugby at the age of fourteen. He went on to read history at King's College, Cambridge, during which time his family moved from Bombay to Karachi, Pakistan. Since his childhood, he had only been back to India once, in the late seventies, when *Midnight's Children* was conceived.
3. From Una Chaudhuri, "Imaginative Maps" (New York: Turnstile Press). A 1983 interview with Rushdie, conducted by Una Chaudhuri, downloaded 3.8.97 from Subir Grewal's Rushdie pages: www.crl.com/subir/rushdie/ucmaps.html).
4. Mukund Padmanabhan, et al., "The Empire Writes Back," in *Sunday,* 4–10 December, 1988.
5. See Narayan's 1983 Bibliography, cited above.
6. See Debashish Mukerji's article, "An Area of Brightness," on the increased acceptance of Indian writers in English both in the west and in India itself (downloaded 11.28.96 from SAWNET:www.umiacs. umd.edu/users/sawweb/sawnet/SAW.books.html).
7. Two examples of Indian critiques of Rushdie's literary influence are Aijaz Ahmed's *In Theory* (London: Verso, 1992) and Harish Trivedi's essay, "The St. Stephen's Factor," Indian Literature (Sept./Oct. 1991):183–87. Trivedi also uses the term "post-Rushdie" critically in his *Colonial Transactions: English Literature and India* (Manchester: Manchester Univ. Press, 1995). Two recent studies of Rushdie as diasporic writer are Vijay Mishra's "Postcolonial Differend: Diasporic Narratives of Salman Rushdie," Ariel 26.3 (1995): 7–45, and Jean Kane's "The Migrant Intellectual and the Body of History: Salman Rushdie's *Midnight's Children,*" Contemporary Literature 37 (Spring 1996): 94–118.
8. Rushdie accidentally (-on-purpose?) calls him the scribe of the Ramayana.
9. These are too numerous to list, but some of the scholars who have discussed the relationship of history, politics, and the individual in *MC* are Uma Parameswaran, R. S. Pathak, Dieter Reimenschneider, Aruna Srivastava, Neil ten Kortenaar, and Jonathan White. Thanks to Michael Reder for his useful review of the critical literature in "Narration and Identity in Salman Rushdie's *Midnight's Children,*" Unpublished Master's Thesis, 1994.
10. "The Empire Writes Back."
11. Timothy Brennan, *Salman Rushdie and the Third World: Myths of the Nation* (New York: St. Martin's Press, 1989), p. 85.
12. Talk given at Amherst College (4/4/97) on the occasion of its award of an honorary degree to Rushdie.
13. Hence Saleem's desperate anxiety to set down his story before it is too late and his recognition that his son-who-is-not-his-son's generation will not live by his generation's ideals. Incidentally, "out of touch and out of time" also evokes a popular Rolling Stones' song of Rushdie's teen years, "Out of Time," whose lyrics express a lover's contemptuous rejection of a former love who has "been away for much too long."
14. Una Chaudhuri interview, 1983.
15. Salman Rushdie, *The Moor's Last Sigh* (London: Jonathan Cape, 1995), pp. 173; 178–79.

16. For an excellent discussion on the vexed relationship between literature and the post-independence Indian nation-state, see the Introduction to *Women Writing in India. Vol. II: The Twentieth Century,* S. Tharu and K. Lalita, eds. (New York: The Feminist Press, 1993).

17. For some of the ideas in the above paragraph, I am indebted to Shiv Visvanathan of the Center for the Study of Developing Societies in Delhi. He used Rushdie's phrase "collective failure of the imagination" in our 1993 conversation.

18. *Indian Literature* 25.1 (1982): 128.

19. Kumkum Sangari, "The Politics of the Possible," *Cultural Critique* (Fall 1987): 157–86.

20. Salman Rushdie, "Imaginary Homelands," in *Imaginary Homelands: Essays and Criticism 1981–1991* (New York: Viking, 1991), p. 21.

21. These passive-aggressive forms of resistance are reminiscent of suffragettes' tactics and—more relevant here—of Gandhi's use of mass non-violent civil disobedience. See Ashis Nandy's discussion of Gandhi's "feminine" modes of anti-colonial resistance in *The Intimate Enemy: Loss and Recovery of Self Under Colonialism* (Delhi: Oxford Univ. Press, 1983), pp. 47–57. For a feminist critique of these tactics, see Ketu Katrak's essay, "Indian Nationalism, Gandhian 'Satyagraha' and Representations of Female Sexuality," *Nationalisms and Sexualities,* Andrew Parker, et al., eds. (New York: Routledge, 1992), pp. 395–406.

22. R. S. Pathak, "History and the Individual in the Novels of Salman Rushdie," in *The Novels of Salman Rushdie,* G. R. Taneja and R. K. Dhawan, eds. (New Delhi: Indian Society for Commonwealth Studies, 1992), p. 123.

23. Thakur Guruprasad, "The Secret of Rushdie's Charm," in *The Novels of Salman Rushdie,* G. R. Taneja and R. K. Dhawan, eds. (New Delhi: Indian Society for Commonwealth Studies, 1992), p. 169.

24. Anita Desai, "Where Cultures Clash By Night," *The Washington Post,* 3/15/81.

25. Una Chaudhuri interview, 1983.

26. The depth of Rushdie's current disillusionment with socio-political trends in India is reflected in *The Moor's Last Sigh,* in which Saleem's son Adam, his last repository of hope in *MC,* has grown up to be a power-hungry, amoral, nineties-style yuppie capitalist.

27. William Safire, "On Language: Janus Lives," *New York Times Magazine,* 5.4.97: 22.

28. Homi K. Bhabha, *Nation and Narration* (London: Routledge, 1989), p. 3.

29. *The Moor's Last Sigh,* pp. 163–64.

30. Ibid., p. 155.

31. M. Keith Booker, "Beauty and the Beast: Dualism as Despotism in the Fiction of Salman Rushdie," *ELH* 57 (1990): 977–97.

32. "The gander is the animal mask of the creative principle, which is anthropomorphically embodied in Brahma . . . a symbol of sovereign freedom through stainless spirituality. . . . The Hindu ascetic . . . freed from the bondage of rebirth, is said to have attained to the rank of "gander" (*hamsa*), or "highest gander" (*paramahamsa*) . . . The wild gander . . . exhibits in its mode of life the twofold nature of all beings. It swims on the surface of the water, but is not bound to it. Withdrawing from the watery realm, it wings into the pure and stainless air, where it is as much at home as in the world below . . . Thus it is the homeless free wanderer, between the upper celestial and the lower earthly spheres, at ease in both, not bound to either . . . it symbolizes the divine essence, which, though embodied in, and abiding with, the individual, yet remains forever free from, and unconcerned with, the events of individual life . . . On the one hand earth-bound, limited in life-strength, in virtues and in consciousness, but on the other hand a manifestation of the divine essence . . . we, like the wild goose, are citizens of the two spheres." See Heinrich Zimmer, *Myths and Symbols in Indian Art and Civilization* (New York: Harper Torchbooks, 1962), pp. 48–49.

33. In his essay, "The Riddle of Midnight: India, August 1987," Rushdie returns for the 40th anniversary of Independence and the 40th birthday of the "Class of 47." In view of the

increasing exclusiveness of the nationalist idea in India, he muses over the "paradox: that, in a country created by the Congress's nationalist campaign, the well-being of the people might now require that all nationalist rhetoric be abandoned." Given the continuing nationalist history India has been rehearsing, that does not look very likely anytime soon. See *Imaginary Homelands* (New York: Viking Penguin, 1991), pp. 32–33.

34. Kathleen Flanagan, "The Fragmented Self in Salman Rushdie's *Midnight's Children*," *Commonwealth Novel in English* 5.1 (Spring 1992): 38–45.

35. Whether it was either or both, M.C.C. is also the Marylebone Cricket Club. This is typical Rushdiesque deflationary humor, but with a serious point—the English democratic institutions inherited by independent India may have held promise at Independence, but it is increasingly being asked whether they hold the seeds of their own destruction.

36. To Rushdie, the fragment implies a whole, even if the whole is itself composite; it loses meaning in isolation. While he defends the fragment's right to a voice and an independent existence and condemns the coerciveness of the centralized State, he is clearly ambivalent about the loss of a controlling center. For a 1990s perspective, see Partha Chatterjee's *The Nation and Its Fragments* (Princeton NJ: Princeton Univ. Press, 1993).

37. Two of the protagonists in I. Allan Sealy's 1988 epic family-chronicle/national-narrative, *The Trotter-Nama,* are also ballooning miniaturists, literally and figuratively. As the Seventh Trotter's body balloons grotesquely, his paintings (ironically, copies of Mughal miniatures), get smaller and smaller. He claims that they do not simply imitate the original, but progressively improve upon it, eventually "dispensing with the world" altogether. His illustrious ancestor, also a portly figure, was killed while hot-air ballooning.

38. Richard Cronin, "The Indian English Novel: *Kim* and *Midnight's Children*," *Modern Fiction Studies* 33.2 (1987): 201–02.

39. "Washing dirty linen" inevitably calls to mind the episode of the washing-chest. If you hide in dirty laundry, you are bound to get exposed. You can only retreat "from the demands of parents and history" for so long before they catch up with you. And as with Saleem, both exposing and exposed, so also with Rushdie himself.

40. Anita Desai, Personal Interview, S. Hadley, Massachusetts, November 1992. For a discussion of Anita Desai's novels in the sixties and seventies, see my essay, "Codes in Conflict: Post-independence Alienation in Anita Desai's Early Novels," *Journal of Gender Studies* 5.3 (November 1996): 317–28.

41. Two recent India collections of essays on new Indian English writers of the 1980s are Viney Kirpal, ed., *The New Indian Novel in English: A Study of the 1980s* (New Delhi: Allied Publishers, 1990) and Nilufer E. Bharucha and Vilas Sarang, eds., *Indian-English Fiction 1980–1990: An Assessment,* New World Literature Series 77 (Delhi: B. R. Publishing Corporation, 1994).

42. The Parsis came to India in the 7th Century A.D., and Anglo-Indians have been a presence since at least the late 18th Century.

43. Here I must acknowledge my colleague Pennie Ticen, who first used "on the hyphen" years ago in a conversation with me, long before it was in common use.

44. Antonio Gramsci via Nadine Gordimer, from the epigraph to her novel *July's People:* "The old is dying and the new cannot be born; in this interregnum there arises a great diversity of morbid symptoms." Gramsci's position here is that, while the precise direction is unknown, it is clear that the mass of the people have become "detached from their traditional ideologies . . . through the crisis of authority." There can be no easy resolution through a "restoration of the old," he asserts; it is necessary to create a new culture. "State and Civil Society," in *Selections from the Prison Notebooks,* Quintin Hoare and Geoffrey Nowell Smith, eds., p. 276.

45. Rajeswari Sunder Rajan, "The Feminist Plot and the Nationalist Allegory: Home and World in Two Indian Women's Novels in English," *Modern Fiction Studies* 39 (Spring 1993): 71–92.

46. Sanjay Iyer, "East, West: No Home Is Best," *Indian Review of Books* 4.3 (Jan.-Feb., 1995): 2.

47. Mukul Kesavan, *Looking Through Glass* (New York: Farrar, Straus and Giroux, 1995). A young student in Delhi when Rushdie read on his 1983 tour of India, Kesavan has likened the event to a religious experience.

48. In her reading of *Midnight's Children,* Fawzia Afzal-Khan says that Saleem is trying to "debunk myth" when he declares that he will not see his son's miracles, that he will not see them "because, in fact, they will not happen." While it is true that Saleem does suggest that his son's generation will be more "pragmatic" than his own, I do not believe that he rules out "new myths" altogether. Saleem cannot partake of a new collective myth because he has been formed by the old one, and with its demise will come his own. See *Cultural Imperialism and the Indo-English Novel* (University Park, PA: Penn State Univ. Press, 1993), p. 159.

49. Amitav Ghosh, *The Circle of Reason* (New York: Viking, 1986), pp. 416–17. This is what Ghosh sets out to do in his next novel, *The Shadow Lines* (1988), in which he uses the structures of nation only to step out of them altogether.

50. For the history of the novel (including the historical novel) in colonial India, see Meenakshi Mukherjee's *Realism and Reality: The Novel and Society in India* (Delhi: Oxford Univ. Press, 1985) and Sisir Kumar Das's *A History of Indian Literature, 1800–1910, Western Impact: Indian Response,* and *1911–1956, Struggle for Freedom: Triumph and Tragedy* (New Delhi: Sahitya Akademi, 1991, 1995).

Midnight's Children, History, and Complexity: Reading Rushdie after the Cold War

M. Keith Booker

> **sophisticated:** 1. Mixed with a foreign substance, adulterated, impure. 2. Altered from or deprived of natural simplicity or innocence; (of a text) altered in the course of being copied or printed. 3. Falsified to a greater or lesser extent; not plain, honest, or straightforward. b. Of a book: having the content, binding, etc., altered so as to deceive.
>
> —*The New Shorter Oxford English Dictionary*

Salman Rushdie's Saleem Sinai, in the first paragraph of *Midnight's Children,* announces as he begins to tell his life story that he has been, throughout his life, "handcuffed to history," thus indicating the central importance that history will play throughout the text.[1] Indeed, Saleem's personal biography, beginning with his birth at the moment of Indian independence at midnight on August 15, 1947, serves in a rather obvious way throughout Rushdie's novel as an analog to the public history of the postcolonial Indian state. Critical reception of the book has thus, quite appropriately, tended to focus on the topic of history. On the other hand, the complexities of *Midnight's Children* (and for that matter, of Indian history) are such that critics have been able to reach no real consensus regarding the implications of Rushdie's engagement with history in the book. Granted, it has, by now, become a sort of mantra of Rushdie criticism to chant that his book challenges conventional Western Enlightenment notions of linear, cause-and-effect history, but there seems to be very little agreement about what Rushdie is proposing instead. Proclamations of Rushdie's supposed subversions of conventional Western historiography are almost equally split between critics who read this aspect of his work as a postcolonial characteristic and those who see it as a postmodern one. In both cases, however, critics seem to take it for granted that simply by providing historical accounts that are complex, multiple, nonlinear, and unreliable, Rushdie is somehow striking an effective blow against Western scientific his-

---

This essay was written specifically for this volume and is published for the first time by permission of the author.

toriography and therefore against the bourgeois hegemony that this historiography represents. But accounts of Rushdie's subversion of conventional historiography tend to be insufficiently theorized (if theorized at all), failing to specify exactly how and why the exuberant presentation of Saleem's memory as erratic, confused, and often fabricated (combined with a liberal seasoning of "transgressive" images ranging from naturalist turds to supernaturalist telepathy) somehow shakes the mighty ideological foundations upon which the global power of Western capitalism has been built over the past three centuries.

I do not mean to be especially hard on Rushdie critics. After all, I myself have been there and done that, though I hope I have learned a few things in the years since my early essays on the "transgressive" power of Rushdie's fiction.[2] Moreover, a quick look at the essays in this very volume should be enough to show that Rushdie critics are actually more sophisticated than most, his highly complex work (somewhat like that of Joyce or Shakespeare, or at least Thomas Pynchon) tending to attract complex (and ambitious) critics. Indeed, the criticism of both postcolonial and postmodernist literature is nothing if not sophisticated and complex, to the point that the disquisitions of the scholars involved in producing this criticism are becoming increasingly opaque and indecipherable. Which is, of course, part of the problem. These days, such scholars almost always claim to be politically committed, even if it is virtually impossible to discern to *what* they are committed. But a political program that is vague, ambiguous, and inaccessible to all but a few learned initiates is surely of relatively little value. Moreover, the seemingly automatic assumption that "sophisticated" works such as Rushdie's somehow pack a potent (if nebulous) political punch is closely related to the assumption, by now thoroughly ingrained in the discourse of Western literary studies, that complexity is by definition a good thing, a clear sign (and for that matter, a prerequisite) of "genuine" art and thorough thought.

Rushdie himself is an unabashed apostle of complexity, presumably because of his own complex background. And to an extent, he is rightfully so. Who could argue, for example, with commonsense observations, such as his plea that "if history creates complexities, let us not try to simplify them"?[3] On the other hand, one could also argue that if history creates simplicity, we should not try to complicate it, even if the charge of being "simplistic" has become the most dreaded one that can be hurled against a literary critic, functioning for most of us like daylight on Dracula or water on the Wicked Witch of the West. But there is a certain value in clarity, especially when crucial political issues are involved, and literary critics, especially those who have concerned themselves with postcolonial and postmodernist fiction, have not always been able to distinguish among complexity, confusion, and obfuscation—in their own work or in that of the novelists they so admire.

Timothy Brennan, who wrote the first doctoral dissertation entirely devoted to Rushdie's fiction (which then became the first, and remains the best, book-length study of Rushdie's work), has some claim to being America's leading authority on Rushdie.[4] Appropriately, then, it is Brennan, in his new book, *At Home in the World,* who has recently called needed critical attention to the infatuation with complexity in contemporary literary studies. Brennan notes the way in which so many critics and theorists have accepted all too uncritically and untheoretically the notion that "complexity is the unassailable quality, the sign of intelligence and care, and therefore of a quiet modesty comporting with an image of solitary lucubrations."[5] Among other things, Brennan understands full well that this emphasis on complexity helps to keep the labors of American intellectuals safely separated from the world of real work and therefore to drive a wedge between intellectuals and the working class. After all, it is presumably the ability to appreciate complexity that qualifies us to do our work in the groves of academe, while those less gifted must labor in far less inviting surroundings. Somebody has to clean the toilets, as the saying goes. Brennan also understands this entire phenomenon as a key strategy of bourgeois hegemony, drawing in his discussion on the work of Antonio Gramsci, who insisted so vehemently on the importance of an alliance between antibourgeois intellectuals and the working class. Brennan also draws on the French Marxist thinker and novelist Paul Nizan, whom he quotes as stating, "[O]nly the bourgeois have a real need for subtlety in their classifications and palpable profundity in their intellectual exercises, because they alone have something to hide—and vulgarity is a much less effective mask than subtlety and nuance."[6]

One of the central points Brennan makes throughout *At Home in the World* is that this emphasis on complexity, perhaps especially in postcolonial studies, has the effect, intended or not, of obscuring the importance of Marxist thought in a variety of antibourgeois struggles, including the postcolonial one. Indeed, within the context of the Cold War (which is, we should not forget, the context within which most of our basic assumptions about the nature of "literary studies" developed), the ideological outlines of the glorification of complexity are clear. In the rhetoric of the Cold War West, complexity means, of course, capitalism and all its attendant cultural and political operations (open-mindedness, democracy, etc.), while simplicity means communism (especially Stalinism), with its vulgar emphasis on binary oppositions, such as class struggle and its unseemly insistence on maintaining intellectual contact with the unwashed masses and with people who actually do physical work and are therefore marked as incapable of real thought.

This Cold War tendency to glorify complexity, especially in the realm of culture, is surely part of the secret behind the enthusiastic reception of Rushdie's work in the West, the recent Booker of Bookers having made *Midnight's Children* something like the official Western masterpiece of the late Cold War years. After all, Rushdie's book is certainly more complex than all those socialist realist novels produced by Soviet writers, even if works such as Gorky's *Klim Samgin,* Sholokhov's *Quiet Flows the Don,* and Alexei Tolstoy's

Peter the Great have a monumental and masterly quality of their own and can be dismissed as simplistic only by the most myopic and narrow minded of readers. How better, then, to demonstrate the sophistication of Western bourgeois culture than by adopting Rushdie, with all his complexity and inherent cultural multiplicity, as the paradigm of both the postcolonial and the postmodern and as the official poster boy of the Booker McConnell Corporation and of corporate capitalism as a whole?

Of course, one cannot assume that Rushdie's work has no subversive force simply because it has been so enthusiastically endorsed by the culture industry of global capitalism. However, given that the works of Soviet writers such as Gorky, Tolstoy (Alexei), and Sholokhov (and Kataev, Gladkov, Platonov, Ostrovsky, Serafimovoch, Furmanov, Ivanov, etc.) mount such a powerful assault on bourgeois ideology, even if they are written in a calm, accessible, realistic mode, we should probably be extremely cautious in assuming that a work such as *Midnight's Children* is automatically subversive of Western bourgeois ideology simply because it is complex and breaks the rules of nineteenth-century historiography and realistic fiction. Indeed, a close look at Rushdie's book within the context of recent critical discourse on both postcolonialism and postmodernism reveals the difficulty of demonstrating that *Midnight's Children,* on the basis of form alone, contains a powerful political critique of either imperialism or global capitalism. As I have already said, the very complexity of the book closely conforms to the Cold War aesthetic of the West. Moreover, a look at the actual content of the book also tends to suggest that the book serves as a prop for the ideological structures deployed by Western capital during the decades of the Cold War, which was, like Saleem Sinai, born at approximately the same time as the Indian state.

Midnight's Children and the Postcolonial Challenge to Colonialist Historiography

At first glance, the central importance of Indian history in *Midnight's Children* (and for that matter, in Rushdie's other novels) would seem to place the book firmly within the mainstream of postcolonial fiction, despite Rushdie's own expressed discomfort at being considered a postcolonial writer.[7] Of course, the term "postcolonial" has become drastically multiple and overdetermined in recent years. I will use it here to indicate cultural activity that seeks to contribute to the development of new cultural identities that contest the legacy of the colonial past in formerly colonial areas, a definition that sets the postcolonial distinctly apart from the postmodern. History has, in the course of the twentieth century, emerged as a crucial ground for the contestation of postcolonial cultural identities. From the pioneering work of W. E. B. Du

Bois in African-American history and early anticolonial histories such as C. L. R. James's *The Black Jacobins* to the recent, theoretically informed work of the subaltern studies group of Indian postcolonial scholars, numerous historical projects have begun to mount an impressive challenge to the hegemony of white, European historiography.

The grounds for this contestation are, of course, well chosen given the extent to which colonialist historiography has served as a principal justification for both colonialism and racism. In any number of Western historical accounts, the advent of colonialism rescues the colonized world from a timeless malaise, propels it into the flow of history, and opens it to the limitless opportunities for democratization and wealth that are presumably associated with the process of capitalist modernization. Thus, in the colonial situation, the only true historical event is the process of colonization and its aftermath, leaving no room for the colonized world to have a history of its own independent of the history of the European bourgeoisie. A classic statement of this attitude comes from the work of G. W. F. Hegel, one of the leading theorists of bourgeois historiography, in his view of Africa as

> the land of childhood, which lying beyond the day of self-conscious history, is enveloped in the dark mantle of Night.... For it is no historical part of the World; it has no movement or development to exhibit.... What we properly understand by Africa, is the Unhistorical, Undeveloped Spirit, still involved in the conditions of mere nature.[8]

Famously, Hegel's view of world history as the unfolding of a sort of divine plan leads him to the ethnocentric conclusion that his contemporary European culture is the farthest point thus far toward the culmination of that plan and to the nationalistic belief that his own Germany is supreme among the nations of the earth.

Little wonder, then, that so many postcolonial historians have felt it necessary to contest this situation, though it is worth remembering that in doing so they follow, though with their own distinctive strides, in the footsteps of a long line of Marxist historians, from Marx's monumental challenge to Hegel on down, in attacking bourgeois ideology on its own historicist grounds. Meanwhile, postcolonial novelists have quite frequently chosen to contribute to this same project by writing historical novels that challenge the premises of bourgeois historiography or, for that matter, of bourgeois historical novels, which arose at very much the same time as bourgeois scientific historiography and for very much the same reasons. Thus writers of postcolonial historical novels are also challenging bourgeois ideology on its own turf, again, however, pursuing a course originally mapped out by European Marxists. Particularly relevant here is Georg Lukács's reminder that the European bourgeoisie, in their emergent phase, turned to the realist novel in general and the historical novel in particular as the appropriate expression of their revolutionary historical energies.[9] Consequently, Lukács urges modern socialist writers to pursue realist writing strategies, and in particular to employ the genre of the historical novel, in their own quest for literary expression of a revolutionary social and political vision.

It is no accident, then, that the historical novel has been such a favorite genre of both European leftist writers and postcolonial writers, the latter of whom are, of course, quite frequently heavily influenced by Marxist ideas but who also draw upon alternative visions of the historical process derived from their own indigenous cultural traditions and historical experiences. Thus Gorky, Sholokhov, and Tolstoy produce their most impressive challenges to bourgeois cultural hegemony in the genre of the historical novel, even if their own Marxist historiography is scientific and their own historical narratives linear and well behaved. And the same can be said for the works of numerous leftist postcolonial novelists, even if these novelists draw upon important indigenous cultural energies as well.[10] Rushdie has long been considered by many of his critics to be an important participant in this phenomenon. The contours of Rushdie criticism on this topic were mapped out early on, as when Anna Srivastava points out that the British domination of India involved, among other things, the imposition on India of Western rationalist notions of history, notions on which "an imperialist venture . . . depends . . . for its sustenance" (63). Rushdie's presentation of his own historical narrative through the use of nonlinear narrative modes—presumably derived, if one accepts his own testimony, from the characteristic forms of Indian oral culture—thus potentially presents a challenge to some of the most fundamental assumptions on which the rhetoric of British colonial superiority in India (the same rhetoric that was also used to explain bourgeois class superiority back in Europe) was based.

A quick review of the postcolonial novel indicates the centrality of historical fiction in the attempts of such novels to contribute to the development of viable postcolonial cultural identities. For example, each of the novels of the radical Kenyan writer Ngugi wa Thiong'o focuses on a particular moment in the history of Kenya, and together his novels, ranging from *The River Between* to *Matigari,* constitute a sweeping historical narrative that tells the story of Kenya from the early days of British colonization to the contemporary postcolonial period, focusing on the strong Kenyan tradition of resistance to colonial oppression. Indeed, Ngugi has openly proclaimed that Kenyan history provides the principal inspiration for his fiction, especially in the sense that "the Kenyan peoples' struggle against foreign domination" is the "one consistent theme" of this history over the past 400 years.[11] In a similar (if less politically specific) manner, Chinua Achebe, in works such as *Things Fall Apart,* seeks to provide his African readers with a realistic depiction of their precolonial past, free of the distortions and stereotypes imposed upon that past in European accounts. Meanwhile, Achebe's novels, from *Things Fall Apart* to *Anthills of the Savannah,* collectively trace the colonial and neocolonial history of Nigeria. Other representative examples of African historical novels include Ousmane Sembène's dramatization of a 1947–1948 railway strike in French colonial Africa in *God's Bits of Woods,* M. G. Vassanji's imaginative retelling of the history of Tanzania in *The Gunny Sack,* Nuruddin Farah's elaboration in his trilogy "Variations on the Theme of an African Dictatorship" of the Siyad Barre period in Somalia, Ben Okri's attempt to capture the spirit of modern Nigerian history through an Africanized magic realism in *The Famished Road,* Yambo Ouologuem's somewhat notorious depiction of African history as a never-ending cycle of abject violence in *Bound to Violence,* and Ayi Kwei Armah's *Two Thousand Seasons,* a more positive and mythic version of African history (written partially in response to Ouologuem).

The Caribbean novel has displayed a similar historical focus, often with a specifically anticolonial, antibourgeois emphasis. Indeed, many early Caribbean historical novels have been important influences on later African novelists. One might note, for example, Vic Reid's *New Day* (1949), a sweeping historical epic that details the modern history of Jamaica in a way that places leftist politics and (especially) the Jamaican trades union movement at the very center of the growth of the Jamaican nation. Also especially impressive is Ralph de Boissière's two-volume account, in *Crown Jewel* (1952) and *Rum and Coca-Cola* (1956), of the history of Trinidad during the crucial decade from 1935 to 1945. De Boissière's novels also focus on trades union activity as a key to anticolonial liberation, while making clear the Marxist model of history on which they rely. Strongly recalling the aesthetics of Lukács, de Boissière deftly presents Trindadian society as an interlinked totality in which the fundamental social category is class.

History has long been a crucial concern of the Indian novel as well, remaining a central preoccupation of contemporary English-language novelists such as Shashi Tharoor, Nayantara Sahgal, Rohinton Mistry, and Vikram Seth. Many of these recent novelists are directly inspired by the work of Rushdie, to the point that they are often collectively referred to as "Rushdie's Children." However, with the (monumental) exception of the work of Mulk Raj Anand, the most politically radical Indian novels have tended not to be written in English, which may largely account for the fact that until very recently, Indian literature has been rather marginal to the field of postcolonial studies, despite the prominent (some would even say dominant) position occupied by Indian intellectuals in the field of postcolonial theory. There is, for example, a powerful tradition of anticolonial novels in Bengali that goes back to Bankim Chandra Chatterjee's *Anandmath* (1882), which became a major source of inspiration for the nationalist movement in subsequent decades. Through the middle decades of the twentieth century, nationalism remained one of the most important trends in the Indian political novel; many of these novels were devoted specifically to a glorification of Gandhiism and thus tended to take a rather nostalgic approach to the traditional past in their treatment of history. In English, Raja Rao's *Kanthapura* is perhaps the most important product of this movement. Meanwhile, Anglophone novels such as Manohar Malgonkar's *The Devil's Wind* (1972), about the 1857 revolt; Khushwant Singh's *Train to Pakistan* (1955), about Partition and the ensuing riots; and Bhabani Bhattacharya's *Shadow from Lladakh* (1966), which revolves around the 1962 border conflict with China, treat specific important historical events from an Indian perspective that often differs significantly from Western accounts.

Malgonkar's *A Bend in the Ganges* (1964) is a sweeping historical novel about decolonization in India that in many ways suggests comparison with *Midnight's Children*. Malgonkar includes in his novel virtually all important political tendencies that informed this crucial moment in Indian history, ranging from radical anticolonial violence to gullible admiration for British efficiency—with subtle suggestions that Gandhian nonviolence, intermediate between the two, may sometimes have a tendency to deteriorate into the latter. Anticipating Rushdie's Saleem and Shiva, Malgonkar employs central characters such as Debi-dayal Kerwad and Gian Telwar as an opposed, almost allegorical pair, using them to represent militancy and nonviolence, respectively. But Malgonkar presents his historical narrative in a strictly realistic, rationalist mode, differing dramatically from Rushdie in this sense. As Asha Kaushik puts it, "Malgonkar's fictionalization of history is a resolved quest for an ordered, patterned and logical past," which puts his work in stark contrast to Rushdie's treatment of history, which "moves through various 'fragmented' aspects into both a comprehensive fantasy and reality."[12]

Predictably, Malgonkar's realistic, accessible fictions have received very little critical attention in the West, but in point of fact Malgonkar is far more in tune with the main thrust of postcolonial fiction than is Rushdie. Despite the enthusiasm of Rushdie critics over the subversive possibilities of his complex, nonlinear narrative forms, the vast majority of postcolonial historical novels are narrated in realistic modes that employ linear narratives and clearly accept the validity of rationalist models of history, especially Marxist models, in which men (including postcolonial ones) have the ability to make their own history and are not, as often seems to be the case in *Midnight's Children,* at the mercy of inexplicable turns, supernatural forces, and random accidents. Moreover, realism (of the nineteenth-century, rather than the magic, variety) has long been the dominant mode not only of the postcolonial novel in general but of the Indian novel in particular.[13]

All of the Caribbean novels just mentioned are realistic and assume that history is a rational process that proceeds in an explicable, linear fashion, though some Caribbean novelists (Reid, Thelwell) make particularly good stylistic use of dialect in ways that anticipate Rushdie's notion of "decolonizing" the English language through injection of elements derived from the languages and cultures of the formerly colonized world. The same can be said for most of the African novels as well, including those, like Ngugi's *Devil on the Cross,* that make extensive use of traditional African cultural forms and supplement their realistic matrices with magic realist and other devices that set them apart from conventional European realistic novels. However, Ngugi's principal historical model is Marxist, and his call is not for a return to the traditional African past but for a working-class revolution and a move forward in history toward socialism. Even *Things Fall Apart,* with its vivid evocation of traditional Igbo culture and its clever adaptation of various elements of Igbo oral narrative to the novel form, does not really challenge the fundamental Western narrative of history, to the point that Michael Valdez Moses, perhaps going a bit too far, has argued that Achebe's book is essentially Hegelian in its acceptance of the inevitability of modernization.[14] And even *Two Thousand Seasons,* which presents the most direct challenge to Western bourgeois historiography, still assumes that history is a linear, rational process, despite its central use of elements derived from African myth and oral narratives.[15]

Writers such as Achebe and Vassanji (who seems to have been influenced directly by Rushdie) often again seek to find new forms of English in which to write, though Ngugi has vehemently rejected Rushdie's call to decolonize English, writing his fiction from *Devil on the Cross* onward in Gikuyu and arguing that projects such as Rushdie's only strengthen the hegemony of English by injecting new energies into it.[16] Of the African novels listed previously, only those of Ouloguem and Okri abandon the realistic mode altogether. But Ouloguem's novel, often considered to be postmodern, has problems of its own, including its tendency to verify European notions of African savagery, not to mention that large portions of it seem to have been plagiarized from Western novels.[17] Meanwhile, Okri's use of Yoruba folk culture as a basis for his magic realistic narratives, however brilliantly done, comes dangerously close to a mere exoticization of Africa for the consumption of Western readers.[18] That novels such as *The Famished Road* poses no real threat to the hegemony of Western bourgeois culture can perhaps be seen in the fact that, of all the postcolonial novelists mentioned previously, only Okri has joined Rushdie in winning the Booker Prize.

One would be hard pressed to demonstrate that there is anything inherently anticolonial in the form of *Midnight's Children,* either. For example, noting the similarity between the nonlinear narrative structure of *Midnight's Children* and that of traditional Indian oral storytelling, Rushdie himself has stated in an interview that the similarity is intentional and that "everything about Laurence Sterne, García Márquez, and all that comes a long way behind" Indian oral narratives as an influence.[19] Yet it is also the case that the illiterate Padma, the character in Rushdie's book who is its principal representative of oral culture, is the one character who insists on rational, linear narratives, becoming increasingly frustrated by Sinai's digressions and time jumps. Other "anti-Western" aspects of the book are equally problematic. For example, one is tempted to see the fuzzy boundaries that exist among individuals, families, and states in *Midnight's Children* as the sign of an ongoing sense of community long lost amid the radical alienation of the individualist West. Until, of course, one considers the various ways in which the ever-present Hegel, in *The Philosophy of Right,* sought to overcome the centrifugal implications of bourgeois individualism by depicting the family as a structure in which the individual could comfortably feel himself part of a larger community, in turn depicting the state as a sort of "universal family." But Hegel's vision leads to a privileging of the state over other forms of community and ultimately reinforces, rather than transcends, the gap between public and private existence that is a central characteristic of bourgeois social life.[20] Meanwhile, as I have noted elsewhere, the sheer obviousness of Sinai's role as a figure of India, combined with the ironic postmodern playfulness of Rushdie's text, suggests that *Midnight's Children* is not so much a national allegory proper as a parody of such allegories.[21]

Still, Rushdie, on the basis of his after-the-fact comments elsewhere, seems to have been quite serious in his attempt to construct *Midnight's Children* as a distinctively Indian sort of national allegory. In a recent *Time* magazine article (part of the brief hoopla in the Western press surrounding the 50th anniversary of Indian independence), Rushdie suggests that the "idea of India" has been quite central to his life and his writing. Moreover, he argues that despite the vast complexity and multiplicity of the Indian subcontinent, the idea of India as a single entity remains viable, largely because "the country has taken the modern view of the self and enlarged it to encompass almost 1 billion souls. . . . It works because the individual sees his own nature writ large in the nature of the state."[22] In short, for Rushdie, to think in terms of national allegory, and in particular in terms of direct parallels between the nature of the individual and the nature of the state, is central to the Indian sense of both national and individual identity, an idea he enacts quite directly in *Midnight's Children.* But this particular vision of the Indian state as an aggregate of unique individuals aligned by little more than a sense that this aggregate somehow mirrors each of them individually also sounds suspiciously Hegelian, which could mean that Hegel here is showing a submerged longing for community of a kind unavailable in bourgeois society, but it could also mean that Rushdie, even as he attempts to be at his most Indian, remains firmly within the imperial grip of the bourgeois ideology of the West.

Perhaps realizing the difficulty of such problems, postcolonial historical novels have always relied more on content than on form to present their challenges to the hegemony of the West. And rightfully so. Ngugi's attempt to construct a usable past from the legacy of radical Kenyan anticolonial resistance (as in the Mau Mau rebellion) or the central use of radical labor activism, as in Sembène, Reid, or de Boissière, surely have a subversive force that cannot be denied, while the subversive power of unconventional narrative forms is highly debatable. Perhaps the classic case here is Du Bois's monumental, but neglected, trilogy of historical novels, *The Black Flame* (1957–1961). Drawing upon his own encyclopedic knowledge of history, Du

Bois constructs in these volumes a magisterial history of America, in a global context, from Reconstruction to the mid-1950s. In the process, Du Bois works virtually every important historical personage and event from that period into his narrative, while at the same time maintaining a focus on his semiallegorical fictional protagonist, Manuel Mansart. Du Bois's narrative entirely conforms to the conventions of realism, and his Marxist vision of history is highly rational and scientific. Yet by emphasizing formerly repressed aspects of American history, especially African-American history, and by reinterpreting well known historical events from the point of view of the central assumption that all history is the history of class conflict, Du Bois mounts a mighty challenge to received notions of history. Little wonder, then, that the books received little attention in the Cold War West, despite Du Bois's towering reputation (which had, by the end, anyway, been "tarnished" by his move to Africa, his renunciation of his American citizenship, and his enthusiastic endorsement of the Communist Party).

From this point of view, the famed encyclopedism of *Midnight's Children* would seem, at least potentially, to offer an analogous challenge to official Western history. Unfortunately, a close look shows that Rushdie's text, despite its reputation for heteroglossic richness and its liberal sprinkling with references to popular culture, does very little to reveal aspects of Indian historical experience that are not already present in conventional Western accounts. Here, one might recall David Lipscomb's discovery that Rushdie seems to have lifted most of his information about Indian history directly out of a Western introductory textbook, Stanley Wolpert's *A New History of India* (166).[23] However, Lipscomb ultimately comes not to bury Rushdie but to praise him. Rather than charge Rushdie with ignorance or laziness, Lipscomb is generous enough to suggest that this discovery implies that in constructing *Midnight's Children* in a textual form so different from that employed by Wolpert (a UCLA professor whose book was published by Oxford University Press, that ultimate voice of Western academic publishing authority), Rushdie challenges the authority of Western historians to represent the Indian past.

Lipscomb does not, however, explain the dynamics of this challenge in any convincing way. Meanwhile, a continued look at the content of *Midnight's Children* shows that there is a surprising lack of actual anticolonial material in this story of Indian independence. As Brennan pointed out long ago, there is a striking absence of coverage of the anticolonial nationalist movement in Rushdie's book, which narrates the 1919 Amritsar Massacre in an appropriately horrifying mode but then skips directly to 1942, and then rushes on to independence.[24] In the process, Gandhi and his followers disappear from the text altogether (except for a later passing reference to his assassination),[25] not to mention the more radical opponents of the British raj, such as Subhas Chandra Bose and Balwantrao Gangadhar Tilak, whose appropriation of the Hindu god Ganesh as a symbol of anitcolonial Indian nationalism would have made him a perfect forerunner to Saleem Sinai, whose principal mythical analog is Ganesh.[26] Meanwhile, as Neil ten Kortenaar points out, Rushdie still emphasizes the same kinds of political events that Western historians like Wolpert do, while the fictional retelling of Indian history in *Midnight's Children* makes little or no attempt to challenge, in the mode of the Subaltern Studies historians, traditional Western histories of India by reflecting the experiences of groups traditionally ignored by those histories.[27] Indeed, the most obvious fact about the point of view of *Midnight's Children* is that it focuses on the upper classes and gives undue weight to the experiences of India's Muslim minority, something that can also be said for most Western historians of India, from James Mill on down.

MIDNIGHT'S CHILDREN AND THE POSTMODERN CHALLENGE TO RATIONALIST HISTORIOGRAPHY

To a large extent, of course, the lack of an effective critique of colonialism in *Midnight's Children* can be explained by the fact that it is a postcolonial novel in a sense more literal than that in which I am using the term. The political critique of *Midnight's Children* is aimed at Indian society after independence, not before, and the villains of the piece are not Thomas Babington Macaulay and General Dyer but Indian politicians such as Indira and Sanjay Gandhi. It is perhaps from this point of view that the assault on rationalist historiography in *Midnight's Children* should be understood. "Secular rationalism" was always a crucial component of the ideology of the nationalism movement, becoming even more dominant as an official ideology of the Nehru-led Indian state after independence. Moreover, as Alok Rai points out, numerous Indian intellectuals in Rushdie's generation have become disenchanted with the secular rationalism, so that Rushdie is in this sense participating in an important movement in postcolonial Indian political thought.[28] In this sense, *Midnight's Children* resembles Ngugi's various critiques of the Kenyatta regime in Kenya or Armah's satire of Nkrumah in *The Beautyful Ones Are Not Yet Born*. Yet both Ngugi and Armah manage simultaneously to level withering attacks on colonialism and on its neocolonial successor, global capitalism, while Rushdie does not.

Indeed, if Rushdie's target is secular rationalism per se and not simply colonialist secular rationalism, then readings that treat his work as more properly postmodern than postcolonial may be more to the point. After all, part of the problem involved in any attempt to discern the subversive anticolonial thrust of Rushdie's particular narrative forms, in *Midnight's Children* and elsewhere, is that these forms have so many Western analogs and precedents, from *Tristram Shandy* and *Ulysses* to *Gravity's Rainbow*.[29] Such narratives, while not specifically anticolonial, are frequently seen by critics as subversive, presumably challenging the rationalist legacy of the Enlightenment. Yet such narratives have been absorbed quite comfortably within the confines of Western bourgeois culture. This is especially true in the wake of the Cold War, when modernist art, most of which was originally designed by its makers as a conscious assault upon the increasing conservatism of the European bourgeois elite, was suddenly adopted as the official high culture of the bourgeois West, thereby presumably making the socialist realist culture of the Soviet Union appear simple (with all the attendant negative implications) by comparison. One might, then, define postmodernist culture as that which is produced in the modernist mode after that mode has been canonized, thus allowing postmodernism to pursue the complex aesthetic strategies of its modernist predecessors but without the antibourgeois charge. Postmodernism, from this point of view, is merely the cultural logic of late capitalism, which Fredric Jameson tried to tell us long ago.[30] As Christopher Norris notes, postmodernist attacks on "the old enlightenment meta-narrative of progress, reason, and truth" quite consistently pose as radical assaults on authority and equally consistently end up as neoconservative props for the status quo by throwing out the baby of Marxist critique with the bathwater of bourgeois ideology.[31] This is not to say that Rushdie should be somehow required to employ Marxist models of history in his work. It is, however, to say that he should be perhaps more responsible in discerning between historical models rather than rejecting out of hand any and all metanarratives regardless of their nature. However fashionable the postmodern rejection of metanarratives in theory, the fact remains that, in practice, the metanarrative of capitalism is still firmly hegemonic in the world; to ignore this fact in a sweeping declaration that all metanarratives are now irrelevant is simply to leave the currently hegemonic metanarrative safely in place. If, in short, Rushdie's complexity is of a postmodern type, then its status as a subversive challenge to Western bourgeois hegemony is seriously called into question.

Of course, *Midnight's Children,* with its strong connection to Indian history and culture, is surely postmodern in a different way than, say, the novels of Pynchon or the lucubrations of Jean-François Lyotard and Jean Baudrillard. Still, the challenge to "official" modes of history posed in Rushdie's work is in many ways precisely of the kind Linda Hutcheon associates with postmodernist fiction in general. Hutcheon, in fact, specifically identifies *Midnight's Children* as one of the central examples of what she calls "historiographic metafiction," a typical postmodernist mode that for her mounts powerful challenges to accepted modes of historiography and received accounts of the historical past. There is, however, nothing particularly anticolonial in Hutcheon's vision of historiographic fiction, and she specifically associates the historical vision of Rushdie's novel not with traditional Indian culture but with the work of Michel Foucault.[32] Rushdie's novel is thus lumped into the same category as numerous other works of historiographic metafiction, including Pynchon's *Gravity's Rainbow,* D. M. Thomas's *The White Hotel,* Gabriel García Márquez's *One Hundred Years of Solitude,* Günter Grass's *The Tin Drum,* E. L. Doctorow's *Ragtime,* John Berger's *G.,* John Banville's *Doctor Copernicus,* and Umberto Eco's *The Name of the Rose.* In short, Hutcheon's postmodernism, which supposedly has a subversive political charge, includes works with such diverse backgrounds that it is not exactly clear of *what* it is supposed to be subversive. The vague nature of Hutcheon's vision of opposition to "official" histories becomes completely clear when one recalls that the most powerful challenge ever mounted to the official scientific historiographies of the post-Enlightenment West arises from the even more scientific, but decidedly oppositional, perspective of Marxism, which in Hutcheon's formulation gets blithely lumped in with bourgeois historicism in a sweeping indictment of "official" historical accounts even as García Márquez and Doctorow somehow wind up in the same category as Pynchon and Banville and, of course, Rushdie.[33]

Among other things, Hutcheon acknowledges that her notion of the subversiveness of historiographic metafiction flies directly in the face of Lukács's well-known argument that one of the most effective ways to oppose bourgeois ideology is probably through the writing of socialist-oriented historical novels in very much the same realist vein as the early historical novels of the European bourgeoisie, when they were still in their revolutionary phase. However, Hutcheon is able to rebut Lukács only by assuming what she wants to prove, that is, by showing that postmodernist historical novels do not meet his criteria for politically effective historical fiction, which for her means that Lukács must be wrong because postmodernist historical fiction is by definition effectively subversive.[34] She does not, however, look at specific cases, which is probably for the best, because she would probably have a very hard time arguing that *Midnight's Children* poses a more powerful challenge to "official" history than, say, *The Black Flame.*

Meanwhile, Hutcheon formulates her reading of the politics of postmodernism in direct response to Jameson's Lukácsian notion that postmodernism represents the "cultural logic" of late capitalism, with which it is thus in direct ideological complicity. Yet by lumping such diverse works together and labeling them all "postmodern," Hutcheon comes dangerously close simply to verifying Jameson's point about the global homogenization of culture in the postmodern era, that is, in the era of late capitalism. Indeed, while Hutcheon pays little attention to the cultural specificity of the texts she categorizes as historiographic metafiction, Jameson is always aware (some would say *too* aware, in some cases) of the cultural differences that make texts from Africa or Asia operate on different premises than texts from Great Britain or the United States. Meanwhile, Hutcheon's inattention to cultural and historical diversity is particularly problematic given the similar tendency of so much postmodernist discourse, as in the outrageous Orientalist ramblings of postmodern maven Baudrillard.[35]

All of which is, of course, highly relevant to the work of Rushdie, which clearly meets so many of the criteria usually associated with postmodernism but that also presumably derives important energies from the particular historical experience of Indian colonialism and postcolonialism. For Hutcheon, there would be no contradiction between these two positions—both of which are, for her, subversive in their "ex-centric" refusal of the well-behaved linear narrative forms of high bourgeois history, but only because she does not really grant that the second position has any significance that cannot already be comprehended within the rubric of the first. For Jameson, on the other hand, postmodernist fiction is precisely aligned with the worldview of late capitalism, while postcolonial (and other marginal, in the geopolitical sense) fiction is one of the few remaining forms of world culture that still retains an ability to get outside of the ideology of late capitalism and thus make statements that are potentially subversive of it. Thus he remarks that "the only authentic cultural production today has seemed to be that which can draw on the collective experience of marginal pockets of the social life in the world system," a category that for him includes such heterogeneous entities as Third World literature, black American literature, British working-class rock, women's literature, gay literature, and the *roman québecois*.[36]

However problematic the inclusion of such diverse cultural forces in a single grouping or the description of a phenomenon as broad as third-world literature as a "marginal pocket," Jameson's point is that these diverse cultural phenomena seem to share a common ability to resist the homogenizing tendencies of global capitalism and to tap into collective experience in ways that are denied the more mainstream culture of a world system thoroughly saturated with the capitalist market and commodity system. Conversely, Ziauddin Sardar has recently argued that postmodernism itself tends to extend the Western imperial domination of the third world and to aim at "nothing less than the total annihilation of the Other."[37] For Jameson or Sardar, then, the question of whether Rushdie's fiction is postmodern or postcolonial is a crucial one indeed, except that Jameson is subtle enough to know that texts cannot be neatly categorized in the manner of different-size nuts and bolts but in fact can (and usually do) contain a number of different, even contradictory, impulses. One would certainly expect that to be the case for *Midnight's Children,* though it is still worth asking whether Rushdie's novel is dominated by either postcolonial or postmodern impulses.

Sardar, in fact, identifies Rushdie as one of the principal culprits in his impassioned critique of postmodernism. And indeed, virtually all aspects of Rushdie's text, even those that seem most postcolonial or distinctively Indian, can be comprehended within Jameson's theorization of postmodernism. For example, *Midnight's Children,* despite its ostentatious literary artifice, shows little sign of the separation of the political and poetic typical of the West. Rushdie himself has suggested that his work is inherently political and that the intermingling of politics and art is an inescapable fact of life in the third world. For Jameson, of course, it is precisely the bridging of the gaps between the public and the private and between the poetic and the political that permits what he sees as a consistent use of individual characters as markers of national identity in postcolonial texts.[38] In short, Jameson seems to admire third-world texts because they necessarily, as a result of their own historical origins, effect a politicization of aesthetics of the kind Walter Benjamin calls for as a response to the aestheticization of politics by the German Nazis.[39] But within the radical uncertainty of *Midnight's Children,* it is not really possible to determine whether Rushdie is politicizing aesthetics or aestheticizing politics. Which is not to say that Rushdie may be a fascist but simply that Western societies can also collapse the boundary between the poetic and the political, and sometimes in sinister ways. In fact, in postmodernism, all such boundaries and distinctions collapse by definition.

To take another example, the radical fragmentation Saleem Sinai experiences in the course of *Midnight's Children* might at first glance appear to serve as part of his function as a national allegory of India. Sinai feels that as a result of his physical fragmentation, he will eventually "crumble into (approximately) six hundred and thirty million particles of anonymous, and necessarily oblivious dust" (37). His total number of particles, in short, will equal the total population of India. Indeed, Sinai's fragmentation is quite closely and directly tied to Indian history, especially to the traumas of the postindependence Partition of India and the subsequent bifurcation of Muslim Pakistan into East and West wings. One might compare here Naipaul's encounter in *India: A Million Mutinies Now* with the Muslim Rashid, a member of an old Lucknow family who feels that the Partition has led to his own subjective fragmentation as a Muslim in India: "I can never be a complete person now. I can't ignore partition. It's part of me. I feel rudderless. . . . The creation and existence of Pakistan has damaged a part of my psyche."[40]

The scattered and multiple sense of self Sinai experiences may seem particularly Indian, but it certainly has any number of Western analogs. Consider, for example, the attempts of the narrator of Karel Čapek's *An Ordinary Life* to sort through his past in Czechoslovakia as he constructs his autobiography: "Well, look here, it was to be a quite simple yarn, the story of an ordinary and happy man; and now, look, all sorts of people are crowding in: the ordinary man, the one with elbows, the hypochondriac, the former poet, and the Lord knows what else; there's a whole pile of them."[41] Meanwhile, the fragmentation that Sinai experiences in *Midnight's Children* may indicate a more general splitting of the colonial subject, but it can certainly also be comprehended in terms of Jameson's own analyses of the fragmentation of the hyperalienated subject of Western late consumer capitalism. Fragmentation, in *Midnight's Children,* extends to the generic, stylistic, and linguistic multiplicity of the text, much in the mode of the schizotexts

Jameson identifies as typical products of the postmodern condition. Further, Sinai's fragmentation is a motif found in numerous postmodernist texts. Compare, for example, the scattering of Pynchon's Tyrone Slothrop as a result of his loss of a sense of "temporal bandwidth" in *Gravity's Rainbow*.[42] Indeed, Sinai's fragmentation provides a vivid enactment of the schizophrenic sense of self that Jameson has identified as representative of subjectivity (or lack thereof) in late consumer capitalism. Using Jacques Lacan to update Marx's analysis of the alienation of workers under the capitalist division of labor, Jameson suggests that like the schizophrenic patient, the postmodern self is highly unstable, lacking any firm sense of continuity over time:

> [H]e or she does not have our experience of temporal continuity . . . but is condemned to live a perpetual present with which the various moments of his or her past have little connection and for which there is no conceivable future on the horizon. . . . The schizophrenic thus does not know personal identity in our sense, since our feeling of identity depends on our sense of the persistence of the "I" and the "me" over time.[43]

Interestingly, Sinai's subjective (and perhaps physical) fragmentation derives largely from an inability to maintain a sense of connectedness over time of precisely this kind. He himself suggests that his very project of writing the text that *Midnight's Children* supposedly represents is motivated by his poor memory, which would otherwise lead to a complete loss of the events being narrated, thus among other things suggesting his own belief (however parodied in the text) in the superiority of written forms of history to oral ones. And his fragmentation occurs specifically because he has lost "the awareness of oneself as a homogeneous entity in time, a blend of past and present, . . . the glue of personality, holding together our then and our now" (*MC*, 420). Moreover, though Sinai himself claims that the resultant lack of a historical memory is a specifically Indian national characteristic, the waning of historical sense is crucial to all of Jameson's characterizations of the postmodern. Sinai even specifically labels his fragmentation and the accompanying amnesia as a form of schizophrenia, and there are hints in the text that what Sinai sees as his literal fragmentation is merely a figment of his imagination, thus a symptom of his hyperalienated (postmodern) mental state.

Neither the textual fragmentation of *Midnight's Children* nor the personal fragmentation of its narrator is necessarily subversive of the ideology of late capitalism, which revels in such fragmentation. And by now it should be clear that Rushdie's use of a complex, nonlinear narrative form for the presentation of the postcolonial history of India is not necessarily subversive, either. In short, *Midnight's Children* is certainly an example of historiographic metafiction, but Jameson's discussions of postmodernism, to my mind, thoroughly negate Hutcheon's notion of such fictions as automatically subversive.

MIDNIGHT'S CHILDREN AND THE
MARXIST CHALLENGE TO BOURGEOIS HISTORIOGRAPHY

Midnight's Children seems to epitomize Jameson's description of certain postmodernist historical novels, which employ a "fantastic historiography" to

> make up a chronicle (generational or genealogical) whose grotesque succession and unrealistic personnel, ironic and melodramatic destinies, and heartrending (and virtually cinematographic) missed opportunities mime real ones, or to be more precise about it, resemble the dynastic annals of small-power kingdoms and realms very far from our own parochial "tradition."[44]

Moreover, Rushdie's book also seems susceptible to Jameson's charge that such postmodern historical narratives are generally "allergic to the priorities and commitments, let alone the responsibilities, of the various tediously committed kinds of partisan history."[45]

It is certainly the case that Sinai's undisciplined ramblings in *Midnight's Children* differ dramatically from the smoothly rational notion of historical procession that underlies bourgeois ideology and that is epitomized in the philosophy of Hegel. But the same can be said for most postmodernist fiction, which in Jameson's vision has no real subversive charge (or historical vision) whatsoever. For Jameson, of course, the real alternative to bourgeois scientific historiography must be Marxist scientific historiography. And it should be pointed out that many, and perhaps most, postcolonial historical novelists have appeared to agree with him. After all, the specific forms of bourgeois scientific historiography are not merely colonialist; they are deeply inscribed within the ideology of capitalism itself, having evolved during the period of the historical rise to power of the European bourgeoisie and being clearly designed to explain, legitimate, and even glorify Europe's new ruling bourgeois class. As Jameson puts it, bourgeois historiography was specifically designed during the emergent period of the bourgeoisie to describe the "bourgeois cultural revolution," that is, the long, slow historical process (extending roughly from the fifteenth to the nineteenth century) through which the bourgeoisie gradually supplanted the aristocracy and the Catholic Church as the most powerful ruling force in Europe. In particular, Jameson argues that the story of "the transition from feudalism to capitalism is what is secretly (or more deeply) being told in most contemporary historiography, whatever its ostensible content." Further, Jameson points out, this view of history makes the bourgeois cultural revolution "the only true Event of history."[46]

From this point of view, colonialism is merely one stage in the larger process of bourgeois modernization. Meanwhile, simply to question rationalist historiography undermines not only bourgeois ideology but also the Marxist challenge to that ideology. Put in an Indian context, to reject altogether the rational historicist premises upon which Nehru and his daughter attempted to found a modern, secular Indian state is also to challenge the historicist basis of the ideology of the Communist Party of India. Perhaps, then, it is no surprise that most of the criticism on Rushdie's engagement with history in *Midnight's Children* seems to ignore the Marxist tradition altogether (or at least to lump Marxist historiography in with other "Western" forms) and therefore does little to acknowledge that Western scientific historiography takes both bourgeois and antibourgeois forms. As Brennan notes at several points in *At Home in the World,* the same can be said for postcolonial studies in general, in which a call to respect traditional third-world cultures all too often translates into the suppression of the proud heritage of Marxist anticolonialism. And Brennan is not alone. Postcolonial theorists such as Aijaz Ahmad, Epifanio San Juan, and Arif Dirlik are also beginning at last to question the suspicious absence of Marxism (or of any specific critique of capitalism) in postcolonial discourse.[47]

Midnight's Children participates in this same suppression. For example, in addition to the absence of Indian nationalism from the text, also missing is the crucial role played by the Indian trades union movement in the fight for independence. Meanwhile, Rushdie does virtually nothing to critique capitalism, his few feeble jabs at the "Businessism" of postcolonial India having no real force. Almost needless to say, Rushdie also does not acknowledge the central importance of the Indian Communist Party in the development of the forms of political organization that were necessary to make the challenge to British rule effective. I say "almost" because Rushdie does at least grant the existence of a communist movement in India. However, he treats the movement in a consistently ironic mode that tends to make it look ridiculous and inept. For example, one of the central events in the book occurs when the midwife Mary Pereira, in an attempt to impress her communist boyfriend, Joseph D'Costa, exchanges the newborn infant son of the relatively rich Sinai family with that of the impoverished Wee Willie Winkie and his wife Vanita, who dies in childbirth. The latter infant, Saleem, then grows up thinking he is the child of the Sinais, only later to discover that he is actually the child of an illicit liaison between Vanita and the Englishman William Methwold. Meanwhile, the real son of the Sinais, Shiva, grows up in poverty and eventually becomes Saleem's alter ego and nemesis. One can unpack this overdetermined episode in any number of ways, but the switching of the infants certainly suggests a comically ineffective mode of social protest that changes essentially nothing, reversing the roles of the haves and have-nots but leaving the gap between them firmly in place. Joseph himself, it turns out, is equally ineffectual and is killed by the police soon afterward, despite the huge stockpile of weapons he has been accumulating for use in undefined terroristic activities (*MC,* 174).

Rushdie's treatment of communism in the remainder of the text is similarly snide and condescending, even if his description of communists seems, on the surface, reasonably sympathetic by Cold War standards. To an extent, communism functions in the text as a sort of road not taken, especially if one reads Saleem as an allegorical stand-in for the Indian nation. Thus one of the major communist figures in the text, the politician Qasim the Red, is originally introduced as the Muslim activist poet Nadir Khan, hiding out in the basement of Aadam Aziz's household for fear that he will be assassinated by terrorists. There, Nadir falls in love with Aadam's daughter, Mumtaz, who will later be renamed Amina Sinai. Nadir and Mumtaz are secretly married but cannot consummate the union because of his impotence. In short, if it had not been for his own inability to function, the budding communist Nadir might have fathered Saleem (and thus India).[48]

Later, Joseph's ghost returns to haunt Mary, while Nadir and Amina continue a clandestine relationship, both motifs suggesting communism's stubborn refusal to go away and India's continuing (illicit) flirtation with communism in the postcolonial years. In *Midnight's Children,* this flirtation peaks in 1957, when young Saleem first discovers that his mother is secretly meeting Nadir/Qasim and when the Communist Party poses its first serious electoral challenge to Nehru's Congress Party, emerging from the elections of that year as the leading opposition party. Meanwhile, in these same elections, 10-year-old Shiva begins his career as a Congress Party thug by leading his gang in attacks on voters who might otherwise vote against the Congress candidates. Qasim, who has for some time been doing good works (with Amina's help) among the poor, emerges as a serious candidate for parliament but is narrowly defeated under suspicious circumstances that include not only Shiva's childhood terrorism but the stealing of ballots and the stuffing of ballot boxes (*MC,* 265).

Communists again emerge as important figures later in the book, but again, communism is treated by Rushdie essentially as a joke. In particular, Saleem becomes involved with a group of communists whose figuration in the book as "magicians" not only runs counter to the materialist basis of Marxism but suggests that communists are charlatans whose political program is primarily composed, as it were, of smoke and mirrors. After a comic invocation of the rhetoric of anticommunism in which the magicians are announced as "reds! Insurrectionists, public menaces, the scum of the earth—a community of the godless" (*MC,* 474), Saleem, his true heritage of poverty having been revealed, discovers that he finds the communists a congenial group. He begins to work with them, impressed that they seem able to grip reality "so powerfully that they could bend it every which way in the service of their arts" (*MC,* 476). Picture Singh, the snake-charmer leader of the communist magicians, struggles against factional disputes, attempting to formulate a distinctly Indian form of socialism free of foreign influence, but of course he fails to do so, despite his considerable skills as an illusionist. Meanwhile, Rushdie subtly suggests that Saleem's attraction to the communists is misguided, as when he informs us that Picture Singh was "no lover of democracy," a fact Saleem earlier failed to appreciate because he was caught "in the grip of my fever-for-revolution" (*MC,* 477). In short, communist revolutionary fervor is presented as a sort of sickness.

Tellingly, Picture Singh's true ineffectuality comes to the fore soon afterward when he initially fails to oppose Indira Gandhi's declaration of the Emergency, the single political event that comes in for Rushdie's most sustained and virulent criticism.[49] Appalled by Mrs. Gandhi's move, Saleem turns to Picture Singh for leadership, but the latter does nothing, causing Saleem to wonder if he is, in fact, nothing but a snake charmer after all (*MC,* 508). By the time bulldozers and government troops, armed, significantly, with Russian-supplied weapons, move in to raze the slum long occupied by the magicians, it is too late: "What chance do Communist wizards have against socialist rifles?" (*MC,* 512). Picture Singh is driven into hiding, eventually becoming little more than a shadow of his former self, meanwhile forgetting what Mrs. Gandhi did to him and the other magicians during the Emergency and therefore failing to mount any real opposition to her rule. In short, Rushdie seems to be suggesting, Picture Singh proceeds very much like Indian Communism itself, of which he is clearly an allegorical representative. Picture Singh's deterioration is attributed largely to the effect of the washerwoman and wet nurse Durga, whose massive breasts are matched only by her bulging biceps. Meanwhile, Mother Durga, described by Gayatri Spivak as a "luminous fighting figure," was sometimes employed as a figure of nationalist resistance to the British rule of India. *Midnight's Children* seems to suggest in a number of ways that both Indian nationalism (which for him seems almost synonymous with the Congress Party) and Indian Communism suffered from an unhealthy collusion between the two.

Durga is only one of the numerous images of feminine menace that occur with disturbing frequency in Rushdie's text. Working-class women, who typically have massive muscles and large, hairy arms, seem especially threatening, though the central image of sinister feminine menace in *Midnight's Children* is Indira Gandhi, who is generally identified simply as the Widow and in ways that often quite explicitly suggest that she may have been responsible for her husband's death (*MC,* 502). Later, Mrs. Gandhi quite literally becomes the epitome of the castrating female, divesting Sinai of his testicles and thus, presumably, cutting off the original promise offered to future generations by the new Indian state at the moment of independence. Gender is crucial to Sinai's account of the Emergency and of Mrs. Gandhi in general, and we should not be too quick to equate Sinai's attitude toward Mrs. Gandhi with that of Rushdie. After all, Rushdie goes to great pains to suggest that Sinai's contempt for Mrs. Gandhi is part of a larger pattern of the narrator's misogynism and sexual insecurity. Further, Rushdie also makes it clear that Sinai is in many ways simply jealous that it is Indira Gandhi, and not him, who eventually comes to be considered the embodiment of the Indian state. Moreover, Sinai's description of the Emergency clearly relates to his own megalomania, as when he concludes that "the truest, deepest motive behind the declaration of the State of Emergency was the smashing, the pulverizing, the irreversible discombobulation of the children of midnight" (*MC*, 427).

Still, however problematic Sinai's own position, Rushdie also does nothing to dispute Sinai's account of Mrs. Gandhi as the menacing Widow.[50] Rushdie's treatment of Mrs. Gandhi and the Emergency in his essay "Dynasty" is quite similar to Sinai's treatment of the same topics in *Midnight's Children*.[51] A careful look shows that Rushdie's treatment of Mrs. Gandhi (born, the text notes, in November of 1917, that is, during the same month as the Russian Revolution) may be part of the basic anticommunist subtext of *Midnight's Children*.[52] Indeed, the figuration of the Widow, during the Emergency and otherwise, is quite typical of Cold War anticommunist rhetoric, and it is important to recognize the central role Cold War politics play in the generally negative perception of the Emergency in the West. It was, for example, typical of Indian opponents of Mrs. Gandhi to claim that she was playing into the hands of the communists in declaring the Emergency. Note the description of Mrs. Gandhi, by her imprisoned political opponent Jayaprakash Narayan, as little more than a communist dupe:

> As for the Congress party, I do not understand its spinelessness. Of course, quite a number of Congressmen are disguised communists.... Behind them is the Right CPI [Communist Party of India] and then behind it is Soviet Russia. Russia has backed Mrs. Gandhi to the hilt. Because the farther Mrs. Gandhi advances on her present course, the more powerful an influence will Russia have over this country. A time may come when, having squeezed the juice out of Mrs. Gandhi, the Russians through the CPI and their Trojan horses within the Congress will dump her on the garbage heap of history and install in her place their own man.[53]

Weirdly, Narayan then goes on to suggest that the establishment of this communist dictatorship will make of India another Pakistan—as if Pakistan had not long served as an *anti*communist dictatorship and as a key pawn in the anti-Soviet strategies of the West in the Cold War. But then Cold War propaganda was never particularly concerned with making sense as long as it achieved the desired emotional effect. Indeed, the basically irrational character of official Western rhetoric during the Cold War should give pause to any who want to assume that any discourse, merely by being opposed to rationality, is somehow opposed to official authority.

In the "Dynasty" essay, Rushdie himself quite openly and intentionally attempts to link his depiction of Mrs. Gandhi to the anti-Stalinist rhetoric of the Cold War when he argues that the political power of the Nehru-Gandhi family is based on a "cult of personality," thus borrowing the phrase Khrushchev employed, in the famous denunciation of 1956, to describe Stalin's political strategies.[54] Similarly, the criticisms of the Emergency in

Midnight's Children often appear to have been directly borrowed from Cold War descriptions of the Stalinist "Terror," descriptions of which Rushdie has shown evidence of uncritical acceptance.[55] In addition to the obligatory charges of torture, terror, repression, censorship, suspension of civil rights, persecution of political enemies, and so on, Rushdie's central charge against Mrs. Gandhi and her regime is that they manipulated history to their own advantage, rewriting and reconstructing the past as it suited the political needs of the present moment. Among other things, this theme in *Midnight's Children* recalls Western works like Orwell's *Nineteen Eighty-four,* a central motif of which is the thoroughgoing attempt of the Party of Oceania (a satire of the Communist Party of the Stalinist Soviet Union, though with critiques of Western bourgeois society thrown in as well) to manipulate the past in ways that further their own power.[56]

Of course, Rushdie himself is attempting to rewrite history in his description of the Emergency, which calls attention to aspects of that phenomenon that were legitimately problematic but which also blatantly falsifies historical fact to make a rhetorical point. For one thing, the dictatorial powers Mrs. Gandhi invoked during the Emergency were consistent with the Indian Constitution, derived from the political legacy of the British past, not from Stalin. For another, Rushdie, showing a typical Western Cold War contempt for the economic, brushes off the very genuine economic progress that was made during Mrs. Gandhi's years in office. Thus, in a line made inherently sarcastic because of the time-worn cliché about Mussolini's fascist Italy (and apparently borrowed from his old mentor Wolpert), Rushdie has Sinai admit that during the Emergency, India's trains for once ran on time (*MC,* 517).[57] Moreover, unable to uncover any actual horrors that could be attributed directly to Mrs. Gandhi and that would make the economic advances made under the Emergency appear insignificant in comparison, Rushdie simply manufactures horrors, including a graphic description of the forced sterilization of Sinai and the other children of midnight.[58] Lipscomb, in the typical admiring style of Rushdie scholars, tries to argue that this motif subverts official historical accounts by including the "too-horrible-to-be-true," which is missing in the work of "area experts" such as Wolpert.[59] But surely something that is not true *should* be omitted from historical accounts.

Lipscomb's move here is not, of course, unusual, the truth having come in for considerable attack as a somehow authoritarian (or at least simplistic and unsophisticated) category in much recent critical discourse. But to undermine the truth is surely the central strategy of global capitalism, as Terry Eagleton has almost desperately argued in the face of the recent postmodern distrust of the true:

> Gross deception, whitewash, cover-up and lying through one's teeth: these are no longer sporadic, regrettable necessities of our form of life but permanently and structurally essential to it. In such conditions, the true facts—concealed,

suppressed, distorted—can be in themselves politically explosive; and those who have developed the nervous tic of placing such vulgar terms as "truth" and "fact" in fastidiously distancing scare quotes should be careful to avoid a certain collusion between their own high-toned theoretical gestures and the most banal, routine political strategies of the capitalist power-structure.[60]

Again, one should be cautious in attributing the misrepresentation of the Emergency in *Midnight's Children* directly to Rushdie, who goes to great pains to inform us that his narrator is an inveterate liar. Indeed, Sinai directly links his own manipulation of historical facts to the Orwellian attempts of the postindependence Indian government to manipulate perceptions of reality: "I have been only the humblest of jugglers-with-facts; . . . in a country where the truth is what it is instructed to be, reality quite literally ceases to exist" (*MC,* 389). Again, however, Rushdie does nothing to challenge Sinai's fundamentally negative account of Mrs. Gandhi, while critics have tended to see Sinai's mendacity as a sign of sophistication. Of course, to an extent, Rushdie's conflation of Indira Gandhi with Stalin, and of India during the Emergency with the Soviet Union during the "Terror" of the 1930s, is not surprising. By 1980, after decades of Stalinist propaganda, it was almost inevitable for anticommunist intellectuals to attempt to equate any political regime they disliked with that of the Stalinist Soviet Union. Moreover, Rushdie's mention of the Russian rifles Mrs. Gandhi's troops wielded during the Emergency also calls attention to the ability of Mrs. Gandhi, following in this sense in the footsteps of her father, to avoid being drawn into the gravitational field of the anticommunist West and to maintain disturbingly (from a Western point of view) good relations with the Soviet Union, especially during the Emergency, when the Soviet presence in India became increasingly prominent.[61] Indeed, if Mrs. Gandhi's policies during the Emergency were reminiscent of Stalin's efforts at rapid modernization of the Soviet Union in the face of the earlier emergency posed by the rapidly growing threat of fascist invasion, it is also the fact that Nehru, with his intense emphasis on centralized planning of modernization and industrialization (implemented through a series of "Five-Year Plans"), had already drawn on Stalin's successes in the 1930s as a developmental model. Mrs. Gandhi went even further. Not only did she originally consolidate her power in 1969 by leapfrogging the Congress Party with the support of a left-wing coalition that included Communists but she helped solidify her power in 1971 by adding the Keralan Communist leader S. Mohan Kumaramangalam to her cabinet and by signing a 20-year pact of friendship and mutual cooperation with the Soviet Union.

It should also be pointed out that Rushdie's use of Cold War rhetoric to condemn Mrs. Gandhi (and the widespread critical acceptance of his use of that rhetoric) may be part of the sweeping rejection of modernization as a whole that has somehow become central to postcolonial discourse in recent years. For postcolonial scholars, modernization and the entire legacy of the Enlightenment seem to have become synonymous with colonialism, so that a genuine respect for the peoples and cultures of the formerly colonized world requires a rejection of the entire phenomenon of modernization, however much those peoples and cultures might profit from a large dose of technological and industrial progress. Thus, paralleling the postmodern rejection of Enlightenment metanarratives, such postcolonial scholars reject bourgeois and antibourgeois narratives alike, forgetting, as Dirlik notes, that the Enlightenment, however complicit in capitalism and colonialism, "was also the source of new critiques of oppression and exploitation in societies both in an outside of Europe."[62]

Rushdie is perfectly right, of course, that the urban-renewal projects that were part of the Twenty-Point Program were sometimes administered with insufficient sensitivity to the slum dwellers who were displaced by this renewal. Similarly, there were no doubt local instances of overzealous implementation of the government's official policy of offering incentives to encourage sterilization. Urban renewal, however, was designed to help slum dwellers, not persecute them, while, contrary to the account given in *Midnight's Children,* there were no instances in which suspected dissidents were rounded up, imprisoned, and then forcibly castrated because of their perceived threat to the Gandhi regime. Moreover, the fact remains that urban renewal was, and is, sorely needed in India and that (however blasphemous such remarks might seem within the context of most recent postcolonial discourse) India, as a nation crippled by overpopulation, can use all the sterilizations it can get.

Both urban renewal and radical population control were crucial to Mrs. Gandhi's attempts to modernize India, and we should recall that modernization, not totalitarianism, was the major goal of the Emergency. Meanwhile, it seems necessary to ask, given my previous argument, whether the wholesale rejection of modernization in postcolonial studies might in fact be a legacy of the anti-Soviet propaganda of the Cold War. Here, one might note Eric Hobsbawm's recent argument that in retrospect, we will eventually see the major event of the twentieth century as the culmination of "the seven or eight millennia of human history that began with the invention of agriculture in the stone age, if only because it ended the long era when the overwhelming majority of the human race lived by growing food and herding animals."[63] Hobsbawm, in short, sees modernization as the principal movement of history, based on a relatively conventional Marxist notion of the movement of history as shifts in mode of production. In addition, while Hobsbawm argues that the Russian Revolution was far and away the most important single historical event of the twentieth century, he does not see the twentieth century as centrally informed by the Cold War opposition between capitalism and communism. For Hobsbawm, the Soviets, thwarted in their initial plans to export revolution worldwide, had little choice but to set about the desperate project of building socialism in the huge, impoverished, and unruly political entity that had been imperial Russia. Recognizing that this could not be done in a poor, backward country, the Soviets set forth on an astonishingly ambitious (and sometimes frightfully ruthless) campaign of rapid modernization based on a combination of "an all-out offensive against the cultural backwardness of the notoriously 'dark,' ignorant, illiterate and superstitious masses with an all-out drive for technological modernization and industrial revolution" (*AE,* 376).

This project was not without its impressive successes. As Hobsbawm points out, Soviet economic policies "turned the USSR into a major industrial economy in just a few years and one capable, as czarist Russia had not been, of surviving and winning the war against Germany in spite of the temporary loss of areas containing a third of her population and, in many industries, half the industrial plant." (*AE,* 382). Moreover, Soviet policies provided a social safety net unheard of in the centuries of czarist rule, while in education the "transformation of a largely illiterate country into the modern USSR was, by any standards, a towering achievement" (*AE,* 382). Nevertheless, the intense emphasis on modernization under Stalin meant that the socialist project of social and political emancipation had to take a backseat. The ultimate result was the demise of the Soviet state, which should not necessarily, according to Hobsbawm, be interpreted as discrediting Marxism. Indeed, that demise proves Marx to have been right in his insistence that socialism could be established only after human beings have reached a certain stage of material development, a stage that postrevolutionary Russia had clearly not reached (*AE,* 496–97).

The upshot is that Stalinism turned out to be an extremely effective way to modernize and industrialize a backward nation, even if it was not a very successful program for building socialism. Indeed, the Stalinist transformation of the Soviet Union served as a model for would-be modernizers throughout the third world, thus posing a potentially serious threat to global capitalism, which depends upon the continuing economic backwardness of the third world to maintain the new international division of labor on which global capitalism centrally depends. This threat may perhaps help account for the seemingly inexplicable level of hysteria that informed Western Cold War propaganda, which thus had to discredit Stalinism at any cost. But if the anti-Stalinist propaganda of the Cold War was thus designed with the ulterior motif of helping to retard the modernization, and thus to enable the continued exploitation, of the third world, then postcolonial scholars probably need to take a long look at their own recent adoption of so many Cold War strategies, including a thoroughgoing rejection of modernization as a form of neocolonial exploitation designed to destroy traditional cultures and further the cultural hegemony of the West. Indeed, from this point of view, the recent tendency of postcolonial scholars to see modernization as a capitalist plot is precisely backward: modernization may be the only way to overcome capitalist exploitation, and it may be the recent demonization of modernization that is the real capitalist plot. After all, nobody seems to be opposing modernization in America or Britain; it is only in Africa and Asia that modernization is supposedly evil.

These are weighty issues that obviously go well beyond the world of literature and culture. Still, literature and culture played crucial roles in Cold War rhetoric, especially in the concerted efforts of Western capital to portray its own culture as complex, sophisticated, and multivalent, in opposition to the supposedly simplistic, authoritarian, and monological culture of the Soviet Union. Critics of postcolonial (or postmodernist) literature should think twice before adopting these same aesthetic criteria in their promotion of the subversive potential of "complex" and "sophisticated" texts such as *Midnight's Children*. Similarly, if I am right that the demonization of Soviet modernization during the Cold War was at least partly motivated by a capitalist desire to impede the development of the third world, then postcolonial scholars should probably think twice before concluding that all-out assaults on modernization (and attendant concepts such as rationality, progress, and technology) are the best way to oppose the exploitation of the third world by global capital.

There can be no doubt that multiculturalism in literary studies is a good thing insofar as it seeks to further intercultural communication and respect. But an insufficiently theorized multiculturalism that simply repeats the clichés of the Cold War is by no means automatically desirable. Further, however good it might be that the literature and culture of the third world have received such increased visibility in first-world academic discourse in recent years, it is also the case that pointing out that third-world novels are just as rich as first-world ones potentially diverts attention from the fact that first-world people, in a material sense, are vastly richer than their third-world counterparts—and largely at the expense of those counterparts. In our attempts to call attention to the positive virtues of third-world culture we should seek to avoid this kind of obfuscation. Meanwhile, detailed consideration of the complex cultural relationship between the first and third worlds threatens to divert attention from the economic realities that define the true, and ultimately rather simple, relationship between the two "worlds," which are by now really just part of a single world system structured around international class differences. We should therefore eschew the uncritical endorsement of fashionable postcolonial concepts, such as complexity and hybridity, that tend to obscure these differences. Rushdie's texts, with their inherent complexity and hybridity—and with their widespread critical acceptance in the West as masterpieces of either postcolonial or postmodern sophistication, or both—should provide a fertile ground for the exploration of these issues. Rushdie scholars should therefore take the lead in the effort to ensure that multicultural literary scholarship actually achieves what it sets out to do rather than simply advancing the cause of global capitalism in ways that were mapped out during the Cold War effort both to destroy the Soviet Union and to preserve the uneven development that makes the current global division of labor possible.

Notes

1. Salman Rushdie, *Midnight's Children* (1980; reprint, London: Penguin, 1991), 3; hereafter cited in the text as *MC*.
2. M. Keith Booker, "Beauty and the Beast: Dualism as Despotism in the Fiction of Salman Rushdie," *ELH* 57 (1990): 977–97; M. Keith Booker, *"Finnegans Wake* and *The Satanic Verses:* Two Modern Myths of the Fall," *Critique* 32 (Spring 1991): 190–207.
3. Salman Rushdie, *Imaginary Homelands: Essays and Criticism, 1981–1991* (London: Penguin, 1991), 65.
4. Brennan's 1987 Columbia dissertation later became *Salman Rushdie and the Third World: Myths of the Nation* (New York: St. Martin's, 1989). To give credit where credit is due, note that Fawzia Afzal-Khan's earlier (1986) Tufts dissertation was devoted to Rushdie and three other "Indo-English" novelists. This dissertation was later published as *Cultural Imperialism and the Indo-English Novel: Genre and Ideology in R. K. Narayan, Anita Desai, Kamala Markandaya, and Salman Rushdie* (University Park: Pennsylvania State University Press, 1993).
5. Timothy Brennan, *At Home in the World: Cosmopolitanism Now* (Cambridge, Mass.: Harvard University Press, 1997), 71.
6. Paul Nizan, *The Watchdogs: Philosophers of the Established Order,* trans. Paul Fittingoff (1932; reprint, New York: Monthly Review Press, 1971), 40. Brennan quotes this passage on p. 40, where he notes that it "might well have come from Gramsci."
7. Actually, Rushdie has expressed a discomfort with being placed in *any* single category, though the category he seems to dislike most is that of "commonwealth literature." See his essay " 'Commonwealth Literature' Does Not Exist," in *Imaginary Homelands,* 61–70.
8. G. W. F. Hegel, *The Philosophy of History,* trans. J. Sibree (New York: Dover, 1956), 91, 99.
9. Georg Lukács, *The Historical Novel,* trans. Hannah Mitchell and Stanley Mitchell (Lincoln: University of Nebraska Press, 1983).
10. For a discussion of the numerous parallels between the historical novels produced by African postcolonial writers and those produced by writers of Soviet socialist realism, see M. Keith Booker and Dubravka Juraga, "The Reds and the Blacks: The Historical Novel in The Soviet Union and Postcolonial Africa," *Studies in the Novel* 29, no. 3 (1997): 274–96.
11. Ngugi wa Thiong'o, *Moving the Centre: The Struggle for Cultural Freedoms* (London: James Currey, 1993), 97.
12. Asha Kaushik, *Politics, Aesthetics, and Culture: A Study of the Indo-Anglian Political Novel* (New Delhi: Manohar, 1988), 71.
13. On realism in the Indian novel, see Meenakshi Mukherjee, *Realism and Reality: The Novel and Society in India* (New Delhi: Oxford University Press, 1985).
14. Michael Valdez Moses, *The Novel and the Globalization of Culture* (New York: Oxford University Press, 1995), 108.
15. See M. Keith Booker, "The Historical Novel in Ayi Kwei Armah and David Caute: African Literature, Socialist Literature, and the Bourgeois Cultural Tradition," *Critique* 38, no. 3 (1997): 235–48.
16. See Ngugi's discussion of the language question in "The Language of African Literature," in his *Decolonising the Mind: The Politics of Language in African Literature* (London: James Currey, 1986), 4–33.

17. Ouloguem has been widely criticized for lifting passages almost verbatim from novels by authors such as Graham Greene, André Schwartz-Bart, and Guy de Maupassant. But for a spirited (poststructuralist) defense of Ouloguem's textual strategies, see Christopher Miller, *Blank Darkness: Africanist Discourse in French* (Chicago: University of Chicago Press, 1985), 216–45.

18. A similar charge has frequently been leveled against Rushdie, especially by Indian critics. Note Kaushik's concern that Rushdie, in *Midnight's Children,* shows an "essential western tendency to present India as either exotic or antiquated" (111).

19. Salman Rushdie, "*Midnight's Children* and *Shame:* An Interview," *Kunapipi* 7, no. 1 (1985): 8.

20. On Hegel's attempt to naturalize the notion of the state by making it a mirror of the family, see Partha Chatterjee, *The Nation and Its Fragments: Colonial and Postcolonial Histories* (Princeton, N.J.: Princeton University Press, 1993), 230–34.

21. M. Keith Booker, *Colonial Power/Colonial Texts: India in the Modern British Novel* (Ann Arbor: University of Michigan Press, 1997), 139.

22. Salman Rushdie, "India at Five-0," *Time* (11 August 1997). For a detailed meditation on the paradoxical viability of India as a political entity that in some ways reads almost like a companion to Rushdie's work, see Sunil Khilnani, *The Idea of India* (London: Hamish Hamilton, 1997).

23. David Lipscomb, "Caught in a Strange Middle Ground: Contesting History in Salman Rushdie's *Midnight's Children,*" *Diaspora* 1, no. 2 (1991): 163–88. See Stanley Wolpert, *A New History of India* (Oxford University Press, 1977). Wolpert's book has now gone through several editions (at this writing, the fifth edition was just released), but only the first edition was available to Rushdie when writing *Midnight's Children.*

24. Brennan, 84.

25. Meanwhile, the main reaction to Gandhi's death in the text is Amina Sinai's ecstatic expression of relief that he was not killed by a Muslim, which might have caused Hindu mobs to seek retribution against Muslim families such as the Sinais (169).

26. Rushdie was no doubt aware of this fact; see Wolpert, 260.

27. Neil ten Kortenaar, "*Midnight's Children* and the Allegory of History," *Ariel* 26, no. 2 (1995): 41–62.

28. Alok Rai, "Black Skin, Black Masks," in *Indian-English Fiction, 1980–90: An Assessment,* ed. Niufer E. Bharucha and Vilas Sarang (New Delhi: B. R. Publishing Corporation, 1994), 96–97.

29. In another interview, Rushdie emphasizes the commonality between the techniques of the Indian oral tradition and those typically associated with Western postmodernism. See David Brooks, "An Interview with Salman Rushdie," *Phoenix Review* 19 (Spring-Winter 1984): 57.

30. Fredric Jameson, *Postmodernism, or, the Cultural Logic of Late Capitalism* (Durham, N.C.: Duke University Press, 1991). Jameson's identification of postmodernism as the "cultural logic of late capitalism" dates back at least as far as his essay with the same title as his book, published in *New Left Review* 146 (1984): 59–92.

31. Christopher Norris, *What's Wrong with Postmodernism: Critical Theory and the Ends of Philosophy* (Baltimore, Md.: Johns Hopkins University Press, 1990), 4.

32. Linda Hutcheon, *A Poetics of Postmodernism: History, Theory, Fiction* (New York: Routledge, 1988), 162–63. See Hutcheon's attempt elsewhere to argue that postcolonial and postmodernist fiction are pursuing very similar projects, apparently because, in her view, both employ irony as a central rhetorical strategy. In addition to its obvious deficiencies (irony being, among other things, the favorite mode of bourgeois and colonialist literature as well), Hutcheon's argument is further undermined by the fact that her principal examples of "postcolonial" literature are texts written by white Canadian writers, who certainly participate in the

postcolonial project but are surely postcolonial in a weaker sense than, say, Ngugi or Lamming. See Linda Hutcheon, " 'Circling the Downspouts of Empire': Post-Colonialism and Postmodernism," *Ariel* 20, no. 4 (1989): 149–75.

33. It is not, of course, that Hutcheon literally forgets about Marxism, which she addresses at several points in her book. But apparently offended by the refusal of many Marxist critics to share her enthusiasm for the postmodern, she dismisses Marxist critiques of postmodernism essentially as so much sour grapes, claiming that Marxist critics are jealous because postmodernist texts "make overt what certain kinds of Marxist criticism . . . claim is hidden and only revealed by their particular kinds of analysis" (211).

34. Hutcheon, 113–15.

35. For a discussion of Baudrillard's Orientalism, see Neil Lazarus, "Doubting the New World Order: Marxism, Realism, and the Claims of Postmodernism Social Theory," *Differences: A Journal of Feminist Cultural Studies* 3, no. 3 (1991): 94–138, 97–98.

36. Fredric Jameson, *Signatures of the Visible* (New York: Routledge, 1992), 23. A similar notion is at stake in Jameson's somewhat notorious essay "Third-World Literature in the Era of Multinational Capitalism," *Social Text* 15 (1986): 65–88. See my discussion of this essay in the introduction to this volume.

37. Ziauddin Sardar, *Postmodernism and the Other: The New Imperialism of Western Culture* (London: Pluto, 1998), 197.

38. Jameson 1986, 69.

39. Walter Benjamin, *Illuminations,* trans. Harry Zohn (New York: Harcourt, Brace, and World, 1955), 243–44.

40. V. S. Naipaul, *India: A Million Mutinies Now* (London: Penguin, 1990), 387.

41. Karel Čapek, "An Ordinary Life," in *Three Novels by Karel Čapek,* trans. M. Weatherall and R. Weatherall (Highland Park, N.J.: Catbird Press, 1990), 313–464. It should be pointed out, however, that Čapek, though writing from the geographic center of Europe, is also writing in a multicultural situation, and his Czechoslovakia, born in the breakup of the Austro-Hungarian Empire after World War I, is a postcolonial society of sorts.

42. Interestingly, Ahmad, in his response to Jameson's discussion of third-world national allegory, evinces *Gravity's Rainbow* as an example of a similar allegorical phenomenon in Western literature. Ahmad, *In Theory: Classes, Nations, Literatures* (London: Verso, 1992), 110.

43. Fredric Jameson, "Postmodernism and Consumer Society," in *The Anti-Aesthetic: Essays on Postmodern Culture,* ed. Hal Foster (Port Townsend, Wash.: Bay Press, 1983), 119.

44. Jameson 1983, 368.

45. Ibid., 369.

46. Jameson 1992, 226–27.

47. See Ahmad; Epifanio San Juan, *Beyond Postcolonial Theory* (New York: St. Martin's, 1998); Arif Dirlik, *The Postcolonial Aura: Third World Criticism in the Age of Global Capitalism* (Boulder, Colo.: Westview Press, 1997).

48. That Mumtaz/Amina is not the biological mother of Saleem does not change this point. Saleem is reared by Amina and her family and becomes who he is through them.

49. Note that Rushdie's later treatment of Mrs. Gandhi in *The Moor's Last Sigh* is somewhat more conciliatory; there, he at least acknowledges the widespread sense of genuine grief Indians felt after her assassination.

50. Rushdie himself was a consistent critic of the Thatcher regime in Britain, which is in itself understandable, even laudable. However, to criticize both Mrs. Gandhi and Mrs. Thatcher in similar terms tends to suggest a hostility toward strong women in positions of political power. See, for example, Rushdie's suggestion of parallels between Thatcherite Britain and Nazi Germany (made using the rhetorical device of continually repeating that he realizes the two are different) in his essay "The New Empire within Britain," in *Imaginary Homelands,* 129–38.

51. *Imaginary Homelands,* 47–52.

52. In a text that so often calls attention to the significance of fatidic dates, one should not discount the fact that Rushdie calls attention to the date of Mrs. Gandhi's birth (*MC,* 501).

53. Jayaprakash Narayan, *Prison Diary, 1975,* ed. A. B. Shah (Bombay: Popular Prakashan, 1977), 3–4.

54. *Imaginary Homelands,* 50–51.

55. In his essay "Outside the Whale," for example, Rushdie repeats one of the most overworked (and inaccurate) clichés of the Cold War, conflating Stalin with Hitler as examples of the "horrors" of the 1930s (*Imaginary Homelands,* 96). Perhaps the most widely disseminated account of the Stalinist "Terror" is Cold War hack Robert Conquest, *The Great Terror: Stalin's Purge of the Thirties* (New York: Macmillan, 1969). For a far more balanced and scholarly account that disputes the centrality of terror to the Soviet experience of the 1930s, see Robert W. Thurston, *Life and Terror in Stalin's Russia, 1934–1941* (New Haven, Conn.: Yale University Press, 1996).

56. In an obvious reference to the continual revisions of history under Stalinism (but also in a general reference to the fact that the official history of the past is written by those who hold power in the present), the key element of the ideology of Orwell's party involves what they call the "mutability of the past." "Who controls the present," runs a related slogan, "controls the past." See my discussion of this motif in *The Dystopian Impulse in Modern Literature: Fiction as Social Criticism* (Westport, Conn.: Greenwood Press, 1994), 86–88.

57. Wolpert notes that Indian supporters of the Emergency, apparently with no irony, proudly proclaimed the new punctuality of India's railway system as an example of the success of the Emergency's Twenty-Point Program of economic reform (411).

58. Scenes of such genital violence are a favorite motif of postmodernist literature. See my discussion of this phenomenon in *Techniques of Subversion in Modern Literature* (Gainesville: University of Florida Press, 1991), 132–61.

59. Lipscomb, 177.

60. Terry Eagleton, *The Ideology of the Aesthetic* (London: Basil Blackwell, 1990), 379.

61. See Hemen Ray, *The Enduring Friendship: Soviet-Indian Relations in Mrs. Gandhi's Days* (New Delhi: Abhinav Publications, 1989); Vinod Bhatia, *Indira Gandhi and Indo-Soviet Relations* (New Delhi: Panchsheel Publishers, 1987); S. S. Rai, *The Red Star and the Lotus: The Political Dynamics of Indo-Soviet Relations* (New Delhi: Konark Publications, 1990).

62. Dirlik, xi. In this same mode, see Göran Therborn's characterization of Marxism as a critique of modernity from within in his essay "Dialectics of Modernity: On Critical Theory and the Legacy of Twentieth-Century Marxism," *New Left Review* 215 (1996): 59–81.

63. Eric Hobsbawm, *The Age of Extremes: A History of the World, 1914–1991* (New York: Pantheon, 1994), 9; hereafter cited in the text as *AE*.

Index

◆

Abrahamian, Ervand, 52, 73, 75
Achebe, Chinua, 132–33, 151, 196, 204, 277, 288, 291
Adams, Ian, 151
Adnan, Etel, 127
Adorno, Theodor, 68
African literature, 132–33, 174, 194, 288–91, 293, 310. *See also individual authors*
Ahmad, Aijaz: critique of Jameson on national allegory, 6–7, 167, 176, 186, 248; and postcolonial theory, 15, 301; on Rushdie's *Shame*, 13, 20–24, 29, 39, 47, 48
Ahmed, Eqbal, 59, 73, 75, 90–91, 94, 100, 104, 153, 221, 252, 279
Akhtar, Shabbir, 59, 61, 64, 66, 74–76, 127
Aksyonov, Vassily, 10, 182, 186
Albee, Edward, 114
Alcoff, Linda, 48
Ali, Agha Shahid, 118, 127
Ali, Ahmed, 79
Ali, Tariq, 119, 112, 190, 214
Alighieri, Dante, 32, 68
al-Shaykh, Hanan, 127
Amis, Martin, 110
Anand, Mulk Raj, 2, 10, 115, 148–49, 180, 289
Anantanarayanan, M., 2
Anderson, Benedict, 48, 55, 74, 246, 252
Appadurai, Arjun, 69, 76, 141
Appiah, Kwame Anthony, 130, 150
Appignanesi, Lisa, 49, 73
Arabian Nights, The, 80, 93–96, 104, 113
Aravamudan, Srinivas, 119, 128, 153

Armah, Ayi Kwei, 167–68, 186, 289, 294, 310
Asad, Talal, 73–74, 76
Attar, Farid ud-din, 93, 104

Babri Mosque, 10, 63, 138, 143, 161
Bader, Rudolph, 13
Bahri, Deepika, 150
Baker, James, 108
Bakhtin, Mikhail M., 76, 170–72, 175, 185–86, 227, 239, 245–46, 248
Banerjee, Ashutosh, 232–33, 247
Banville, John, 296
Basu, Latika, 132
Baudrillard, Jean, 295–96
Beckett, Samuel, 4
Belsey, Catherine, 48
Ben Jelloun, Tahar, 128
Benjamin, Walter, 11, 205–24, 298
Berger, John, 119, 125, 296
Bhabha, Homi, 3, 15, 48, 73, 83–88, 102, 104–5, 134, 136, 140, 150, 152, 194, 203, 247; on hybridity, 12, 20, 133, 204; on nationalism, 252, 264, 280
Bharatiya Janata Party (BJP), 11, 70, 126, 160, 197
Bharucha, Rustom, 13, 185, 245, 281
Bhattacharya, Bhabani, 290
Birch, David, 14, 215, 224
Booker Prize, 1–3, 5–6, 251, 278, 291
Booker, M. Keith, 166–67, 185–86, 222, 224, 249, 311; on African literature, 168, 186, 310; on Rushdie, 1–15, 185–86, 226, 234, 238, 245, 247–48, 264–65, 280, 283–313

315

Brennan, Timothy, 5, 15, 53, 68, 72–73, 76, 78, 190, 203–4, 207, 221, 254, 293; dissertation on Rushdie, 6–7, 284, 310; on postcolonial theory, 12–13, 101–2, 128, 190, 285, 301; on *The Satanic Verses* Affair, 5, 9, 14, 77, 86, 104, 107–28
Brooks, David, 248
Brooks, Geraldine, 127
Brown, Judith M., 214, 222–23
Butler, Judith, 48

Calvino, Italo, 113
Cantor, Paul, 14
Capek, Karel, 298
Carey, Peter, 183, 187
Caribbean literature, 178–79, 194, 289–90. *See also individual authors*
Cary, Joyce, 106, 233
Chakrabarty, Dipesh, 228, 246
Chatterjee, Bankim Chandra, 289
Chatterjee, Partha, 74, 252, 281, 289, 311
Chatterjee, Upamanya, 12, 273–74
Chrisman, Laura, 151, 247
Christian, Barbara, 101
Clark, Katerina, 173, 185
Cold War, 13, 109, 116, 123, 125–27, 185, 252, 293, 302, 304, 313; impact on literary studies, 285–86, 295; impact on postcolonial studies, 12, 305, 307–10
Collins, Larry, 79, 105
Communism, 59, 61, 177, 263, 285, 306, 307
Communist Party, 181, 218, 293, 301–2, 304–5
Congress Party. *See* Indian National Congress
Conrad, Joseph, 46, 50, 172, 233
Conroy, Jack, 173
Coppola, Carlo, 94–95, 105
Couto, Maria, 3, 13
Cronin, Richard, 203–4, 270, 281
Cundy, Catherine, 15

Dahl, Roald, 53, 74
Das, Sisir Kumar, 282
Dasenbrock, Reed Way, 105
Datta, Jyotirmay, 132
De Boissière, Ralph, 289
Derrida, Jacques, 69, 246, 248
Desai, Anita, 149, 194, 203–4, 260, 272, 280–81

Desai, Boman, 12, 273–74
Desai, Morarji, 177, 209
Desani, G. V., 2, 127, 133–34, 152, 194–95, 204
Deshpande, Shashi, 1, 275
Devi, Mahasweta, 149
Dharwadkar, Aparna, 151
Dharwadkar, Vinay, 151
Dhondy, Faruk, 1
Dickens, Charles, 202
Dirlik, Arif, 150, 301, 307
Djebar, Assia, 127
Dobrenko, Evgeny, 173, 185
Doctorow, E. L., 296
Du Bois, W.E.B., 185, 286–87, 292–93
Duffy, Andrew Enda, 13
During, Simon, 151, 225, 245
Durix, Jean-Pierre, 13, 245, 247

Eagleton, Terry, 50, 151, 218, 220, 222, 224, 305
East, West, 6, 46–47, 105, 275, 282
Eco, Umberto, 296
Edmundsen, Mark, 14
Ellerby, Janet Mason, 14
El-Saadawi, Nawal, 127
Emergency (1975–1977), 11, 55, 190, 205–25, 249, 254, 263, 303–7. *See also* Gandhi, Indira

Fanon, Frantz, 12, 20, 178, 186, 192, 233; *Black Skin, White Masks*, 83, 105, 247; *The Wretched of the Earth*, 10, 56, 74, 154–68, 196–97, 203–4
Flanagan, Kathleen, 186, 267–68, 281
Fletcher, M. D., 13, 15, 185
Foley, Barbara, 170, 172, 185
Forster, E. M., 67, 233
Foucault, Michel, 295
Franco, Jean, 67, 69, 74, 76
Friedman, Jonathan, 133, 152
Fuentes, Carlos, 125, 126
Fuss, Diana, 48

Gandhi, Indira, 11, 48, 190, 197, 200, 222, 254, 294, 312–13; in *Midnight's Children*, 13, 28, 49, 55, 86–87, 180–81, 197, 200, 205–25, 252, 255, 280, 303–7. *See also* Emergency (1975–1977)
Gandhi, Mohandas K., 121, 132, 180, 189, 256, 289–90, 311

Gandhi, Rajiv, 63, 73, 76, 116, 188
Gandhi, Sanjay, 294
Garber, Marjorie, 32, 49
García Márquez, Gabriel, 4, 13, 80, 100, 291, 296
Gates, Henry Louis, Jr., 15
Ghosh, Amitav, 1, 12, 186, 273, 277, 282
Ghosh, Bishnupriya, 9, 129–53
Gibb, H.A.R., 92, 105, 123
Gokhale, Namita, 12, 273
Gordimer, Nadine, 6, 10, 178, 180, 186, 281
Gorky, Maxim, 185, 285–86, 288
Gorra, Michael, 10–11, 167, 188–204
Gramsci, Antonio, 166, 281, 285, 310
Grass, Günter, 4, 71, 74, 80, 112, 123, 127, 248; *The Tin Drum*, 13, 169, 201, 296
Greenblatt, Stephen, 48, 247
Greene, Graham, 111
Greer, Germaine, 119
Grewal, Inderpal, 13, 20–22, 24, 39, 47–48
Grimus, 3–4, 20, 31–33, 40–41, 47, 49, 86, 123
Gunn, Giles, 48
Guruprasad, Thakur, 260, 280

Habermas, Jürgen, 64, 75
Hai, Ambreen, 8, 16, 48
Hali, Altaf Husain, 84, 94, 95, 97–98, 100–101, 105–6
Halliday, Fred, 109, 119, 125, 127
Hamilton, Ian, 48
Hanaway, William L., Jr., 96, 99, 105
Hariharan, Githa, 275
Haroun and the Sea of Stories, 93–94, 96, 105, 113, 135, 152
Heffernan, James A., 48
Hegel, G.W.F., 233, 247, 287, 291–92, 300, 310
historical novels, 12, 68, 169–70, 184, 255, 282, 287–90, 292, 296, 300, 310
Hitchens, Christopher, 119
Hobsbawm, Eric, 252, 307–8
Hodge, Bob, 130–31, 134, 150–51
Hollander, John, 48
Howe, Geoffrey, 108, 124
Hume, Kathryn, 15
Huntington, Samuel, 127
Hutcheon, Linda, 31, 49, 76, 295–97, 299

Idris, Farhad, 10, 154–68

Imaginary Homelands, 47, 49, 77, 82, 105, 128, 136, 152–53, 166, 168, 210, 222–23, 245–46, 249, 259, 280–81, 310
Indian National Congress, 180, 189, 197, 213, 219, 223, 255, 256, 268, 276–77, 302–3, 306
Iyer, Sanjay, 275, 282

Jackson, Stevi, 48, 105
James T. Farrell, 173
James, C.L.R., 287
Jameson, Fredric, 170; on postmodernism, 67, 76, 186–87, 295–97, 299–300, 311; on Third-World literature, 6, 53–54, 74, 162, 167, 175, 176–78, 180–87, 235, 248, 252, 298
JanMohamed, Abdul, 12, 15, 105, 233, 247
Jinnah, Muhammed Ali, 90, 189
Johnson, Adrienne, 124, 153
Joyce, James, 4–5, 7, 14, 172, 244, 248–49, 284
Juraga, Dubravka, 10, 169–87, 310
Jussawalla, Feroza, 8, 9, 14, 78–106, 122, 128

Kakutani, Michiko, 167
Kane, Jean M., 15, 207, 221–22, 245, 279
Kapur, Geeta, 130
Karamcheti, Indira, 229, 246
Kaufman, Michael T., 79–80, 105
Kaushik, Asha, 290, 310
Kesavan, Mukul, 276, 282
Khan, Sayyid Ahmad, 73, 75, 79, 100, 104, 270, 302
Khomeini, Ayatollah, 5, 9, 61, 72, 73, 74, 75, 81–82, 87, 116, 191
Kidwal, A. R., 127
Kipling, Rudyard, 11, 48, 67, 115, 193, 203, 233, 270
Koran, The, 39, 58, 60, 62, 64, 70, 81, 84, 91, 93, 95, 103, 110, 112–13, 121–23
Kramers, J. H., 92, 105
Kureishi, Hanif, 86, 88–89, 105

Lacan, Jacques, 299
Lal, P., 132
Lamming, George, 10, 174, 178–80, 184, 186
Lapierre, Dominique, 79, 105
Lazarus, Neil, 178, 186
Le Carré, John, 53, 74

Lehmann-Haupt, Christopher, 115
Lenin, V. I., 185
Leseur, Gita, 185
Lévi-Strauss, Claude, 151
Lipscomb, David, 13, 185, 223, 245, 293, 305
London, Bette, 46, 50
Lu Hsun, 177, 178
Lukács, Georg, 170, 178, 184, 186–87, 268, 287–89, 296, 310

Macaulay, Thomas Babington, 104, 195, 198, 294
magical realism, 4, 53, 68, 80, 130, 172, 239, 273, 276, 289, 291
Mahabharata, 197, 230, 252, 271, 274
Mahfouz, Naguib, 127
Maitland, Sara, 49, 73, 167
Majid, Anouar, 14
Malak, Amin, 14
Malgonkar, Mahonar, 2, 290
Mann, Harveen Sachdar, 35–36, 38–39, 47, 49, 136–37, 152, 185
Mann, Thomas, 172
Markandaya, Kamala, 149, 245, 310
Marx, Karl, 127, 167, 287, 299, 308
Marxism, 12–13, 50, 127, 146, 158, 178, 198, 246, 285, 287–91, 293–96, 300–302, 307–8
Marzorati, Gerald, 14, 87, 89, 105, 204
Mazrui, Ali, 118, 127
McClintock, Ann, 20, 48, 150
Mehdi, Mohammad T., 127
Merivale, Patricia, 13, 169, 185
Mernissi, Fatima, 60, 75
Midnight's Children: allegory in, 10–11, 147, 205–24, 231–36; as bildungsroman, 10, 169–87; Booker Prize and, 1, 3, 5, 285; contemporary Indian literature and, 1–2, 129, 132, 147, 250–58, 272–77; critical attention to, 7, 176, 184; Indian national identity and, 11, 12, 43, 53, 55–56, 90, 135, 162, 176–78, 189, 198, 207, 258–61; Indira Gandhi in, 13, 28, 49, 55, 86–87, 180–81, 197, 200, 205–25, 252, 255, 280, 303–7; Jawaharlal Nehru in, 54, 141, 176–77, 188, 203, 216, 218–19, 232, 237, 258, 276–77; language in, 3, 114, 188–204; Marxism and, 300–310; oral culture and, 55, 80, 93; postmodernism and, 10, 13, 182–84, 294–99; treatment of Emergency (1972–1977) in, 55, 209, 213, 221; treatment of gender in, 8, 18, 20, 25, 27–29, 34; treatment of history in, 4, 11, 12, 14, 80, 137, 169, 186, 225–49, 283, 286–313; treatment of intellectuals in, 54, 56, 221; treatment of Islam in, 82, 91–92, 97, 110, 112; Western culture and, 67–69, 80, 270, 311
Miller, Christopher, 311
Miller, J. Hillis, 31, 49, 215, 222, 224
Mishra, Vijay, 130–31, 134, 136, 150–51, 279
Mistry, Rohinton, 1, 289
Mitchell, W.J.T., 24, 48, 187, 310
Modood, Tariq, 151
Mohanty, Chandra Talpade, 75
Moharam, Radika, 151
Moi, Toril, 48
Moore, Jane, 48, 68
Moor's Last Sigh, The, 1, 6, 8–10, 14, 16–18, 121, 126, 130, 135, 137, 154–68
Moretti, Franco, 170–75, 185
Morson, Gary Saul, 76, 246–47
Moses, Michael Valdez, 291, 310
Mufti, Aamir, 5, 8–9, 14, 51, 119, 127
Mukherjee, Meenakshi, 130, 149, 151, 282, 310
Munif, Abdelraman, 112
Musil, Robert, 172

Nabar, Vrinda, 253
Naipaul, V. S., 10, 102, 131, 167, 181, 188, 199, 200, 202, 204, 298, 312; on Islam, 85, 92, 103, 105
Nairn, Tom, 264
Nandy, Ashish, 145, 152, 280
Narayan, Jayaprakash, 304
Narayan, Shyamala, 251, 279
Narayan, R. K., 2, 102, 149, 194
Narayan, Shyamala, 251, 279
Nehru, Jawaharlal: in *Midnight's Children*, 54, 141, 176–77, 188, 203, 216, 218–19, 232, 237, 258, 276–77; in *The Moor's Last Sigh*, 156, 162, 164, 167; as secular modernizer, 84, 137–38, 149, 175, 189, 193, 197, 267, 294, 301, 306; writings, 74, 79, 105
Ngugi wa Thiong'o, 10, 132, 135, 151, 174, 179–81, 184, 288, 290–92, 294, 310

Nietzsche, Friedrich, 136, 222, 248
Nimbkar, Jai, 275
Nizan, Paul, 285, 310
Noor, Ronny, 14
Norris, Christopher, 295

Omer, Mutaharunnisa, 127
Orwell, George, 21, 111, 127, 305
Ouologuem, Yambo, 289
Ozick, Cynthia, 117, 127

Padgaonkar, Shri, 103
Pamuk, Orhan, 50
Paquet, Sandra Pouchet, 179, 186
Parameswaran, Uma, 4, 13, 48, 185, 279
Partition of India, 188, 216, 298
Pathak, R. S., 259–60, 279, 280
Phillips, Lily Wiatrowsky, 173, 185
Pipes, Daniel, 14, 95
popular culture, 9, 11, 53, 113, 120, 125, 139, 141, 183, 293
postmodernism, 53, 67, 89, 258; and postcoloniality, 12, 231, 283–84; and Rushdie, 2, 4–5, 9–14, 31, 80–82, 98, 100, 102, 129–53, 175, 177, 181–86, 199, 235, 244, 253, 286, 291–300, 305, 307, 309
Prager, Karsten, 103, 105
Price, David, 14, 222
Prince, Gerald, 26, 49
Pritchett, Frances W., 94–96, 99–100, 105
proletarian fiction, 173
Pynchon, Thomas, 248, 284, 295–96, 299

Quran. *See* Koran
Qur'an. *See* Koran

Rabelais, Frannçcois, 80, 182, 231, 248
Rai, Alok, 294
Rajan, Gita, 151
Rajan, Rajeswari Sunder, 48–49, 275, 281
Ramayana, 143, 197, 230, 279
Rao, Raja, 2, 102, 105, 132–33, 149, 152, 193, 203, 289
Ray, Hemen, 313
Ray, Satyajit, 113–14, 145–46, 152–53, 198
Reder, Michael, 11, 225–49, 279
Redfield, Marc, 185
Rege, Josna, 11, 12, 246, 250–82
Reid, Calvin, 102, 105
Reid, Vic, 289–90, 292

Rosenthal, Andrew, 77
Roth, Henry, 173
Roy, Arundhati, 1, 29, 49, 129, 133, 153
Russel, Ralph, 95
Ruthven, Malise, 14

Sahgal, Nayantara, 1, 289
Said, Edward, 20, 31, 49, 175, 197, 204
Samad, Yunus, 102
San Juan, E., Jr., 12, 15, 301
Sangari, Kum Kum, 13, 115, 127, 130, 138, 147, 151, 153, 215, 224, 234–35, 248, 257–58, 280
Satanic Verses, The, 1–9, 14, 51–106, 129, 136–40, 152–53, 167, 191–92, 194, 198–99, 202–203; controversy over, 3–8, 51–128, 135, 148, 176, 182, 251, 253; treatment of gender in, 17, 20–25, 32–39, 43–44, 47–49
Sarkar, Bhaskar, 151
Schimmel, Annemarie, 104, 106
Scott, Paul, 10, 68, 193
Scott, Sue, 48
Sealy, I. Allan, 1, 12, 273, 281
Sedgwick, Eve Kosofsky, 48
Sembène, Ousmane, 177, 178, 289, 292
Sen, Suchismita, 135, 145, 146, 152
Seth, Vikram, 1, 289
Seyhan, Azade, 207, 220, 222
Shahabuddin, Syed, 58–59, 63, 66, 74–76, 89, 111
Shame, 1, 4, 13, 53, 56–57, 74, 110, 112–13, 121, 125, 191, 221–22, 224, 245, 248; treatment of gender in, 16–31, 34, 36–37, 39–41, 43–44, 47–48; treatment of Islam in, 80, 82, 86, 91–93, 98, 105
Shepherd, Ron, 232, 236, 248
Shohat, Ella, 150
Sholokhov, Mikhail, 285–86, 288
Sibal, Nina, 12, 273, 275
Sidhwa, Bapsi, 1
Singh, Khushwant, 116, 290
Slemon, Stephen, 130, 233–34, 247–48
Smedley, Agnes, 173
socialist realism, 310
Sokolov, Sasha, 10, 182–83, 186
Soviet Union, 59, 64, 109, 126, 173–74, 178, 182–83, 185–86, 222, 285–86, 295, 304–10
Soyinka, Wole, 132–33, 151
Spielberg, Steven, 113

Spivak, Gayatri Chakravorty, 14, 20–21, 35–36, 39, 48–49, 51, 67, 73, 76, 87, 106, 150, 303
Spurr, David, 227, 234, 245, 248
Srivastava, Aruna, 13, 245, 288
Stalin, Joseph, 182, 186, 304–6, 308
Steel, Laurel, 173
Sterne, Laurence, 80, 112, 248, 291; *Tristram Shandy*, 190, 198, 234, 294
Suleri, Sara, 3, 12–15, 20, 35, 37, 48–49, 65, 76–77, 82–83, 85, 89, 106, 125, 128

ten Kortenaar, Neil, 13, 15, 185, 207, 221, 224, 247, 279, 294
Tharoor, Shashi, 1, 12, 273–74, 289
Thomas, D. M., 296
Tiffin, Hellen, 151, 228, 246
Tolstoy, Alexei, 285
Tompkins, Jane, 49
Turner, Victor, 133, 152

Vassanji, M. G., 181–82, 186, 289, 291
Vasudeva, Mary, 150
Viswanathan, Gauri, 131, 151, 193, 203

Waxman, Barbara Frey, 14
Welch, Stuart Cary, 104, 106
Weldon, Faye, 119
Werbner, Pnina, 133, 151–52
Wheatcroft, Geoffrey, 127
Williams, Patrick, 151, 247
Wolpert, Stanley, 85–86, 106, 123, 213, 223, 245, 293–94, 305
Wood, James, 129, 147
World War II, 163, 180, 186
Wright, Peter, 118

Young, Robert, 152

Zaheer, Sajjad, 94–95

Notes on Contributors

◆

Timothy Brennan is the author of *Salman Rushdie and the Third World: Myths of the Nation* and *At Home in the World: Cosmopolitanism Now.* His first English edition of Alejo Carpentier's *Music in Cuba* is forthcoming from the University of Minnesota Press. He is currently at work on a book on New York Bohemia.

Bishnupriya Ghosh is assistant professor of English at Utah State University, where she teaches postcolonial literature and theory, cultural studies, and film. She is also vice chair of the Women's Studies Program. She has published several essays on Indian writing in English, Indian film, the South Asian diaspora, and postcolonial pedagogies. Her most recent work comprises an anthology that she coedited and introduced, entitled *Interventions: Feminist Dialogues on Third World Women's Literature and Film.* She is currently working on a manuscript on postmodernity and the Indian novel in English.

Michael Gorra is associate professor of English at Smith College. He has published numerous essays on modern British and postcolonial literature. He is the author of *The English Novel at Mid-Century* and *After Empire: Scott, Naipaul, Rushdie.*

Ambreen Hai is assistant professor of English at Smith College, where she teaches Anglophone postcolonial literature and theory, with a focus on South Asian literature. She completed her doctoral dissertation, focusing on Rushdie and Rudyard Kipling, at Yale University in 1994. She is currently writing a book on Kipling, Forster, and Rushdie, portions of which have appeared in *English Literary History* and *The Journal of Commonwealth and Postcolonial Studies.*

Farhad Idris is a doctoral student in the Department of English at the University of Arkansas. He is currently completing a dissertation on the treatment of Indian nationalism in the writings of Salman Rushdie and V. S. Naipaul.

Dubravka Juraga has published essays on postcolonial, Russian, and east European literature. She is the coauthor of *Bakhtin, Stalin, and Modern Russian Fiction: Carnival, Dialogism, and History* and of *The Caribbean Novel in English: An Introduction*. Her current research focuses on postcolonial literature and the global literature of socialism. Currently, she is editing a volume entitled *Rereading Socialist Cultures after the Cold War.*

Feroza Jussawalla is associate professor of English at the University of Texas at El Paso, where she has taught since 1980. She is the coeditor, with Reed Dasenbrock, of *Interviews with Writers of the Postcolonial World*, editor of *Conversations with V. S. Naipaul,* and author of *Family Quarrels: Towards a Criticism of Indian Writing in English* (Peter Lang). She has published on postcolonial literature and on composition and writing across the curriculum in *Public Culture, Massachusetts Review,* and other journals.

Todd M. Kuchta is a graduate student in the English Department at Indiana University, Bloomington. He studies twentieth-century literature and culture, with particular emphasis on imperialism and postcolonialism.

Aamir R. Mufti is assistant professor of English at the University of Michigan.

Michael Reder is currently completing his doctorate in English at the University of Massachusetts, Amherst. His dissertation addresses recent English fiction in a postcolonial context. He is currently editing a volume entitled *Conversations with Salman Rushdie* for the University of Mississippi Press.

Josna Rege is assistant professor of English at Dartmouth College, where she teaches postcolonial literature and theory and twentieth-century British fiction. She is currently working on a book on Indian nationalist discourse in the postindependence period. She is also studying postcolonial women's writing that dispenses with the language of nation. She completed her doctoral dissertation, focusing on Rushdie and other postcolonial Indian writers, at the University of Massachusetts in 1995.

The Volume Editor

◆

M. Keith Booker is professor of English at the University of Arkansas. He is the author of numerous essays and of more than a dozen books on modern literature and literary theory. His most recent books include *The Modern American Novel of the Left: A Research Guide, The Modern British Novel of the Left: A Research Guide, The African Novel in English: An Introduction,* and *Colonial Power, Colonial Texts: India in the Modern British Novel.*

The General Editor

◆

Zack Bowen is professor of English at the University of Miami. He holds degrees from the University of Pennsylvania (B.A.), Temple University (M.A.), and the State University of New York at Buffalo (Ph.D.). In addition to being general editor of this G. K. Hall series, he is editor of the James Joyce series for the University of Florida Press and the *James Joyce Literary Supplement*. He is author and editor of numerous books on modern British, Irish, and American literature. He has also published more than 100 monographs, essays, scholarly reviews, and recordings related to literature. He is past president of the James Joyce Society (1977–1986), former chair of the Modern Language Association Lowell Prize Committee, and current president of the International James Joyce Foundation.

Wake Tech Libraries
9101 Fayetteville Road
Raleigh, North Carolina 27603-5696

DATE DUE